MW01089433

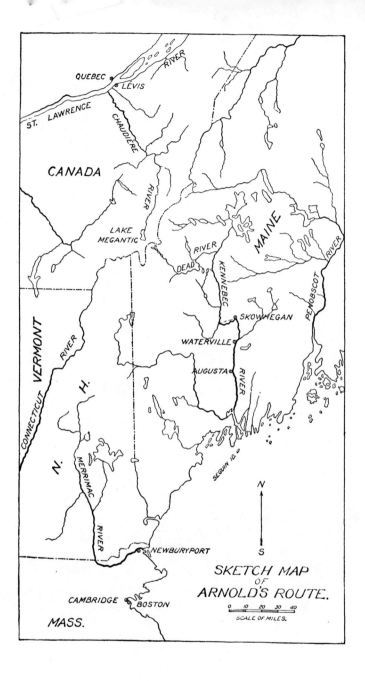

QUEBEC
LEVIS
ST. LAWRENCE
CHAUDIÈRE
RIVER
CANADA
LAKE MEGANTIC
RIVER
DEAD RIVER
KENNEBEC
MAINE
PENOBSCOT RIVER
SKOWHEGAN
WATERVILLE
AUGUSTA
RIVER
VERMONT
CONNECTICUT RIVER
N. H.
MERRIMAC RIVER
SEGUIN ID.
NEWBURYPORT
CAMBRIDGE
BOSTON
MASS.

N
S

SKETCH MAP
OF
ARNOLD'S ROUTE.

0 10 20 30 40
SCALE OF MILES.

ARNOLD'S MARCH
FROM
CAMBRIDGE TO QUEBEC

A Critical Study

Together with a Reprint of Arnold's Journal

By JUSTIN H. SMITH

A HERITAGE CLASSIC

HERITAGE BOOKS
AN IMPRINT OF HERITAGE BOOKS, INC.

Books, CDs, and more – Worldwide

For our listing of thousands of titles see our website
at
www.HeritageBooks.com

A Facsimile Reprint
Published 2003 by
HERITAGE BOOKS, INC.
Publishing Division
1540 Pointer Ridge Place #E
Bowie, Maryland 20716

ORIGINALLY PUBLISHED
1903

International Standard Book Number: **ISBN 1-55613-194-1**

TO MY FRIEND
THE HONOURABLE CHARLES T. GALLAGHER
OF BOSTON
WHO HAS FOUND TIME IN THE
ACTIVE PRACTICE OF THE LAW TO CULTIVATE
LETTERS AND ART
AND TO SERVE THE PUBLIC IN MANY
POSITIONS OF TRUST AND HONOUR

PREFACE

IT seems very singular that no thorough-going history of the American invasion of Canada in 1775 and 1776 has yet been written. This may be due partly to a preconceived idea that nothing of real importance was involved in it, partly to the fact that in appearance the campaigns proved a total failure, and partly to the prominence of the ill-starred Arnold from beginning to end.

On turning my attention to this neglected field, I soon discovered that Arnold's march from Cambridge to Quebec would have to be studied as if nothing had ever been written upon it. When the data for this inquiry were mostly in hand, the announcement of a book on the subject appeared, and seemed to promise an escape from the labour of clearing so much of the way. The promise was not perfectly fulfilled, however, as may be discovered from the notes of the present volume; and

now, after a number of delays, the results of
my investigations are offered.   The purpose
here is to ascertain facts, not paint a picture ;
and the foliage of the subject has been ignored.

I wish it were feasible to acknowledge in
detail my indebtedness to the hundreds of persons who have courteously given me items of
information.   After beginning a list of their
names, I have felt that it would be unfair to
stop short of completeness ; and a complete
list would be hard to make as well as too
long for any one to read.   Let me record a
general but sincere acknowledgment of obligation and of gratitude.

Mention must be made, however, of the
Historical Societies of New Hampshire, Massa-
chusetts, Connecticut, New York, Maryland,
Virginia, and, still more particularly, Rhode
Island and Pennsylvania ; the Congressional,
Lenox, Dartmouth College, Harvard Univer-
sity, and Boston Public Libraries ; the Archives
Office, Ottawa, and the Public Records Office,
London ; and the notes tender acknowledg-
ments to a few individuals, also, for special
assistance.

J. H. S.

Hanover, June 15, 1903.

CONTENTS

The second number refers to the Notes.

MAPS AND PLANS

AUTHORITIES

References in the Notes are by number. To save space titles are in many cases abbreviated, but not in a way to cause confusion. It will be noted that thirty-nine of the numbers refer to unpublished or inaccurately printed manuscripts.

ABBOTT AND ELWELL.—**1.** Hist. of Maine. 1892.

AGRY, T.—**2.** Document (MS.).

AINSLIE, T.—**3.** Journal of the Siege of Quebec (MS.).

ALLEN, W.—**4.** Amer. Biography, 3d ed. Boston. 1857. **5.** Hist. of Norridgewock. Norridgewock. 1849.

ALMON, J.—**6.** Remembrancer. 1776.

ANVILLE, SIEUR D'.—**7.** Amérique Septent. Paris. 1746. **8.** Canada, Louisiane, etc. 1775.

ARNOLD, B.—**9.** Journal (MS.). **10.** Letters (see Nos. 54 and 106).

ARNOLD, I. N.—**11.** Life of B. Arnold. Chicago. 1880.

BAILEY, J.—**12.** Invasion of Canada (MS.).

BANCROFT, G.—**13.** Hist. of the U. S., 15th ed., 10 vols. Boston. 1855-74.

BERKSHIRE HIST. AND SCI. SOC.—**14.** Collections. Pittsfield. 1894.

BERRY, S.—**15.** Letter (MS.).

BISHOP, H.—**16.** Guide Book. Boston. 1887. **17.** Map of the Lake Megantic Region.

BOUCHETTE, J.—**18.** Desc. Topog. . . . du Bas-Canada. Londres. 1815.

BREWER, J.—**19.** Letter (MS.; also in No. 54).

BRITISH ARCHIVES.—**20.** (Public Record Office.)

BROOKS, C.—**21.** Hist. of Medford. Boston. 1855.

BULLETIN DES RECHERCHES HISTORIQUES.—**22.** Lévis.

BUSHNELL, C. I.—**23.** Crumbs for Antiquarians, I. N. Y. 1864.

CALDWELL, H.—**24.** Letter to Gen. Murray (MS.; also in No. 98).

CAMPBELL, C.—**25.** Hist. of Virginia. Phila. 1860.

CANADIAN INSTITUTE.—**26.** Transactions.

CANADIAN REVIEW.—**27.**

CODMAN, J.—**28.** Arnold's Expedition to Canada. N. Y. 1901.

COLBURN, R.—**29.** Documents (MS.).

CONN. ARCHIVES.—**30.** Revol. War. III. (MS.)

CONN. HIST. SOC.—**31.** Collections.

COREY, D. P.—**32.** Hist. of Malden. Malden. 1899.

COWELL, B.—**33.** Spirit of '76. Boston. 1850.

CROSSLEY, P. A.—**34.** Lovell's Gazetteer of Brit. No. Amer. Montreal. 1874.

CURRIER, J. J.—**35.** Ould Newbury. Boston. 1896.

DAVIS, M. L.—**36.** A. Burr, 2 vols. N. Y. 1838.

DAWSON, S. E.—**37.** North America. London. 1897.

DEARBORN, H.—**38.** Journal (MS.; also No. 113, April, 1886). **39.** Letters, etc. (MS.).

DELISLE, G.—**40.** Carte d' Amérique. 1722. **41.** Carte des Nouv. Découvertes, etc. 1750. **42.** Carte du Canada. Amsterdam.

DEMERS, B.—**43.** La Paroisse de St. François. Québec. 1891.

DOMINION OF CANADA.—**44.** Archives (MS.). **45.** Electoral Atlas. 1895.

DRAKE, F. S.—**46.** Amer. Biography. Boston. 1872.

EGLE, W. H. (Ed.).—**47.** Journal of . . . a Party of Provincials, etc. (No. 138, series 2, XV., p. 21).

ESSEX INSTITUTE.—**48.** Collections.

FADEN, W.—**49.** British Colonies in North America. London. 1777. **50.** Inhabited Parts of Canada, etc. London. 1777. **51.** North American Atlas. London. 1777.

FEBIGER, C.—**52.** Documents (MS.).

FOBES, S.—**53.** Account of the Kennebec Expedition (see No. 77).

FORCE, P.—**54.** American Archives.

FOSTER, J.—**55.** A Private Soldier in the Revolution. Manchester (N. H.). 1902.

GAMMELL, W.—**56.** Life of Sam. Ward. Boston. 1846.

GARDNER, A. B.—**57.** The R. I. Line. Providence. 1878.

GARNEAU, F. X.—**58.** Hist. du Canada, 3 vols. Montreal. 1882.

GEOLOGICAL SURVEY OF CANADA.—**59.** Map of the Eastern Townships.

Authorities

GETCHELL, D.— **60.** Letter (MS.).

GOODWIN, MAJ. (U. S. A.).—**61.** Map of the Dead River Region (MS.).

GOODWIN, D., Jr.—**62.** The Dearborns. Chicago. 1884.

GRAHAM, J. D.—**63.** Map of Boundary Lines between the U. S. and the adj. Brit. Prov. 1843.

GRAHAM, J.—**64.** Life of D. Morgan. N. Y. 1856.

GRANT, G. M.—**65.** Picturesque Canada, 2 vols. Toronto. 1882.

GREENLEAF, J.—**66.** Mem. of Rev. J. Parsons. Boston. 1841.

HANSON, J. W.—**67.** Hist. of Danvers. Danvers. 1848. **68.** Hist. of Gardiner, Pittston, etc. Gardiner. 1852. **69.** Hist. of Norridgewock and Canaan. Boston. 1849.

HASKELL, C.—**70.** Journal (MS.; also in No. 219).

HAZARD, S.—**71.** Register of Penn.

HENRY, J. J.—**72.** Account of Arnold's Campaign, etc., 3d ed. Albany. 1877. **73.** Letters (MS.).

HILDRETH, R.—**74.** Hist. of the U. S., 6 vols. N. Y. 1851-56.

HILTON, D.—**75.** Document (MS.).

HINMAN, R. R.—**76.** Conn. in the Revol. Hartford. 1842.

HIST. COLL. OF THE MAHONING VALLEY.—**77.** Vol. I. Youngstown. 1876.

HISTORICAL MAGAZINE.—**78.**

HOLLISTER, G. H.—**79.** Hist. of Conn. Hartford. 1857.

HOPKINS, J. C. (Ed.)—**80.** Canada : An Encyclopædia. I. Toronto. 1898.

HUMPHREY, W.—**81.** Journal (MS.).

IRVING, W.—**82.** Life of Washington, 5 vols. N. Y. 1855-59.

JEFFERYS, T.—**83.** Explan. for the New Map of Nova Scotia, etc. London. 1755. **84.** Natural and Civil Hist. of the French Dominions in No. and So. Amer. London. 1761. **85.** New Map of Nova Scotia, etc. London. 1755.

JOHNSTON, H. P.—**86.** Conn. Men in the . . . Revol. Hartford. 1889.

KINGSBURY AND DEYO.—**87.** Hist. of Kennebec County. N. Y. 1892.

KITCHIN, T.— **88.** British Dominions in America. **89.** New Map of the Prov. of Quebec.

LAVERDIÈRE, C. H.—**90.** Hist. du Canada. Québec. 1874.

LeMOINE, J. M.—**91.** Album du Touriste, 2me. éd. Québec. 1872. **92.** Explorations in Eastern Latitudes. Quebec. 1889.

93. Picturesque Quebec. Montreal. 1882. **94.** Quebec Past and Present. Quebec. 1876.

LINCOLN.—**95.** Hist. of Worcester County, Mass.

LINDSAY, W.—**96.** Hist. of the Invasion of Canada (in No. 27).

LINN AND EGLE.—**97.** Penn. in the . . . Revol. Harrisburg. 1880.

LIT. AND HIST. SOC. OF QUEBEC—**98.** Transactions and Publications.

LOCKE, J. G.—**99.** Book of the Lockes. Boston. 1853.

LONDON MAGAZINE.—**100.**

LUNT, P.—**101.** Diary (Ed. by S. A. Green. Boston. 1872).

McCONKEY, R.—**102.** Hero of Cowpens. N. Y. 1885.

McMULLEN, J. M.—**103.** Hist. of Canada, 2 vols. Brockville. 1891.

MAGAZINE OF AMERICAN HISTORY.—**104.**

MAGAZINE OF NEW ENGLAND HISTORY.—**105.**

MAINE HISTORICAL SOCIETY.— **106.** Collections (particularly Vol. I., 1831). **107.** Proceedings.

MARCEL, G.—**108.** Réproductions de Cartes, etc. Paris. 1893.

MARSHALL, J.—**109.** Life of George Washington, 2 vols. Phila. 1804.

MASSACHUSETTS.— **110.** Archives (MS.). **111.** Soldiers and Sailors of the Revol. War (in process of pub.).

MASS. HIST. SOCIETY.—**112.** Collections. **113.** Proceedings.

MEIGS, R. J.—**114.** Journal (in Nos. 5, 23, 112). **115.** Documents (MS.).

MELVIN, A. A.—**116.** Journal of J. Melvin. Portland. 1902.

MELVIN, J.—**117.** Journal (in Nos. 116 and 219a).

MITCHELL, J.—**118.** Brit. and French Dominions in No. Amer. London. 1755.

MONTRESOR, J.—**119.** Map of a Rout undertaken in Winter, etc. (1760) (MS.). **120.** Map of the Journey of 1761 (MS.). **121.** Journal (in No. 106).

MORISON, G.—**122.** Journal, etc. Hagerstown, Md. 1803.

NEW DOMINION MONTHLY.—**123.**

NEW ENGLAND HIST. AND GENEAL. REGISTER.—**124.**

NEW ENGLAND MAGAZINE.—**125.**

NEW HAMPSHIRE.—**126.** Provincial Papers. **127.** Revolutionary Rolls.

NEW HAMPSHIRE ANTIQUARIAN SOC.—**128.** Collections.

Authorities xviiNEW HAMPSHIRE HIST. SOC.— **129.** Collections. **130.** Proceedings.

NEW YORK HIST. SOC.—**131.** Collections.

NOLIN, J. B.—**132.** Carte du Canada, etc. 1756.

NORTH, J.—**133.** Document (MS.).

NORTH, J. W.—**134.** Hist. of Augusta. Augusta. 1870.

OSGOOD AND BATCHELDER.— **135.** Hist. Sketch of Salem. Salem. 1879.

OSWALD, E.—**136.** Journal (in No. 54).

PARTON, J.—**137.** A. Burr, 2 vols. N. Y. 1879.

PENNSYLVANIA.—**138.** Archives. Two Series. Harrisburg. 1852–93. **139.** Colonial Records. Phila. and Harrisburg. 1852–53.

PENNSYLVANIA HIST. SOC.—**140.** Bulletins.

PENN. MAG. OF HIST. AND BIOG.—**141.**

PHILLIPS, P. L.—**142.** Maps of America. Washington. 1901.

PORTLAND (Me.) PRESS.—**143.**

POTTER, C. E.—**144.** Milit. Hist. of N. H.

POWNALL, T.—**145.** Middle Brit. Colonies, etc. 1776. **146.** Topog. Descript. of No. Amer. 1776.

PREBLE, J.—**147.** Report and Map (MS.). 1765.

QUEBEC GAZETTE.—**148.**

REED, P. McC.—**149.** Hist. of Bath, Me. Portland. 1894.

REED, W. B.—**150.** Letters of Washington to J. Reed. Phila. 1852. **151.** Life and Corres. of J. Reed, 2 vols. Phila. 1847.

RHODE ISLAND.—**152.** Colonial Records.

RHODE ISLAND HIST. SOC.—**153.** Collections.

RHODE ISLAND MILITARY PAPERS (MS.).—**154.**

RIERDAN, M.—**155.** Document (MS.).

ROBINSON, A. W.—**156.** Guide Book to the Dead River Region. Boston. 1886.

ROGERS, R.—**157.** Account of No. Amer. London. 1765.

ROUGE, LE.—**158.** Partie Orient. du Canada. Paris. 1755.

ROY, J. E.—**159.** Hist. de la Seign. de Lauzon, 3 vols. Lévis. 1897–1900.

ROY, P. G.—**160.** La Famille Taschereau. Lévis. 1901.

ROYAL SOCIETY OF CANADA.— **161.** Proceedings and Transactions.

SAVAGE, E.—**162.** Document (MS.).

SAVAGE, J.—**163.** Document (MS.).

SAYER AND BENNETT.—**164.** American Atlas. London. 1776.

165. American Milit. Pocket Atlas. London. 1776. **166.** Gen. Map of the No. Brit. Cols. (after Pownall). London. 1776. **167.** New Map of . . . Quebec (Carver). London. 1776.

SEALE, R. W.—**168.** New and Accurate Map of No. Amer., etc. 1771.

SENEX, J.—**169.** North America, etc. 1710.

SENTER, I.—**170.** Account of Arnold's Expedition (MS.). **171.** Journal (MS.; also in No. 140, I).

SMALL, H. W.—**172.** Hist. of Swan's Island. Ellsworth. 1898.

SMITH, E. V.—**173.** Hist. of Newburyport. Newburyport. 1854.

SMITH, G. B.—**174.** Hist. of Canada, 2 vols. Quebec. 1815.

SMITH, J. H.—**175.** Prologue of the American Revolution (Century Mag., Nov., 1902–April, 1903).

SMITH, J. J.—**176.** Civil and Milit. List of R. I. Providence. 1900.

SMITH, W. H.—**177.** Hist. of Canada, 2 vols. Quebec. 1815.

SPARKS, J.— **178.** B. Arnold. Boston. 1835. **179.** Correspondence of the Amer. Revol., 4 vols. Boston. 1853. **180.** Washington. Boston. 1839.

SQUIER, E.—**181.** Journal (MS.; also in No. 104, II., 365).

STEVENS, N.—**182.** Document (MS.).

STILES, H. R.—**183.** Ancient Windsor, 2 vols. Hartford. 1891.

STOCKING, A.—**184.** Interesting Journal, etc. Catskill. 1810.

STONE, E. M.—**185.** Invasion of Canada. Providence. 1867.

STUART, J. H. & Co.—**186.** Atlas of Maine. So. Paris, Maine.

THACHER, J.—**187.** Military Journal. Boston. 1823.

THAYER, S.—**188.** Journal (MS.; also in No. 153). **189.** Letters, etc. (MS.).

THOMPSON, J. P.— **190.** Hist. 2d Co., Governor's Footguards. New Haven. 1895.

TODD, C. B.—**191.** A. Burr. N. Y. 1879.

TOPHAM, J.—**192.** Journal (MS.).

UNITED STATES.—**193.** Archives of Congress (MS.). **194.** Coast and Geodetic Survey Maps. **195.** Journals of Congress. **196.** Map prepared under the Webster-Ashburton Treaty (MS.). **197.** Secret Journals of Congress. **198.** Various Reports, Journals, etc.

VARNEY, G. J.—**199.** Gazetteer of . . . Maine. Boston. 1881.

VAUGONDY.—**200.** Amérique Septent. 1750.

VERREAU (Ed.).—**201.** Invasion du Canada. Montreal. 1873.

VIRGINIA MAG. OF HIST. AND BIOG.—**202.**

WALKER, G. H. & Co.—**203.** Map of the Coast of Maine. Boston. **204.** Map of Upper Dead River, etc. Boston.

WARD, JOHN.—**205.** Lt. Col. Sam. Ward. N. Y. 1875.

WARE, J. **206.** Journal (see No. 124, April, 1852).

WASHINGTON, G.—**207.** Accounts (facsimile). **208.** Letters (MS.). **209.** Life and Works (Sparks, ed.), 12 vols. Boston. 1837. **210.** Writings (Ford, ed.), 14 vols. Boston. 1889–93.

WESTON, E.—**211.** Early Settlers of Canaan (MS.).

WHITNEY, S. H.—**212.** Kennebec Valley. Augusta. 1887.

WHITON, J. M.—**213.** Hist. of New Hampshire. Concord. 1834.

WILD, E.—**214.** Journal (in No. 113, April, 1886).

WILLIAMSON, W. D.—**215.** Hist. of Maine, 2 vols. Hallowell. 1832.

WILLIS, W.—**216.** Journals of Smith and Deane. Portland. 1849.

WILSON AND FISKE.—**217.** Appleton's Amer. Biog., 6 vols. N. Y. 1888.

WINSOR, J. (Ed.).—**218.** Narr. and Crit. Hist. of Amer., 8 vols. Boston. 1886–89.

WITHINGTON, L. (Ed.).— **219.** Caleb Haskell's Diary. Newburyport. 1881.

W. J. D.—**219a.** Melvin's Journal. N. Y. 1857.

BANCROFT COLLECTION.—**220.** (MS., Lenox Library.)

SPARKS MANUSCRIPTS.— **221.** (MS., Harvard University Library.)

GILMORE, G. C.—**222.** N. H. Men at Bunker Hill. Manchester, N. H. 1899.

BOTTA, C. G. G.—**223.** Hist. of the War of Independence, etc. (trans. by Otis), 3 vols. Phila. 1820.

CHALMERS MSS.—**224.** Journal of the Siege of Quebec (Anon).

LE CANADIEN.—**225.**

To this list should rightfully be added the names of a very large number of persons, from whom the author has received valuable items of information relating particularly to family history, local history, and local topography ; see the Preface.

Arnold's March to Quebec

INTRODUCTION

LATE in the summer of 1775, General Schuyler moved against Canada by the way of Lake Champlain; and, to meet this attack, General Carleton, the British Governor, concentrated his forces near Montreal. At this time Washington felt able to spare a portion of the troops besieging Boston, and he concluded to despatch a small force under Benedict Arnold through the Kennebec Valley against Quebec, hoping either to gain possession of the Canadian capital, or to aid Schuyler by drawing Carleton to its defence.

The route of Arnold's detachment lay through an unknown region, a wilderness; and it would be a fascinating as well as difficult problem simply to disentangle the facts of the march, and so clear the way to a sound history of the expedition. Where did the gates of the wilderness open and close upon these daring patriots ?   What lakes were furrowed by their keels ?   At what bastion did they storm the granite wall of the Appalachians ?   How did they surmount the difficulties of the way, and what were the steps of their progress ?

But questions of still greater moment are involved in our inquiry.   The march itself was a campaign,—a campaign against the forest and the flood, against fatigue, sickness, and famine. The contest proved close and pitiless, and the issue remained long in doubt.   In so keen a struggle, the smallest of circumstances was enough to throw the victory this way or that. We cannot understand it at all unless we understand it thoroughly ; and therefore every detail not only enlists attention and repays interest, but in a special degree requires the most careful study.

THE ROUTE BEFORE ARNOLD

A STUDY of the route that Arnold followed might go back a long way, for the geology of the region predestined an expedition like his; but it will be more convenient and quite as useful to begin with attempts at the delineation of it. It is very curious to observe how the truth about this highway between south and north glimmered and faded for many years, before coming clearly out in the full light of knowledge; and it is worth while to see how the region was represented on a few maps out of the many which have been examined.

We may begin with a map of North America preserved in the French Navy Department.[1] * Both the Kennebec and the Chaudière are here beaded with a lake, and a straight waterway lies between them. The drawing is undated, but internal evidence proves that it was done no later than the year 1682. In 1698,

* The " superior figures " refer to notes, which will be found at the conclusion of the text.

however, Hubert Jaillot dedicated to the Dau-
phin a map that parted the two rivers, though
in other respects it was no doubt incorrect
enough.   After another interval of about the
same length, John Senex, of the Royal Society
of London, produced a chart in which the
separation of the St. Lawrence basin from that
of the Atlantic Ocean was emphasised (1710).
Guillaume Delisle[2] followed this fashion presently in two maps published at Paris (1722 and
1750), and in one issued at Amsterdam.[3] The
Sieur d'Anville in his map of 1746 adhered to
the same opinion.

Two maps of 1755 show still further enlight-
enment.   John Mitchell of London drew some
ponds at the extremity of the Kennebec,—
that is to say, the West Branch or Dead
River; and put one of them very near the
"Amaguntick" lake[4]; and he labelled the
upper waters of the Kennebec, "Carriages to
Quebec," signifying, however, not that people
could drive from that point, but that they
could walk and "carry" their vehicles,—their
canoes.   That same year Thomas Jefferys, another cartographer of London, did even better.
He brought the southern and the northern
streams very near together, and inscribed at
this place: "Indian and French Rendezvous

extremely proper for a fort which would restrain
yᵉ French and curb yᵉ Abenaki Indians."

The next year marks a reaction. In 1756
Nolin, in his *Carte du Canada*, induced a continuous line of water to connect the Kennebec
with the St. Lawrence at Quebec, for, as this
indicates, the old opinion had not yet quite
expired ; but Seale, the engraver of an English map dated New Year's Day, 1771, followed
wiser counsels, and refrained from joining the
Kennebec and the Chaudière.

In 1776 appeared " A New Map of the Province of Quebec . . . from the French Surveys connected with those made after the war
[of 1754–1763] by Captain Carver and other
officers in his Majesty's Service." It was
printed for Robert Sayer and John Bennett,
and bore the engraved date : " 16th February,
1776."

Of course Arnold had then crossed the wilderness, and had proved certain things about
its topography; but none of the geographical
fruits of this expedition can be supposed to
have made their way into a London map of that
date. Confirmation of this view is found in the
fact that on August 14th of the same year Sayer
and Bennett appeared with a new map ; and in
this, not only were there substantial changes,

but an attempt was made to indicate "Arnold's rout." The map of February 16th is thus of special interest as illustrating the opinions about this region accepted by well informed cartographers at the time Arnold set out, and for that reason a portion of it is reproduced here.

Dated the very next month (March 25, 1776), we find a map that bears these words: "Middle British Colonies in North America, first published by Mr. Lewis Evans of Philadelphia in 1755, and since corrected and improved, as also extended, . . . by T. Pownall, M. P." Here we observe Dead River drawn fairly near the truth, with a lake at the extreme end, and not far from it a stream running into "Amaguntaëg" Pond.[4] Why not select this, instead of Sayer and Bennett's map, as representing current opinion at the time of Arnold's march? Because there is a look of special knowledge about it, and in a moment we shall find our suspicion confirmed.

Were these maps clear guesswork? By no means. Their authors tried, we may be sure, to obtain good information, and there were certain sources they could tap. Indians, of course, roamed through the wilderness, and

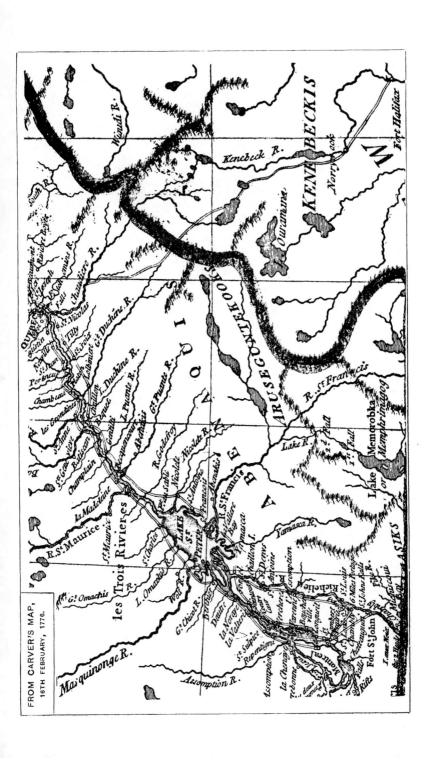

FROM CARVER'S MAP,
16TH FEBRUARY, 1776.

some of them could draw a little, as even the most illiterate of guides can do to-day. Better yet, they could tell a white man how to draw; and there is a map in the possession of the Historical Society at Skowhegan, Maine, drawn in this way by Major Goodwin of our army in 1825, that shows about what the process might be expected to produce,—a rough but valuable sketch. White men also traversed these forests occasionally. French missionaries, and in particular Jesuits, came down from Quebec to labour among the savages. As a regularly settled missionary in the Kennebec wilderness, Gabriel Dreuillettes stands first in order. About the middle of the seventeenth century he found himself domiciled among the Abenakis.[5] His intercourse with Quebec must have been somewhat constant, and we know that he twice went south to Boston.[6] Near the close of the century, the Fathers Bigot were often among the Indians of Maine, and one of them appears to have been a regular missionary in the Kennebec region. Most famous of them all, Sébastien Râle[7] dwelt among his dusky converts on the banks of the Kennebec, in the very track that Arnold followed, for many years, and must have been well acquainted with every Indian path to Quebec.

From the French, at least, these missionaries had no reason to conceal their knowledge, and many hints must have reached the cartographers in this way.

Other sources existed. Thomas Jefferys in his Explanation for the New Map of Nova Scotia (1755) said:

"The Remainder of the Kennebek to its Head, where it interlocks with the La Chaudière, and also the course of this last River to its Exit in the River St. Lawrence, is taken from an Eye-draught made by a French Deserter in 1754."

Pownall, as we have already hinted, possessed special information, and it seems worth while to quote what he said in his Topographical Description of North America (1776), especially as some of his discoveries may have leaked through his agents into the public mind.

". . . As the River Kenebaëg has been now rendered famous as a Pass, by a March of some Spirit and Enterprize made by the Americans, following its Course, across the land to St. Lawrence or Canada River, I shall here give a more particular and detailed Description of it than I should otherwise have entered into.

"This River, in the Year 1754 and 1755, was talked of as a Rout by which an Army might pass, the best and shortest Way, to attack Canada and Quebec. The Rout

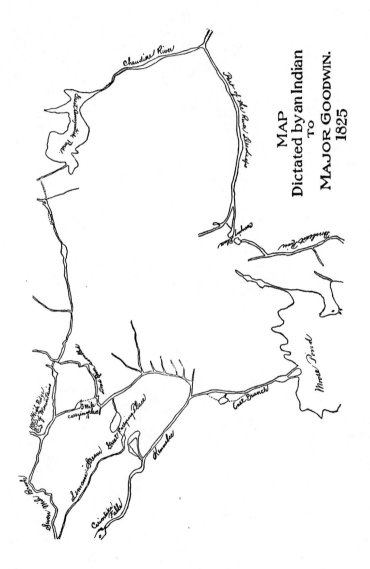

MAP
Dictated by an Indian
TO
MAJOR GOODWIN.
1825

Chaudiere River

Part of the River Chaudiere

Great Carrying Place Pond

Carrying Place

Thundar River

Moose Pond

East Branch

(Foot) High Ridge of Woodland

5 mile carrying place

Dead River

Little River

Lemon Stream

Great Carrying Place

Great Carrying Place

Kennebec

Swan Stone Brook

Carritunk Falls

was supposed to be by an Indian Path and Carrying-place, which, going off from Kenebaëg about Eight or 10 miles above Noridgewaëg, in a North West Course of Six or Seven Miles came to a Pond which issued into the River Chaudière. Some such Information had been given to Government ; it was of the utmost Importance that Government should not be misled. In the year 1756, I had an Opportunity of inquiring into this Matter by scrutinizing a Journal given to me and signed by Capt. Hobbs and Lieut. Kenedy ; and by examining the Journalists themselves as to the Authority of the Particulars, I found enough to be convinced that this supposed Pass was mere conjecture, taken upon trust of Bartholemon, an Indian, who was found to be false and a Spy, and was in 1755 shot by our own People as he was attempting to desert. Government therefore was early cautioned against this misinformation. When I was Governor of the Province of Massachusetts Bay [1757–1760], I had this Rout particularly investigated by Ensign Howard, a Country surveyor, under the Direction of Capt. Nichols, who commanded at Fort Frederick. Instead of a short pass of some Eight or 10 Miles of easy Portage, this Indian Path turned out to be a Rout, on a Line as a Bird flies, of near 50 Miles over Land, *impracticable to an Army that hath a Train of Artillery and heavy Baggage*. It appeared, however, that (although a difficult and very laborious Rout) it was practicable to any Body of Men who should go light armed, as a Scouting Party, either to reconnoitre or to break up settlements. The sort of March which Arnold and his People experienced, has confirmed this Account given 17 or 18 years ago. . . .

"This River Kenebaëg, to begin from its principal Branch, may be described as rising on the Height of the

Land in North Latitude 45° 20', and in East Longitude
from Philadelphia 5° 10' or thereabouts ; its source is
from a little Pond, and the first Courses of its Birth a
Succession of Ponds or drowned Lands, Swamps, and
Falls. Its first general Course is 30 miles South East,
it then makes a great Bow, whose string (lying East and
by South and West and by North) is 12 miles.[8] It then
runs North-easterly Nine Miles and an Half, and then
tumbling over falls North East 10 Miles joins the North
Branch.

"The North Branch is said (I speak not here from
the same Degree of Authority) to arise in and issue
from a little Pond about 16 Miles North of this Crotch,
from whence (it is likewise said) there is a Carrying-
place of 13 or 14 Miles to an Eastern Branch of the
Chaudière River. This was represented to me as the
shortest Rout to Canada, but I do not find in my Journals that I have set this down as confirmed or sufficiently authenticated. After these Two Branches join,
they run South Easterly about Three Miles, when a
small River, tumbling over falls and running between
high perpendicular rocky Banks for Seven Miles and an
Half, and issuing from a great Pond full of Islands,
called Sebaün or by some such Name, North East 12
Miles distant, comes into the Kenebaëg. This stream
is impracticable for any Navigation at these Falls, but
there is a Carrying place on the East side from a Cove
to the Head of the Falls. From the Junction of this
Stream the River has its Course South Westerly 12
Miles when one comes to the Place whence the Indian
Path goes off to the North West, as shall be hereafter
described. Hence with many Windings the River keeps
its Southern Course to Noridgewaëg, where it has the
appearance of a Lake full of Islands. On the Banks of

this was the Indian Dwelling of the Tribe of that Name. A little below are the Falls.

"The River then runs in a winding Course Five Miles East, and at the Point where it turns again South the River Wesseronsaëg[9] comes in from the North East. Keeping on the same Course 12 or 14 Miles more it comes to Tachonaëg Falls,[10] below which Sebastoo-coög[11] comes into it, from a Pond bearing North East and distant about 25 Miles : In the Fork between these two Streams Mr. Shirley built Fort Halifax. From hence the River runs in a course South-westerly 17 Miles to Cushnoög[12]; here is a little Blockhouse called Fort Western. The Fall at Cushnoög is the Head of Tide Water; Sloops of 90 Tons Burthen come up hither from Sea. . . .

"To describe next the River Kenebaëg as a Rout to Quebeck : in the first Place the Reader has been told that Sloops of 90 Tons Burthen can go up to Chesh-noög Falls,[12] about 30 Miles from Small Point. From thence to Fort Hallifax at Tackonic Falls,[10] 17 Miles, is a Waggon Road. Thence a certain Degree of Navigation for Bateaux takes Place, which is interrupted by Falls and Rapids below Norridgewaëg, at which Places all Baggage must be again carried over Land, where a Waggon Road might be made between the Hills and the River. Half a Mile above Noridgewaëg there is a sharp Fall, but for that a good Waggon Road might be made quite up to the Great Carrying-place.

"Hence the Indian Path goes off West from the River over Land about Four Miles and a half to a Pond about Three Quarters of a Mile long; a good Waggon Road might be made here : This First Pond has been found to issue its Waters into the Kenebaëg. Hence the Path runs over like Grounds West-Northerly about a Mile,

and comes to a Second Pond ; this has been found to
issue its Waters into Sagadahoc River.[13]   Hence, over
the like Land and in the˙ same Course about a Mile
More it comes to a Third Pond, which, issuing its
Waters to the North and falling into a river which runs
North-easterly, gave rise to the Misinformation that
here went the Rout to Canada by Chaudière ; but the
River which this Pond Empties itself into is found to
be the Kenebaëg,[14] which in this place runs North-easterly; from this Pond the Path runs West-northerly near
Four Miles, and strikes the southern-most Bend of this
Main Branch[15] of Kenebaëg; up this stream there may
be an imperfect Navigation for Indians, and Traders or
Hunters, somewhat better in the Time of Freshets, but
both the Navigation is bad and the travelling, between
high Ranges of Mountains and in swampy boggy Vales,
very troublesome to Individuals, very arduous and almost impracticable to Bodies of Men.   When you get
higher, towards the Source of the River, you come to a
Chain of Ponds which makes the Navigation better, but
this is interrupted with Falls.   From the Head of the
River to a little stream which falls into Agamuntaëg
Pond,[4] is a Carrying-Place of about Four Miles.   That
is the Indian Carrying-place ; but I apprehend that if a
Body of Men would transport any Baggage which requires a Depth of Water before it can be embarked, the
Portage must be to or near to, the Lake, about 10 Miles.
This Lake is the Head of Chaudière River, and is
about 40 Miles above the present Settlements of the
Canadians." [16]

In 1759, General Amherst sent a messenger
to General Wolfe at Quebec by way of the

Kennebec.   As soon as the conquest of
Canada was secure (1760), General Murray,
the British commander, resolved to investigate
the Chaudière Valley and its communications
with the Kennebec, and the very next year
John Montresor, an able officer, destined
to become the King's Chief Engineer for
America, was despatched with a party of Indians to inspect the region. He accomplished his task, drew a map, and wrote a
journal.[17] Later the map and an imperfect
draft of the journal fell into the hands of
Benedict Arnold; and later still they both
fall into ours.   In the course of our inquiries
we shall very probably need to consult them.

Not long after Montresor made this re-
conaissance from Quebec back again to Quebec, an expedition went north from the
opposite side of the mountains.   In 1764 the
Massachusetts Bay Company sent a well organised surveying party under John Preble up
the Penobscot, with instructions to see whether
a road could not be made that way to Quebec.
January 1, 1765, the party returned to Fort
Pownall, on the Penobscot, and reported in
substance that such a road was not practicable.
Incidentally, the report mentioned the Indian
route by way of the Chaudière and the Dead

Rivers, and on Captain Preble's map it was indicated, or, more exactly, suggested.[18]

This brings us pretty near to the time of Arnold's expedition, and the next step reaches it. Montresor's narrative mentioned another source of information about the Dead River route,— New England surveyors. One of these bore the name of Goodwin and the title Major; and the following letter shows not only that he possessed sketches and minutes of the region, but that Arnold had the use of both.

" POWNALBOROUGH [MAINE].
" October 17, 1775.
" TO HIS EXCELLENCY GEORGE WASHINGTON, ESQ.
" SIR :
" According to your Excellency's verbal orders, by Colonel Benedict Arnold, I supplied him with a plan of the sea-coast, from Cape Elizabeth to Penobscot, and the River Kennebeck to the several heads thereof, and the several carrying places to Ammeguntick Pond[4] and Chaudiere River (which Ammeguntick empties into said Chaudiere River, which Chaudiere empties into the River St. Lawrence, about four miles above Quebeck), and the passes and carrying places to Quebeck ; and also made several small plans for each department, for their guide ; and also gave him a copy of a journal which represented all the quick water and carrying places to and from Quebeck, both ways, viz., east and west; the west is the way to go, and the east to come.[19]   .   .   .

" I think it would be for the general interest for you to

have a copy of said plan, etc., and then you would be a judge of what would be best to be done.   It hath been a great cost and labour to me to obtain those plans, etc., and make them.   Sir, if you think it worth your notice, and will give orders therefor, I will copy one for you, and wait on you with it, and give you the best intelligence I can, as I think I know as much of this country as any one, as I have been travelling, surveying, and settling this part, ever since the year 1750.   .   .   .

                                 "SAMUEL GOODWIN.[20]

"N. B.   Mr. Reuben Colburn informed me you wanted a plan.   I thus began it about 3 weeks before Col. Arnold arrived."

All these things, taken together, show that a good deal was known, in a rough way, of the Dead River passage into Canada before Arnold made it famous.   But a military use of the route,— was that ever considered?   Botta says: " Not only no army was ever known to pass through these rough and dismal solitudes, but never had human being until then [*i. e.,* until Arnold went], imagined it was possible."[21]   Yet it is wonderful how few things men do that were not thought of by other men: was Arnold's enterprise an exception?

In 1697 Iberville proposed to attack Boston by way of the Chaudière, "bursting from the woods with one thousand Canadians and six hundred regulars," as he wrote in a *Mémoire.*

Five years later, Saint Castin took up this plan, and offered to make the expedition with fourteen hundred good men.[22] In the long quotation from Pownall's Topographical Description, the author stated that in 1754 and 1755 it was proposed to invade Canada by way of the Kennebec; and we know that in December of the latter year, Shirley of Massachusetts definitely suggested, in a council of Governors held at New York, to menace Quebec by that route. Roy affirms[23] that during the campaign of 1756 the English actually decided to send two thousand men up the Kennebec and down the Chaudière against the Canadian capital, but that after Montcalm took Oswego the plan was dropped. Pownall in his " Idea of the Service of America " (1758), said[24] : " The People of Massachusetts, in the counties of Hampshire, Worcester and York, are the best wood-hunters in America. . . . I should think if about 100 thorough wood-hunters, properly officered, could be obtained in the county of York, a scout of such might make an attempt upon the settlements by way of the Chaudière River. . . ." More significant still is the fact that just before Arnold's expedition set out, there were fears both in Canada and in Maine of a hostile invasion by this natural route. On the north a post of fusileers was stationed in the valley of the Chaudière to guard against the danger[25]; and on the south the selectmen of Falmouth (Portland), disturbed by a rumour that arrived on the last day of April, sent three men of New Gloucester, with Remington Hobby and John Getchell, of Vassalboro, to "ascertain if any Frenchmen were in motion, or any of the savages were preparing to ravage the frontier settlements."[26] Indeed, an expedition against Quebec by way of the Chaudière was actually proposed in 1775 by Jonathan Brewer, some while before Arnold or Washington seems to have thought of it.[27] Evidently there was nothing very esoteric in the thought of using this route.

Just how all the ideas about this way into Canada came to be crystallised into the expedition under Arnold's command, is a question that lies outside our present field. What seems important is to show that before our American soldiers took ship for the Kennebec, people knew a good deal about this route, and thought of it as available for military uses; and probably facts enough have been cited to establish these points. It only remains to show that in spite of this, all their information

was crude and inexact up to the very day of
Arnold's departure.   Carver's map is evidence
enough, probably, so far as the general intelligent public are concerned; and a letter of the
American Commander-in-chief to the American
Congress reveals that men the most interested
and the best informed had no realization of the
actual difficulties.

" CAMP AT CAMBRIDGE,
"September 21, 1775.

"To CONTINENTAL CONGRESS :
    ". . . I am now to inform the Honourable Congress
that, encouraged by the repeated declarations of the
Canadians and Indians, and urged by their requests, I
have detached Col. Arnold, with one thousand men, to
penetrate into Canada by way of Kennebeck River, and,
if possible, to make himself master of Quebeck.   .   .   .
I made all possible inquiry as to the distance, the safety
of the route, and the danger of the season being too far
advanced, but found nothing in either to deter me from
proceeding, more especially as it met with very general
approbation from all whom I consulted upon it.   .   .   .
For the satisfaction of the Congress, I here enclose a
copy of the proposed route.[28]   .   .   .

" GEORGE WASHINGTON.

" ROUTE TO QUEBECK FROM KENNEBECK RIVER.[29]
    " From the mouth of Kennebeck River to Quebeck, on
a straight line, is two hundred and ten miles.   The river
is navigable for sloops about thirty-eight miles and for
flat-bottomed boats about twenty-two miles.   Then you

meet Jaconick Falls,[10] and from Jaconick Falls to Norridgewock, as the river runs, thirty-one miles; from thence to the first carrying place about thirty miles; carrying place four miles, then a pond to cross, and another carrying place, about two miles to another pond; then a carrying place about three or four miles to another pond; then a carrying place to the western branch of Kennebeck River, called the Dead River; then up that river, as it runs, thirty miles, some small falls and short carrying places around them intervening; then you come to the height of the land, and about six miles carrying place, into a branch which leads into Ammeguntick Pond,[4] the head of the Chaudière River, which falls into the St. Lawrence River about four miles above Quebeck."

II

THE WITNESSES

HAND-CAMERAS were unfortunately not in existence in 1775, and we have no photographs of scenes along the route; but pens and paper were familiar articles, and a number of the soldiers felt moved to use them. In short, a good many reports of the march have come to us from members of the expedition, besides various items and scraps from participants who did not write full accounts.

Of all our first-hand reports, the one most commonly known and relied upon by those who have written on the subject is probably that of John Joseph Henry,[1] one of the riflemen, who become in later life President of the Second Judicial District of Pennsylvania,— in short, a judge. There are sufficient reasons for the vogue of this narrative. It is much more extended than any of the others, and far more readable than most of them; it was

published in book form as early as 1812, while
few of the others got into print until many
years later, or have ever come before the
general public.   And, finally, the high character and standing of the author seemed to
place the seal of truth, and certainly did place
the seal of honesty, upon its face.   For us,
however, Henry's tale, though still the most
enjoyable of all, perhaps, has a number of
defects.   He was only a boy of sixteen when
he joined the expedition, and his lack of rank
barred him from the circle of the officers.

His book was not written until he stood at
the very close of his life, thirty-six years after
the occurrences he narrated.   Indeed, it was
not written by him at all, but dictated to his
daughter, though he had been working on
the subject more or less for several years.
"Casual notes and memoranda" he was aided
by, we are told, and so we can well believe;
but evidently memory supplied by far the
greater part of his account.   In fact, the
Pennsylvania Historical Society has a letter
written by Henry to General Francis Nichols,
November 29, 1808, in which he says of
his proposed book : " It's detailed principally
from my own memory, assisted by the
notes of Genl. Meigs and Wm. McCoy," and

certain questions that Henry asked Nichols
prove that his recollection was in places extremely defective. The author died without
revising his manuscript, and his grandson tells
us that it was not very carefully printed. For
all these reasons Henry's journal seems to
merit only a low place as an authority on
questions of detail, and a close examination of
it proves the justice of this opinion, although
good reasons appear for believing that certain
things fixed themselves very definitely in his
memory.

The first rank must certainly be given to
the one extant journal that has never been
printed in full until now. That is Arnold's.[2]

Arnold was a man of unusual intelligence,
and the commander of the expedition. He
knew all that was known about the route and
the orders to the troops. The main incidents
of the march were pretty likely to be reported
to him. Most of his journal was apparently
written day by day or not long after the
events, and it was prepared with great care
as a kind of report,— in fact, at least the first
part of it was forwarded to Washington.
Only one thing seems to be lacking,— perfect
honesty on the part of the author. Arnold
was always disposed to feel that the end

justified the means, and it is quite possible that we may find some evidence of intentional misrepresentation on his part. But there was little call for this on the march through the wilderness, and especially little concerning the matters that chiefly interest us ; so that Arnold's journal is certainly of prime importance.

A pendent to this narrative is the record of the early weeks of the march[3] signed by Arnold's secretary, Captain Eleazer Oswald.[4] Force has printed this, and we shall have to accept his version, for the original has disappeared from our sight. The journal is similar in character and value to Arnold's own ; indeed, Oswald wrote in Arnold's name, and used the pronoun of the first person as Arnold would have done.

Next in value stands, probably, the diary of Captain Dearborn.[5] The writer was not only a leader in the expedition, but he was a man of unusual ability. Later in life he figured as Secretary of War, Major-General, Commander-in-chief of the army, Collector of Customs at Boston, and Minister to Portugal. The manuscript[6] of his journal as it now exists dates from March 25, 1777, and is not in his own writing, though it bears his name. But we have several journals of other events from his hand, and we naturally infer that he kept an account of the march to Quebec, and later had it copied by a good penman. The manuscript shows corrections, which Mellen Chamberlain, who took a special interest in autographs, declared were Dearborn's. The journal is therefore a first-rate authority, though not quite so good as if it were an original day-by-day record.

Less full, complete, and precise, but still of excellent character, is the testimony of Major Meigs, an intrepid soldier and able officer. Dearborn and Meigs appear to have compared notes, and each may have derived information from the other.[7]

Meigs's journal was published in Almon's *Remembrancer* in 1776, but the version that we prefer is naturally that of the Massachusetts Historical Society,[8] printed in 1814, because we can trace its paternity. The text was a manuscript found among the papers of President Stiles, of Yale College. At the end appeared the name of the author, Return J. Meigs, in the handwriting of his brother, Josiah Meigs, who was a tutor in Yale College during the Revolutionary War. It is easy to infer that the original had been carefully copied, and the

copy given to Stiles by Josiah Meigs; but it
must be admitted that we do not positively
know these things, nor how carefully the printing was done.

The need of reserve is emphasised by finding the journal, as printed in the *Remembrancer*,
quite different in style. Evidently Almon did
not receive the manuscript from the author, for
his name is given as Robert Meigs. It was
doubtless from a copy that the printer worked,
and a copy not always accurate. But the
style of this journal is that of a soldier of 1775,
while the style of the journal printed by the
Massachusetts Historical Society is that of an
instructor in Yale College. In short, one may
believe that in the latter we have Major Meigs's
original faithfully and intelligently edited.[9]
The date of publication in the *Remembrancer*
proves that this journal was composed at
about the time the events occurred.

Next in order should come, probably, the
surgeon of the army, Dr. Senter.[10] He, too,
proved a somewhat notable person, for when
he died, at the early age of forty-six, he
possessed a national—even an international—
reputation among those of his profession.
Senter was for the times a fairly well educated
man, and this fact distinguishes his journal from

a number of the others ; but he was young, he
betrayed occasionally the inattention of the
talkative person, he was not an officer nor
even a military man, he was prevented by his
duties from closely observing many facts, and
there are striking instances of error and even
carelessness. The fulness of his account gives
it an appearance of accuracy above its real
merit. The authenticity of the journal is
beyond question. One curious fact is sufficient
proof. Senter was very proud of a certain
letter that he received from Benedict Arnold,
and states in his journal that it was on the
opposite page. This letter has been abstracted
from the manuscript, but the place where it was
attached is evident. This assures us that we
have before us Dr. Senter's own work. But we
still have to inquire whether it was penned at
the time or later. Later, is my opinion. The
uniformity of the penmanship shows that it
was not a daily record of the events as they
occurred. Some bits of verse relating to the
assault on Quebec, December 31, 1775, are
quoted ; and while I have not been able to
find the date of their publication, it seems
probable that some time was necessary for the
poet to incubate his lines after the event
occurred. Obviously, however, it was written

before Arnold went over to the British (1780), for after that Senter would not have shown pride in his letter. As in other such cases, the author probably made notes as he went, and afterward wrote them out, with some or more likely many additions from memory. An element of uncertainty is therefore to be reckoned with. The printed version [11] is substantially correct, but contains a good many trivial and some important departures from the manuscript.

Besides this, another document attributed to Senter exists, which may be called Senter's Account. It is now the property of the Rhode Island Historical Society, and has not yet been printed. It was given to the Society by a descendant of Dr. Senter, and the natural inference from this fact would be in favour of its authenticity. But it had not been long in the possession of the family; it had had turned up among the papers of Governor Francis, and was forwarded to Senter's granddaughter without careful examination, under the impression that it was the original of the Pennsylvania publication just mentioned. That, however, it is not, by any means.

Still the document seems clearly the work of Senter. There is an extremely close similarity in substance between this and his journal, combined with great independence as to phrasing. We find statements, errors, and expressions in both which we do not meet with elsewhere. Either Senter wrote both, or some unknown author used the journal as the basis for his Account. To accept the latter alternative would require us to believe, not only that this unknown author gave himself extreme trouble to disguise what he took, and even went so far as to invent curious details, but that he then proceeded to defeat himself by imitating certain unmistakable peculiarities of his original. This would be a psychological absurdity, not to say impossibility, and one cannot imagine an adequate motive for such a procedure. Senter, on the other hand, may very naturally have done the Account as a brief summary, intending to give it to a friend or a newspaper or to read it publicly, perhaps. A study of the handwriting of the two manuscripts seems to show as close a resemblance as could fairly be expected, if some time elapsed between the composition of the first and that of the second.[12]

The next three journals will have to be considered as a group. One of them bears the name of Simeon Thayer,[13] of Providence, who served in the expedition as a captain. His diary, annotated by E. M. Stone, has been published, but the editor permitted himself a great number of slight departures from the manuscript, with some of considerable significance. The second is the narrative of John Topham,[14] also a captain, whose residence was Newport. He and Thayer were close friends apparently, and certainly they often joined as comrades in difficult and perilous undertakings. Topham's manuscript, belonging now to his grandson, is mainly in good preservation still, but October 6th is the beginning and May 23d the end of what can be read. It is supposed to be in the Captain's handwriting. I have not been able to find anything certainly traced by his pen to compare with it, yet, in view of the clear family tradition, there seems no good reason to doubt its paternity.

Next, however, appears a manuscript, never listed before among our sources of information, I believe, that must be taken account of. It bears the signature of William Humphrey,[15] a Providence man, who marched as lieutenant in Thayer's company. The document seems clearly to come from him. That is also the family tradition; and this tradition is the more valuable because he lived until 1832, and his

wife until 1843.   Now a comparison between
Thayer and Topham reveals at once remarkable similarities ; and when Humphrey is considered, it is even more evident that we are
not in the presence of three independent accounts.

It will be convenient to compare Humphrey
and Thayer together first.   The simple fact
that both make the error of placing Beverly
between Cambridge and Malden — an error
found nowhere else — is enough to prove a
connection ; but this is only one out of in-
numerable resemblances.   We next inquire
which was the basal document.   It is evident
at once that Humphrey employs a rougher
style than Thayer.[16]   Now if Thayer reworked
his lieutenant's diary, an attempt to improve
its diction can be understood ; but it is impossible to see how Lieutenant Humphrey, had
he used Captain Thayer's journal as an original, could have gone deliberately to work to
roughen it into what we find.   Further, it
seems possible actually to demonstrate that
Thayer used Humphrey's text.   Thayer's
record for October 22d is as follows :

" myself and eight more of the men missing our way by
the freshet of the River and the overflowing of the surface were cast in to the greatest consternation not being

able to make any other way but by wading through the
water in which situation, we were obliged to remain
without vituals or drink untill the next morning about 9
o'clock exhausted with both cold and fatigue reach'd
the detachment as they were beginning their march.

"the storm abated the river rose 6 feet perpendicular
and ran exceeding rapid.   the sun rose with a little rain
but soon grew fair, & we embark'd on board our
Bateaus & after going about 6 miles against the current
which ran at least 5 miles an hour, came to a carrying-
place, entirely overflowed, that our Bateaus went trough
the woods without the trouble of carrying them advanced
about 50 Rodds and encamp'd."

According to this record, Thayer went two
day's journeys on the same day,— one on the
shore and one on the river. We might attempt to explain this apparent absurdity by
assuming that the first paragraph had reference
to events of the 21st. But Thayer and the
others give no hint of moving on the 21st.
In fact they mention how they employed themselves in camp, and Senter, who reached the
camp on that day recorded : "At sunset we
arrived at the encampment of Col. Greene
& his division, who were waiting for provisions." Turning now to Humphrey, we find
that his record is almost word for word like the
second paragraph above, but rougher in style.
We see, therefore, how Thayer came to have

it. Plainly, he composed his journal by
smoothing Humphrey's, adding his personal
experiences, and giving in some cases his fuller
knowledge. A curious illustration of the latter change is Thayer's reporting the number
of men despatched for a certain purpose, while
Humphrey wrote: "The number I do not
know." The value of Thayer's journal is
somewhat lessened by this discovery of his indebtedness; and yet not necessarily very much,
for he was a witness of nearly all the events of
his journal; and, even if he used Humphrey's
statements, he gave them, to a great extent, as
his personal testimony.

Topham's journal resembles Humphrey's
even more closely, perhaps, than Thayer's has
been found to do, and equally clear evidence of
dependence can be found. For example, Topham has no entry for October 26th. His account
of the 25th concludes thus: "Col. Green, Capt.
Topham & Thayer stay by desire of Col.
Enos in order to hold a council of war. Resolved that Col. Enos should not go back,
but afterwards returned with the whole of
his division, viz., Capt. Williams, Scott &
McCobb. We proceeded over three carrying-
places, two small ones, and one half a mile
over, after coming up the river & a pond.

Encamped 20 rods from the pond." Our first
question is, why did not Topham say " I " in
the first sentence? In other places he did not
hesitate to speak of himself in the first person.
Our next is, why does he not mention October
26th? And our third might well be, where
were the carrying-places,— on the river or on
the pond? All these inquiries appear to be
answered by a quotation from Humphrey :

" [Oct.] 25. . . . Here Col Green Capt
Topham & Thayre stay'd by desire of Col.
Enoe in order to hold a countiel of war in
which it was Determined that Enoe should not
go back. 26. This Day we proceeded over 3
Carrying places 2 small ones And one about $\frac{1}{2}$
a mile & through a pond that Is about $\frac{1}{4}$ of a
mile & a carrying place as much more And
came to another pond & encamp'd."

It seems perfectly clear that Topham copied
Humphrey, carelessly omitting a date and
muddling one sentence, yet, on the other hand,
adding a couple of facts. Consequently our
opinion of Topham's journal is about like our
opinion of Thayer's.[17] His testimony is substantially, yet not absolutely, that of an independent witness. In both cases, it must be
remembered, in particular, that we do not know
when the journal was written, and as the

endorsement of Humphrey is valuable in proportion to the freshness of the writer's recollection, this value is an uncertain quantity.

Humphrey's narrative, also, may need to be
discounted somewhat.   The first two months
of it do not appear to be in his handwriting,
and after January 5, 1776, when he was in
confinement at Quebec and ink was taken
away from him, the diary goes on in ink as
before.   But there are hints that Humphrey
kept a record as he went, and it may fairly be
assumed, since his book must have suffered a
good deal of damage on the march, that he decided later to have it copied.

The only other journals throwing light on
our subject, except some written by privates,
are one that has been lost and another that is
anonymous.

Lieutenant Heath,[18] of Captain Morgan's
Virginia riflemen, kept a diary.   It fell to one
of his descendants, a gentleman of Richmond,
Va., but has recently disappeared.   And yet
we do obtain light from this document, for
Marshall used it freely in his *Life of Washington.*   Perhaps Marshall retained the part that
he used, for a gentleman who copied some
years ago what there was of Heath's manuscript informs me that what he saw did not

begin until after the assault on Quebec (December 31st). Reasoning on this hint, I thought the missing manuscript might possibly be found among Marshall's papers. But I had no success in this direction, for it soon appeared that his papers were scattered.[19]

The anonymous journal was published in Glasgow in 1776, and bears this title: *Journal of a March of a Party of Provincials from Carlisle to Boston and from Thence to Quebec.* The editor said in his Preface: "The following authentic Journal, wrote by an officer of the Party, was sent from a Gentleman in Quebec to his Friend in Glasgow, who put it into the hands of the Printers." Evidently the author belonged to the rifle company of Captain Hendricks. Now we are told by Henry that Sergeant McCoy of Hendricks's company, "an excellent clerk," gave Major Murray of the Quebec garrison "a genuine copy of his journal of the route through the wilderness into Canada." Of course a sergeant should not be called an officer, but on the other hand he might be spoken of as such, at least by a civilian. Moreover, this anonymous record has the air of coming from a sergeant. So it seems to me very possible that the "Provincial's" journal is neither more nor less than the

missing narrative of jolly Sergeant McCoy.
This consideration gives it more weight; but
there is no certainty about its authorship, and
we must reckon further on the errors of a
copyist and of two printing offices,—one in
Scotland and another in America,—for I have
had to rely on Egle's version.[20] The testimony of the journal is mainly sound and valuable, but it is seldom full. Distances made
the central point of the author's thought, and
even in this respect he is neither minute nor
precisely correct. Yet the meagreness of the
record adds to the impression of its genuine-
ness and contemporaneity.

Next come a series of reports from the
rank and file, which form a most valuable sup-
plement to the records of the officers. Abner
Stocking, a Connecticut soldier, shows once
more how the last may be first, for his journal
appeared as a book in 1810, while no officer's account has ever done as well. But
here we meet a serious difficulty. Stocking
certainly belonged to Hanchet's company.[21]
The official records of Connecticut, the official British list of the men captured when
Quebec was assaulted, and the similar list attached to what has been called Ware's journal, all agree on this point. Stocking was

a man, too, from whom we might expect a
journal. He was above the average age of
Arnold's men.[22] His father, Captain Abner
Stocking, was a prominent man in the town;
his grandfather, George Stocking, had been a
captain in the militia; one of his brothers became a Methodist minister. It looks at first
a bit suspicious that the diary of a Connecticut
man should have been published by relatives
at Catskill, New York, especially as we have
no record that any of his relatives went there;
but we know that people did go from the
quarries near his home to open quarries at
Catskill. So far we can make our way. But
we find on reading the journal that the auther
of it was not, as a rule, where we have excellent reasons to believe that Hanchet's company was.[23] At the same time Stocking's record
has every appearance of individuality and good
faith.

A reasonable explanation may perhaps lie
within reach. While Stocking was impris-
oned at Quebec, he might naturally resolve to
enliven the tedium of confinement, and obtain
a souvenir of a notable experience, by writing
an account of the incidents that had taken
place. Perhaps he had begun a journal and
given it up. Anyhow, his memory was full of

facts, but he needed a chronological string to hang them on. He might, then, without the slightest intention to deceive, borrow the string from one of his comrades, modifying and extending freely his comrade's narrative according to his personal recollection. Later we shall approach this problem from another point of view. Whatever we conclude about it, we must look upon Stocking's journal with some reserve; yet the author was so evidently a careful, sensible man, observant and also reflective, that we cannot help regarding his narrative as in substance reliable. As for his manuscript, it seems to have disappeared entirely, and we have no means of judging how accurately it was printed.[24]

Journals not so well written as Stocking's, but free from suspicion, have come to us from James Melvin [25] of Dearborn's company, and Caleb Haskell of Ward's.

The whereabouts of Melvin's manuscript are now unknown. It was first printed in 1857, and William J. Davis, who is said to have been private secretary to George Bancroft, prefixed an Introduction. We may probably assume that the printed version represents the original accurately, especially as the Introduction states that Melvin's penmanship was "exceedingly neat." The journalist was a painstaking man, one would say, and there is no reason to question his honesty; but he was merely a private, and possessed only ordinary intelligence. Neither do we know how long after the events his diary was written. However, these are points of no great practical importance, for Melvin adds little to the other journals. Only a few times does his narrative become of special significance, and in those cases the danger of a departure from the original seems to be slight.

Caleb Haskell was a Newburyport man, and according to tradition a cabinet-maker and a sailor at different times.[26] He was a plain, sensible person, and made a plain, sensible narrative of what he saw and heard. Particulars are often wanting, and occasionally there is an error; but in its rather limited way the journal is decidedly valuable. It was first published in a Newburyport newspaper, and afterwards, in 1881, Mr. Withington issued it as a pamphlet. I have been fortunate enough to light upon the copy used by the printer, and, better still, to have a critical comparison made with the manuscript,[27] and so have obtained the reading of the original. The printed copy is substantially correct, though it

contains a few significant errors; but the
grammar, spelling, and capitalisation of Haskell's text were considerably modified. What
is doubtless more important, somebody has
made erasures in the original that blot entirely
what was written.

In the *Proceedings of the Massachusetts Historical Society* for April, 1886, there is printed
a journal of the Kennebec expedition presented by Justin Winsor, and attributed to
Ebenezer Wild.[28] But the Massachusetts archives do not give the name of any Ebenezer
Wild who can have gone to Canada with
Arnold. That, to be sure, is not conclusive,
for some of the Massachusetts members of the
Kennebec detachment do not appear on the
Massachusetts rolls; they seem to have enlisted especially for this expedition. But the
author of the journal was taken prisoner at
the assault on Quebec, and no Ebenezer Wild
appears in "Ware's" list of the men captured.
Neither does he appear on the British list of
prisoners.[29] This is not all. We know of a
Revolutionary soldier who bore that name.
He enlisted on May 12, 1775, as a corporal, and
was reported by his captain, Lemuel Trescott,
as serving at Prospect Hill on October 6,
1775, more than three weeks after the Quebec

detachment had departed. This Wild kept journals. One was devoted to the Ticonderoga expedition of 1776, and at the close of it, he speaks of setting out for the Saratoga campaign in the words: "I marched for my second campaign." But this would have been his third campaign had he gone to Quebec.[30] Finally, the manuscript of the journal attributed to Wild makes no claim that it was composed by a person of that name. The natural inference from these facts is that the document is a copy of a record kept by some one else.[31]

In the *New England Historical and Genealogical Register* for 1852 there appeared a journal almost identical with this attributed to Wild. It was represented as the composition of Joseph Ware, of Needham, Mass.; and it has been so attributed since.[32] Just why there was so much confidence about this does not appear, for according to Mr. Winsor's notes it bore no indication of source except the words "Joseph Ware his book." If this is enough to prove authorship, what must be the number of schoolboys wickedly robbed of their copyright dues on *Webster's Spelling Book*[33]!

The simple fact is that Joseph Ware of Needham cannot have written the journal, for he did not belong to Arnold's army. The

Massachusetts archives contain a roll dated Cambridge, October 5, 1775, which reports him as a corporal in Whiting's company of Heath's regiment on that day.   There was, however, a Joseph Ware in Ward's company of Arnold's army, for the name is down in both our lists of the prisoners of December 31st.[34]   But this is all the information that we have.   Although several Joseph Wares appear on the Massachusetts rolls, no one of that name is reported as " gone to Quebec,"— the usual formula, — and we must conclude that this was somebody who enlisted specially for the Canada campaign, and cannot be identified.   In that case the journal, if written by him, is practically anonymous.

But now comes the explanation of the mystery.   In the book of the Lockes — a genealogy of the Locke family — the author says [35]:

" I have been furnished by Mr. William Tolman of Watertown, N. Y., with a portion of a journal,[36] a part having been lost, which he alleges was ' kept' by his father, Ebenezer Tolman, who was a member of the same company to which Mr. Ware belonged.   A comparison of this journal with what is called the *original* of Mr. Ware establishes the fact that one is a copy of the other, or that both are copies of some other.   They are, with the exception of now and then a word, identically the same, save one important entry, which will be noticed. A comparison also shows with considerable certainty that they were written by the same hand. The writing is very similar, and I think I am not mistaken in the opinion that he who penned the one also penned the other ; and there is a reasonable presumption that Mr. Tolman was the penman, and that the one furnished me by his son is the original ; and for several reasons.

"First, it appears to have been written at different periods, and has an older appearance than Mr. Ware's copy, which looks as though it was written all at one time and almost with the same pen.

"Second, Mr. Ware does not use the personal pronoun 'I' from beginning to end, whereas Mr. Tolman says under date of January 19, 1776 : 'This day I was taken down with the small pox, and carried to the Hospital, and in 15 days was able to return to the prison.'

"And lastly, two sons and two daughters of Mr. Tolman, now living, all unite in saying that they have, time and again, heard their father speak of *his journal* as one that *he* 'kept' on the march and while in prison, and that they have *no doubt* that it is in his handwriting. . . . Mr. Tolman and Mr. Ware had frequent intercourse after the war," and the former may have furnished the latter with a copy of his journal."

There certainly was an Ebenezer Tolman (or Toleman) in Ward's company of Arnold's army, the company in which we find a Joseph Ware. The evidence in Tolman's favour, set over against the facts about Wild and Ware, seems decisive, so that we may boldly discard the two latter names, and attribute their

journals to the former.   Of course, this is not
quite satisfactory, for we have not the original
manuscript, and have only Mr. Locke's testimony that Tolman's copy differed very slightly
from Ware's ; but it is the best we can do, for
the Tolman original appears to have disappeared from our ken.[38]

Unfortunately, we are not quite done with
this journal.   The same difficulty meets us as
in the case of Stocking.   Tolman belonged to
the third division, but his record belongs to
the first.   Is this another case like Stocking's,
whatever be the explanation of that ?   Presently we shall try to make up our minds.

The next document on our list is Morison's.
Morison [39] was only a private in Hendricks's
company of Pennsylvania riflemen, but he certainly possessed what he called "an extensive
imagination," with intensive feelings to match,
and a good deal of general intelligence.   His
record is both interesting and valuable as a
picture of the brave, hopeful, patriotic soldier,
laughing at hardship until too weak to produce
a laugh, and then pushing doggedly on ; but
he wielded the quill of a ready penman, felt
over-anxious for effect, and was too often
incomplete or incorrect in detail.   A tinge of
scepticism is advisable in reading his account.

The original manuscript I have neither seen nor heard of. It was printed at Hagerstown in 1803, and a copy of this edition exists in the library of the Pennsylvania Historical Society. As the title-page of the book states that it was " published from the manuscript," we may probably conclude that the original went the way of other printer's " copy "; and this appears the more likely because Morison was dead, and the publisher, as he issued the book at his own risk, was not likely to increase his bill of costs by having the rather voluminous manuscript copied. How accurately the printing was done, we have, therefore, no means of judging.

With all its plainly marked personal peculiarities, Morison's journal shows a certain family likeness to " Provincial's." This makes a group of four suspicious documents, and it is now time to investigate the problem of origin more fully.

Tolman's case may be taken up first. His journal, at bottom, is clearly not his own, for, as we have seen, it describes things from the point of view of the first division, while he belonged to the third. Further, we have a diary from another member of the same company, Haskell, which agrees with what we

should expect, not with what Tolman gives
us. Further still, there is internal evidence
to the same effect. For instance, here is a
bit of Tolman's journal :

"[Oct.] 5th, 6th & 7th.—Pushed up to the head of
the Kennebec, where we carried out into a pond. These
last three days we came about 20 miles. 8th.—This
day we pushed on very briskly, it being Sunday. The
foremost companies lying still on account of heavy
rains ; we marched all day, it being very wet & cold,
& suffered a good deal from the inclemency of the
weather, and came up with some of them at night. 9th,
10th & 11th.—Carried to the first pond," etc.

How does it happen that on the morning of
October 8th Tolman found himself a "brisk"
day's march behind the riflemen, when, according to his own journal, he left Fort
Western the day they did, and moved as they
moved all the way? Stranger still, how does
it happen that it took him all day Sunday to
reach the point which he has just stated that
he reached Saturday night,— the point where
all left the Kennebec? A glance at "Provincial's" account explains all this : "[Oct.]
5, 6, 7. We poled & dragged against a
shallow stream & encamped at the place where
we leave Kinnebec. Three days made 20
miles. 8. Lay in our tents on account of a

heavy rain." Evidently Tolman relied on "Provincial" or Morison for October 5th, 6th, and
7th, but wished to give the doings of his own
company for the 8th; and so, instead of following his guide for the latter, merely alludes
to the "foremost companies." Haskell confirms this by saying that on the 8th they
went eight miles in the rain. That Tolman
leaned on "Provincial" rather than Morison is
hinted by a great number of close verbal
similarities,— even many whole sentences; and
by the fact that both he and "Provincial"
give figures omitted by Morison. Yet Tolman
was not a slavish imitator. At one time he
did not pursue the same route as "Provincial," and his journal is faithful to the
fact. There are many differences of wording
or arrangement between the two, and in some
cases he makes additions. With proper care,
use may be made of his record.

Stocking's case is by no means so clear.
Resemblances between him and "Provincial"
there certainly are. The whole general course
of the two is the same. Whenever "Provincial"
lumps the record of two days or three days,
Stocking, with two exceptions, does the same.
Where there is a gap in one, the other is silent; and more minute points are not wanting.[40]

Apparently Morison cannot have been his
authority, for Morison's record of October
17th and 18th is : " We ascended this river 36
miles, these last two days, carrying over two
small carrying-places of about 10 rods each ";
while Stocking has it : " 17.   After passing
over a small carrying place of 16 rods we
rowed 16 miles up the river. . . . 18.
This day we rowed 20 miles & passed a short
carrying place. . . ."   But a similar difficulty arises October 5th, 6th, and 7th with reference to regarding either " Provincial's " or
Tolman's journal as Stocking's original.   These
are only specimen cases.   At all times he shows
independence, and he adds matter of his own
liberally.   It may be that he wrote with more
than one journal before him.   Anyhow, it
seems impossible to do more than say that
he made a very independent use of some
journal or journals of the first division as
the thread of his story.   His record is much
more valuable than Tolman's, because fuller
and more individual, but it must be followed
with caution.

Morison belonged undoubtedly where he
represents himself, and he was no mere imitator.   In its way his account is no less individual than Stocking's.   But it has the

look, not of a daily record, but of a free re-working of something else, filled out with many additions. For an example, the record of October 18th may be referred to again: "We ascended the river 36 miles these last two days, carrying over two small carrying-places of about 10 rods each. In this en-campment we were confined the four following days by heavy rains." From the first sentence one would infer that the record was made at the close of the 18th; but the next sentence negatives this idea. Besides this, we find in places, particularly November 5th and 6th, an almost verbal resemblance to "Provincial" and Tolman.

Under date of November 4th, he says: "Last night we got plenty of good beef and potatoes, but not much bread," and Tolman records: "Last night had plenty of beef & potatoes; but little or no bread was to be had"; while "Provincial" writes under date of November 3d: "Here we . . . got plenty of good beef & potatoes, little or no bread." As Tolman's journal was probably not based on Morison, it would seem to follow that Morison's was based here on Tolman. But Morison may have used more than one source. The main point is to remember that his record is not altogether his own, though he was an eye-witness of the march, and in a sense confirms the record that he adopts.

Simon Fobes, a private in Hubbard's company, is next in order.[41] What he gives us is not a journal, but recollections, put in writing sixty years after the events took place. His narrative contains many errors, but it adds a number of items which we seem justified in accepting.

This completes the list of original documents covering the whole of the march to Quebec, but we have also the diary of Ephraim Squier [42] of Scott's company, one of those who turned back in the wilderness and made for Cambridge. As the only account of this retreat, the journal has a special value; and for us it is of considerable importance all the while, because no other pen was going in the fourth division. But the story is that of a common soldier, very plain, simple, and meagre, and not always accurate. So far as authenticity is concerned, however, we are on firm ground, for the manuscript is preserved in the Pension Bureau at Washington. It has been printed, but not carefully. I have gone back to the original. One can scarcely avoid judging from the manuscript that what we have here is a contemporary, unaltered record, as Squier himself stated.

To these sources may be added an account of the expedition by the Rev. Jacob Bailey,[43] a tory clergyman of Pownalborough, on the Kennebec, and a careful and voluminous writer whose work has never been published. The number of facts that he adds is not large, but his point of view makes all that he says interesting. Of course he was not an eye-witness of the march, but he knew about things done in his immediate vicinity, and seems to have obtained information from guides, and perhaps from other persons who traversed the wilderness.

Finally, we have letters bearing on the subject, particularly from Arnold, Captain Dearborn, and Captain Ward.[44]

In short, the witnesses are many and their testimony is full, though it covers by no means every point. A satisfactory harmony of all these varying accounts, often confused and often inaccurate, is hard to secure ; but the problem has to be faced.[45]

III

CAMBRIDGE TO GARDINERSTON

THE Orderly Book[1] of Colonel William Henshaw, who was Adjutant-General at Cambridge until Washington took command, and then served as assistant to Gates, contains this entry :

" Head-quarters, Sept. 5th, 1775. Parole *Waltham ;* countersign *York.* . . . A detachment, consisting of two lieutenant colonels, two majors, 10 captains, 30 sub-alterns, 30 sergeants, 30 corporals, 4 drummers, 2 fifers & 676 privates, to parade to-morrow morning at eleven o'clock, upon the Common in Cambridge, to go upon command with Colonel Arnold, of Connecticut. One company of Virginia riflemen[2] & two companies from Colonel Thompson's Pennsylvania regiment of riflemen[3] to parade at the same time & place, to join the above detachment. Tents & necessaries convenient & proper for the whole will be supplied by the Quartermaster-General immediately upon the detachment being collected. As it is imagined the officers & men sent from the regiments, both here & at Roxbury, will be such volunteers as are active woodsmen & well acquainted with bateaux, so it is recommended that none but such

will offer themselves for this service. Colonel Arnold
& the Adjutant General will attend upon the Common
in Cambridge to-morrow, in the forenoon, to receive
and parade their detachments. The Quartermaster-
General will be also there, to supply tents, &c.   .   .   ."

Adding to the figures of the order about
250 riflemen, a surgeon with his mate and two
assistants, two adjutants, two quartermasters,[4]
a chaplain, and a few volunteers,[5] we reach a
total of almost exactly 1050.[6] Washington
called the detachment "one thousand men";
and, speaking roundly, that was the number
of the rank and file.

On the 8th of September, the Commander-
in-chief issued this order :

"The detachments going under the command of Col.
Arnold, to be forthwith taken off the roll of duty, and
to march this evening to Cambridge Common, where
tents and everything necessary is provided for their
reception. The rifle company at Roxbury[7] and those
from Prospect Hill, to march early tomorrow morning to join the above detachment. Such officers and
men as are taken from Gen. Green's brigade for the
above detachment are to attend the muster of their re-
spective regiments tomorrow morning at 7 o'clock upon
Prospect Hill ; when the muster is finished they are
forthwith to rejoin the detachment at Cambridge."

In view of what followed, the delay in setting out seems extremely unfortunate. Washington's intention was not at fault, and he

felt greatly disappointed at the loss of time. But it proved more difficult than was expected to make the necessary preparations, and Squier informs us that when the men were paraded on Monday, September 11th, " in order to march for Quebec," some of them refused to move without a month's pay,— " so we stayed still in Cambridge." The advance did, however, begin on that day,[8] and on Wednesday the major part set out. Newburyport,[9] a good harbour on the Merrimac River, about three miles from the sea, was to be the rendezvous. First of all the riflemen moved; and after spending one night at Neale's Tavern, and the next at Mr. Bunkam's church, they camped on Wednesday, the 13th, about a mile from the Merrimac.[10] The musket men formed two battalions. The first of these, led by Lieutenant-Colonel Roger Enos and Major Return J. Meigs, consisted of five companies, commanded by Thomas Williams, Henry Dearborn, Oliver Hanchet, William Goodrich, and a captain whom we know only as Scott. Leaving Cambridge toward evening on Wednesday, this battalion spent the night in Medford.[11] The next day, after passing through Malden and Lynn, they stopped in Salem and Danvers.[12] On Friday they crossed Beverly and

SKETCH MAP
OF
NORTHEASTERN MASS.

SCALE

Wenham, and rested for the night in Rowley and Ipswich; and early on Saturday they arrived at Newburyport.

The second battalion was led by Lieutenant-Colonel Christopher Greene and Major Timothy Bigelow. The captains were five in number, and their names were Samuel Ward, Simeon Thayer, John Topham, Jonas Hubbard, and Samuel McCobb. Setting out on the 13th, earlier in the day than the first battalion, this party were able to reach Malden before night, Beverly[13] on Thursday, and Newburyport on Friday.[14] Arnold himself, after lingering at Cambridge until Friday,[15] pushed on so vigorously that he dined at Salem,[16] and lodged that same night in Newburyport.

On Saturday[17] the little army were all near the point of their next departure, but not all together. The riflemen were encamped in Newbury, near the edge of Newburyport, by what was known as the Trayneing Green and is now called the upper Common,[18] while the rest of the soldiers pitched their tents elsewhere or found lodgings in the Town-house, a church, and two rope-walks in the Port.[19] Twenty men from Newbury and the Port were members of the force, besides the Rev.

Samuel Spring, the chaplain, and both officers and men were hospitably treated. Many last preparations proved necessary, and it was a busy time.

Nathaniel Tracy, Arnold's host,[20] was a man of considerable wealth at that day, and particularly interested in ships. It was to him that Washington had addressed himself for vessels to transport the detachment to the Kennebec,[21] and he advanced £700 of lawful money to fit out the expedition. Thanks in part to his exertions the fleet was there, and was adequate; but certainly not all the vessels were grand: "dirty coasters & fish boats" they seemed to Fobes.

Saturday the winds were contrary; but, in accordance with orders from the Commander-in-chief, Arnold sent off three scouting vessels toward the Kennebec, toward the Isles of Shoals, and along-shore, with instructions to report as quickly as possible whether any British cruisers or men-of-war could be seen.

Sunday there were head winds and thick weather, but the preparations to embark went on, and a review was held.[22] Religion also was remembered, and the troops listened to their chaplain, or marched under arms to church.[23]

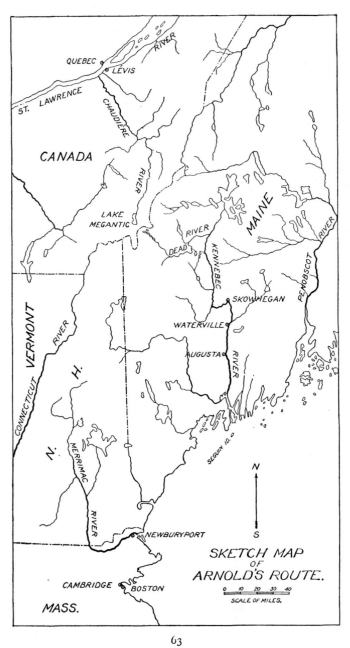

QUEBEC

LÉVIS

ST. LAWRENCE

RIVER

CHAUDIERE

CANADA

RIVER

LAKE
MEGANTIC

RIVER

DEAD

KENNEBEC

MAINE

RIVER

PENOBSCOT

RIVER

SKOWHEGAN

WATERVILLE

AUGUSTA

RIVER

CONNECTICUT

VERMONT

RIVER

N. H.

MERRIMAC

RIVER

SEGUIN ID.

N

S

NEWBURYPORT

SKETCH MAP
OF
ARNOLD'S ROUTE.

0   10   20   30   40
SCALE OF MILES.

CAMBRIDGE

BOSTON

MASS.

63

The transports—eleven schooners and sloops —lay at the wharves near the centre of the town, and on Monday afternoon[24] the men embarked,— none too willingly, it must be confessed, for in at least one case a guard was necessary to keep them aboard. Nothing more was needed but favourable conditions for setting sail, since one of the scouting fleet had come in and reported the coast quite clear.[25]

Tuesday, rather early in the forenoon, anchors were weighed, and at midday ten of the transports were safely off. The schooner *Swallow*, however, ran aground, and could not be floated at that tide.[26] Captain Scott was ordered to remain aboard with eleven others, and follow as soon as he could ; but the rest of the passengers were transferred, and early in the afternoon the fleet set sail for the Kennebec and Canada with a favourable wind.

The following signals,[27] issued to the fleet, show that careful preparations for contingencies were made :

" 1. Signal for speaking with the whole fleet : ensign at main-topmast head.

" 2. Signal for chasing a sail : ensign at fore-topmast head.

5

" 3. Signal for heaving to : lantern at mast head
& two guns, if head on shore ; and three guns, if off
shore.

" 4. Signal for making sail in the night : lantern at
mast head, & four guns.   In the day, for making sail :
jack at fore-topmast head.

" 5. Signal for dispersing & every vessel making the
nearest harbor : ensign at main peak.

" 6. Signal for boarding any vessel : jack at main-
topmast head, & the whole fleet to draw up in a line,
as near as possible.

" N. B. No guns to be fired without orders."

About four o'clock two fishing schooners
were spoken, but nothing was heard of hostile ships; and, after keeping on the course [28]
until about midnight, the fleet hove to off
Wood Island.[29] It was a quick passage,—
nearly or quite one hundred miles [30] in about
eleven hours, for Wood Island lies close on
the left hand as one approaches the Kennebec
from the south-west.

The first look when daylight broke was not
quite an agreeable one.   Rocky islands are
very plentiful at the mouth of the Kennebec,
and the fleet seemed in very dangerous company.   But all went well, though three of the
transports missed their way for a time; and
half an hour after sunrise, as Dr. Senter informs us, the mouth of the river could be

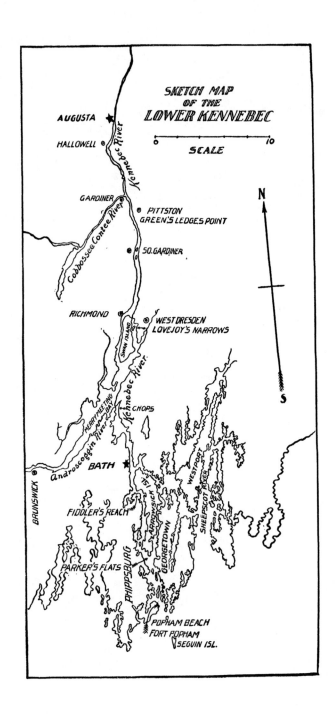

SKETCH MAP
OF THE
LOWER KENNEBEC

SCALE

0   10

N

S

AUGUSTA

HALLOWELL

Kennebec River

GARDINER

PITTSTON
GREEN'S LEDGES POINT

Cobbossee Contee River

SO. GARDINER

RICHMOND

WEST DRESDEN
LOVEJOY'S NARROWS

SWAN ISLAND

Kennebec River

CHOPS

MERRY MEETING BAY

Androscoggin River

BATH

WESTPORT

BRUNSWICK

SHEEPSCOT RIVER

FIDDLER'S REACH

ARROWSICK

GEORGETOWN

PARKER'S FLATS

PHIPPSBURG

POPHAM BEACH
FORT POPHAM
SEGUIN ISL.

made out.   A little later the vessels, one by one, began to enter it.[31]

Whether fortifications existed here in 1775 we do not know; but that seems very probable, for Arnold's fleet was greeted by men under arms, and they could not have expected to keep British cruisers out of the river unless they had cannon and some kind of defences. Old guns may have been put to use again there, for the French and Indian War had come to an end only twelve years before (1763).   Whatever the explanation, a number of soldiers were on the alert, and a pilot was immediately provided.

From this point the fleet separated more or less, for the navigation of the river is not simple, and such a number of sailing craft could not be handled in a body.   Rocks, islands, bold headlands, and confusing bays are numberless in this part of the Kennebec.   However, guided by the pilot, Arnold worked his way up the stream, and anchored for six hours at Parker's Flats, about four miles from the river's mouth.[32]   Next he proceeded about six miles farther up the river, and arrived at Georgetown.   One of the missing transports appears to have rejoined him here.[33]

Georgetown was a generous term at that

day, and included also Arrowsic Island, Bath
and West Bath, Phippsburg, and Woolwich.
Of all this area, Arrowsic Island was the most
populous part.   James Sullivan, afterwards a
noted jurist and a Governor of Massachusetts,
is believed to have been one of its inhabitants [34]
in 1775.   Another of the residents was Samuel
McCobb, town clerk and a delegate to the Provincial Congress.   News of Lexington travelled
to Georgetown in eight days ; and then
McCobb, laying down his pen, took up his
sword,—or, more probably, musket,—organised a company, marched in six days, we are
told, to Cambridge, and fought behind the rail-
fence at Bunker Hill.   When the Kennebec
expedition was decided on, he appears to have
hurried back to Georgetown, raised some
twenty recruits to fill up his quota, and joined
the expedition on its arrival there. [35]

Some of the transports did better and some
did worse than Arnold's top-sail schooner.
Senter passed the night on Parker's Flats, but
Meigs contrived in some way to get up as far
as Pownalborough, about thirty miles from the
sea, while Stocking's yet abler skipper, using
both sails and oars, and aided finally by the
evening tide, succeeded in anchoring his sloop
only six miles below Fort Western.

The next sun was not yet due by a full hour when Arnold's anchor came up and he set out again.   About opposite the present city of Bath, the two other missing vessels of his fleet rejoined him, after working their way across from Sheepscot River.   Then, sailing through Merrymeeting Bay,[36] an enlargement of the Kennebec, and passing Swan Island,[37] Arnold pushed on as far as Gardinerston (September 21st).   " Left the transports in the river, wind and tide unfavourable," recorded Oswald.[38] Dearborn's vessel ran aground,[39] and all the ships found themselves in difficulties.

Swan Island, now the township of Perkins, is about three and one-half miles long, and splits the river into halves.   The western channel, often called at this day Swan Alley, is the one the Boston steamers take, for they wish to stop at Richmond village near the upper end ; but Arnold's vessels appear to have chosen the other and deeper one.   When a little more than half-way to the parting of the two channels above, they came to Little Swan Island,[40] once, according to tradition, the seat of a powerful sachem.   There they found a hard bit of navigation in Lovejoy's Narrows,[41] and finally, rounding the island, they entered once more the full Kennebec.

This was a notable point in their journey.
On the left, a little above the present village
of Richmond, could be seen the remains of
Fort Richmond.   It had been occupied first in
the winter of 1720–21, or in the following
spring,[42] and had been dismantled a generation
later.[43]   On the right or eastern side lay Pownalborough,[44] the Dresden of our day. " A
court-house and gaol and some very good
settlements," was the record of Captain
Dearborn ; and one may still see the big,
square, box-like, two-story house that answered as court-house and jail.[45]   Here lived
Major Goodwin, surveyor for the Plymouth
Company, original proprietors of the region,
and here the Rev. Jacob Bailey minis-
tered to a sizable congregation, a large part
of it loyalists like himself.   Here also could
be seen a fort, and Meigs noted it, though
Dearborn did not.   It stood on the river bank
about a mile above Swan Island.   A court
two hundred feet square was encompassed
with palisades except on the land side ; barracks and two blockhouses were put up within,
and the fort was christened in 1751, its birth-
year, Fort Shirley [46]; but the need of such
defences had passed away, and of course the
fortifications were not kept up.   Pownal-

borough, however, did not detain Dearborn, and four o'clock found him at Gardinerston with Arnold.[47]

Many of his comrades were with him, but not all.   Two of the fleet were now aground [48] some fifteen miles below ; and, as the *Swallow* had come up, Arnold sent her down with some men to their relief.[49]   And so, after hazards of many kinds, the expedition seems to have reached or passed the landing at Gardinerston by Friday night, the 22d of September.

IV

SYLVESTER GARDINER of Kingston, R. I., after studying medicine for eight years in France and England, settled in Boston, practised his profession successfully, made money also in the business of importing drugs, and became the greatest land-owner in the Kennebec valley. The extent of his possessions there was vast : at one time probably not less than one hundred thousand acres belonged to him, and the name Gardinerston covered not only what we know as Gardiner, but half a dozen other towns as well.[1]

It was on the eastern side of the river, in what we now call Pittston, that Arnold and many of his men stopped. There, on the shore of the Kennebec, about a couple of miles below the present city of Gardiner, lived Major Reuben Colburn.[2] He, too, was a land-owner. In 1763 he was granted two hundred and fifty acres ; but that seemed nothing, and on New

Year's Day, 1773, he bought himself a present
of two and a half square miles. The Major
owned a house there, and a good one, too.
It has always remained in the family, and his
granddaughter told me that the present building is substantially as he erected it. One
can easily accept the tradition that Colonel
Arnold lodged there.

There were good reasons why the commander of the expedition halted at this point :
Colburn was the real fulcrum of his enterprise. August 21st Arnold had addressed to
him the following letter [3] :

" WATERTOWN [MASS.], 21st Aug! 1775.
" MR. REUBEN COLBURN
 " SIR
  " His Excellency General Washington Desires you
will Inform your self how soon, there can be procured, or built, at Kennebec, Two hundred light Bat-
toos [4] Capable of Carrying Six or Seven Men each,
with their Provisions & Baggage, (say 100 wt. to each
man) the Boats to be furnished with four Oars two
Paddles & two Setting Poles [5] each, the expence of
Building them & wheather a Sufficient quantity of Nails
can be procured with you. you will Also inquire, what
quantity of Fresh Beef can be procured at Kenebec,
& the price.— at Newbury you will Inquire the Size &
Strength of the two Armed Vessels, If Compleated,
& wheather, bound on a Cruise or not.[6] Also the Condition the Armed Vessels are in at Kenebec [7] — you

will Also get particular Information from those People who have been at Quebec, of the Difuculty attending an Expedition that way, in particular the Number, & length, of the Carrying Places, wheather Low [?], Dry land, Hills, or Swamp. Also the Depth of Water in the River at this Season, wheather an easy Stream or Rapid — Also every other Intelligence which you Judge may be necessary to know, all which you will Commit to writing & Dispatch an express to his Excellency as soon as possible, who will Pay the Charge & expence you may be at in the Matter.

"I am

" Sir

" Your Hble Sv:

" BENED: ARNOLD."

Colburn was evidently an active, enterprising man, and took hold of the matter vigorously. Three times he appears to have gone to Cambridge. Once he was expressly summoned by Washington ; about the other trips we do not know. He was at headquarters on August 21st, and there on September 3d he received his definite orders [8]:

" Orders for Mr. Rheuben Colbourn of Gardnerstone, upon the River Kennebeck in The Province of Massachusetts Bay —

"You are to go with all Expedition to Gardnerstone upon the River Kenebeck and without Delay proceed to The Constructing of Two Hundred Batteaus,[9] to row with Four Oars each ; Two Paddles & Two Setting Poles to be also provided for each Batteau : —

"You are to Engage a Company of Twenty Men consisting of Artificers, Carpenters, and Guides, to go under your Command to Assist in such Services as you & they may be called upon to Execute [10] : —

"You are to Purchase Five Hundred Bushells of Indian Corn, to Provide the Workmen employed in Building the Batteaus : —

"You are also [11] to bespeak all The Pork, and Flour, you can from the Inhabitants upon the River Kennebeck, & a Commissary will be immediately sent [12] from the Commissary General, to agree, and pay for the same ; you will also acquaint The Inhabitants, that the Commissary will have Orders to Purchase Sixty Barrells of Salted Beef, of Two hundred & Twenty pounds each Barrell : —

"You are to receive Forty Shillings Lawfull Money for each Batteau, with the Oars, Paddles, and Setting Poles included [13]; out of which you are also to pay The Artificers & for all the Provisions Nails etc.[14] they shall expend.

"Given at Head Quarters at Cambridge this 3ᵈ day of September 1775

"Gᵒ WASHINGTON

"By the Generals Command
"HORATIO GATES Adjᵗ Genˡ"

The first reason, then, why Arnold stopped at Gardinerston was to see about the bateaux. Major Colburn had a shipyard; and, in the year 1763, Thomas Agry, a shipwright, came and settled just above him at a slight turn in the river, known then as Agry's Point,[15] but now as Green's Ledges Point.   The shore was covered, it is said, with white oaks that would make excellent ribs for the bateaux, and pine for the rest of them could be sawed two miles above at Gardiner's mill, and floated down. Finally, Henry Smith had been keeping a tavern just above Agry's Point for about three years, and could take care of the workmen. So it was here that the bateaux were constructed.

Quick time had been made with them undoubtedly, and the two hundred boats were now lying on the beach. Yet Arnold felt by no means wholly pleased. Whatever the ribs were made of, sides and bottoms had been constructed of green pine, heavy but thin and weak, and many bateaux were undersized. Arnold seems to have accepted the situation calmly, and he provided for lack of capacity by ordering twenty more,[16] with the understanding that they should be ready in seven days ; but later, when the wretched constructions were going to pieces, the poor soldiers were not so mild. After the boats had been in use only four days Morison exclaimed :

" Could we then have come within reach of the villains who constructed these crazy things, they would fully have experienced the effects of our vengeance. Avarice or a desire to destroy us — perhaps both — must have

been their motives,— they could have had none else.
Did they not know that their doings were crimes,— that
they were cheating their country and exposing its de-
fenders to additional sufferings and to death?"

Without a doubt the feebleness of the
bateaux was a vital defect in the preparations
for Arnold's enterprise ; but it does not follow
that the boat-builders were really to be blamed.
The time allowed them was very short.   One
can hardly believe that seasoned lumber for
such a fleet could possibly have been on hand.
The bateaux were to be thrown away, it was
expected, after a service of two or three
weeks, and it would not pay to build them
very expensively.   The need of strong boats
could not have been understood at Cambridge, and perhaps it was not at Colburn's,
for the few people who navigated the upper
Kennebec and Dead River probably did so in
lightly freighted canoes or pirogues, and understood the management of them.   Certainly
there was no sign of a guilty conscience on
Colburn's part, for he marched with the army
close within Arnold's reach.   In reality, this
appears to have been one of many misfortunes
that resulted naturally and almost inevitably
from haste and scanty knowledge of the conditions.   The bateaux would have answered,

had they only been required to navigate
waters like the Kennebec at Colburn's, and
perhaps they would have answered where they
went, had expert boatmen been in charge.

Arnold had another reason for stopping
at Gardinerston. As soon, apparently, as the
expedition was decided upon, or perhaps even
sooner, Major Colburn had been directed by
Washington to send scouts along the proposed
route "in order to see what were the obstacles Col. Arnold would be likely to meet on
his way to Quebeck." [17]   Dennis Getchell and
Samuel Berry of Vassalborough,[18] just above
Fort Western, were engaged to execute this
commission, and now Arnold received their
report in a letter addressed by them to Colburn.[19]   The report was as follows [20] :

"VASSALBOROUGH, 13th Sept'r, 1775.
"SIR. In Compliance with your Orders I proceeded
with Mr. Berry [21] on our intented Journey to Quebeck
as Follows—Fryday 1st Sept'r. P.M. we sat out.[22]   . . .
Wednesday 6th. we Reached the third Pond in the
Great Carrying Place distance 9 miles — Thursday 7th.
we arrived at an Indian Camp 30 miles distance from
the last mentioned pond, up Dead River [23] good water,
of [24] this Indian [25] we got intelligence that He was employed by Governor Charlton to Watch the Motions of
an Army or Spies that was daily expected from New
England — that there were Spies on the Head of Chaudiere River, that Some way down the River there was

Stationed a Regular Officer & Six privates, He possitively Declared that if we proceeded any further he would give information of his Suspicion of our Designs — as otherwise he should Betray the Trust Reposed in him—[26] But Notwithstanding his Threats we thought it of moment to get all possible intelligence & Accordingly on Fryday the 8th. we went up the River aforresaid [27] about 30 miles — We found the water in General pretty Shoal & meeting with nothing new Returned to the Indian Camp — Our Indian Pilot fearing the Consecuence of going any further with us after our first arrival at the Camp, did not go with us, on our last days Journey [28] — in this interval We had a Conference with an Indian Squaw who gave us this intelligence, that the Spy had a Commission from Charlton, that at Shettican [29] the uppermost Settlement on Chaudiere there was a great Number of Mohawks that would have destroyed us if we had proceeded, that all the Young Indians from that Quarter had gone to Johnson [30] — that the Spy was in daily expectation of the arrival of Three Canoes of Indians — We found the Carrying places pretty passible —the water in General pretty Shoal—on Account of the Dry Season—The Trees we found Marked [31] so as the way is pretty direct as far as we went—& may easily be found.[32]   .   .   .

" DENIS GETCHEL
" SAMUEL BERRY."

There was ample basis for at least a portion of this threatening report. Natanis proved a friend, whether he was really in Carleton's pay at this time or not; but there were Indians at Sertigan, about half-way down the

Chaudière,[33] and, as we have found, a British post had been established in that vicinity, though it had been withdrawn about the time Arnold's detachment set out from Cambridge, because the soldiers appeared to be more needed elsewhere.[34]   But Arnold, with characteristic boldness, snapped his fingers at all hints of danger.   The Indian, he wrote Washington,[35] was "a noted villain, and very little credit, I am told, is to be given to his information."

Still another matter of importance appears to have awaited Arnold at Gardinerston. Major Goodwin and his maps have already been mentioned.   His letter to Washington, quoted in Chapter I., proves that he met Arnold ; and, as there is no evidence that Arnold stopped at Pownalborough, and it would certainly have been more natural for Goodwin to wait upon him, we may conclude that their meeting took place at Gardinerston. Some weeks before, Colburn had given notice that maps would be wanted, and Goodwin now delivered them.[36]

These matters, however, were not the only ones that required Arnold's attention.   The lessening depth of water in the Kennebec made it impossible for the transports to go all the way to Fort Western, about nine miles[37] above Colburn's; and in fact some went but a little distance, if any, beyond the shipyard. At Gardinerston, therefore, or some point a few miles above, it was necessary to transfer men and cargoes to the bateaux. A portion, at least, of the provisions that Farnsworth, the commissary, came down to gather had no doubt been brought to Colburn's, and arrangements had to be made for taking these supplies to Fort Western, the real point of departure for the wilderness. A hundred men were now drafted to row the bateaux to that rendezvous.[38] Arnold engaged "two caulkers, some guides & assistants," as Oswald states; and then—by transports as far as they could go,[39] by the boats, and in part by land, some of the detachment stopping over-night at the Gardiner of to-day, or at Hallowell — the troops moved on for Fort Western. Arnold reached that point at six o'clock on Saturday evening, the 23d; and, if we except some belated men and those detailed for work, the whole army had arrived there before Sunday, the 24th.[40]

V

AT FORT WESTERN

FORT WESTERN stood on the eastern bank of the Kennebec, in the Augusta of to-day, the Hallowell of 1775, the Cushnoc [1] of Indian geography, about forty-three miles from the sea. [2] At this point a trading post had been established at a very early time, and in 1754 that was succeeded by what Governor Shirley [3] of Massachusetts called "a strong, defensible magazine."

The principal building, parallel with the river and only a few rods from it, was one hundred feet long and thirty-two feet wide, with posts eleven feet high. There it stands to-day, a little below the carriage bridge, and one may see the kind of work put into those border fortifications. It was a log house, except that the logs were squared beams a foot thick, laid close together, and dovetailed at the ends instead of crossing and projecting. So excellent was the fitting of the timbers that a knife-blade can hardly be inserted in the joints to-day. At present the sides are covered with shingles, and the roof displays dormer windows, but these, it seems likely, are modern.[4] Doors and windows were of solid plank, and the rain was probably kept out with short split boards[5] in lieu of shingles. This was the barrack or living house. Around it lay an area or parade-ground one hundred and sixty feet long and sixty-two feet wide, protected with a palisade. At the north-east and the south-west corners of the area stood a blockhouse[6] with a projecting upper story, pierced for cannon and musketry, and a sentry box of hardwood plank on the top; while the other two corners were strengthened with much smaller blockhouses, a single story in height.

These were the essential features of Fort Western, except that a still stronger palisade, thirty feet distant from the inner one, ran back from the river and around to the river again, and very likely there was a trench outside of that.[7] Certainly this was not a Gibraltar; yet these wooden walls could resist not only any rifle-ball of the time, but the shot of any cannon likely to be transported hither; and so the post was well designed for its purpose,—to serve primarily as a magazine and base for the more advanced position at Fort Halifax, higher up the river.

When the hopes of French and Indians had been killed by Wolfe on the Plains of Abraham in 1759, the need of fortresses on the Kennebec passed away. Fort Western was dismantled not long after, and its garrison withdrawn; but the commander, Captain James Howard, remained at Cushnoc as a settler,— the first resident there ; and the barrack was a lodging very suitable for a good number of Arnold's men. The parade-ground proved no doubt a convenient and suitable spot for the tents of others, and also for the board cabins that some of the troops put up to shield them from the cold and rainy weather.[8]

Arnold, however, does not appear to have lodged at Fort Western. About a mile above, on the Kennebec, stood Captain Howard's Great House,[9] just south of "Howard's Brook." It was here that the proprietor believed the future town would grow up, so it was here that he fixed his home ; and very naturally Arnold and some of the others took up their abode with this "exceeding hospitable, opulent, polite family," as Doctor Senter calls it.[10] No one could doubt that the courtesies of such a man were extended to the officers of the expedition, and tradition has it that a banquet or barbecue was given in honour of the army.[11]

But courtesies and festivities appear to have been only incidental. There was a vast deal of work for the troops to do.

Fort Western marked the head of navigation then as it does now, for just above begins a half-mile of rapids. Here all the stores had to be packed in the bateaux, and from this point the strength of men was to furnish the motive power. Under the supervision of their officers, we may well believe that most of the soldiers devoted themselves to preparing for the onward march, for we find the first three divisions ready to set out when the signal was given, while we know that others were employed in getting up from below the articles of every sort brought in the transports or accumulated at Colburn's.[12]

Arnold himself was not less busy. It was here, perhaps, that he met and talked with Getchell and Berry, the guides whose report had reached him below at Gardinerston.[13] But their information was only what their letter had already given him, and at that Arnold still mocked. On Sunday—or possibly on Saturday evening, as soon as he reached the Fort—

he ordered Lieutenant Steele, of Smith's riflemen, to select six [14] men and a couple of canoes
and go to Chaudière Pond,[15] reconnoitring the
way, obtaining all possible information from
the Indians hunting there, and, in particular,
ascertaining the course of the stream that
empties into the Pond.[16] The same day he
sent forward Lieutenant Church,[17] with seven
men, a surveyor, and a guide, to note "the
exact courses and distances to Dead River."[18]

Monday the attack on the wilderness began
in earnest. For convenience in this new kind
of warfare Arnold now arranged his army in
four divisions.[19] The leading group was very
naturally of rifle corps, for they were regarded
as light infantry, and the men, coming from
the confines of civilisation, were more truly
pioneers than the musketmen ; and Arnold
proposed to have Greene lead the advance
with a company of riflemen and two companies of musketmen. But here a difficulty
arose : Morgan, Smith, and Hendricks objected to the plan. There was no quarrel, no
ill-will ; but they held that no officer should
have authority over the riflemen except Arnold
and Morgan, and the latter declared that such
had been Washington's design. The difficulty
might have proved serious, but Arnold, though

he wrote Washington for instructions,[20] conceded the point; and the three rifle companies set out on Monday under the command of the Virginia captain, Daniel Morgan, the born leader of such an enterprise.[21]

Their orders were to go as quickly as they could to the carrying-place [22] between the Kennebec and Dead River—the Great Carrying-place [23] it was usually called—and "cut a road over to Dead River," as Oswald states.[24] With provisions for forty-five days in their bateaux, but yet freighted less heavily than succeeding divisions appear to have been, the brave fellows embarked.[25] October 7th most of them reached the end of their journey on the Kennebec, and eight days later their bateaux were afloat in Dead River on the farther side of the Great Carrying-place.[26] Later we shall inquire into their journey.

At noon, September 26th, Arnold sent off the second division. This included the companies of Thayer, Topham, and Hubbard, under the command of Lieutenant-Colonel Greene and Major Bigelow.[27] October 7th and 8th brought these men to the Great Carrying-place, and about the 13th they reached Dead River.

Wednesday, September 27th, at three o'clock in the afternoon, Major Meigs embarked with the companies of Dearborn, Ward, Hanchet, and Goodrich, Arnold's third division. They, too, had provisions for a month and a half. On October 10th most of this body reached the Great Carrying-place, and the 15th found a part of it camping on Dead River.

Behind all these companies was Lieutenant-Colonel Enos with Captains Williams, Mc-Cobb, and Scott, the fourth and last division, and also Colburn's company of " artificers."[28] It was their turn to set out on the 28th, and perhaps a part of them did so. But there were many loose ends for the rear to gather up. Some of the men had not yet quit the shipyard. Some of the bateaux[29] also were there. Oars, paddles, and the like proved somewhat lacking, and not all of the stores had been sent up. There were a few sick people to be carried back to Newburyport on the Broad Bay, a criminal—perhaps more than one—to be disposed of in the same fashion, and stragglers—we do not know how many—to be rounded up. Enos himself and the commissary were somewhere below Fort Western. So it was not until ten o'clock on Friday morning that McCobb's and Scott's companies were entirely off ; and, even then, Enos, the commissary, and Williams's company had to be left behind.[30]

Meanwhile Arnold was concluding his adieus to civilisation and his preparations for the fateful plunge into the wilderness. All his doings since Newburyport faded from sight were reported to Washington, and he cast a cheerful glance forward.

" I design Chaudiere Pond," he wrote, " as a general rendezvous, & from thence to march in a body . . . I have engaged a number of good pilots, & believe, by the best information I can procure, we shall be able to perform the march in twenty days; the distance is about 180 miles. . . . There is at present the greatest harmony among the officers."

At last his preparations for the march were all complete ;[31] his armament was perfected by the arrival of some manifestoes[32] designed for distribution among the Canadians ; and about noon on Friday,[33] the 29th, he set out in a birch-bark canoe, intending to overtake the head of the army as quickly as possible. The canoe proved leaky, and at Vassalborough he exchanged it for a dug-out. The next day he arrived at Fort Halifax; Sunday he passed Skowhegan Falls; and, after pausing from October 2d to October 9th at Norridgewock Falls, he reached the Great Carrying-place on the 11th, and Dead River on the 16th.[34]

We have taken pains to note the chief settlements from the mouth of the Kennebec to
Fort Western.   Nothing like a military base
existed there ; nor was anything of the sort
established by Arnold. [35]

VI

FORT WESTERN TO NORRIDGEWOCK FALLS

FOR half a mile beyond Fort Western impassable falls blocked the river, as we have seen; but along the eastern side lay a road,— the road to Fort Halifax, eighteen miles above.[1]   No king's highway was this, we may be sure, for though made passable for wheels the year Fort Western rose, it was used but little, and had not been kept in order. Still it was a road, and very likely it received a little mending at this time.

The first step was to get the boats and stores beyond the falls. One assumes that country people gathered from far and near with their oxen and their horses. Waggons of every description were no doubt employed, and sleds also, probably[2]; and in one way and another the bateaux and all the stores travelled northward to the point of embarkation. Then the boats were launched and loaded; three, four, or five soldiers[3] usually took places

93

in each of them as a crew, and the fleet set off by water, while the rest of the army proceeded by land.[4]	Neither party had much to suffer during this first stage of the long journey.	The footmen were most of the time in the forest, but occasionally the river came into view, and in Vassalborough[5] a number of houses were discovered.

The bateaumen—little used to such work, or not at all—found the task of combating the rapid current of the Kennebec wearisome enough, and it was rather more than wearisome, when, as they approached Fort Halifax, they were compelled to push up through a long piece of extremely quick water[6]; but the labour did no more than stretch the hemlock muscles of the men, and had they known what lay before them, such a pull would have seemed only a pleasure trip.	And so, after a day and a half or two days of toil, all the boats arrived safely at the next landmark.

Fort Halifax[7] came into existence—that is, a portion of it—in the same year as Fort Western; in fact, the two posts were features of the same plan.	It stood about three-fourths of a mile below the present city of Waterville, where the Sebasticook River entered the Kennebec from the north-east.[8]	At the point

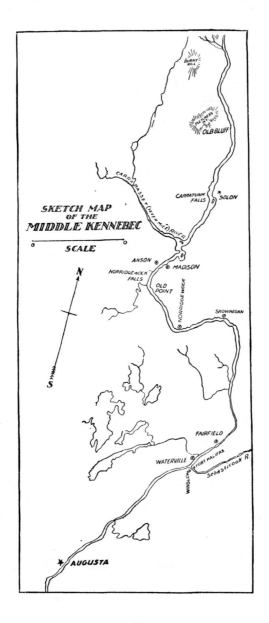

SKETCH MAP
OF THE
MIDDLE KENNEBEC

SCALE

N

S

BURNT HILL

THE RIPS
AT
OLD BLUFF

CARRABASSEC (SEVEN MILE) RIVER

CARRATUNK FALLS

SOLON

ANSON

MADISON

NORRIDGEWOCK FALLS

OLD POINT

NORRIDGEWOCK

SKOWHEGAN

FAIRFIELD

WATERVILLE

FORT HALIFAX

WINSLOW

Sebasticook R.

AUGUSTA

there were a few acres of level ground raised
some twenty feet above the water, while a
tongue of the prevailing plateau of the region,
forty or fifty feet higher still, came to an end
near the Sebasticook about a furlong from the
Kennebec.   There was need of guarding both
the point and the tongue, and the plan provided for both objects.   It was proposed by
General John Winslow, the officer directly in
charge of the works, to build a pretty extensive affair, but only a small part of his design
went into effect.   That, however, was enough
to lodge one hundred men on the point, and
shelter a dozen, with a couple of two-pounders
and a swivel, in a redoubt on the tip of the
tongue.[9]   By the 3d of September, 1754, so
much was accomplished, and a garrison then
took possession.

Winslow was succeeded by Captain William
Lithgow[10] and a less ambitious plan.   A second
and stronger redoubt[11] appeared the ensuing
year on the tongue, but the fort as a whole
was only about a third as large as Winslow
had proposed.[12]   A palisade of posts enclosed
a square of one hundred and seventeen feet
each way.   At the north-east corner stood a
blockhouse twenty feet square, and at the
south-west corner a second one : the latter has

7

survived the storms of time.[13]   Inside the enclosure on the east side were barracks eighty
feet by twenty, one story high, while on the
north side a building supposed to have been
of the same length but twice as wide contained
the officers' quarters, armory, and some other
departments.

Naturally, when the French and Indian War
had ended, Fort Halifax appeared valueless,
and soon it was dismantled and abandoned by
the military.[14]   Even before that, it had not
been kept well in repair, for the victory at
Quebec in 1759 seemed to make the Kennebec
safe.   Montresor described the post in his
journal of 1761 :

"It is square; its defence a bad palisade . . . by
two blockhouses, in which there are some guns mounted;
but, as the fort is entirely commanded by a rising ground
behind it, they have been obliged to erect two other
blockhouses and to clear the woods for some distance
around.   They [*i. e.*, the upper blockhouses or redoubts]
are capable of making a better defence, and it must be
confessed that either of them are more than sufficient
against an enemy who has no other offensive weapons
than small arms."

When Arnold and his party arrived, the
fort retained no doubt the same general appearance.   Dearborn speaks of the two blockhouses, "a large barrack," and the palisade.

But the whole affair had greatly decayed. " In a ruinous state" it was, wrote Henry, so that it "did not admit of much comfort." Ezekiel Pattee lived in one of the redoubts, but a "Captain Harrison or Huddlestone" seemed to Henry's party a real godsend when he invited the company to his house.[15] In short, Fort Halifax was not a fort at all in 1775, and could render no assistance to Arnold's expedition. Still less than Fort Western could it be called a base, except as Arnold ordered his surplus provisions stored there.

Half a mile above Fort Halifax the Kennebec ran over a series of ledges, and broke into what we call the Ticonic Falls.[16] No boat could possibly ascend the stream here, and so this became the first carrying-place.[17] The most irksome and fatiguing sort of labour was now required. As each bateau came to the bank on the western side of the river just below the falls, the crew leaped into the water and rapidly took the lading ashore. Two handspikes were then passed under the bottom of the craft,[18] and four men raised and carried it up the bank. If a portage were short and the load not too heavy, the bateau might not be emptied, but here, as often, it was necessary to divide the weight, and even to make a number

of journeys back and forth. The length of
the Ticonic Falls was about half a mile,[19] but
apparently it proved possible to find smooth
water along the shore at each end, and so the
portage measured only three-fifths as long.[20]

Still the labour was immense. According to
Senter's Account, each bateau weighed "not
less than four hundred pounds,"—a total of
forty tons. Provisions for forty-three days,[21]
at the rate of twelve ounces of flour[22] and of
meat for each man, would make about thirty-
five tons, besides the sugar, salt, yeast, butter,
and other extras of the commissary's department. If a hundred rounds of ammunition
were provided for every man, we must add
four tons for this, besides five and one-half
tons of rifles and muskets.[23] Tents, blankets,
and all the other camp equipments we may
call at a venture ten tons, though here we are
very much in the dark. Extra shoes and
clothes and everything else in the way of personal baggage, if it averaged ten pounds each
for the men and something more for the officers, may easily have amounted to six tons.
Two hundred shovels and as many axes do
not seem an excessive allowance for such an
expedition, and these would have counted a
ton. Medical and surgical stores, nails, tools,

kitchen utensils, and a dozen other categories we ignore ; but even without them our estimates figure up to something over one hundred tons. A part of this fearful weight was probably dragged across the carry by horses or oxen, but all of it had to be unloaded, taken up the river bank, and finally replaced in the boats by the men, and probably the greater part of it was taken across by them.[24] In general, at Ticonic Falls, the better part of a day seems to have been required for this work by each lot of men. Evidently the land party crossed the river and assisted, else the toil would have been still harder. Finally it was done, the footmen marched on again, and the boats breasted the stream once more.[25]

Not far beyond Ticonic Falls began the "Five Mile Ripples," a long stretch of swift water, not violent enough to be genuine falls, but still, as Arnold[26] wrote, "very dangerous and difficult to pass."[27] Arnold himself avoided them by hiring a settler named Crosier to convey his baggage by team to the slower current beyond; but for the army no such happy escape was possible. It began to be "cold and uncomfortable," too ; and the bateaux were already leaking profusely.

But the wilderness was not yet reached ; the

men did not yet feel the abandonment of complete exile from inhabitants and homes.   Not
far above the Five Mile Ripples was a little
settlement, and scattering families may have
settled elsewhere; but there were not many,
for the oldest inhabitant had been on the
ground but a year.[28]   Farther on, about eighteen miles beyond the Sebasticook, were
Great Island and Ten Acre Island, with a
few pioneers on each.   The army had now
reached Canaan, or, as the town is named at
present, Skowhegan.[29]

Five men had come here in the spring of
1772, but three of them went back to Massachusetts; yet the tide had flowed again, and
not only was Arnold's little party able to get
a dinner in Canaan, but his army secured two
energetic helpers, if not more, for the next
thirty or forty miles of their journey.[30]   Compared with unbroken forests, a region like this
would seem inhabited, and Arnold felt able to
speak of the country as "well settled" all the
way to Norridgewock Falls.

Three miles farther on, but still in Canaan,
there came another battle with the Kennebec,
—Skowhegan (or, if one choose to follow
Thayer, "squhegan") Falls, about twenty-one
miles from Fort Halifax.[31]

Even the approach to the falls was arduous. About half a mile below, the course of the river made about a right angle, and perhaps created then, as it does now, a triple whirlpool. Just above the turn stood a sort of natural gateway. Two ledges, projecting from the two sides of the stream, left a passage only some twenty-five feet wide between them, and forced the river to drive on like a mill-race. Through this gateway the shaky bateaux were somehow driven, for there is nothing in the records to suggest their being taken from the water at this point,[32] and local tradition agrees with the records. Then came the long run of exceedingly swift current. At the foot of the southern side log-drivers are able to walk, and it seems likely that men on the shore drew the bateaux along by the painters, while men in the boats kept them off the rocks with the poles. Finally they reached a pretty abrupt fall that is now called more than twenty-two feet high,[33] where Colburn had a primitive sort of a mill. A Mr. Howard resided at this place.

The stream was divided here by a rocky, craggy islet in the middle of it, so that about a half of the falls was in each of the channels; and the Indians were accustomed to take their

canoes up through a slight break in the almost vertical wall at the lower end of the
islet, twenty-five or thirty feet high. It must
have been a hard task to carry up even a
birch canoe, for one can see—aided by tradition—where the ascent was made, and far
worse to transport the heavy bateaux of green
pine by such a route[34]; but up they went, and
we can believe that the tired soldiers rested a
while on the point of the island above, which
the Indians are said to have cleared for a
camping-ground. The portage itself was only
sixty rods long,[35] but we are not surprised when
Stocking tells us that "it occasioned much delay and great fatigue." Dearborn was able to
make only three miles the day he passed these
falls. Nor was that all. A touch of cold
weather saluted a part of the army here on
the night of the 29th, and the soldiers had to
sleep in clothes that would have been wet had
they not been frozen "a pain Glass thick"[36];
and it was already necessary to caulk the
bateaux, or at least some of them.

For about five miles above these falls the
current of the stream is at present gentle, and
the river seems almost like a pond. But that
is evidently owing to the dams at Skowhegan,
for Arnold records that a great part of the

way there were small falls—that is to say,
rapids—and quick water. So much the pleas-
anter was it no doubt when he arrived at the
Widow Warren's, near the present village of
Norridgewock, and was able to sleep off his
fatigue under a roof.

Then the river veered around once more,
and began to come from the north-west, and
serious trouble for the boatmen was again in
order. First it was the Bombazee Rips,[37] or
at least this was the first nodal point, not
quite three miles above the widow's. Here
two ledges approached each other from the
opposite sides of the river and pinched it
pretty closely. The water rushed down like
a torrent; but fortunately the change of level
was not great, and the boatmen were able to
get through.

About six miles and a half from the widow's,
in the midst of a natural garden, opposite the
mouth of Sandy River, appeared the site of
Old Norridgewock,[38] once the capital of an
Indian tribe called by that name, where Râle[39]
had preached. Remains of the town were
still visible, though nothing can be discovered
there now. A fort and chapel were noted by
Dearborn; Meigs observed the signs of en-
trenchments and of a covered way to the

river, as well as the grave of a priest, no doubt the unfortunate Râle, and Thayer tells us that on the grave a cross had been erected.

Two or three families had recently settled in this vicinity,[40] and one of them possessed a baby, fourteen months old. But no base of operations existed here, not even as much as at Georgetown or Gardinerston, Fort Western or Fort Halifax. And this was the end. Civilisation ceased; and, a mile[41] farther on, the army found itself confronted by the great falls of Norridgewock.[42]

VII

FROM NORRIDGEWOCK FALLS TO THE GREAT CARRYING-PLACE

FROM Fort Western the part of the army that went by land followed the left or easterly bank[1] of the river to Fort Halifax, and there it evidently crossed.[2] The marching to Skowhegan was probably better on the right bank,[3] and the distance was less that way on account of the angle in the Kennebec. Just above Skowhegan Falls another crossing appears to have been made, for this would give the troops a short route across the next great bend of the river, and, marching on the northern side, they would not have to cross the Sandy River.[4]

In this way the army arrived at Norridgewock Falls on the left bank, and so had to cross again, since the carrying-place was on the other side.[5] Of course the bateaux had to be unloaded anyway at all these falls, and with so large a number of boats to use, the men could cross very quickly.

Norridgewock Falls are not in the present Norridgewock at all, but near the northern edge of the town of Starks. Very far indeed they appear from Lossing's picture of them. The reality is about a mile of swift water, with low but violent falls at each end and in the middle. No high cataract exists anywhere; each series of falls is a rather short but very tumultuous course of rapids. The upper one appears to be the longest and the greatest in actual descent, but the second is the most dramatic. No boat could possibly live a moment there. The total drop of the river in the course of a mile or so is given as ninety feet.[6]

To carry the boats and all they contained such a distance [7] and up such an ascent was a herculean labour. The people of the region turned out, of course, with all their "teams." Two sleds drawn by oxen [8] were "going constantly" with baggage. But, as Dearborn tells us, there were only two or three families, and all they could do was little. The men had to transport the bateaux on their shoulders, we learn from Morison, and no doubt much besides. Indeed, the labour was so great that all the divisions lost a good deal of time, and this became, perforce, a sort of rendezvous, though the earliest companies left before the

last arrived.   When Arnold reached there,
Monday forenoon, October 2d, the first division had just got its baggage well across, and
the second was approaching ; while Meigs and
the third division came up two days later,
and Enos with the fourth division appeared on
the 6th.

Arnold himself remained at the falls a week,
for there was a deal of work to be supervised.
Not merely had the boats and baggage to be
carried ; they required to be thoroughly over-
hauled.   Caulking had been necessary at
Skowhegan; now many of the bateaux were
"nothing but wrecks," as we are told by Senter, and "some stove to pieces."   On the 4th
Colburn arrived, doubtless with his company
of artificers, and then the work of patching
up the miserable boats proceeded still more
vigorously.

But this was by no means the full extent of
the mischief.   Moisture had no doubt entered
the bateaux both at bottom and at top, — at
bottom because the bateaux leaked, at the top
because the boatmen were not expert at their
business, and could not get up through the
"ripples" without shipping water.   The consequence was that the provisions had been
much injured.   A great part of Greene's bread

had been damaged,[9] says Oswald, and probably most of it had to be examined; while
Dearborn tells us that all his pork needed to
be repacked.   The dried fish, piled loosely
in the boats, had lost its salt, and could only
be thrown away.   Casks of biscuit and dried
peas had absorbed water, burst, and spoiled.
Worst of all, perhaps, the salt beef, which had
been put up in hot weather, was found worth-
less.   Flour and pork were to be the two
crutches of life henceforward, though no doubt
the remnants of biscuit and other supplies
lasted a little while.   But finally the disheart-
ening and tiresome work of patching bateaux,
of inspecting and throwing away provisions
was done, and before the close of October 9th
the last company had probably moved on.[10]

Arnold camped that night with McCobb of
the rear division, while Scott of the same division, though behind them, had advanced nine
miles beyond the falls during the day.   The
troops going by land were now perhaps on the
eastern side of the river again, for they seem
to have crossed back after passing the carry.[11]
In that way they avoided meeting the Seven
Mile Stream.   With no great difficulty, though
the water was all the way pretty rapid, the
army now went on, and about six miles, as

Dr. Senter reckoned it, from the end of Norridgewock Falls, passed the mouth of Seven Mile Stream, or Carrabasset River, as it is known to-day. A little below this point the Kennebec flowed more than a mile around a long projection of land to make thirty rods. Arnold, who gives us this information, crossed the neck of land with his light boat, and saved the long, hard pull; but the rest of the army had to toil on. About eight miles above[12] came another portage at Carritunk Falls,[13] which are said to produce more water-power than any others on the Kennebec. At present the drop is given as twenty-one feet, for a dam has been built. In 1775 it was about six feet less, according to Arnold, but still the falls were very impressive. The carry over such a pitch was of course a hard one, but fortunately not very long, probably not more than a quarter of a mile, and perhaps considerably less than that.

As soon as the army left Norridgewock the men began to feel they were now in the wilderness, for no more inhabitants could be looked for until the French settlements were reached. But while the fact of the wilderness had met them, the reality of it had not. Between Norridgewock Falls and Carritunk

Falls lay the Eden of the Kennebec,—perhaps the Eden of Maine. "The land we passed to-day was exceeding good," wrote Dearborn. In particular there were many islands of extraordinary fertility; Arnold dined at one and spent the night on another. But when Carritunk Falls had been passed, the outlook became extremely dark. That name itself was ominous. It is said to mean something very rough or broken, and to have been applied to the whole district beyond the falls. Anyhow, this point marks now, and marked then, the transition from lowlands to mountains, the entrance to the real wilderness.

The Kennebec, minus now the waters of the Carrabasset, assumed the guise of a highland stream, shallow, swifter even than before, and broken by many islands.[14]   On the western bank, foothills came down to the very water, leaving no passage for the soldiers ; but on the other side, the hills were more hospitable, and by marching on the high ground [15]—sometimes half a mile from the river—the troops were able to avoid both the tangled growth of the moist ground, and the many "logans," as the people call them now, where the water of the Kennebec "made up" into depressions between the hills.

Frequent tracks of moose testified to the wildness of the surrounding country. The weather turned bleak, and heavy, cold rains set in, drenching the men and injuring the stores. Minor difficulties were not small, even if there were a temporary surcease of major ones. The river did not fail to be vexatious and fatiguing now, when it was nothing worse, and marching over rough ground through pathless forests is not all pleasure. Finally the third and largest division reached the Great Carrying-place October 9th and 10th, and found there both of the preceding divisions.[16] Arnold arrived the next forenoon, and a part of the fourth division came later in the day.

The Kennebec River is formed by the junction of the East Branch, the outlet of Moosehead Lake by the way of Indian Pond, and the West Branch, the outlet of a series of ponds extending to the "height of land." The West Branch, or Dead River as it is usually called, pursues a south-easterly course aimed at the Kennebec valley, but just when it has arrived within some ten miles of its destination, the mountains drive it sharply toward the north for about that distance, and then send it eastward, to join the East Branch about fourteen miles above the Great Carrying-place. For

much of the way on this last stage, Dead
River is wide, rapid, and shallow, and it has
one large break, called Grand Falls; so that
the stream is not navigable. Partly to atone
for this, Nature has placed between the Kennebec valley and the place where Dead River
turns north a triad of sizable ponds or small
lakes, to suggest that boatmen "carry" across
from the Kennebec to Dead River here; and
since the earliest days of boating in this region
the suggestion has been followed.

The precise point where the army left the
Kennebec is readily found. As Arnold wrote
in his journal, it

"is very remarkable, a large brook emptying itself into
the river just above, which comes out of the first lake—
when abreast of the carrying-place in the river you will
observe at ab.ᵗ four hundred yards above you a large
mountain in shape of a shugar loaf—" at the foot of which
the river turns off to the Eastward.—This mountain, when
you are at the carrying-place seems to rise out of the
middle of the river.—"

Tradition accords perfectly, so far, with
Arnold's indications, but local vagaries are
not slow to appear. Beside the river, just
below the brook just mentioned, are four or
five acres of cleared ground and a couple of
small farm-houses. I inquired of the venerable

proprietor of one of these places, as I did everywhere, for traditions and especially for relics.

" Oh, yes, there used to be a big rock in my mowing field, with ' B. D. A. 1775' on it; but the durned thing was in the way, and I blasted it out."

" What did those letters mean,—' B. D. A.'?"

" Why, Bennie Dick Arnold, of course."

And this illustrates very fairly a great part of the local information that one may pick up from uneducated people along the route.[18]

We have now reached another nodal point of the march : Arnold leaves the Kennebec, a stream partially known, and certainly a highway back to civilisation.   So far the difficulties have been many enough and trying enough ; but they have been difficulties that human energy and human intelligence could combat. The general health of the troops has been excellent.[19]   Their exertions, however arduous, have not endangered either physique or morale.   Provisions have been ample,—too ample, perhaps ; for this is a democratic army serving the cause of independence, and there is reason to believe that a salutary closeness in dealing out the supplies would have been resented,

as the strictness of Morgan's discipline was.
And besides the free use of army stores, which
we may be sure was tolerated, other sources
of supply have been found.   Certain articles
of food, such as beaver tails, dried salmon,
and dried moose-meat, have been purchased
of the people to an extent that we cannot
measure, and carried by the men until used up.
Some fresh meat has been obtained.   Oxen
have been driven along, and slaughtered at
the proper time, very probably.   Just below
Carritunk Falls, Hendricks's company have
killed a young moose, estimated to weigh two
hundred pounds ; farther on Dearborn tells us
of catching fish ; and we cannot doubt that
other such prizes have found their way into
the larder, though of course the forward companies frighten most of the game away.   So,
in spite of rapids and falls, the army come to
this pivotal point in high spirits, health, and
vigour.

VIII

ON THE GREAT CARRYING-PLACE

SETH ADAMS, who lived on the Kennebec near where Arnold left it, died in 1882 at the age of about eighty-five. He had two sons who used to go to the first of the ponds mentioned in the last chapter to fish. In fact they made a business of fishing. In a single season, it is said, they took eleven hundred pounds of trout. This means that they went back and forth a good deal, and for years kept the trail pretty well marked.

Now when they began, Arnold's road was distinctly traceable. So people say, and so we can readily believe. They began as boys, and, as we may assume, about 1830, fifty-five years after the American army was here. It is well known that when evergreen woods are cut down—and, as the journals prove,[1] the forests of this region were of evergreens—a growth of hardwood takes their place. This is a fact constantly relied upon by woodsmen in finding

old roads and clearings. In 1830, there is
good reason to suppose that Arnold's road
was marked by a line of hardwood trees which
could not be mistaken; and it is very natural,
in the absence of anything to oppose that
theory, to accept the tradition that the Adams
boys followed this line,—especially as Arnold's
road, based on an Indian trail, was doubtless
the best route. It is even easier to believe
that the path so long travelled by them was
the path one finds to-day, for people soon began to be numerous, and they were very sure
to keep the trail alive, since it became the
regular route from the Kennebec valley to
Dead River. We appear, then, to have a
pedigree for the present road.

Even were that not the case, we could hardly
miss Arnold's trail. The point of departure,
the destination, and the direction by compass
are known; and for a part of the way, a deep
gorge, where the outlet of the first pond flows,
bounds the possibilities on that side. So we
may safely be confident that we are here on
the route of the army.

For about two miles[2] one ascends,—and
sometimes pretty rapidly, though none of the
way could fairly be called steep; and then
about a mile and one-fourth over fairly level

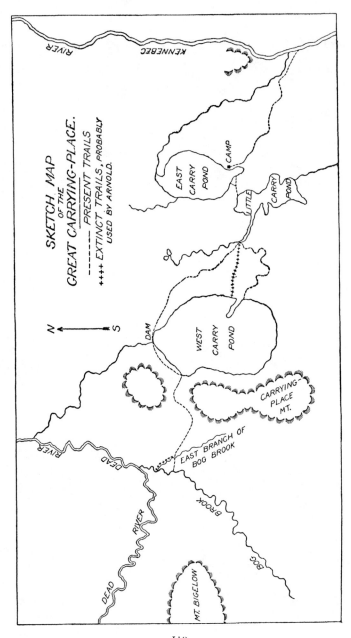

SKETCH MAP
OF THE
GREAT CARRYING-PLACE.
—— PRESENT TRAILS
++++ EXTINCT TRAILS, PROBABLY
USED BY ARNOLD.

KENNEBEC RIVER

RIVER

EAST CARRY POND

CAMP

LITTLE CARRY POND

N

S

DAM

WEST CARRY POND

CARRYING-PLACE MT.

DEAD RIVER

EAST BRANCH OF BOG BROOK

BOG BROOK

DEAD RIVER

MT. BIGELOW

ground brings one to the pond.   Near where this level ground begins, the trail crosses diagonally what is called the Old Canada Road, a lane four rods wide, it is said, cut through the forest some fifty years ago, the first waggon road from the Maine settlements to Quebec. As one approaches the pond, the present path turns abruptly toward the north a short distance from the water, and runs a strong quarter of a mile along the shore to a group of sportsmen's cabins called "Arnold Camp"; but the soldiers, we may be sure, carried their burdens as short a distance as possible, and laid them down at the south-eastern extremity of the pond.[3]

Morgan's division was sent forward, it will be remembered, to clear a road across the Great Carrying-place.   The route was not hard to discover, for, according to Henry, Steele's party had found the trail "tolerably distinct," and had made it still more so by blazing the trees and "snagging" the bushes with tomahawks.[4]   The road, if we call it by that name, was of course bad, but "capable of being made good," as Lieutenant Church reported, because the ground was generally firm; and the pioneers proceeded at once to clear it for the army.

Unfortunately they had but very little time. Hendricks's company of riflemen did not reach the Great Carrying-place until October 7th, and were prevented from working the next day by a heavy rain. Morgan was probably a little in advance, but not much, for all the "riflars" left Norridgewock at about the same time[5]; and the rest of the army began to arrive on the 7th.[6] Consequently it became necessary to detail men of later companies to assist in the road-making.

Unfortunately, also, the hard rains of October 8th and 9th soaked the firm ground very thoroughly, while soft spots—and there are many of them on this portage—became positively miry. It was impossible for the riflemen to find a dry place to camp, and for two nights the men passed the hours chiefly in sitting around the fires. Staggering along under the weight of a bateau,— often filled or partly filled with lading[7]—they sank "half-leg deep" in the wet earth, and now and then, slipping in the mud, fell and brought their burden down with them. Too often the rickety boat smashed in the process, and the strain of such a tussle fatigued and even exhausted the men.

Doubtless the ground became firmer after a time, and the later divisions experienced less difficulty.   But the labour was tremendous at best.   Some of the commanders, if not all, had the pork unpacked and strung on sticks for convenience of transportation, but the heavy bateaux had to be carried up the hills and across the sloughs on the sore and aching shoulders of the men ; and Senter's Account assures us that seven trips, or even eight, were necessary to get everything across.   Happily youth, strength, patience, and pluck are equal to any hardship.   Every mishap was turned into a joke.   The officers took their full share of everything disagreeable,[8] and cheered the men with inspiring words ; and so at length all came to the first pond, where, according to Arnold, the soldiers "caught a prodigious number of fine salmon trout, nothing being more common than a man's taking eight or ten dozen in one hour's time, which generally weigh half a pound apiece."   The main thing, however, was to get across.

This body of water—-East or Big Carry Pond, it is called—is quite irregular in form, though very roughly lemon-shaped, and according to Lieutenant Church's estimate— doubtless the best, for he had a surveyor, and made a business of measuring and estimating —one and one-fourth miles long.   Unluckily the great rain was followed by a great wind, with occasional squalls of snow. One man was fatally injured by the blowing down of a tree, and for several days boating was hindered or prevented. When the water became passable, half a mile of rowing brought the army to the other side.[9]

But where? Certainly not at the trail used now. Perhaps the voyage ended at a huge overhanging boulder, called Arnold's Rock, which is half a mile or so from the point where the army probably struck the pond. Signs of a path from this point are still visible, and it was formerly the usual trail, for the distance to the second pond is thought by the guides to be less by that route than by any other. It is natural to suppose that the shortest line was the one the Indians and the army took, but certainly we can feel no confidence here.

The second portage, running almost due west according to the surveyor's compass, measured twenty rods more than half a mile, and was not only short but pretty good, for the ground, though rough, was hard. Probably it reached the second lake, Little Carry Pond, about where the trail of to-day finds it, for on crossing the pond in the same direction as Arnold, one arrives where he did.

Little Carry Pond was half a mile wide and two and one-half miles in length, according to Arnold,[10] but other estimates of the voyage across run from three-fourths of a mile to a mile and a half. In this case a reason may be found for the differences. After the pond, a muddy, unattractive piece of water, surrounded then, as now, with dead and moss-grown trees, had been crossed, the course lay, as it still lies, up an inlet or arm about three-fourths of a mile long,[11] and some of the journalists might very naturally include this distance in their figures for the width of the pond.

The trail between the second and the third ponds has been completely lost. The way was "very bad" then, and is very bad now,—so much resemblance there is. Arnold describes it as "extremely bad, being choaked up with roots which we could not clear away, it being a work of time." This indicates that a part at least of the road lay through low and swampy ground, and such ground may be seen to-day on the eastern side of the next pond, quite a little north of the termination of the path most used at present. However, the route had one thing in its favour: it was only a mile and three-eighths in length,[12] and certainly bateaux could be transported that distance through pretty deep mud more easily than twice as far by a trail like the present one.

West Carry Pond, the last of the series, is also the largest. Three miles long and two miles wide it was called by the surveying party, while Arnold himself added half a mile to each figure. Its form is quite regular, but one distinguishing feature is very noticeable, — a long, narrow arm of land projecting into the lake from the south-eastern side. The present path, alluded to above, reaches the lake just south of this arm, but the boggy ground, where it has been suggested that Arnold may have arrived, is on the other side of it.[13]

Then came the fourth and hardest carry, only twenty rods less than three miles long.[14] Here again we find local information to guide us. Samuel Parsons of Dead River Post-office, a mile or so beyond the end of this portage, settled here about 1850; and he tells us that at that time it was easy to follow with the eye the line of the Arnold road as it came down the side of the mountain, for the foliage there was clearly different from the foliage on either side; and further, he tells us, the line marked out by this lighter green of the hard-wood trees ran substantially as the road goes now. One can believe — and so the woodsmen assure us — that such a difference could easily persist from 1775 to 1850; but, aside from this aid to identification, we find a sufficient argument in the general correspondence between the present road [15] and the descriptions of 1775.

First there was a short mile of ascent. At the very start it was, and is, decidedly steep, and Captain Dearborn described it as a "Very-high-Hill." Next came about a mile of easy downward slope, and, finally, for nearly the same distance, a "savanna."

It was this last division of the portage that nearly broke the hearts of the toiling soldiers. At a distance the savanna seemed like "a beautiful plat of firm ground, covered by an elegant green moss," [16] divided by a large grove of spruces and cedars, with grey moss and half-withered bushes here and there, and in places almost impenetrable thickets; but at every step the men sank eight or ten inches through the treacherous moss into mud, and found at the bottom the sharp snags of dead trees. In a word, as Squier declared, the first part of this carrying-place was very bad, and the rest of it a hundred times worse; and Squier, we recall, belonged to the fourth division, and therefore crossed after the road-makers had done what they could. But at last, with infinite patience and effort, this difficulty also was overcome. The army arrived then at what is called Bog Brook,[17] a small serpentine creek, running toward the north and emptying into Dead River. The distance to be navigated on this stream was a mile or a little less.[18]

Nowadays the brook is not navigable at all, for deposits of sand and mud have choked it up, but in 1775 it was about a dozen feet wide most of the way, and, according to Senter, " much deeper than wide." Joyfully the bateaux were launched in this natural canal, and in a little time Dead River came in sight.[19]

It was October 6th or 7th when the first of the soldiers[20] appeared at the Great Carrying-place ; on the 13th, portions of the first and second divisions reached Dead River, and on October 20th the last of the troops were in motion up the river.[21] Arnold himself arrived at the carrying-place on the 11th, and left it five days later. During the interval he was of course attentive in a general way to the progress of the men, but there were certain special cares to occupy him.

So far the health of the army had mostly been excellent,[22] but that good fortune could not be expected to last for ever. The weather grew bad. Rain fell again on the 14th and the 19th, and some of the troops had no tents. Exposure and fatigue began to tell upon them, and indeed a small number were already ill. Of their own motion, the first division had thrown together a "bush hut"[23] for the sick on the second portage, but that was inadequate. So Arnold ordered the construction of a log hospital there, and the soldiers christened it "Arnold Hospital" and "Fort Meggs."[24] Dr. Irvin[25] and eight or ten sick men took immediate possession, and soon the number of invalids began, of course, to increase.

On the first portage a small log house was erected near the Kennebec the same day,[26]— the day after Arnold reached the Great Carrying-place. Its purpose was to serve as a dépôt for "men and provisions," so Arnold explains; and in order to carry out his plan of accumulating here a reserve of provisions for an emergency,—in particular to secure his retreat, as he informed Washington,—he ordered Colonel Farnsworth, his commissary, to hire men and bring up to this house the hundred barrels or so of provisions left behind.[27]

9

Architecture, however, was the least of the commander's employments. On his arrival the day before, Lieutenant Church had reported the courses and distances from the Kennebec to Dead River.[28] Now came Lieutenant Steele with his budget. The scouting party under his command left Fort Western on the 24th of September, as we recall, made their way to the last pond at the head of Dead River, crossed the height of land, and reached what they called the Chaudière River.[29] One of them, climbing a tree, was able to follow the meandering course of the stream, and even —as he thought—make out Chaudière Lake at a distance of fourteen or fifteen miles. This appeared to prove that the army was on the true path to Canada, and the company turned back at once.

The journey of the scouting party downstream was unfortunate. Their canoes were broken, and provisions ran out. Steele with two of his men, however, leaving the others to recruit their strength—as it was supposed they could—on the meat of two moose that were fortunately killed, hurried on to meet Arnold, and reported cheeringly a route free from Indians, a "fine deep river most part of the way," and a plenty of game. The distance to

the carry over the height of land he reckoned
as eighty miles.[30]

Upon this the two lieutenants were immediately sent forward again [31] with twenty axe-men
and a surveyor. They were "to clear the
portages and take a survey of the country" to
Lake Megantic,[32] and then Steele was to go
down the Chaudière River till he approached
the settlements, examine the falls and portages, and report at Lake Megantic.

The next day (October 13th) was not less
busy for the commander. Washington had
urged him to communicate with Schuyler if he
could, and it now seemed time to make an
attempt. Washington had also suggested that
Indians of the St. Francis [33] tribe might be
employed as messengers, and apparently one
or more of them, who had been making a visit
at the Cambridge camp, were now with Arnold
for that purpose. However this may be,
Arnold wrote a letter to friends [34] of his in
Quebec, with an enclosure to be forwarded
on to General Schuyler. The object of both
letters was to announce his approach and request information. His purpose in coming
was "to frustrate the arbitrary and unjust
measures of the ministry and restore liberty to
our brethren of Canada." The state of things

at Quebec, and whether anything was known
of his expedition, he was of course peculiarly
anxious to learn.   The ships, the troops, and
the sentiments of the people were inquired
after, and he promised rewards to any of his
acquaintances who would come to meet him.
The letters were entrusted to Eneas and another Indian, and John Hall, who could speak
French, went with them.[35]

So far as announcing his approach was concerned, these letters proved successful,— only
it was the British Lieutenant-Governor who
received the information ; in other respects
they were a total failure.   Whether the Indians
became traitors or captives, surrendered their
charge willingly or unwillingly, we cannot be
sure, but Arnold was disposed to look upon
them as false.[36]   The white man, however, may
be supposed to have done good service.   His
orders were to ascertain the sentiments of
the people, gain all the information of every
sort that he could, particularly about the British troops and that other enemy, the river,
and meet the army at Lake Megantic, where
Arnold counted on arriving in " about seven or
eight days."   So much for the onward view.

There was also a look behind.   Arnold sent
his journal through October 13th to General

Washington, adding in a letter that he now had some nine hundred and fifty effective men and provisions for about twenty-five days.[37] It appears also from this letter that he did not feel sure of pushing on to Quebec. Only at Lake Megantic did he intend to determine his plan finally. Should it then be deemed necessary to retreat, there would still be sufficient provisions, he reckoned, to bring the army back to the Kennebec; and there, in the log house, would be found enough to carry them down to civilisation. For the men he had only praise, though he regretted that in general they did not understand the management of bateaux, and were compelled to wade and haul them more than half the way. But now he hoped the greatest difficulties were over.

Enos, the commander of the rear, was ordered to station a bateau on each of the ponds, so that sick men could pass back toward home, and to make other needful arrangements for them.[38] These matters all attended to, Arnold went on, and October 16th began to ascend Dead River.[39]

As the pioneers of the van were beginning to make the semblance of a road through the savanna of the last carry, a group of feeble and emaciated men staggered across it, and

came up to them.   These were the remainder
of the scouting party.   Steele and two others
had gone on, as we have seen, and met Arnold
at the second pond; they despatched an expedition to relieve their comrades, but for
some reason it did not reach them; and the
rest of the scouting party, after waiting several
days for the promised succour to arrive, and
starving meanwhile on a diet of nothing but
lean moose meat, concluded that the army had
retreated, and set out with their remnant of
strength to overtake it.[40]

IX

LOWER DEAD RIVER

IT was an interesting spot where the army found itself after crossing the morass of the fourth portage. Below this point, Bog Brook and Dead River were nearly parallel, though soon to unite. Between the two lay a meadow covered with a luxuriant growth of native grass, and apparently extending westward for several miles. Out of this floor rose a lofty mountain, the front of a short but rugged chain, Mt. Bigelow.[1] Still more interesting to the army, and hardly less beautiful, were the smooth black waters of Dead River, about sixty yards wide, as Arnold thought.[2]

The first stage of a considerable part of the army on this highway seemed a backward move, for a journey of a mile up the river brought them back to the grassy meadow that lay between it and Bog Brook.[3] But, of course, it was vastly easier to make the two miles, or something less, down the brook and up the river, than to transport the boats and baggage across a wide field.

Regular rations were fixed on October 15th as three-quarters of a pound of flour — almost exactly a pint — and an equal weight of pork each day, and after devouring a yoke of oxen that were driven to this point, the army settled down to this limited regimen with good grace. So mild was the current of the river, apparently, that rapid progress appeared sure, but this natural expectation was disappointed. As Arnold remarked, the river seemed reluctant to leave Mt. Bigelow, and meandered to and fro without permitting the impatient army to advance. "Two hours passed away, and we had gained nothing in our course," wrote Arnold. But gradually the stream "returned to its proper course." The river was very uniform in width, and the water deep and still.[4] The banks rose probably eight or ten feet high, well clothed with bushes, and on either side stretched a large expanse of flood-plain,—covered thinly with trees which sometimes grew to be large, or with grass that stood waist high in places, but faded out in the spots of cold soil,—bounded at a distance of a few miles with hills or mountains. Unfortunately, the current proved stronger than

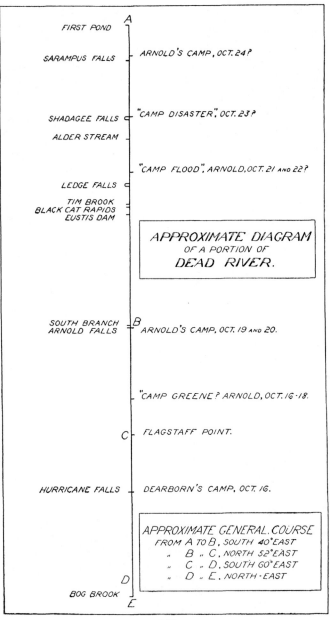

FIRST POND

A

SARAMPUS FALLS — ARNOLD'S CAMP, OCT. 24?

SHADAGEE FALLS — "CAMP DISASTER", OCT. 23?

ALDER STREAM —

"CAMP FLOOD", ARNOLD, OCT. 21 AND 22?

LEDGE FALLS —

TIM BROOK
BLACK CAT RAPIDS
EUSTIS DAM

APPROXIMATE DIAGRAM
OF A PORTION OF
DEAD RIVER.

SOUTH BRANCH
ARNOLD FALLS — B
ARNOLD'S CAMP, OCT. 19 AND 20.

"CAMP GREENE? ARNOLD, OCT. 16-18.

C — FLAGSTAFF POINT.

HURRICANE FALLS — DEARBORN'S CAMP, OCT. 16.

APPROXIMATE GENERAL. COÜRSE
FROM A TO B, SOUTH 40° EAST
„ B „ C, NORTH 52° EAST
„ C „ D, SOUTH 60° EAST
„ D „ E, NORTH · EAST

D

BOG BROOK

E

it seemed, and as the boats were not all supplied with enough oars or paddles, perhaps, in
spite of Arnold's anxiety about them at Fort
Western, and as the water was too deep for
the poles to serve, progress had to be made or
aided in some cases by pulling at the bushes
of the river's bank.[5]

Eight miles or a little more from Bog Brook
by the river came a pronounced interruption,
called nowadays Hurricane Falls, which it was
necessary to carry forty yards around.[6]   Like
most of the other falls that annoyed the army
in its passage up the stream, this was not a
vertical drop, a cataract, but a series of tumultuous ripples,—in short, violent rapids.
The drop in the level of the river was about
eight feet, and it was useless for Arnold's boatmen to think of taking their loaded bateaux
through such water.   Five miles farther on,[7]
a point of land some twenty feet higher than
the river made out against it from the north,
and seemingly drove the stream the opposite
way.   The point was indeed "beautifully situated," as Dearborn wrote, commanding an
outlook on the river both up and down, and a
noble view of the whole range of Bigelow on
the other side of the valley.

Here, in a considerable clearing, Natanis,

the Indian already known to us, had a hunting
lodge, apparently a pretty substantial cabin,
and since that day the cabin has grown into
something still more substantial, the village of
Flagstaff.[8] Steele and the scouting party were
given particular orders to capture or kill this
"noted villain," as Arnold styled him, because
he declared himself a partisan and spy of the
British.   Steele did what he could, but in vain,
for instead of letting himself be caught, the
Indian was hovering about the party, and observing its manœuvres, from the moment it
built a fire in Dead River valley.   Nothing
was lost and much was gained by this failure,
for Natanis—whether or no he was making
sport of Berry and Getchell, when he called
himself a scout of Carleton's — joined the
Americans later, as we shall see, and proved a
faithful friend.

Morgan's division was intended to lead the
army.   It left Fort Western in the van, and it
arrived first at the Great Carrying-place.   But
there it seems to have been delayed by its
engineering duties, and Greene's command,
the second division, began the voyage on
Dead River in advance of it.   Passing Hurricane Falls, then, a few miles in front of Morgan's company, the leaders pressed on, and

camped on the evening of October 16th three
or four miles beyond the house of Natanis, on
the south side of the river, at a place that
may be named for convenience Camp Greene.
They were eager to get on as far as possible,
and must have been grievously vexed by the
aimless wanderings of the stream.[9]   The distance from Flagstaff to Eustis is eight miles
by land, but more than twice as much by
water.   In paddling for two hours beyond the
Point they cannot have gained a mile, and
the veerings of the course did more than "box
the compass."   What was far more vexing
still, after finally reaching Camp Greene, the
division could not leave it for five days.

The cause was even more disquieting than
the fact: provisions were on the point of giving out.   According to Humphrey and Topham, the men were "brought to one-half pint
of flour for each" on the morning of the 16th.
Thayer also mentions half rations that day, and
both he and Humphrey speak of beginning the
next with "but 5 or 6 lb. of flour" for fifty or
sixty men.[10]   Arnold's account of the situation
is more favourable, but certainly alarming.

We cannot possibly understand the case:
on the 15th, as already mentioned, Arnold
wrote Enos that the first three divisions had

provisions enough for more than three weeks; yet the very next day Greene's men were put on shortened rations, and saw starvation at the tent door. No journal undertakes to explain the situation. There is no mention of any disaster since the Kennebec was left behind; there was no occasion for any serious accident. Humphrey, Thayer, and Topham only state the facts; Arnold merely adds in parentheses, "great part of their bread being damaged." Perhaps we are simply to conclude that all of the damage was done on the Kennebec, but much of it not discovered until this time. Yet how could it escape discovery? The worst of the navigation on the Kennebec was below Norridgewock Falls, for the journals have little to say of difficulties above that point, except the ordinary trouble of a fast current and shoal water. Probably we must suppose that the full extent of the loss was not understood, that some further losses occurred, and also that the supplies were lavishly used. It was not until October 15th that a regular scale of allowance was ordered. The very fact that rations were fixed before a shortage had been discovered is a suggestion of previous extravagance. We know that the men were hard to control.

The attempt to replenish the store of provisions was even more alarming than the discovery of a lack.   Arnold himself had reached
Camp Greene on the evening of the 16th,[11]
and the next day undertook to help the division obtain supplies.   Major Bigelow was
directed to go back with men and boats for
provisions,[12] and Enos was ordered by letter to
give him all that could be spared.   Bigelow set
out accordingly with twelve bateaux, three
lieutenants, six sergeants, and eighty-seven
men to get the supplies, while the rest of the
men were ordered to employ their time in
making cartridges.   Judge of the astonishment
of the division, when the boats returned four
days later with nothing but a barrel or two of
flour.[13]   It was a desperate dilemma; yet the
officers did not hesitate.   They decided to send
back all who were unfit for " actual duty," and
the next day, October 22d, they pushed on.
They counted on getting supplies at the French
settlements on the Chaudière, and supposed
that these were not far away.

Meantime the rest of the army had been
advancing.   Morgan's division passed Greene's
at noon on the 17th, and resumed the lead.
Meigs and his division spent the night of the
18th in Camp Greene,[14] and went forward the

next afternoon with orders to make all haste to the Chaudière River, prepare a supply of cartridges while waiting for the rear, and in the meantime detail men to clear the carrying-place over the height of land [15]; and on the 21st a part of the fourth division arrived at the camp.[16]

But an unexpected enemy now assailed the army. On the 19th there were "small rains," as Arnold called them, all day ; but at three o'clock the storm abated,[17] and Arnold pushed on to a carrying-place of fifteen perches,—evidently at what we now call Arnold Falls ; for before this Arnold mentions nothing of the sort except what may be identified clearly as Hurricane Falls, and he calls this "the second carrying-place." Besides, this is in about the right spot for Arnold Falls, and he records no other such obstacle, until, after advancing nine miles farther, he came to a group of rapids not at all like Arnold Falls. As the latter are not small, and the boats certainly must have been carried here, it seems perfectly safe to say that we have now reached Arnold Falls. At this point he camped for the nights of October 19th and 20th. Meigs had been outstripped, but about noon on the 20th he passed Arnold with the intention of camping early. Meanwhile the storm continued.

The next day (October 21st), more rain fell.
The river had already risen several feet, and
still it poured, while a furious gale from the
south-west [18] filled the river with broken or up-
rooted trees, and the men in camp listened
in terror to the smashing and crashing near
them in the forest. In spite of weather the
army moved,—all but the hungry division
in Camp Greene,[19] which had made its cartridges and packed them in casks " ready for
immediate embarkation," but had still to wait
for provisions. Arnold himself camped a mile
in advance of Morgan that evening, while the
third division (Meigs's) lay between them and
Arnold Falls, and the fourth division was
partly in Camp Greene, and partly a little
way below. Then came the flood.

Dead River drains a large number of ponds,
and now all these natural reservoirs were combining their forces. Suddenly in the darkness the river swelled portentously. In nine
hours it rose eight feet.[20] At four o'clock in
the morning, Arnold and his party were awak-
ened by the rush of waters, and before they
could remove their baggage, it was all in the
flood.[21] The riflemen, just below, had camped
in a bad place, and they also were driven away
from their beds during the night by the rising

10

stream.[22] The rest of the divisions were more fortunate, but Squier noted that in the morning four feet of water stood where the fire had been the evening before.[23] And this was not all. The weather grew rapidly cold ; and, as many of the soldiers had no protection but the boughs of trees, they suffered greatly.[24]

Sunday, the 22d, found the army in a desperate plight. Many of the boats were now under water or half submerged. The current of the river proved so swift that head could scarcely be made against it. All the landmarks were altered. Portages had disappeared under water, and in one or two instances the boats were floated over a carrying-place. The soldiers who went by land fared no better,— perhaps even worse. All the brooks had become rivers, and the meadows were lakes. Long detours became necessary, and it was almost impossible to know what course to follow.[25] Sometimes the shore parties could advance only by felling trees, and using them for bridges. But, in spite of everything, the army pushed slowly and painfully on.[26]

X

UPPER DEAD RIVER

HERE we come to a crisis of the expedition, and also to a crisis of our study. We are now to share the embarrassments of the troops. Up to Arnold Falls one can easily keep pace with the march of the expedition; beyond that point it is hard to do so.

There are several reasons for this. As we have already found, estimates of distance differed widely even in the case of a short course by land. To estimate distances by water was far more difficult, because the rate of speed could not be so accurately gauged; and on Dead River this difficulty was increased by having to allow for a current of unknown and varying swiftness. Embarassment arises also from the fact that not one of the journals is complete in enumerating the natural features of the river, particularly falls and affluents, and most of them are very incomplete indeed. Again, we find on comparing the journals that

our various authors give widely differing accounts of the same courses. Take, for instance, the series of portages between Arnold
Falls and the first pond above, as figured in
rods.   Arnold's series is : 10, 26, 75, 73, 7, 12,
6, 40, 100; Dearborn's: 35, 30, 74, 74, 74, 4,
4, 90.   It is of course impossible to harmonise
the two series, though some of the numbers
appear to correspond.   The distance from the
outlet of Bog Brook to Camp Greene is reckoned almost as variously : Arnold, eighteen
miles ; Dearborn, twenty-six miles ; Meigs,
(apparently) twenty miles ; Melvin, twenty-
five miles.   Many such differences may be
due — in part, at least — to the flood, which
changed the whole aspect of the river just at
this time ; but whatever the cause they are
extremely troublesome.

Finally we are not a little embarrassed by
the fact that changes have taken place in the
river itself, — due largely to the lumbermen.
At a number of places blasting has been done,
and possibly an entire fall has been obliterated
in the process of opening a better passage for
the logs.   No records have been kept of such
operations, and one has only the imperfect
recollections of this man or that man to rely
upon.   The logs themselves have dug and

hammered the banks, and very possibly have shortened the stream in some places by cutting through the isthmus of an "ox-bow." As they come down over falls they dig up the bottom, and perhaps they have in this way closed the old channel; and of course the usual wearing process of a rapid stream has to be counted upon.

But an effort at least must be made to solve the mysteries of the next few days, and in Arnold's journal we may find a guide that is mainly satisfactory.

According to his account, no carrying was necessary for nine miles beyond the violent rapids which we have identified as Arnold Falls, and in fact one can paddle easily there now for a distance reckoned as about nine miles by the most competent guides and residents. Five "ripples" are met with, but none of them is at all serious. At one point, at least, blasting has been done, but nothing suggests that falls of any importance existed there before. So close an agreement between Arnold's figure and the present estimate is almost suspicious; but this is the easiest place on the river to guess distance, perhaps, and Arnold had not exceeded the truth very much below this point. We are surprised to find

no mention of the South Branch,[1] which empties about forty rods above Arnold Falls;
but, as that stream could be forded without
serious difficulty, Arnold seems to have considered it, as well as other affluents, not worth
mention.   Yet it is a considerable river.   In
fact, at the point of junction it looks larger
than Dead River itself; and, according to
Henry, some of Morgan's men went that way
for quite a distance, believing it the true
course.

At the upper end of the nine-mile stretch is
the village of Eustis, the last settlement, with
a dam across Dead River.   The high water
of the mill-pond disguises the natural character of the stream, but it looks as if rather long
rapids had existed formerly at this place.
That, however, does not appear to have been
the fact, for a careful and trustworthy resident
states that when a former dam was carried
away by a freshet many years ago, the falls
were only a few rods in extent.   There has
been blasting here, yet little more than was
necessary to secure a good foundation for the
present dam.   It seems probable, then, that
Arnold's next portage — ten rods long — took
him past this obstruction.[2]

Above the dam, our river makes a wide

turn.   The bow is half a mile long, while the
string is considerably less than a quarter of a
mile.³   At present the boatmen travel by the
string, taking their canoes from the water a
little way below the dam.   In 1775, however,
when the present road was covered with trees,
they seem to have made a short carry at the
falls, and returned to the water, for Arnold
now speaks of going half a mile by the river.
This distance would have brought him to the
next bar encountered by the boatmen of to-
day.   That is Black Cat Rapids, not quite two
hundred rods by water above the dam.   Arnold mentions here a portage of twenty-six
rods.   At present a rod or two suffice; but
the dam has raised the water considerably,
and it may well be that in 1775 the rapids
were longer.   Besides, gunpowder or dynamite
has been at work there.   Perhaps wet ground
made a slight detour necessary.

We come now to a difficulty.   The next
carrying-place at present is at Ledge Falls,
which begin about a mile and a half above; but
Arnold reports only half a mile of paddling here,
which, with the twenty-six rods of portage,
would be less than three-fourths of a mile.
That is not the whole truth, however, for
while his items of water travel for the day

foot up to only about eleven miles and a quarter, he says in conclusion that he had "paddled up near four leagues," and this distance is about enough to accommodate the facts of the river.   The character of the falls that he describes, also, seems to indicate that we are still on the right track, and that his journal—if no error has been made in copying it — is simply mistaken about the figure that seemed to create our difficulty.

The most pronounced feature in the navigation of Dead River between Bog Brook and the ponds is undoubtedly Ledge Falls.   They are usually spoken of as Upper and Lower; but the Lower Fall itself may be called double. The length of the first part of the latter is about sixty rods; then come thirty or forty rods of navigable water; and finally some fifty rods of almost continuous rapids would bring one to the dam at Upper Ledge Falls. This last stretch is so bad, however, as to be almost impassable; and, according to a tradition which seems highly reasonable, the Indian practice was to avoid it by making a long carry.   As the rapids formerly extended some distance above the dam, it is easy to believe that the portage was nearly a quarter of a mile in length.[4]

Arnold's journal shows no evidence of this
great obstruction except at one point.   That
point we reach in his account precisely where
we meet Ledge Falls in the river, if we accept
the theory of a slight mistake proposed above,
and the features of the account seem to fit
pretty closely the peculiar nature of the spot,
for there was a portage of seventy-five rods
separated by navigable water from a portage
of seventy-three rods, and the fall avoided by
the latter was " very considerable and long."[5]

The length of the navigable water, however,
Arnold called ninety rods.   Possibly there is a
copyist's error here.   A figure four is often
written so that it looks like a nine, and one of
the other journalists, referring apparently to
this piece of water, calls it forty rods long.
Possibly, too, the appearance of the river has
changed.   At present there are two half-dams
— wing-dams, they are called — in the course
of the Lower Falls, designed to throw the
entire stream into the channel best fitted to
be a sluiceway for the logs ; and perhaps,
were they not in existence, the intermediate
space would be longer.   In that case the
seventy-five rods of the first portage would be
obtained by beginning to carry a little lower
down, so as to cut off an angle of the river.[6]

The direction of the portage, compared with the bearings of the two sides of the angle, suggests that this may have been done. If we suppose that it was, our difficulty about the distance to Black Cat Rapids is somewhat lessened.[7] But the main argument is that the facts, all taken together, seem to prove that Ledge Falls belong at this point in the journal, and therefore some explanation must exist for slight apparent disagreements.

At the upper end of this hard stretch Arnold overtook the riflemen on the evening of October 21st; but, as they had encamped in a bad place, he went on a mile farther, and there pitched his tents in what we may call, for convenience, Camp Flood. Here, a mile above Upper Ledge Falls, he was assailed by the rising waters before morning, and here he remained through the following day, drying his baggage and preparing to move again, while Morgan passed with his company at nine o'clock in the morning, and Meigs, with a part of his division, came up at five o'clock in the afternoon.

Arnold's record for October 23d is this:

"At 7 A. M. Capts Smith, Hendrickson,[8] and Major Meigs with his division came up and passed on.[9]—At 10 A.M. embarked and proceeded up the river — the

stream by reason of the freshet very quick; in ab!
3 miles we came to the crotch of the river. Our Co
[urse] was ab! W! Here we found that the land
[party] had by mistake taken the S. W. or wrong course
which we rowed up two miles, and sent men ahead to
inform them of their mistake and direct their march.
This mistake occasioned a detention of the Battoes and
whole division near 2 hours; when the whole were
formed, we proceeded up the river against a very rapid
stream ab! 3 miles to 7th carrying place, Co[urse] over
N? 35 E. distant ^{10} 7 perches; here we had the misfortune of oversetting 7 Battoes and loosing all the
provisions. Here the whole division encamped, the
river continues high and rapid, and as our provisions
are but short and no intelligence from Canada, I ordered a counsell of Warr."

About three miles beyond the place where
we have fixed Camp Flood, Alder Stream
enters Dead River. The junction may properly
be called a crotch, for the two streams are
nearly equal in apparent size, and the angle
between them is only half of a right angle.
Dearborn states that he sent his bateau four
miles up the affluent in search of the land
party, and found that the party had struck
across to Dead River. Now Alder Stream
is navigable for that distance, and the nature
of the country is such that the lumbermen
often make such a "cross-cut." One difficulty, meets us, however: Arnold's statement

that at the mouth of the affluent Dead River was running from the west, while the other stream flowed from the south-west, for in 1775 Dead River ran here from about twenty-five degrees west of north.[11]   But Meigs states that the affluent came from the westward, and this he could hardly have done had he understood that Dead River was flowing there from the west.   In short, we must conclude that Arnold spoke loosely, if he wrote what we now have.[12]

Two miles or something more, as is es- timated, above the mouth of Alder Stream are Upper Shadagee Falls,[13] which answer to the description of the next obstruction mentioned by Arnold, for there is a sharp though short pitch,[14] such as his portage of seven rods would circumvent, with a long piece of swift, hard water below.   Just as one approaches the pitch, going up-stream, the river makes a short double turn around a cliff, running very swiftly.   Meigs's account seems to fit the spot precisely : " At this place the stream is very rapid, in passing which, five or six battoes filled and overset " ; and at these falls we must fix what may be called Camp Disaster,[15] where Arnold passed the night of October 23d.

The council of war was composed, according

to Arnold's account, of "such officers as were
present," and apparently these were Meigs and
his subordinates, Captain Hendricks, Captain
Smith,[16] and very likely Captain Morgan, also.[17]

In accordance with the decisions of the
council, twenty-six invalids[18] were sent back
the next morning under the care of an officer
and doctor, while Captain Hanchet of Meigs's
division hurried forward, with a picked company[19] of fifty men, to secure provisions for
the army in the French settlements of the
Chaudière valley. At the same time Greene
and Enos were ordered to press on with as
many of their best men as they could supply
with rations for fifteen days, and send all the
rest back.[20] The next day, after seeing these
matters attended to, exhorting the soldiers to
persevere, and getting them also started forward, the commander set out with a small
party, and pushed for the head of the column.

Here came the part of the river where estimates of distance are most likely to err. One's
only helps in reckoning are time and fatigue,
and in rapid, shallow water like this, where
oars and paddles can seldom be used, where
every yard of advance means a dead thrust
against the current, and where time is constantly lost by grounding or by catching on

obstructions, the most experienced of guides is very liable to overestimate. Probably, too, as he is compelled to keep his eyes constantly on the swiftly passing water, he receives in that way an impression of moving more rapidly than he does. For these reasons we must now be prepared to discount Arnold's figures a good deal.

Setting out at noon on October 24th, he records advancing "about 7 miles — very rapid water," and then arriving at a pair of short falls about a hundred yards apart. This description seems to fit Sarampus Falls, four or five miles above Upper Shadagee. The upper one of the pair is a sharp drop of about five feet, and the blasting that has been done about it does not seem to have altered its essential character. Only a short carry is needed at such a place, and Arnold's figure for the one he made is six rods. The portage of twelve rods at the lower rapids is likewise sufficient. We still seem to be on the right track.[21]

Beyond these falls, Arnold thought he advanced a mile before camping ; but, as darkness was coming on and rain falling, his tired boatmen were likely to exaggerate the distance greatly. Nearly all night it rained and snowed,

but at four o'clock in the morning the wind
swung around to the north, and the weather
cleared. Daylight found two inches of snow
on the ground.[22]

From Sarampus Falls to the first pond is
perhaps three miles, but in 1775 the foot of
the pond was about a quarter of a mile above
the present dam. Arnold reports proceeding
a mile and a half, crossing a portage of forty
rods, advancing a mile, carrying a hundred
rods, and finally pushing on half a mile more
through rapid water to the pond. This would
make, in all, a little less than four and a half
miles by his reckoning, against about three
and a quarter according to present estimates.
All things considered, the difference is not
surprising, and — in a word — we seem to have
made the journal fit the river as well as could
reasonably have been expected. With but
very slight allowances for error in the original
or the copy of Arnold's report, we have found
all the principal features of the stream, both
the falls and the long reaches of smoother
water, dropping into their proper places.[23]

The other journals do not compare with
Arnold's in completeness or carefulness. In
general, they confirm us at some points, differ
at others, and at still others add more or less

useful details ; but their evidence is no way
decisive.[24]

At Camp Disaster the third division, the companies of Smith and Hendricks, and perhaps
Morgan's company also, passed the night of
the 23d. The next morning they set forward
again. Several boats were capsized, and not a
little baggage, provisions, and ammunition —
besides a few guns and considerable money —
was lost.[25] Whether the first division passed
from river to pond late on the 25th or early on
the 26th, we are unable to determine. Close
behind followed the third division. Nothing eventful seems to have marked its hard
labour for these two days. Like those who
went before, it had to cross one carrying-place
more than a quarter of a mile long, where the
water proved too swift and rocky, and perhaps also too shallow, for navigation ; and on
the 26th all arrived — some early and some
late [26] — at the first pond.[27] The land-party,
meanwhile, had continued to struggle with
difficulties that constantly increased. The
only testimony bearing upon the matter shows
that they travelled on the west side of the
river, and the topography of the district seems
to confirm this. More and more sternly the
valley closed upon them, and at places the

precipices came sheer to the water's edge as they do at present.[28]

Experiences decidedly more dramatic befell the rest of the detachment at this juncture. Greene and his division were proceeding a few miles ahead of the fourth division.[29] Just how far they had advanced by the night of the 24th we cannot say with any certainty, for neither Humphrey, Topham, nor Thayer has given a precise account of his doings at this time; but apparently they were not far from Camp Disaster.[30]   Here they remained in camp the next forenoon, while forty-eight sick men were sent off with a subaltern to the rear, and Greene went forward to inquire of Arnold, what could be done about provisions[31]; and before long Enos with some of his officers came up.   Greene returned before or about noon, quite unsuccessful, for Arnold was beyond his reach[32]; and then the division went on three miles, while the leaders held a conference with Enos and his officers.   Next, sending some boats back to bring provisions from the fourth division, Greene's troops encamped to await their return.[33]

The essential question before the conference was a momentous one: Should these two divisions keep on or turn back?   Or what should be done? The situation was discouraging enough[34]; but duty and honour bade the troops advance, until the order to retreat had been given by the commander; and the commander, instead of sending such an order, had just written Greene and Enos to press on.

Evidently the officers of the fourth division had resolved upon returning, and perhaps the council was called in the hope that it might give them a semblance of authorisation. That it did not do. Williams, McCobb, and Scott, Adjutant Hyde and Lieutenant Peters — all of the fourth division — voted for the return of the whole party, while Greene, Bigelow, Topham, Thayer, and Hubbard[35] voted that only a portion — doubtless the sick, and those who could not be fed — should go back. Enos, who presided, then gave the casting vote in favour of advancing, but none the less he and his captains decided upon immediate retreat. Evidently he voted as he did for the sake of appearances; and then, pretending, or perhaps persuading himself, or possibly persuaded by others, that he was compelled by the urgency of his officers to join them, he went back with the rest. Anyhow, the retrograde movement was ordered not later than two o'clock that afternoon.[36]

The officers who resolved at all hazards on going forward counted, at least, on a division of supplies. In fact they had been given ground for doing so. But they were mistaken. Thayer and a volunteer, borrowing a boat of Major Colburn, "ran rapidly down with the current" until they met the fourth division; but, to their utter astonishment, no supplies were given them. Enos declared that his men were beyond his control, and had resolved to keep all they possessed. He declared also, we may assume, since that was his contention later, that he had only enough provisions left for four days. Entreaties, arguments, and reproaches were used in vain for a long while; but finally Captain Williams aided the petitioners, and they were given two barrels of flour.[37] With this "small pittance," as Senter calls it, the resolute on-goers had to be content; and some of them, throwing aside everything except what each man could carry on his back, pushed on at once,[38] resolved to perish rather than abandon the expedition.[39] The rest followed the next day.

XI

ARNOLD CROSSES THE HEIGHT OF LAND

ON Tuesday, October 24th, Arnold, as we saw, embarked at noon in a bateau,[1] passed his troops, and pushed on with all speed, intending to reach the French settlements in the quickest possible time, and send provisions back to the army. The next day, quite early in the forenoon, he passed from Dead River into what is now called the Chain of Ponds, and for a considerable distance followed a route that is unmistakable, though a very high dam[2] has been placed at the outlet, and the aspect of all the lower ponds a good deal modified by the resulting change of level.

According to Arnold's account, the first pond—or lake, as he called it—was three and one half miles long, but contracted to a width of two rods a mile and a half below the upper end. Evidently one might as well say there were two ponds; and in most cases people now give the names Lower Pond and Bag Pond to

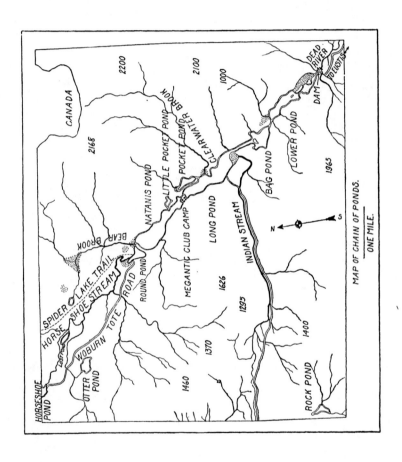

MAP OF CHAIN OF PONDS.
ONE MILE.

this portion of the Chain.³   By the best surveys
the total length of the two is only a couple of
miles ; though, as already mentioned, the first
pond is longer than it used to be.

Next, Arnold came to some marshy ground,
—covered pretty well with water at present,—
found a rivulet, which has become now a wide
strait, and after half a mile of rowing entered
what is to-day Long Pond, though the upper
end of it, partly cut off by a projection from
the western shore,⁴ bears also a name of its
own, Natanis Pond.⁵   To Arnold the two lakes
appeared to be five miles long, while we can
allow but half that extent ; but his mistake is
not surprising—indeed he suspected the error
himself—for the wind was blowing heavily
against him, blustering snow squalls cut off his
view, and several times his party had to go
ashore to bail out the bateaux.⁶

Natanis Pond is closed by a very long sandy
tongue of land running out from the western
side.   So it was in 1775.   Arnold noted that
a passage or strait only three rods wide was
left open for a short distance, and that beyond
it lay "a small round Pond or rather the north
end of the Lake."   This description is clear
and correct, and the body of water beyond the
tongue is now called Round Pond, though, to

tell the truth, it is far from circular after all.

Here the party "were a long time at a loss," as one still is, unless thoroughly familiar with the place. It looked as if they could not leave the pond except by land, and no portage could be found. At length they discovered "a small brook,"—in effect a part of Dead River, but at present more commonly spoken of by the guides as Horse Shoe Stream. The water in the brook was shallow, the current often swift, and the way barred with drift logs in many places. Night began to approach ; and, after forcing his way a mile and a half, as he thought, Arnold found himself compelled to halt. It was eleven o'clock before the party "could get comfortable to lie down"; and even then sleep was not easy, for either the scouts had made no marks, or Arnold had missed them, and he could not feel satisfied whether he had been going right or not.

Thursday morning one of the party was despatched up the stream to look for signs of a portage, while the rest had breakfast and packed up ; but his quest proved fruitless, and after his return Arnold advanced again. Evidently he was reluctant to follow the brook, as he called it ; and one cannot wonder, for, although the "loggers" have probably widened it somewhat in clearing the way for their "drives," it must be still very much as it was a century and a quarter ago, and at present its frequent shallows and swift water and its endless meanderings make it seem interminable. The region itself added to the tediousness of the stream, for while the ponds had been walled up with what Arnold called " prodigious high mountains," the country on either side for a considerable distance was now either swampy or monotonously rolling.

The journey on Horse Shoe Stream was reckoned by Arnold as five miles,—at least a mile too much, probably ; and then he came to the portage so long expected. Carrying the bateaux a dozen rods or so to the left, he found a lake, which—as none of the many guides and sportsmen whom I consulted about the topography of the district, knew of it—we may name the Lost Pond.[7]   It was almost a perfect ellipse, walled completely around, except for two narrow breaks at the lower end, with a high wooded rim. One of the breaks permitted the overflow of the pond to find its way into Horse Shoe Stream ; and it was here that Arnold's party, forcing a passage through a screen of alders, made their entrance across the portage.[8]

Lost Pond seemed a quarter of a mile long.
On reaching the farther end, the travellers
might have lifted their boats over the rim of
the lake, and replaced them in the brook,
but as they had now passed above a considerable affluent of the Stream,[9] it would have been
even harder and more wearisome than before
to boat it.   So the bateaux were shouldered,
and transported—no doubt along the level
top of the ridge[10]—to Horse Shoe Pond, a distance only twenty-seven rods less than a mile.

Just half a mile was the extent that Arnold
assigned to Horse Shoe Pond,[11] and probably
this figure represented fairly the length of his
passage across it.   Then it became necessary
to carry again; and the party, turning almost
due west,[12] struck through the woods to a
somewhat roundish lake called Mud Pond,[13]
a trifle less than a quarter of a mile distant.
In Arnold's eyes this rather unattractive lake
was about half a mile wide; but probably he
doubled its real size, and in fact an unfamiliar
body of water is always likely to seem larger
than it is.   Once more the party carried.
This time the portage ran exactly west, and
measured only a little more than an eighth of
a mile.[14]   At the farther end of it, the shaky
bateaux were placed in the last of the series,

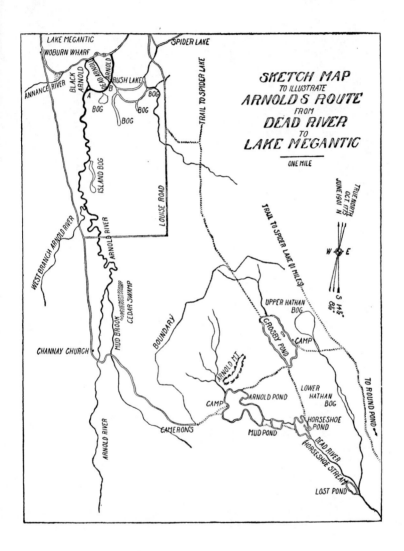

SKETCH MAP
TO ILLUSTRATE
ARNOLD'S ROUTE
FROM
DEAD RIVER
TO
LAKE MEGANTIC

ONE MILE

Moosehorn or Arnold Pond, the largest and perhaps the most beautiful of all.[15]

But the impatient leader could not pause to enjoy the scene, and without delay he began the long portage over the height of land, which has frequently been called the Great Carrying-place, though we, to prevent confusion, will name it the Boundary Portage.

Our quest now becomes more difficult. Thus far, lake and river have guided us. Chances of erring there have been, as we may discover soon ; but they were only at certain points. At present we have before us, after leaving the few regular trails, only mountains, valleys, swamps, and trackless woods,—trackless except as here and there the deer have worn a path. The guides who conduct hunters and fishermen through other parts of the region have little acquaintance here, and the compass has to be one's reliance, aided only by the sun and the occult signs of woodcraft.

Indeed, the territory is not only trackless, but in many places impassable. Here and there are " blow-downs," where many acres of trees have been laid flat, and one must go far around, recovering the line as best one can. Mire-holes, swamps, treacherous bogs, thickets where the dead twigs snap into one's eyes, precipices, ravines,—all these abound; but here must be found the solution of problems vital to our inquiry.

The first and main problem is to discover a line fitting certain conditions. If the line then prove to connect with Arnold Pond, our conclusions as to the route will seem verified; if not, it will be necessary to lay out a different approach to the height of land. The conditions are these: Arnold went two miles about north [16] from the last pond on this side of the present boundary, and came to the height of land "at an elevation of about 35°"; then he made an abrupt wheel to the left of 10° more than a right angle, and advanced a mile and a half; an equally abrupt return to the north for half a mile brought him next to a "beautiful Meadow"; and finally, after marching a quarter of a mile more in the same direction, he came to a very crooked stream. Down this he paddled about ten miles, and then arrived at Lake Megantic.

Montresor's account also requires our attention. He too, reached the height of land after walking two miles from the last pond. Then he descended three miles, traversed a very disagreeable tract of low, swampy ground, crossed a large brook, entered a "most beau-

tiful meadow," decorated with occasional
"knots of most beautiful elms," as well as a
few oaks and ash trees, came then to the Megantic River, and after six miles of rowing, as
he thought, entered Megantic Lake. According to Arnold the distance from pond to river
was four miles and sixty rods ; but Montresor
said: " The New Englanders who measured
this carrying place call it a little more than $4\frac{1}{2}$
miles. This must be understood only from the
last lake to the river Megantick ; though even
that did not seem less to us than 6 miles."

In the course of my trips I crossed the height
of land seven times, and became rather familiar
with the district. Then, with the aid of one of
the first settlers in the Lake Megantic region,
I found where the meadow is likely to have
been,— not a very difficult matter, since there
is at present a particular place where the
ground is low and flat, where the wild grass
reaches to one's shoulder, and where elms and
ash trees at least may still be admired, while
below are swamps, and above are highlands.
Looking eastwardly from this point at the
mountains, I saw a gap, and said to my guide,
" That is probably where we ought to cross the
height of land from the other side, if I have
calculated rightly."

On inquiry I was told that by the river it was about ten miles to Lake Megantic from the place where we stood. Behind us ran a crooked brook, and beyond that Arnold River, the Megantic River of Montresor. And on the other side, between us and the foot of the mountains, lay a tract of cedar swamp, quite sufficiently "disagreeable." "If now," I said to myself, "we go back to the pond, follow the indications of Arnold's journal, and arrive at this spot, we can feel satisfied that he came by about the same route."

That is just what happened. Entirely out of sight of our destination, of course, guided only by the compass, and reckoning distance as carefully as possible, though pretty roughly, we climbed and descended the mountain, crossed the cedar swamp, and arrived almost exactly at the place where we had stood before. Then, looking back, we saw that unless greatly mistaken, we had come over the mountain through the gap that had appeared likely to have been Arnold's way. Only one point was unsatisfactory: we had spent more time than seemed equivalent to four miles and sixty rods. But as there was no trail, frequent aberrations from the true direction and efforts to regain the line were necessary; and

besides, as we have seen, Montresor felt that
the measurement was a good deal too small,
while Washington, in describing the route for
Congress, gave the length of this portage as
six miles.   In short, there seems to be a fairly
complete correspondence between this route
and Arnold's journal, and the route is further
supported by its correspondence with Montresor's account of it, for we have no reason to
doubt that Arnold intended to pursue Montresor's course, or to suppose that he could
not do so.

There are certain other confirmations. Following Arnold's direction, we found the final
ridge, the height of land, rising before us at
an angle that looked like 35°, and then understood, as I thought, what had seemed a very
mysterious passage in his account: "which
brought us to the heighth of Land at an elevation of ab! 35°."   I believed we understood,
too, why the trail took so eccentric a course—
north, south of west, north—instead of about
north-west all the way, for this enabled one,
first, to keep the easily ascending ground of
the valley, and then to avail oneself of the
gap in the mountains, whereas a direct line
would not have been very feasible.   Probably
there was another reason.   One of my guides,

12

an experienced woodsman, called attention to
a log about two feet below ground and a few
inches below the surface of a brook running
to Arnold Pond, which looked as if cut off
to open a passage by the stream. He was positive that we saw axe-work, and as no logging
has ever been done hereabouts, and such a
piece of hackmatack would never decay under
water, he felt no doubt that one of Arnold's
men swung the axe; for the Indians did not
work in that way. Now one of the journals
makes mention of trailing the bateaux here.[17]
Finally, this route seems to be corroborated,
not only by Montresor's journal, but by his
map, for his representation of the last pond
east of the height of land is an evident though
not quite successful attempt to draw the shape
of Arnold Pond, and is not in the least like
Crosby Pond.

Shall we then conclude that Arnold passed
this way ?[18]

All have not been of that opinion. Some
of the guides—for Arnold's expedition is a
very interesting subject to them—believe that
he went by the way of Crosby Pond, north-east
of Arnold, because in their judgment it would
have been a preferable route. William Allen,
who became President of Bowdoin College in

1820, and wrote an account of Arnold's expedition, speaks of "the erroneous belief that it [*i. e.*, Arnold River] was passed by the detachment under his command." [19] In 1777 Sauthier brought out a map of " The Inhabited Part of Canada," engraved by Faden.   Arnold's route is indicated, and the army would not have passed by Arnold Pond.   A " Map of the Boundary Lines between the United States and the Adjacent British Provinces . . . as settled in 1842 by the Treaty of Washington, Compiled . . . under the direction of Major J. D. Graham, Corps of Topographical Engineers, one of the Comm[rs] for surveying and exploring the North Eastern Boundary of the United States under the Act of Congress of July 20, 1840,"—this portentously entitled map indicates what the maker supposed to have been Arnold's route, and a copy presented to the Bowditch Library of Boston by Major Graham himself has the line emphasised with little dots of red ink.   Now in this map the ponds are not correctly done, but the route seems quite clearly intended to pass by Crosby Pond, and meet Arnold River far below the point referred to above. [20]

Admitting, then, that our line of march seems to fit Arnold's journal, one asks whether

there may not be another that would fit it
equally well or better.

So far as Round Pond and the lower part
of Horse Shoe Stream there can be no question, for the topography of the country led the
Colonel by a firm and not over gentle hand.
But let us suppose that when he came to
Hathan Stream, opposite Lost Pond, he followed that to Lower Hathan Bog,[21] proceeded
then to Upper Hathan Bog and Crosby Pond,
crossed the height of land by a gap opening
toward the north-west, and so reached Arnold
River a little distance above Lake Megantic.
This would bring him to his destination, undoubtedly; but the number of ponds, every
direction, and every distance but one, would
be out of keeping with the journal.

Another supposition: did not Arnold ignore Lost Pond, keep on up the Stream till he
came to Horse Shoe Pond, and then strike
for Crosby Pond? He could have done so;
I found an old trail connecting these two
lakes. But the same objections arise as before, and in some respects are even stronger.

There is no other plausible course for him,
and it seems clear that our hypothesis must
be accepted.[22]

So much for Arnold's route; now a word

about his passage over it. At four o'clock in the afternoon of October 26th, the second day after he left the army, his party entered upon the Boundary Portage. By nightfall they had gone up the brook to the height of land and crossed the ridge,—three miles in all. The day's work had been an arduous one, and they now halted for repose, thoroughly fatigued. But repose was slow in coming. The whole of the baggage did not arrive until very late, and it was nearly midnight before the tents could be pitched.

Meantime Arnold had something to think of. His army was liable to find even more trouble than he, so he sent back Nehemiah Getchell[23] "to pilot up the rear." On the other hand, Steele and Church were ahead, and no doubt he had been impatient for advices from them; here twenty of their men appeared, and of course they could give the desired information.[24] The next morning a letter was addressed to the second and fourth divisions, advising them to leave their bateaux, urging them to "make all possible despatch," and giving advice and encouragement about the travelling beyond the height of land.[25] Then the party set out, the rest of the portage was soon crossed, and at 11 o'clock they launched their boats on Arnold River.

XII

THE ARMY CROSSES THE HEIGHT OF LAND

ON the morning of October 26th, as we know, Arnold himself was breaking camp on Horse Shoe Stream, about a mile from Round Pond.[1] The "axe-men" under Steele and Church were engaged in clearing the trail over the Boundary Portage, though the lieutenants themselves had gone forward.[2] Hanchet and his advance party seem to have been not far from Arnold.[3] The first division, with the third close behind it,[4] was crossing the first pond of the Chain. The second division was toiling along on the upper Dead River; and the fourth division, led by Enos, could have been seen going rapidly downstream.[5]

By this time, it should be remembered, the army had been well sifted.[6] The sick, the faint of heart, and the weak of limb had gone back. Those who remained must, then, have numbered about six hundred, besides the ad-

vanced parties,[7] and their one thought now
was to reach the French settlements.

But here rises a question: did the whole army
take the same route as Arnold? At first sight
the inquiry may seem unnecessary,—almost im-
pertinent. The trail marked by the scouting
and surveying parties, and followed by Arnold
and Hanchet with their companies, must have
been distinct enough, we naturally say ; and,
besides, the commander had thought it prudent to send a guide back to pilot the army.
Under such circumstances who would venture,
we are inclined to ask, to strike out on a route
not followed by the leader?

But we shall presently find the army splitting up, and pursuing different courses. There
may have been guides at that day, as we find
now, who did not consider Arnold Pond the
best gateway from Dead River to Lake Megantic. Finally, none of the descriptions of
the route given us by the other journalists
tallies exactly with Arnold's, and some of them
appear to differ irreconcilably. No definite
directions are found in these journals, and the
statements of distance are incomplete ; and this
vagueness widens the range of possibilities.

As far as Round Pond the army must have
followed its head.[8] The lakes were a plain

and indeed compulsory route for the bateaux, while the land parties could easily see the water, and had no temptation to leave it.

From Round Pond a trail now conducts one all the way across the height of land to Spider Lake, and there are hints, though not in the journals, that such a trail existed in 1775. The route is an easy and convenient one; but, as the army had its bateaux to care for, water navigation was extremely desirable.

Nor can a land party have gone this way, for the men took turns in the boats, and all were accustomed to help at the carries. Even the possibility of using the two Hathan Bogs does not make this route available, for they could have given only two miles of water in a total of eleven. Still other objections could be urged, but this one seems fatal.

Suppose, however, that a carry were made from Round Pound to Lower Hathan Bog, and another from that to Crosby Pond. In this case we should have the army choosing a carry of three and a quarter or three and a half miles instead of using Horse Shoe Stream, and that is not thinkable. We are, in short, driven to believe that the troops went up Horse Shoe Stream as far as the outlet of the lower bog, at least. It must be admitted that none of the journalists,[9] except Meigs, Dearborn, and probably Senter, alludes to the Stream; but certainly no one mentions at this point a carry of three miles or more, so that we must simply consider some of the narratives defective on this point, as they clearly are on other points, particularly at this stage, and admit that what evidence they give is distinctly in favour of this view.   Were other arguments needed, they could be offered; and several will appear before the end of the chapter.

Now let us suppose that the army went up Horse Shoe Stream and thence up Hathan Stream,[10] rowed the length of Lower Hathan Bog, made its way next to Crosby Pond by a direct carry or via Upper Hathan Bog, and finally proceeded over a convenient gap in the mountains straight on, between Spider and Rush lakes, to Lake Megantic; or to Spider Lake on the right, or perhaps to the lower Arnold River on the left.

Let us try this route by Meigs's journal. Meigs does not agree with Arnold, for he records finding only three ponds after he entered the "crooked river," evidently Horse Shoe Stream, while Arnold mentions four; and, if he followed the route just suggested, he did find three ponds, provided he touched

the upper bog, and only three.   But other
points are not so favourable.   He says that he
went about three miles by the crooked river,
but the distance by water from Round Pond to
Lower Hathan Bog is between five and six
miles, and would have seemed to him over
six.   Then he came to a portage of fifteen
rods, which would oblige us to suppose that
some large obstruction existed at the lower
end of the bog, which nothing suggests at
present.

He next found a pond " 100 perches across,"
whereas the bog is nearly a mile in length
and very narrow indeed.   The carry of a mile
that followed would have brought him to the
upper bog ; but his next pond was " 50 rods
wide," a description that no way fits the spot.
Possibly he could have found a carry only
forty-four rods long between the bog and
Crosby Pond, but one may doubt very much
whether he could have done so.   His figure
for the last pond, two miles, fits Crosby better
than Arnold.   The distance to the height of
land, two miles, is about right for this route
also, but his estimate of the Boundary Portage
as a whole, four miles and sixty perches, will
not answer at all here, for one must walk not
less than six miles from Crosby Pond to reach

Spider Lake, and at least a mile more than that to pass around the swamps to Arnold River.

In short, our hypothesis does not agree with Meigs's journal, and it seems still less credible to us when we reflect that Hathan Stream, instead of being navigable, as—for the sake of the argument—we have assumed, is only a narrow, shallow, tumbling brook, full of rocks and little falls. On the other hand, if we suppose that Meigs accidentally omitted a pond in his count, he agrees almost perfectly with Arnold. The carry into Lost Pond appears as fifteen rods, a mere variant from Arnold's twelve, and his estimate of the length of the pond—one hundred instead of eighty— may be understood the same way. At this point, too, he makes a remark that is decidedly significant. After crossing Lost Pond he " encamped on the northwest side, upon a high hill, which is a carrying place."   North-west from the upper end of this pond the rim is at least one hundred and fifty feet high, one may guess, and, in order to reach the level ridge mentioned in the preceding chapter, it was necessary to carry up the hill. Finally, if we are not mistaken, we shall discover Meigs in the grassy meadows beside Arnold River, and there he would not have arrived by the suggested route.

Dearborn's ponds and carries, while they do not measure exactly the same as Meigs's, correspond so nearly that the same discussion covers both. The other accounts are too fragmentary to throw any light on our present theory.

Next let us suppose that Meigs went on like Arnold to Horse Shoe Pond, but there turned north, carried over to Crosby Pond, nd then made his way across the height of land. This would agree with the number of his ponds, but the length of the portage, about a mile and an eighth, would not agree with his "44 perches," and several of the other difficulties would confront us.

One more scheme presents itself. Let us assume that Meigs did not find Lost Pond at all, but followed Horse Shoe Stream to the pond of that name, underestimating the length of the stream and the width of the pond. Let us assume further that a few rods north of the pond there existed a body of water which does not exist now; that this pond, which Meigs called "50 rods wide," was a mile in length; and that Meigs crossed it the longest way on his passage to Crosby Pond.

This assumption that a pond has vanished, is
not so extravagant as one might imagine.
Formerly the beaver abounded here, and some
have outwitted the trappers even down to the
present hour. In Horse Shoe Pond, the dome
of a beaver house may be seen on a bit of an
islet.   Not far away I counted twenty poplars
freshly gnawed off,—one of the stumps not
less than eight inches across.   In Lower Pond,
one night, as we were paddling silently along,
we suddenly heard a loud splash close by, as
if an aërolite had dashed into the lake : it was a
beaver that had come up just there, and, finding enemies near, had made the customary
signal by slapping the water with his tail, as
he dove under.   There can be no doubt,
probably, that some of the ponds and streams
have been changed by the destruction or
natural decay of old beaver dams.   Little
Carry Pond, on the Great Carrying-place, is
said to have a lower level than formerly for
this reason.   The proprietors of the dam were
caught or frightened away, their works fell out
of repair, and the lake broke through.

Has this been the case between Crosby and
Horse Shoe Ponds ?   Certainly one finds low
ground there, and flowing water.   It is said
that Crosby Pond, instead of having a brook

for an outlet, sends its overflow in an oozing
or rushing sheet, according to the season,
across this area.[11]   There is a hill, too, at the
north-west sufficiently high, perhaps, to fit
Meigs's narrative.   On the other hand, one
finds no signs of a beaver dam; the assumption that a pond a mile long once existed
there is rather violent; Meigs could not have
estimated the whole length of Horse Shoe
Stream as only "about 3 miles"; and, besides
these objections to the hypothesis, we should
have all the other difficulties of the route by
Crosby Pond to encounter.

But there is one other possibility.   We
know that the Colonel went north from Arnold
Pond, but we do not know in what direction
Meigs turned from that point.   May he not
have gone where the present path—almost a
road—leads from the permanent camp on the
western side of the pond to the beginning of
the highway at Cameron's house on the Canada
side?   This distance is something less than a
mile, and it presents no difficulties except a
few short, but rather steep, pitches.   A man
can run the entire distance.   Scores of people
pass between Arnold Pond and Arnold River
by this route every summer, and in winter
sleds go back and forth.

It does not seem probable, however, that Meigs went this way. He says that it was two miles from the pond to the dividing ridge of the height of land; but by this western course the distance is less than one mile. Again, it was easiest to march where a trail existed; the trails were made by Indians; the Indians usually followed water-courses, as did the trail pursued here by Arnold; and there is no water-course running toward Cameron's.

Meigs tells us further that the length of the portage was four miles and sixty perches. This reminds us at once of the portage that Arnold took; and while the distance by Cameron's to the meadows, where Meigs will presently appear to have been, is not very much longer, it is enough longer so that we cannot suppose it was called precisely the same. Neither would Meigs have been likely to know the exact length of his portage, if he went by another path than the regular one. Finally, those who kept on after their leader had not only a trail, but a trail cleared by the pioneers. All things considered, it seems plain that Meigs followed his chief.

The same reasoning holds all the way along for Dearborn, but at the last stage we have a curious corroboration. About half a mile forward on the Boundary Portage, Dearborn found a fine canoe, apparently an Indian's, carefully laid up.   Why had it been brought so far from the pond?   Not merely for concealment,—twenty rods would have been far enough for that.   Apparently it had gone by water from the pond to the point where it was found, and this argues that Dearborn went north by the brook, as Arnold did.

If both Meigs and Dearborn adopted this route, the presumption that all the rest did so is a good deal strengthened.   None of the journalists in the first division helps us here. Henry and Morison are plainly inaccurate, and they, like " Provincial," are very incomplete. Thayer, Topham, and Humphrey give the length of the Boundary Portage as four and one-quarter miles, which eliminates the route by Crosby Pond, but otherwise they help us little.   The rest of the journalists are too confused and incomplete to be worth considering, except that Senter calls the last carry four and one-half miles, as Dearborn does, while Tolman and Stocking call it four miles and fifty rods.[12] Our conclusion must be, no doubt, that the rest of the army followed on after Steele, Church, Arnold, Hanchet, and their parties, all of whom went evidently by the same route.[13]   It only remains, then, to note the incidents of the journey.[14]

They were not many. During Thursday, the 26th, all moved forward, the bateaux on the water and the land parties on the south-western side of them.[15] The weather was cold, the ground covered with several inches of snow, and the journey on foot extremely arduous; for below Round Pond the men had to struggle against rocks and mountains, and beyond that point against swamps. The boatmen, too, had difficulties apparently, even after the Chain of Ponds was entered, for several of the journals mention one carry a quarter of a mile in length.[16] At night the first division appears to have camped between Horse Shoe and Mud ponds, the third division at the two ends of Lost Pond, and the second division somewhere on the Chain of Ponds, very likely on the level ground near the foot of Long Pond, where the " Upper Farm " now is.

Friday, October 27th, all advanced again. The first division reached the Boundary Portage early in the day, crossed the height of land, and encamped in the meadows by Arnold River to await the rest of the army. It was a fearful day's work. In consequence, very likely, of the letter written that morning by

the commander,[17] the captains appear to have
decided that it would not be worth while to
try to carry the bateaux across this long
portage; but Morgan saw that bateaux would
be useful beyond the mountain, and would be
needed, in particular, to carry his military
stores.[18]   So he ordered his command to take
their boats along; and they obeyed, though
we are told that their shoulders were worn to
the bone. Smith's and Hendricks's companies
carried only one bateau each to Arnold River,[19]
but, even so, Morison drew a heartrending
picture of what he named "The Terrible
Carrying Place."

Meigs and the third division made no
attempt to transport their bateaux (except a
very few) across the carry, for Dearborn says
that as they entered on the portage they "received orders[20] here to Leave our Batteaus."
Naturally the men desired to carry as little
weight as possible over the mountain. The
stores were examined, and when most of the
powder proved unfit for use, it was promptly
thrown away. Relieved in this manner the
division moved on. Meigs encamped on the
height of land, and Dearborn about a mile and
a half in the rear.[21] Meanwhile the second
division was pushing forward, and probably

it encamped that night at Horse Shoe Pond.[22]

Saturday, the third division found it easy to join the first on the meadows, while the second, making greater exertions, and taking but one boat for each company across the height of land, was able to arrive at the same place by the middle of the afternoon.

XIII

FROM THE BOUNDARY PORTAGE TO LAKE MEGANTIC

AS Arnold came to the river, about 11 o'clock A.M., October 27th, important and welcome news greeted him. Steele and Church were there, or soon met him, and with them Jaquin, a man who had been sent down to the French settlements to learn the state of sentiment among them.[1]

Steele, we may assume, reported on the character of the river and the path below Lake Megantic, for it was a part of his mission to obtain this information, and we find Arnold immediately sending such intelligence to his officers. Jaquin's packet of news was even more interesting. He reported the people in the settlements as glad to hear that Americans were coming, and ready to supply them with provisions; and he said that, as few or no regulars were then in Quebec, the city could be taken easily.

Arnold, after writing — but not despatching [2] — a letter of cheer, advice, and orders to
his men, set out down-stream, reached the lake
at four o'clock, rowed about three miles farther
— as he called it — to a "very considerable
wigwam," or house of bark, on the eastern
shore, and stopped for the night.

A letter to Washington was next in order.[3]
Arnold explained that he found he had been
greatly deceived as to the difficulties of the undertaking, gave an account of the situation and
the army, expressed the opinion that his troops
would not all reach fresh supplies in less than
eight or ten days, and finally announced what
course he should adopt on arriving at Quebec.
The letter was despatched to Enos, for Arnold
had not yet heard of his defection; and Enos
was directed to forward it to Cambridge, and to
"take particular care of the sick and those who
are returning, as well as of any other matters
that are necessary."[4]

Hanchet and sixty men[5] left the Boundary Portage with Arnold, but their course was
by land.[6] The journey proved not a pleasant one, but finally, after wading "two miles
thro' water to their waists," they reached
"at ab^t Sun set" a low, marshy point on the
eastern side of the lake, some two miles from

the bark wigwam.[7]   Arnold, seeing them in
that place, divined their difficulty, and sent his
bateaux for them.   "Three and four" trips
proved necessary, but a little before midnight
the men were all brought off.

The next day was Saturday.   Arnold despatched his letters, and ordered Hull,[8] the
bearer, to "pilot up" the fourth division,
which he still counted upon.   Then, with
Steele, Church, Oswald, and thirteen men, he
embarked about 7 o'clock, A.M., in four bateaux and a birch canoe,[9] paddled briskly down
the lake a distance that he called thirteen
miles, though it was really much less, and at 10
o'clock reached the outlet.   By that time his
rear bateaux were nearly four miles astern, so
he went ashore and kindled a fire; but at 11
o'clock the little fleet was together once more,
and entered Chaudière River.   Hanchet, meanwhile — his number reduced to fifty-five —
marched along the shore.

For the rest of the troops, this Saturday,
October 28th, was a striking nodal point in
their march.   Apparently the entire army,
with the exception of Arnold's company and
Hanchet's advanced party, gathered in the
meadows by Arnold River; and Senter expressly states that by four o'clock all had ar-

rived, and been "embodied" in their proper commands.[10]

Here all heard of the defection of Enos.[11] Earlier news of this had reached, of course, the hindmost companies. Dearborn learned of it on the Boundary Portage. But the riflemen, we may infer, first knew of the misfortune on the meadows, and indeed this is evident from Henry's narrative. That men in the rear, whose way had been made easy for them by the preceding companies, should have been the quickest to give up, roused bitter resentment ; and such a reduction of numbers, with the loss of so much ammunition, seemed to doom the expedition to certain failure.

In order that all might know what provisions there were to count upon, and also, no doubt, that all might share justly, whatever supplies the army still had were now brought together, and a distribution made.[12] How much was a soldier given to support him during the fatigues and hardships of the coming six days ? Four or five pints of flour, but no meat at all, except, in some cases, two or four ounces of pork. The distribution took place before Arnold's letter arrived,[13] and the forward movement began at once.

Morgan seems to have found it necessary

to let his men rest a little more after the excessive toil of bringing their boats across the Boundary Portage, but Goodrich's and Dearborn's contingents were in good trim, and set off immediately down the river, followed by Smith's riflemen and later by Ward's company.[14] Enterprise, however, was this time a mistake. At four o'clock, after these troops had moved, Arnold's letter to the field officers and captains arrived, and the soldiers that had already gone forward missed several important things.

One was the announcement that in three days Arnold hoped to reach the inhabitants, and in as many more to have provisions halfway up the Chaudière River to meet the army. The second was a most emphatic warning against undertaking to march down beside the river to Lake Megantic,— a route that would land them, so the Colonel declared, in a swamp they could not possibly get out of. In the third place, the letter told the army how they should proceed. They should avoid the swamp by keeping the high ground between the river and the mountains, pursue a direction "about north and by east," and follow the eastern shore of Lake Megantic. Besides all this, Arnold's messenger [15] brought good news

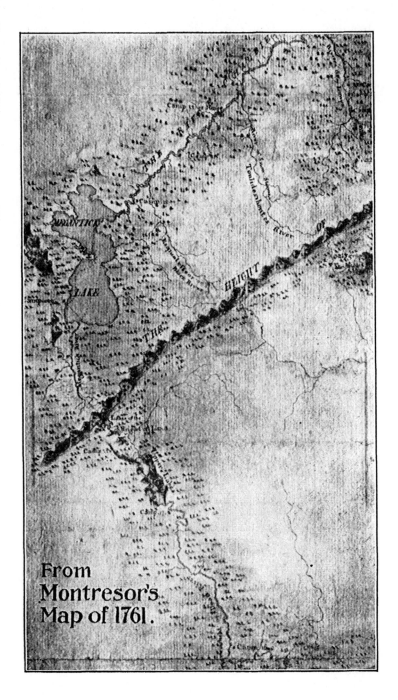

From
Montresor's
Map of 1761.

of Schuyler's operations, and the whole army — Meigs in particular — rejoiced exceedingly.

The danger of starvation now seemed almost over. In fact, the story went abroad among the hungry soldiers that provisions would *reach them* in three days. The consequence was that rations began to be eaten extravagantly, and we are told that some of the men actually hastened to devour their whole share.

The army was now split into three parts. Four companies had begun to march down beside the river; Morgan, having his boats, naturally determined to proceed by water; and the remaining five companies, in obedience to their colonel's directions, moved back to the high ground, and either camped on the portage, or advanced a little way to the north before stopping for the night.[16]

We come now to the grand crisis of the march, a crisis threatening nothing less than the complete extinction of the whole army, except the parties under Arnold and Hanchet. Our first step must be to study the ground.

Arnold River takes its rise not far from the sources of the Connecticut, but on the northern instead of the southern side of the New Hampshire boundary; and thence it flows almost due north, receiving a number of tributaries.

One, Muddy Brook, enters it in, or close by,
the meadows where Arnold's men encamped,
and not very far below this it is joined by
its largest affluent, a stream called the West
Branch.   The descent of the river is considerable ; it winds interminably ; it must rise
quickly and high in the spring and after heavy
rains, for its basin is narrow and bounded
chiefly by high, steep slopes ; and as a consequence of these conditions, it has carried a
large amount of earth toward the lake.

The last few miles of its course lie through
low and swampy ground.   About a mile and a
half below the meadows the land begins to be
wet, and is covered with a fairly dense growth
of alders ; while in some places many small
cedars and spruces may be found, and in others grassy swamps and open bogs are seen.
When one arrives within about a mile of the
lake, its main channel turns more than 90° to
the right, flows about three-eighths of a mile
toward the east, and receives what we may
name Rush River, the outlet of a large pond
called Rush Lake, into the other end of which
a small river or large brook pours the overflow
of Spider Lake.   (See the map on page 171.)

It is about twenty-five or thirty rods from
Rush Lake to the point where its outlet enters

Arnold River. There the latter turns again, and flowing north for about three-quarters or seven-eighths of a mile, empties into Lake Megantic. About eight rods above the juncture of the river and the outlet, Arnold River sends a very small part of its waters into a lagoon-like stream called the Dead Arnold, which seeks the lake by a course considerably west of north; while from the point where the Arnold veers so sharply eastward (A on the map), another small part of its volume finds its way, through a very crooked stream called the Black or Little Arnold, to the common receptacle. Most of this lowest region is occupied with standing water, swamp grass, many dead and a few living trees, some alders, and scattering bushes of other kinds.

In 1775 the state of things was unmistakably similar. Doubtless the many floods of turbid water have extended the delta somewhat, but not nearly so much as if the stream had not been free to spread over the miles of swamp, and lay down its burden of mud before arriving at its mouth. A dam has been constructed recently in the Chaudière River about two miles below its source; but, although the dam is a high one, it has not raised the level of the lake very much, because, as we know,

the descent of the river in the intervening distance was quite rapid. Eighteen inches probably would measure the change of level ; and,
while this was rise enough to kill a great
many trees, I believe the change in the plane
of the water, compared with that of the soil,
cannot have been great, for the spring floods
and the storm floods of more than one hundred and twenty-five years must have built up
the swamp a good deal.

Turning now to the advance of Goodrich's
and Dearborn's men, we find that they reached
the border of the lake [17]; but, on attempting to
proceed along to the eastern shore, they were
soon stopped by two rivers, the second even
deeper and wider than the first. Only one
spot can be found that corresponds to this description : it is the shore of the lake on the
left bank of the Dead Arnold. The second
river must, then, have been the combined
volume of Arnold and Rush rivers, a really
formidable stream.

But here we discover a difficulty. To reach
this point it was necessary to cross the Arnold
where it ran eastwardly — the eastward Arnold, we may call this part — and at present
that is not a fordable stream (on the map,
between A and B). Melvin gives us the clue,

and he alone; but, as he was in a canoe with Captain Dearborn and Mr. Ayres, leader of the pioneers, his opinion very likely reflects theirs. Melvin says that the first of the two rivers crossed Sunday morning in a boat, was one which they had forded the night before. Now a moment's reflection will show that his statement was the only natural one to make about the Dead Arnold, if they had waded the eastward Arnold the previous evening, for that eastward Arnold was of course bound for the lake, and they were sure, therefore, by all ordinary reckoning, to come to it again before they could come to any other river, when they moved toward the east along the shore. So it is evident that according to Melvin's statement, the eastward Arnold was crossed Saturday evening.[18] But, as we saw, that stream is not fordable. How then did they ford it?

Montresor's map is the next thing to consider. It represents the direction of the Arnold River as essentially north all the way to the lake, and shows that Montresor entered the lake near its western — not its eastern — side, turned to the left, and camped. Plainly he went down the Black Arnold, and did not see Rush River or Rush Lake, for neither his map nor his journal gives a hint of them. Had the

Arnold flowed at that time as it flows now, there is not one chance in a hundred that he would have gone down the Black Arnold. He would have paddled through the eastward Arnold, noted Rush River, noted also Rush Lake, which is visible from the junction of the two rivers, followed the Arnold to Lake Megantic, and camped close by on the eastern — not the western— shore. Even had he chosen, for some unimaginable reason, to follow the Black Arnold, he could not possibly have failed to observe the eastward Arnold, for although he passed that river after sunset, there must have been some light, or his men could not have made their way along such a stream. Able engineer that he was, sent expressly to survey the region, had he observed a river there he would have explored it the following day, and found Rush Lake; but this he did not do. The conclusion is that in 1775 the eastward Arnold was comparatively small.

This is confirmed by Arnold's course. He knew that his officers relied on Montresor's map. Had he passed through the eastward Arnold, he would have seen Rush Lake, and would have given the officers notice of it in his letter. He would also have seen that the greatest danger ahead of men coming down the river was not the swamp, but the complete trap formed by Arnold and Rush rivers and Rush Lake. Still further, he would have seen that Hanchet's men were sure to get into trouble, and would have stayed by to help them.

There is evidence even more convincing. Arnold, after entering Lake Megantic, paddled a distance that he called three miles to reach the bark house or wigwam on the easterly shore, but Hanchet was stopped by a river at a point considerably nearer the bark house. This was of course impossible, unless Arnold passed down the Black Arnold, and so entered the lake west of the river that stopped Hanchet.

But how can we explain such a change in the eastward Arnold?

The Black Arnold is exceedingly crooked, and, I should think, about a couple of miles long. To drive logs through it would be extremely tedious. On the other hand the eastward Arnold and the lower Arnold, while there are two great bends, do not meander, and probably measure less than a mile and a quarter together. It was very natural for loggers to clear out the eastward Arnold and use it. The removal of obstructions quickened the current, and that of course both deepened and

widened the channel, especially as the soil is
extremely soft and watery ; and at the present time this is the regular and sole highway
of the logs.   Natural causes assisted.   The
crookedness of the Black Arnold checks the
current, and the stream has become so clogged
that continuous navigation is impossible, even
for a canoe.

Late Saturday afternoon, then, Goodrich's
men waded the eastward Arnold, and forced
their way through the swamp, waist deep in
mud and water most of the time, to the edge
of the lake or near it.   One bateau belonged
to the company, but it carried their stock of
flour and went ahead, and there was no boat
within reach to convey them across the Dead
Arnold.   Goodrich himself, discovering that he
was in a trap, explored the swamp up and down,
wading — as he thought — several miles, in
the hope of finding a way to cross the river ;
but no way could be discovered.   Next, with
some of his men, he pushed on to a little
island near the shore, probably in the hope of
attracting the attention of his bateaumen or
some one of the advanced party.

Just then Dearborn arrived in his canoe, followed by his company.   At first his men proposed to build a raft, but Dearborn said he

would paddle farther, and look for a place to wade the river. Going then into the lake, he discovered Goodrich, and learned that no ford could be found. He was told also that probably the bateau was not far off. So Goodrich clambered into the canoe, and, as it was now beginning to be dark, and a light became visible, apparently three miles away, the captains made off in that direction in the hope of overtaking the bateau.

The light proved to be at the bark wigwam or house where Arnold had stopped. One of Hanchet's party had used up his provisions, and so was left here to " join his Company " [19]; and he had built a fire. As this point the officers halted, while their crew went on in search of the bateau. Unable to overtake it, the canoe returned an hour and a half later; and, as nothing more could be done at that time, the two captains remained at the wigwam, very anxious about their companies.

The soldiers had been able, meanwhile, to arrange with a dismal show of comfort for the night. Dearborn's men got onto a knoll, very small and very low, and at last, dragging wood from the water, succeeded in making a blaze. A mouthful of pork was eaten, and they lay down with their feet to the fire and their heads close to the water.   The other company did about the same.

As soon as day broke, Sunday morning, Dearborn and Goodrich went back to their men, and began to ferry them over the rivers in the one boat.   It was an exceedingly slow process and very ticklish also, for merely to get into a canoe from a swamp without splitting the bark was a difficult feat.   But luckily Captain Smith's bateau came along, attended more or less closely by his company.   This boat was hired by Dearborn and Goodrich, and finally, before nightfall, the three companies crossed the Dead Arnold, marched forty or fifty rods to the main stream, crossed that also, and set out for the bark house. Dearborn undertook to lead his men around through the forest, but his compass was bad, and after advancing about a couple of miles, they had to return and make a fresh start.

While they were in the woods, Morgan's company came down the river.   Whether all of his men could get into the bateaux we cannot say, but with seven boats he was of course able to pass the swamps without serious difficulty.   Stopping at the bark house, the men helped themselves to some provisions left there by Dearborn, Melvin,[20] and others, and then

pressed on for the Chaudière River. Dearborn's company finally reached the bark house,
and there camped for the night. Goodrich's
men hurried on in the hope of overtaking
their bateau and flour, Smith's,[21] if we may
trust Henry's account, pushed forward with
equal speed, and Ward's, we have evidence,
were not far behind.[22]

Greene with his three companies, Meigs with
Hanchet's company, and Hendricks with his
riflemen remain to be accounted for. At four
o'clock on Saturday afternoon all of these appear to have been together in the meadows by
Arnold River, as we saw.[23] There the general
distribution of provisions took place,[24] and
there Arnold's letter arrived. The advice of
the letter was heeded, and all moved back to the
high ground. The second division, resuming
its place before what there was of the third,
then proceeded a little distance toward Lake
Megantic, and all encamped for the night in
fine spirits.[25]

Early on Sunday morning the advance began. Greene, Topham, Thayer, Senter, the
guide,[26] and some of the other officers led, and
the men followed, though in separate companies.[27] The general course of their march
was a little east of north.[28] At first they were

in woods, and the spurs of the mountains in-
tersected their line of advance. After a time
they came to a brook that ran from the height
of land in a north-westerly direction.[29] No attention should have been paid to it; but, as
they knew of no lake in the region except
Lake Megantic, it was very natural to suppose
that the brook would conduct them there.
Whether they followed it or not, they certainly
left the high ground and descended into the
miserable swamp south of Rush Lake, full of
slippery roots and icy water. Their feet were
soon reduced to a state of insensibility, and
at every step they risked a fall and a sprained
or broken limb that could only mean abandonment and death, — for a helpless man could
not be carried. At eleven o'clock the head of
the straggling procession reached Rush Lake.
Not much over a mile away to the north-west,
Dearborn and Goodrich were then at work
ferrying their men across the two rivers; but
they were too far off to be heard, and the
woods north of the lake stood partly in the
way of seeing them.

A turn was now made to the right, for the
high ground lay on that side, and after a time
the stream that empties Spider Lake into
Rush Lake was encountered. This offered a

grand opportunity.[30]   Had the stream been
crossed, and a course toward the north-west
pursued, Greene and his followers would soon
have stood on the shore of Lake Megantic,
where the other companies had passed or were
soon to come.   But the guide was ignorant of
this fact, and indeed no better posted than the
rest.   It seemed far safer, we may suppose, to
follow the water, than to strike off into a
trackless forest; and so the march continued
until Nepiss Lake, as it was then called, appeared in view.   The modern name of this
piece of water—Spider Lake—suggests its irregular outline.   Not daring to leave its mar-
gin, the men toiled on, in and out of the
tongues of land between the bays, and in and
out of the low and swampy spots along the
shore, and finally had to encamp for the night
with no idea where they were.[31]

The next morning an early start was made,
for the preparation of breakfast consisted only
in stirring a gill of flour with some water, and
baking it a little on the coals or the ashes.[32]
In a short time Spider River[33] was met.   It
seemed too deep to cross, and the leaders
took their followers a considerable distance
toward the south in search of a way around
the stream.[34]   That idea, however, was soon

given up, and when a place about four feet
deep and three or four rods wide presented
itself, all waded through, some in their clothes
and others naked, though there was ice on
both margins. The leaders proceeded then to
a high eminence,[35] and, after getting such an
outlook as they could, changed the course of
the march to west-north-west.

By this time the soldiers began to despair.
Many were soon ready to give up. What
semblance of military order had been maintained until now was discarded, and those who
could walk fastest went ahead. But their
wanderings were nearly over. According to
Fobes, a young Indian, who possessed " some
practical knowledge of the country," was found
among the soldiers, and he assumed the place
of guide. However this may have been, after
a march of about fifteen miles that day, as it
was estimated, the men came upon the track
of other troops.[36] They did not know where
it led, but at least it was a sign of comrades.
Gladly they camped for the night.[37] Lake
Megantic was not far below, and the Chaudière
River lay only six miles or so to the north.

XIV

FROM LAKE MEGANTIC TO THE FIRST INHABITANTS

SATURDAY morning, October 28th, Arnold set out from the bark house, or wigwam, on Lake Megantic with four bateaux, a birch-bark canoe,[1] and fifteen men besides Captain Oswald, "being Resolved to proceed on to the french Inhabitants, & at all events send back provisions to meet the rear." He seems to have chosen the canoe as his own conveyance, and his men paddled on so briskly that at ten o'clock, when he reached the outlet of the lake, the Chaudière River, he was—as we recall—four miles in advance of his rear bateaux ; but by eleven o'clock the bateaux had arrived, the baggage was lashed to the boats, and the descent of the river began.

The word Chaudière means caldron, and it pictures very well the boiling, foaming stream. Lake Megantic lies almost eleven hundred feet[2] above the St. Lawrence near

Quebec, and the air-line distance between the two is only about seventy-five miles. To make matters worse, the channel bristles with rocks. Everybody familiar with the stream stands in awe of it. In looking for a boatman, I heard of a few guides who had attempted to go down, but only one had succeeded — partially, at that — and he showed no desire to repeat the experiment.[3]

The danger of Arnold's party was very great. They probably had had little experience, or none at all, in such navigation. Only the best of canoes could hope to defy the swift water and avoid the rocks; and Arnold sat in a brittle thing of bark, while most of his party had only the clumsy and rickety bateaux. However, they bravely committed themselves to the current, and rushed along at the rate of eight or ten miles an hour.[4] Fifteen miles had been passed, Arnold thought, when suddenly the little fleet capsized amidst the rocks of some bad rapids. Three of the boats were damaged, and two of them smashed to pieces. Four men lost their baggage, arms, and provisions; and six of the party, after swimming a long time in the perilous water, were saved with difficulty.

Serious as this misfortune was, Arnold soon

thought it a mercy in disguise, for no sooner
were the men dry and in their boats again,
than one of them, who was in advance, cried
out that falls lay just ahead.   These were decidedly worse than the rapids that had just
caused their mishap ; and had no warning
been given, it looked as if the boats must
have been dashed in pieces, and the lives of
all been destroyed.[5]

On examining the shore, Arnold found a
portage of 146 rods, carried across it, embarked again, with eyes and ears alert, went
a half-mile or so, observed "more dangerous
Rapids," reconnoitred them from the shore,
and concluded to encamp.   Provisions were
then re-distributed, and it appeared that each
member of the party had eight ounces of pork
and two ounces of flour.[6]

Sunday, while one part of his army was
getting across the rivers at the head of Lake
Megantic, and another wandering through
the swamps and thickets near Rush and
Spider lakes, Arnold again took his chances
on the Chaudière.   Embarking at seven o'clock
in the morning with only about one-third of his
party, while the rest proceeded by land, he
reckoned that he made some forty miles in
the course of the short day.   His two bateaux

survived the journey; but the canoe, running against the rocks, sprung a leak, and had to be abandoned.   Meanwhile the stream, though it received no large affluents, was growing in volume and even faster in width, until, as Arnold estimated, it was twenty rods across in most places.[7]   Less width and greater depth would have rendered it easier to pass.

Monday morning the party made an early start, and after going about ten miles, as they estimated, came to some very swift water and filled a bateau.   Luckily nothing was lost, and, by lowering the boats with the painters, they were got safely through.   Two miles more, and the Great Falls appeared.[8]   These, a cataract fully twenty feet high, one may guess, it was of course vain to think of running.   In fact some rapids quite a distance above seemed too fierce to be attempted.   A portage of half a mile provided a way of escape; and, as two friendly Penobscot Indians were met there and aided in the work, it was crossed without much delay.   Another half-mile of paddling, as Arnold reckoned it, brought him to the Lesser Falls and a carrying-place of fifteen rods.   About three miles beyond this point, the principal tributary of the Chaudière, the River du Loup, emptied.

It was now evening, but the party hurried on ; and, some four miles below the junction, the first house of the French settlements gave them a welcome to civilisation.[9]

At this point Arnold's account, as we have it, suddenly breaks off in the middle of a sentence ; but we know that he lost no time in redeeming his promise, and sending men, with cattle and other supplies, to meet his famishing army.[10] We must now turn back and inquire how that army fared.

Hanchet's party, leaving the bark house at six o'clock on Saturday morning, October 28th, made their way as rapidly as possible, we may assume, to the pale of civilisation. We know nothing as to the details of their march.

To understand the order of the next men requires a bit of calculation.[11] Of the companies that went down Arnold River, Smith's would naturally have been the one to cross the two streams at the lake first, for it owned the bateau ; Goodrich's, having led the advance and being anxious to overtake its provisions, was probably given the second place ; Dearborn's would come next, for it had arrived next, and, after Goodrich's, it had suffered most ; Ward's would then follow, as we find suggested by Haskell's statement that when he reached the lake, he got a bateau (it was no longer needed to take soldiers across the two rivers), and went along in it.

While Dearborn's men were marching through the woods, Morgan's probably passed them, and went forward; but a misfortune which overtook this company soon after it began to descend the Chaudière, checked its advance. Goodrich's company also, we shall see, became demoralised by a disaster. The result was that Smith's and Dearborn's men were, as Dearborn states, the first of the main body who reached the settlements.

As for the companies that rounded Spider Lake, they did not begin the descent of the Chaudière until Tuesday forenoon, while Dearborn, Smith, and Ward had made a good march there on Monday; and so they found themselves considerably in the rear. Greene, with his three companies, went first, and Hendricks followed, for the former appears to have camped that evening nearly six miles below the latter. Hanchet's men were doubtless not far away. Questions of precedence were of but very little moment, however, now.

Morgan, who deserved reward for saving his boats, met with the bitterest misfortune

DIAGRAM OF THE MARCH
ON THE UPPER CHAUDIÈRE.
LARGELY CONJECTURAL.

LAKE MEGANTIC — A

GENERAL DIRECTION FROM A TO B
ABOUT NORTH 30° EAST

{ARNOLD, MORGAN, McCLELLAN WRECKED?
DEARBORN'S CAMP, OCT. 30?
HENDRICKS'S CAMP, OCT. 31?

GREENE'S CAMP, OCT. 31?

WARD'S CAMP, OCT. 31?
"PROVINCIAL'S" CAMP, NOV. 1?
DEARBORN'S CAMP, OCT. 31?

ST. GÉDÉON — B   SENTER'S CAMP, NOV. 1?

GENERAL DIRECTION
FROM B TO C ABOUT
NORTH 8° WEST

{200 CAMPED, NOV. 2?
SENTER MET CATTLE, NOV. 2?

ST. MARTIN   DEARBORN'S CAMP, NOV. 1.
WARD'S CAMP, NOV. 2
DEARBORN MET CATTLE, NOV. 2.

GREAT FALLS   SENTERS CAMP, NOV. 2.
GREENE'S CAMP, NOV. 3.

RIVER DU LOUP   60 MILES, AS THE MEN MARCHED,
C   FROM LAKE MEGANTIC?

223

of all, for his seven bateaux were capsized, his precious freight of ammunition was lost, substantially all of his provisions met the same fate, one man was drowned, and the rest barely escaped with their lives.[12] Unless other companies divided their starvation supplies with these unfortunates, it is very hard to see how they existed for the next three or four days.

Captain Smith also was wrecked, and he, too, lost everything. Poor Lieutenant Mc-Clellan of Hendricks's company, lying sick with pneumonia in the bateau that was carried expressly for him across the height of land, happily escaped drowning at the same falls; but his bateau was ruined, and the invalid had to be left there, in the care of two lads, after Dr. Senter had done everything possible for his disease. Goodrich's boat was wrecked and all the flour of the company lost, reports Melvin, with details that seem to confirm the truth of his account; and Tolman records a similar misfortune as befalling Ward's company, though his language has a suspicious resemblance to Melvin's, and Haskell, travelling at that time in a bateau, does not mention it. Both of these companies are reported as eating dog-meat afterward, and certainly Goodrich's did so.[13]

15

Those who went by land — that is to say, almost all — fared little better. The distance they travelled cannot be given exactly, for we do not know the length of the river from Lake Megantic to the Du Loup, and precisely where the army marched is of course unknowable; but we may pretty safely call the journey about sixty miles.[14] The trail, if a trail existed, was very probably a wretched one.[15] While the country is reasonably level, the river had cut through it a deep channel, bounded — now closely, now at a distance — with high bluffs; and at times the army had to march up and then down the steep bank, because it crowded sheer against the stream. Swamps were to be crossed, gorges passed, and cold streams waded. It would have been a hard experience for fresh and well-fed soldiers; but for tired men, who had been on half-rations or less for a considerable time, and now possessed but the meagerest supplies, the hardship was extremely distressing.

Tuesday night, October 31st, found Dearborn's and Smith's[17] companies six or seven miles, perhaps, above the present village of St. Gédéon, Ward half a dozen miles behind them, Greene's division an equal distance below the scene of Arnold's disaster, Hen-

dricks's and Hanchet's companies a little way
north of that unfortunate spot, and Morgan's
and Goodrich's men somewhere at intermediate points.[18] On November 1st, all pressed
forward as rapidly as possible, leaving behind
those who could not keep up, for it was
thought best that the strong should save
themselves and send back relief, rather than
make a vain effort to help their comrades
along. In fact, Goodrich's company, at least,
had broken up two days before. No military
order was observed, and many of the men
had no food whatever.

The next day Arnold's relief reached the
head of the column. Dearborn appears to
have met the cattle before noon, four miles
above the Great Falls, apparently a little
earlier than his men and Smith's. Ward's
company seem to have been still farther behind, though not far; they were about six or
seven miles above the Great Falls when the relief party came in sight.[19] At evening Morison
and " Provincial " met the cattle ; and, according to the former, two hundred men camped
together at that point,—six miles above Ward.
Hendricks's rifle company and a considerable
part of the second division, with stragglers
from the three forward companies, probably

composed this body. Greene was there, we
may believe, for the next day, when the relief
squad had had time, as we may estimate, to
work their way nine miles farther, they reported that they had succoured Greene that
distance below. This camp appears to have
been about five or six miles above St. Martin. The evening was spent by the rescue
party in looking for those who had fallen by
the way, and many such men were picked up
and brought into camp on the horses.[20]   November 3d, Thayer and Topham, who had
been behind, urging on the stragglers, met
the relieving party at about noon, but did not
permit it to stop. Meigs reports getting provisions at the same hour.[21]   Beyond this point
we lose sight of the rescuers, but may assume
that they kept on until all the soldiers appeared
to have been found.

Dearborn reached the first house at four
o'clock P.M. on November 2d. Smith's company and fifty-two members of Dearborn's arrived an hour later. The first of Ward's men
appeared at about two o'clock the next day.[22]
Hendricks's company came in the evening.
Rather early on the 4th, Humphrey and Thayer
gained the same point, but we may infer that
most of Greene's division arrived the day be-

fore, as Topham did.[23] Meigs and the rest followed on.

Once the relief party had come in sight, all danger of starvation was over, especially as the natives appear to have grasped the idea that a good business could be done by furnishing the troops with eatables. Thayer obtained some potatoes at an Indian's hut.[24] And, at the first house, Arnold had ready a sufficient stock of simple food.

Three questions arise here. To begin with, the relief party described by Arnold does not correspond to that pictured in the journals. Arnold wrote of sending Lieutenant Church, Mr. Barrin, and eight Frenchmen with a quantity of flour[25]; while the journalists mention horses, cattle for slaughter, oatmeal and mutton, eighteen Canadians, and two persons in a canoe. But it is only necessary to suppose that Arnold sent a second party, not only to the falls, but beyond them. As the forward one stopped, the second would overtake it, and the two might appear, and be described, as one.

The next question is whether the soldiers did in reality suffer very much. Most of the men seem to have received about five pints of flour[26] on the afternoon of October 28th; so that if they were economical and met relief on November 2d, they had half rations for the whole time. In other words, while very inadequately supplied, they fared as well as many or most of them had been faring for some while before. No doubt this was the case with a considerable number. Dearborn states that when he met the relief party he was not in need of provisions.[27] Fobes, of Hubbard's company, speaks of the men as "nearly" without food for several days, adding that none of his company died.

Those who had the same supply, but failed to meet the relief before November 3d, must have been severely pinched, even if they husbanded their flour closely. Many, no doubt, permitting themselves to be optimistic, consumed more than a pint a day at first, and had to pay the penalty later. Those who received only four pints of flour originally, came to the end of their supply the sooner, and "Provincial," a sober witness, informs us that "several" of his company were out of provisions on October 31st. Some, as we have seen, devoured their allowance almost as soon as they received it, and their sufferings were certainly dreadful. Fobes, whose conservative statement has just been quoted, says: " I was told that some of the soldiers, who ate their whole allowance the morning after our provisions were divided in the wilderness, were obliged, in order to sustain life, to eat their dogs, cartridge-boxes, old shoes and clothes."

To these we must add a perhaps larger class, the unfortunates.[28]   It is impossible to see how Goodrich's and Morgan's men can have escaped extreme suffering, and Ward's appear to have been little better off.   Haskell of Ward's, a matter-of-fact man, wrote October 31st : "There is scarcely any one who has any more than one day's provision, and that small, and a great number none at all.   Some have had none at all for two days.   Captain Goodrich's company have nothing but a large dog, which they killed and ate tonight."

Finally, there were the tender-hearted, who gave to others.   Some of this kind belonged to Hendricks's company, and shared their flour with McClellan.   Perhaps Topham was of the same class, for November 2d we find him saying,[29] "I have now been 48 hours without victuals."   And no doubt many more showed equal kindness to unfortunate comrades.

Perplexities still remain, and probably we cannot fully understand the situation.   Dearborn wrote, for example, on October 30th :

" Some Companies have but one pint of Flour
for Each Man and no Meat at all." Unless
" Some Companies " was a loose expression
for " men in some companies," it is difficult to
explain the statement. Yet one thing is clear :
there is ample evidence of hunger to the verge
of starvation; only we must not think of
every soldier as undergoing this extreme suffering.[30]   Having to march barefoot, as many
did at this time, was a real though minor
hardship.

Our third question is, How many perished
at this crisis of the march? It is impossible
to answer with definiteness.   Some undoubtedly died.   Fobes, who escaped from captivity
the following year and fled up the Chaudière,
reports finding " a number " of bleaching
skeletons in this part of the route.   Dearborn's journal, under date of November 3d,
contains these interlined words, apparently in
his own hand : " Many of our men died within
the last three days " ; but this is a very general
statement.   Morison wrote :

" It will be recollected that the detachment consisted
originally of 1100 men, including officers.   Col. Enos
returned with 300.   My 3[d] lieu[tenant], Mathew Irwin,
who took sick at the first Pond, was left there in the
care of 4 men, all of whom returned.   The sick sent

back from Dead River including those ordered to take
care of them amounted to 200. The force that escaped
the perils of the Wilderness and reached the banks of
the St. Lawrence, amounted to 510. We, therefore, lost
in the wilds between 70 and 80. But I am inclined to
believe that some of these got to the inhabitants, in a
state no doubt that required weeks to revive."

This is the only attempt in the journals to
give details, and it is not at all reliable.[31]   Arnold himself had no precise information on
these points.   October 13th he wrote Washington, "I intended making an exact return,
but must defer it until I come to Chaudiere."
At the Chaudière, of course, nothing of the
sort received attention.   Morison, a private,
cannot have been better posted than his commander.   The original number was less than
he states, and the number who reached the
St. Lawrence was more.   December 5th Arnold wrote Washington :   "Enclosed is a return of my detachment amounting to 675 men,
for whom I have received clothing of Gen.
Montgomery."[32]   It is possible that he included a party of Indians ; but the Indians
did not in fact belong to his "detachment"
and he would not be likely to include them in
an official return to the Commander-in-chief.
We have no reason to suppose they specially
needed clothing at that time ; and even had

they, Montgomery very likely would not have dressed them in the uniforms that he gave Arnold's troops. The names of a few men who perished can be stated; but, after all has been done, we can only say that "a number" were lost.[33] The escape of others was an extremely narrow one, however. A single day would have made a vast difference; and had the weather been severe, instead of warm and fair, during the most critical period, many a soldier must, no doubt, have succumbed.

XV

FROM THE FIRST INHABITANTS TO
ST. MARY

THE American troops had now reached inhabitants; but the question remains, where were they? According to the journals, the first houses were at Sertigan [1] or Sartigan, and this name has been accepted as an adequate reply to our question. In fact, we find indicated on many of the old maps a place bearing one of these names.

But how does it happen that no village so named exists in the region now, or has existed there within the recollection of the oldest inhabitants? How does it happen that on the maps it appears at various points on the Chaudière between the Du Loup and the St. Lawrence? [2] Why was it customary in Quebec, years ago, to say of any rough-looking fellow hailing from the general direction of the Chaudière that he came "from Sertigan"? And how does it happen that Dearborn speaks of St. Mary, many miles below, as "the middle Parish of what is Commonly call'd Sattagan?"

The explanation of the whole matter is suggested in these words of Dearborn's. Sertigan was not a village or spot, but a vaguely defined region, though it is not at all surprising that our soldiers, knowing that Sertigan was where people would be found, should have noted down, on coming to a settlement, that they had reached "Sertigan." Neither would it have been strange had these first people, when asked the name of the place, replied that it was "Sertigan," for the good reason that it lay in the district so named, and had no other title. The very name suggests its application, for it is a word of the aborigines, and signifies "shady river." In short, Sertigan meant the region watered by the Chaudière, from the Du Loup to St. Isidore de Lauzon,— that is to say, almost to the St. Lawrence.[3]

Rightly or not, however, the Americans applied the name to a particular spot, and Arnold used it in the headings of three letters. Where, then, was the "Sertigan" of the Americans?[4]

According to William Allen it lay at the mouth of the Du Loup[5]; and he is rather good authority, for Dearborn had given him inform-

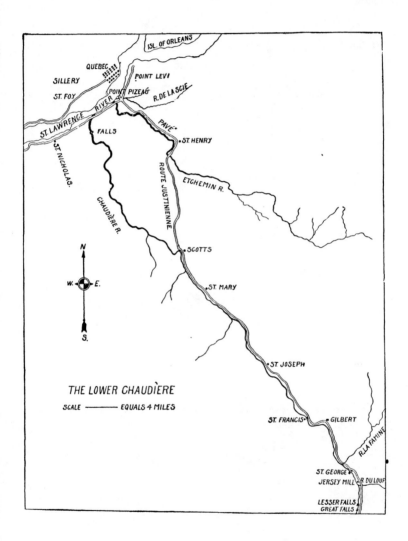

THE LOWER CHAUDIÈRE

SCALE ———— EQUALS 4 MILES

237

ation about the matter, and he visited the spot
in 1824.   These are his words:

"There were then [1824] two houses at this fork of
the river, one of them, inhabited by Mr. Annah or
Hanna, who is called the Seigneur, having a venerable
appearance. . . . It was probably Mr. Hanna's
which was '*the first house*,' and inhabited by a Frenchman, as its situation accords with a description of it given
me by General Dearborn.   The settlement was called
Sertigan, the distance was 25 leagues from Quebec."

On the other hand, the first settlement
appears actually to have been several miles
below the Du Loup.   Arnold says that he
found no house until four miles beyond that
point.[6]   Dearborn calls it in his journal eight
miles from the Falls to the first stopping place,
and thus agrees substantially with Arnold.
Thayer, after camping a mile beyond the
Great Falls, proceeded to a river (which we
take to be the Du Loup, since there is only
a brook between that stream and the Falls),
and after fording it had to march five miles,
as he estimated the distance, before he "could
get to any house to warm" himself.

Topham went six miles beyond the Falls
— that is to say, about three miles beyond
the Du Loup — before coming to "the first
house," while Humphrey called the distance

about five miles.   Senter lodged at the Falls;
and the next day, after fording two rivers,
he arrived, at half-past ten o'clock, at " the
first town, principally inhabited by the Aborigines."   As no doubt he was in motion by
eight o'clock, this town must have been a
considerable distance below the Du Loup.

Haskell and Senter give a clue to the
explanation, perhaps.   The manuscript of
Haskell's journal contains the statement —
omitted in the printed version — that he
"forded two rivers" the day he reached inhabitants, and Senter states that after wading
one stream he came to another — and that a
large one — just as he entered the town.[7]
The first of the rivers was evidently the Du
Loup,[8] and the second was apparently the
Rivière la Famine, a sizable stream, which
enters the Chaudière about four miles lower
down.[9]

The first settlement we may place, then, on
the northern side of the Rivière la Famine.
Mr. Allen's opinion can be disposed of by
thinking that when Dearborn described the
first house as situated on a stream, he meant
Famine River, while Allen understood him
to mean the Du Loup; and by reflecting
that half a century is not required to make

an unpainted house look "venerable." [10]   This
place, then, was what Arnold referred to as
"Sartigan," for of course he would have
stopped, under circumstances so pressing, at
the first settlement, and from "Sartigan" went
his relief party. [11]

It was only a frontier village of the meagrest
sort.   Three or four small houses represented
budding civilisation, and the wigwams of the
savages outnumbered them.   But it must have
been a busy place after Arnold arrived there.
Very possibly the work of collecting provisions for the army began on the evening
of October 30th.   In the morning it was certainly going on, and we are told by Arnold
that the first instalment of relief was then
despatched.

Hanchet arrived in the course of the 31st
probably, and very likely the prosecution of
the work at this point was turned over to him.
For Arnold there were other things to do.
Several times on the march he had tried to
open communication with his acquaintances in
Quebec ; but no reply had come, and he feared
his Indian messengers had betrayed him.   Yet,
as it would be exceedingly helpful to get
information from the city and secure allies
there, one more attempt was certainly worth

making; and so, November 1st, Arnold sent another letter to Mercier, begging to know the number of troops in Quebec and Montreal, and the sentiments of the French.[12] He inquired whether any ships of war were lying at Quebec, asked for news of General Schuyler, and declared that it would be " a particular favour" if a friend or two would come to meet him. Of course he was anxious to know also whether the authorities expected him.

Another letter was written that day. It was directed to Meigs, who seems to have acted as paymaster-general, and authorised him to let each captain have about $20 or $30 for himself and his men. The amount seems niggardly, but Arnold is entitled to so much the greater credit, for it had been extremely difficult to raise hard money for the expedition, and Washington had enjoined upon him the strictest frugality.[13] These matters attended to, Arnold pushed on some half a dozen miles to about where the present village of Gilbert stands,[14] and probably continued to collect supplies for the army.[15]

Thanks to these labours, the soldiers found provisions awaiting them at " Sertigan," as we have already seen, and the men also purchased more or less for themselves. The people showed hearty good-will and a real zeal to supply their wants. The instincts of humanity, Washington's reassuring manifestoes, and admiration for the courage and endurance of the Americans, not unmingled with awe, contributed to make the natives friendly. Yet all these considerations might have counted little had they not been re-enforced with a liberal use of good money. Washington had particularly ordered that full value should be paid for supplies, and men on the point of starvation were easy to bargain with. Equal emphasis was laid by the journalists on the politeness and helpfulness of the peasants, and on their disposition to charge excessive prices.[16]

Provisions were plentiful,— indeed, even too much so, for some of the men made themselves ill by indulging their appetites, in spite of urgent warnings, and one at least died. But it was hardly the same with lodgings. Not until the army reached the more thickly settled parts below could men be provided for in houses; and it cannot be supposed that all were lodged under roofs anywhere along the Chaudière. At "Sertigan" there were practically no such accommodations. The weather, which was fine and warm on Thursday (November 2d), turned suddenly cold, and it snowed on Friday and Friday night. Fires were built, and huts of one sort or another put up, but there was no little discomfort.

Besides the French, Arnold had Indians to reckon with, and these were soon in evidence. Melvin saw seventy or eighty of the braves, Thursday evening, at the first settlement, all decked out with "broaches, bracelets & other trinkets," their faces well painted. But Arnold was of course the object of their quest, and on Saturday a regular council met at his quarters near Gilbert.[17] Although doubtless the redskins understood well enough the aim of the expedition, they pretended the opposite, and through an interpreter demanded formally of Arnold the reason for this warlike invasion.

Arnold replied shrewdly, and brought his harangue to an end with these words[18]: " Now if the Indians, our brethren, will join us we will be very much obliged to them, and will give them one Portuguees per month, two dollars bounty, and find them their provisions, and they [shall have] liberty to chuse their own officers." This proposition appealed forcibly to the savages, and forty or fifty of them enlisted forthwith, took their canoes, and proceeded.[19]

Meanwhile the army was getting together.

Stragglers were coming up hourly with tales of misery and escape.[20] Lieutenant McClellan, though left behind, had not been forgotten. Two Indians were sent up the river for him in a canoe as promptly as possible, and on the third evening they returned successful; but nothing could save the poor fellow, and he died the next day.

The first settlement was reckoned to be about seventy or seventy-five miles from Quebec. The greater part of the distance lay along the river.[21] Whether the village of St. Francis had begun to exist is more than doubtful, for no journalist mentions it; but St. Joseph already possessed a name. Gradually the country became thickly settled. Taverns and victualling houses, which were now to be found, made it easier to supply the army; and the people continued kind, "with few exceptions."

Their satisfaction over the visit of the liberal Americans received, however, a shock. Robbisho, Arnold's messenger from "Sertigan," was captured. News of this unfortunate accident arrived on November 5th, and with it came a story that the British were going to "burn and destroy all the inhabitants in the vicinity of Quebec, unless they came in and took up arms in defence of the garrison."

The Americans wasted no time. Expresses hurried back toward the rear, urging on the soldiers. As much as possible was done for their comfort. Arnold had beef and potatoes ready every ten or twelve miles, according to Melvin; though some of the men, hardly able to relish meat as yet, preferred to eat bread and butter, milk and eggs, when they could, and many necessaries — even shoes — were lacking. In this wise, the Colonel and a part of his officers and men, including Hanchet's advanced party, we may believe, reached St. Mary [22] by the 5th, and the main body of the troops arrived a day later. On the 6th Captain Dearborn, who had been ailing all the way from Lake Megantic, found himself compelled to take lodgings, and go to bed with a fever; for three weeks he did not leave the house, and he could not rejoin the army for nearly a fortnight more. Henry, too, fell sick, and no doubt many others were in the same state; but in general the strength of the troops began quickly to revive.

XVI

FROM ST. MARY TO QUEBEC

ST. MARY was a village of some importance, especially because the manor-house
of a gentleman and landed proprietor, Gabriel
Elzéar Taschereau, stood near it. Taschereau is said to have been away from home
when the Americans arrived, as was very
natural[1]; but even had he been at hand, he
would not have welcomed them as the peasants did, for the peasants desired freedom
from the oppression of the noblesse, while
the noblesse, realising that the British had
treated them far more handsomely than the
democratic Americans would do, were from
the first our enemies.

But Messire Taschereau could not carry his
mansion away; and there Arnold appears to
have established his headquarters on Sunday,
November 5th. This point became, then, a
rendezvous for the army, and those who came
early, besides ample rations, had a breathing

space.   As for lodgings, LeMoine quotes a tradition that Father Verreau, the priest, mounted
his pulpit that afternoon at vespers, and ad-
vised his people that the best thing they could
do, under the circumstances, was to provide for
Americans in need of accommodations; and
this appears to be confirmed by Humphrey's
statement that " the Minister was kind and let
us have all that he had To spare."

The next morning, November 6th, " orders
were given for every captain to get his company
on as fast as possible," says Dr. Senter, " and
not to leave a man behind unless unfit for
duty "; and by afternoon a considerable part of
the detachment had gathered at the rendezvous.   Not all the officers occupied their
places.   Meigs tells us that he was up and
down both sides of the river on business for
several days at this time; and from other
accounts it appears that, in part at least,
his business was to hire or purchase canoes
to carry ninety-six invalids down the river,
and later transport the army across the St.
Lawrence.   Topham and Thayer seem to have
been employed in the same work, and in
urging the rear along.[2]   But the greater part
of the army, probably, was got into some
shape at St. Mary, and set out, November 6th,

at two o'clock in the afternoon, for Point Levi on the St. Lawrence.

For about four miles the highway continued to follow the Chaudière; but a little beyond the present village of Scotts, the river suddenly turned a great angle toward the left, and the road sheered off almost as sharply to the right. Soon began a forest nearly or quite a dozen miles across, the "forest of Sertigan," not yet wholly cut down, which formed the boundary between the seigneurie of Beauce, whence the Provincials came, and the seigneurie of Lauzon, to which they were bound.

There was no uncertainty as to the route, however. Here lay the Justinian Road,[3] named after Father Justinien, the first missionary priest of the Beauce country. But direction was about the only good quality of the highway. For at least twelve miles not a dwelling was to be seen, and the soldiers tramped along through snowy mire half-leg deep. Supper was out of the question. Night set in, and still the march continued. Finally near midnight the woods came to an end, and the troops emerged at the village of St. Henry[4] on the Etchemin River, about twenty miles from St. Mary.

The next day they advanced along the right

bank of the Etchemin by what was called the
Pavement Road,[5] because covered in the cor-
duroy fashion with small logs.   Some ten miles
more, and Quebec would be in sight; but
Quebec was another word for enemy, and caution became necessary.   Scouting was in order,
and no doubt received attention.   It is even
said that Jaquin and two Indians were sent to
Quebec this day in a canoe.[6]   Arnold understood that his coming was expected there, and
he knew that no boats would be found on the
south side of the St. Lawrence.   Under the
circumstances he deemed it wise to halt; and
so, after marching three miles in a snow-storm,
and perhaps an equal distance later in the day,
the army rested until night.[7]

Meanwhile he wrote another letter[8] to General Schuyler, not yet knowing that Montgomery now commanded the western army of
invasion.   All his troops were with him or
within two days' march, he said and in two
or three days he hoped to cross the St. Lawrence.   Should an attack seem likely to succeed, he would make it at once; while, in case
Quebec were reinforced from Montreal, as he
feared it would be, he proposed to march up
the river and join Schuyler.

At nightfall a lieutenant and twenty or

thirty men, probably riflemen, were sent forward to see whether the road was clear, and at two o'clock nothing but air and water lay between them and their destination, Quebec.[9] During the 8th, the army followed along the Pavement Road, crossed the highway that traversed the heights of Point Levi[10] to St. Nicholas,[11] a number of miles above on the St. Lawrence, then took the Mill Road,[12] arrived finally at the St. Lawrence, and found quarters in houses along the bluff, though many of the troops appear to have halted for the night a few miles back.[13]

At one o'clock that morning Arnold received Montgomery's letter of October 29th, and, when he found himself seven and one-half miles from Point Levi, wrote a reply, still calling himself, by mistake, at "St. Marie." Before the message was despatched, a friend arrived from Quebec and supplied a postscript. Only the previous Sunday a frigate of twenty-six guns was said to have reached the town, and also two transports with one hundred and fifty recruits from Newfoundland. These, with citizens forced to take up arms, made nearly three hundred men ; but Arnold proposed to sever the communications of the city, and felt sure of taking it, or at least keeping it sealed up until Montgomery could arrive. This makes it evident that he now intended to cross the St. Lawrence at all events, and not attempt to march up the right bank of the river toward Montreal.

About a quarter or a third of a mile above the end of the Mill Road, and some 3600 feet below the mouth of Etchemin River, a stream,[14] called in English "Saw River," brought down to the St. Lawrence the overflow of two ponds lying in Bellechasse County near St. Charles. It was a small stream, only a dozen miles in length; but it had no little importance at that day, for perhaps fifty rods from its mouth there was a sharp little fall, whence a conduit, possibly twenty rods long, conveyed water to the second story of a very solid stone mill,[15] and poured it on an immense overshot wheel. This is known as Caldwell's mill, for later it became his property; but at that time it was owned by General Murray, who preceded Carleton as Governor of Canada, and belonged to Caldwell only as a part of the seigneurie of Lauzon leased by him. This place appears to have marked the left of the American line; but the troops extended a considerable distance along the bluffs, and a guard was posted four miles below, opposite Quebec.[16]

The approach of the Provincials had been known in the town on November 3d, and at that time the Lieutenant-Governor, Cramahé, took steps to remove or destroy all the boats found on the southern shore of the St. Lawrence and on the Island of Orleans.[17] On the 8th, Cramahé received notice that Arnold's advance guard had arrived the evening before "within two Leagues and a half of the St. Lawrence."[18] But it was not known precisely what their later movements had been, and on the 8th or 9th[19] a bold attempt was made to obtain some property[20] from Caldwell's mill. A boat rowed from the *Hunter*, a sloop-of-war lying in the river, under the command of a midshipman named McKenzie, a brother of the captain[21]; and after the midshipman had stepped ashore, the boat pushed off again[22] — perhaps, as Henry says, to find a better place to land—and McKenzie was captured. No information could be extracted from the prisoner, however. The *Hunter* opened fire on the Americans, but without effect.

Fortunately some one else made amends for McKenzie's silence. That same day appeared at Arnold's headquarters an Englishman named Halstead,[23] Caldwell's superintendent at the mill. Whatever his motives, he had espoused the cause of the invaders, and detained at that place a quantity of flour and wheat, extremely valuable to the Americans: now he came over in person to give information and advice. Though not a soldier, he proved a most serviceable ally, and a few days later piloted the Provincials across the river.

The rest of the troops came up slowly, and when all were mustered the sight was more pitiable than formidable. Their clothes, torn by thickets and bushes, hung in strings. Many had no shoes except the roughest of moccasins made of fresh hides.[24] Many had no hats.

Still worse, it was not possible to reach the enemy. The river before them, about a mile wide, was guarded by the *Lizard* frigate and the *Hunter* sloop-of-war,[25] and all night long their guard-boats were passing to and fro. And then, to cap it all, even an attempt to cross the stream became impossible, when Arnold had men enough to go. For three nights, the 10th, 11th, and 12th, the winds were so high that canoes dared not venture upon the water.[26]

But, in spite of all, Arnold kept at work, and tried to make the time valuable. Provisions were gathered. Prudent measures increased the number of boats,[27] and in all some thirty-five or forty canoes and dugouts were collected.[28]   Preparations were also made for scaling the walls, and the troops passed in review.

Monday, November 13th, the winds moderated. A council of war was held at three o'clock in the afternoon, and it resolved to cross the coming night.

Caldwell's mill was the rendezvous, for it afforded some shelter, provided a convenient place for embarkation, and stood nearly opposite a somewhat narrow part of the river. The canoes and dugouts, which had been kept out of harm's way in a cove of the Chaudière,[29] were brought down. At nine o'clock the work of crossing began.[30]   It certainly looked like a desperate undertaking, for, according to the evidence, the Americans had to pass between the *Lizard* and the *Hunter*, and the British guard-boats were "plying every hour from ship to ship."[31]   It was calm, cold, and "exceeding dark," as Senter informs us. No lights were used, and the utmost silence prevailed. In this way, three voyages back and forth across the mile or more of water[32] were made without discovery.

On the north side of the river, Point Pizeau makes out into the stream a little above the mill, and it would seem as if that had been the proposed landing point[33]; but the bluff was high and steep, and the troops felt their way down to a small bay called Wolfe's Cove, where, since the French war, a fair road had been constructed to the plains above. One canoe, at least, broke on the voyage. Lieutenant Steele was dangerously chilled, and some guns and clothes were lost; but no fatal accidents occurred. No sentinels were encountered. Guards immediately took post above and below, and Captain Smith was sent off with a detachment to reconnoitre.

By four o'clock about five hundred men had been landed in safety on the north shore, though by no means all at the same point. Then the business came to an end. The tide had been ebbing rapidly, and when the tide is out a large tract of rocks is exposed near Caldwell's Mill. The wind became boisterous,[34] and the moon began to shine.[35] Besides these new difficulties, the Americans on the north shore were discovered. A fire had been lighted there in a vacant house,[36] and one of the patrol boats, observing it, pulled in to investigate. Arnold seems to have felt that detection was now inevitable, and that he could only hope to prevent the men in the barge from reporting their discovery.   So the boat was hailed, and ordered to come in. When it disobeyed, it was fired upon, with the intention, doubtless, of frightening the crew into compliance.   But even this persuasion proved vain, and the barge pulled off with no little crying and lamentation.[37]

At about four o'clock, then, Arnold gave up trying to get more men across at that time, and after some discussion as to the best course to take,[38] he marched up to the plains with his men, and soon found quarters in the farm buildings where Major Caldwell had been living.   The next night, or soon after,[39] all the rest, except a guard of sixty men under Hanchet, joined their comrades.[40]   And so Arnold's march from Cambridge to Quebec was at last over.[41]

17

NOTES

The references by number are to the List of Authorities.

I : PAGES 2–23.

1. In No. 108.
2. Also written " De l' Isle."
3. Supposed to have been issued in 1732.
4. Lake Megantic.
5. Râle spelled the name " Abnaki," and that form of the word is not uncommon. " Abenaqui " also is found.
6. He crossed from the St. Lawrence to the Kennebec, and passed down that river to its mouth in 1646. See No. 74, ii., 102, and No. 106, i., 327.
7. There are six ways to spell this name, it is said. On the monument that stands where he preached, it is Rasles. Râle was killed in 1724.
8. This evidently refers to the Great Carrying-place (Chapter VIII.).
9. The Wesserunsett. Similarly Noridgewaëg means Norridgewock, and Kenebaëg means Kennebec.
10. The Ticonic, or Taconic Falls, at Waterville.
11. The Sebasticook River.
12. That is to say, Cushnoc, Fort Western, or Augusta.
13. It empties, in fact, into a branch of the Kennebec.
14. That is, the great bow of Dead River,—the West Branch of the Kennebec.

15. Dead River.

16. This must be understood as an air-line distance.

17. John Montresor (son of James G. Montresor, an eminent engineer of the British army) was born April 6, 1736, at Gibraltar. He served four years with his father as an assistant, and in 1754 came to America as chief engineer under General Braddock. He was present at the siege of Louisburg, in 1758, and at the capture of Quebec the following year. He was very actively engaged in America from this time on. In December, 1775, the King appointed him "Chief Engineer of America." June 26, 1799, he died at London.

Some confusion has existed about his work in the region crossed by Arnold. Even No. 218 is not quite correct. It states that the route was suggested to Arnold by Montresor's journal of *1760* (vol. vi., p. 217), and it gives the map of 1761 in rough facsimile as that of 1760 (p. 224). The facts are that he made two trips across this region. January 26, 1760, he left Quebec with verbal despatches from General Murray for General Amherst, and on February 3d he struck the Chaudière River. He followed this stream to " Amaguntic Pond or Lake St. Augustine " (Lake Megantic), kept on toward the south, reached the "Ammerascagin" (Androscoggin) River on February 16th, after suffering greatly, and four days later entered Topsham, opposite Brunswick, Me. He drew a map to illustrate this journey, and a copy of it in colours, bearing the date *20 February, 1760*, and what appears to be his signature, belongs to the New Eng. Hist. Geneal. Soc. of Boston, by which I was permitted to see it. As the name is variously spelled, we may note that it is written on this map *Montresor*.

The reconnoitring expedition went in 1761. Montresor's narrative of this trip relates first how he travelled from Quebec by the Chaudière and Du Loup Rivers to Moosehead Lake, or, as he called it, Lake Original, and then down the Kennebec to Fort Halifax, just below the present city of Waterville. On his return he followed the route taken later by Arnold.

When Arnold's papers were confiscated by the State of Connecticut, after he went over to the British, his copy of Montresor's journal was found among them. Pierpont Edwards, a Commissioner under the Act of Confiscation, took possession of it. On his death, the document passed into the hands of Ogden Edwards, and by him it was furnished to the Maine Historical Society for publication in the initial volume of its Collections (No. 106, 1831).

18. An account of this Report was printed in the *Sunday Times*, of Portland, Me., on January 27, 1901; but it gave an incorrect version of what the Report had to say about the Kennebec route. I am indebted to the owner of the MS., Mr. Thos. F. Murphy, for extracts from the original and a copy of the map.

19. This has reference to the East Branch and the West Branch (Dead River) of the Kennebec. Montresor came by the East and returned by the West Branch. In a similar way the River Du Loup was called the East and the upper Chaudière the West Branch of the Chaudière. For this letter see No. 54, series 4, vol. iii., col. 1084.

20. Goodwin's letters to the Rev. Jacob Bailey (MS.) prove that he was a royalist at heart; but, as he was probably a "trimmer," he desired very likely to stand well with both sides. "Sam" Goodwin, his son, was an ardent patriot, and there is a tradition that he insisted on his father's letting Arnold have these documents. On the other hand, it has been objected that he was only a boy in 1775; but this is doubtless a mistake.

Colburn, according to a tradition among his descendants, helped secure the maps. The letter shows that Goodwin, if the data had to be used against the British, was not unwilling to make all he could out of them.

21.   No. 223, vol. i., p. 414.

22.   Roy cites the documents: No. 159, ii., 192, 193.

23.   No. 159, iii., 47.

24.   This I quote at second hand, as I have not been able to find a copy of the book.

25.   See Chap. IV., note 34.

26.   Consult Nos. 215 and 216.

27.   The object was to draw Carleton and his forces to the eastward, and so lessen the danger of an invasion from the north by way of Lake Champlain.

28.   No. 54, 4th series, vol. iii., col. 761.

29.   No. 54, 4th series, vol. iii., col. 763.

II : PAGES 24–55.

1.   John Joseph Henry was born November 4, 1758, at Lancaster, Pa., and was trained as a gunsmith. Thirst for glory led him to volunteer clandestinely in the company of riflemen that Mathew Smith, of Lancaster, raised in 1775. After his return from Quebec, a captaincy under Morgan in the Virginia Line, as well as a lieutenancy in the Pennsylvania army, was offered him ; but the scurvy, a sequel of his Quebec prison life, disabled him for two years. He then studied law, and from 1785 until 1793 practised his profession. Gov. Thomas Mifflin appointed him a judge. After years of suffering he died April 15, 1811. Just when Henry began to dictate his book we cannot say, but we are told that he finished "very shortly" before his death. For his grandson's testimony as to the printing, see No. 72, p. x.

2. No extended biographical note on Benedict Arnold
is required here, but a few facts will be found pertinent.
He was born at Norwich, Conn., January 14, 1741 ; and
so was thirty-four years old in 1775. From boyhood, he
was noted for strength and activity, enterprise, audacity,
a domineering temper, fertility of mental resources, moral
indifference, and hasty judgment. He was a fine shot,
a skilful horseman, no mean seaman, fearless, indefatig-
able. His exploits on Lake Champlain had already
proved his energy, alertness, ability, and ambition. In
his operations there he was a Massachusetts colonel ; but
he resigned in June, 1775, and returned to Cambridge to
settle his accounts with the State. He was then appointed by Washington to lead the Kennebec expedition ;
for which he evidently possessed many special qualifica-
tions.

I have tried in vain to discover the original MS. of
Arnold's journal. Formerly it belonged to Mr. S. L.
M. Barlow of New York ; but Mr. Barlow's library was
sold at auction in 1889, and the dealer who finally purchased this MS. is unable to say how he disposed of it.
Besides making many inquiries personally, I have written
to about one hundred gentlemen and libraries that seemed
most likely to be posted, but without result. However,
the copy among the Sparks papers in the library of Harvard University, was no doubt carefully made, though
imperfections clearly exist (compare Arnold's journal
with Oswald's, October 3d, for example). This copy of the
journal is printed without abbreviation in the appendix
of this volume. Apparently Arnold penned the journal
with his own hand, for he wrote Washington on October
27th : " As soon as I can get time, shall send your Excellency a continuation of my journal," *i. e.* a continuation
of the journal (through October 13th) sent previously.

He may, however, have dictated it. But Arnold must
have made notes as he went along, I think, for the data
are minute in very many cases. The MS. begins in the
midst of an entry for September 26th, and comes to an
end in the middle of a sentence, October 30th.

3.   September 15th to October 13th, both inclusive.
Mr. Codman speaks of this (No. 28, p. 314) as the missing first pages of Arnold's journal ; but Arnold's journal
begins more than a fortnight before Oswald's comes to
an end, and during this period the two are not identical.

One may, however, suspect very strongly that it is the
(free) "copy of my journal" that Arnold sent to Washington on October 13th.   In that case it *represents* the
missing pages of Arnold's journal.   But this is not certain ; and, for several reasons, it seems best to speak of
the journal as Oswald's.

4.   Eleazer Oswald was from New Haven, Conn.   He
served under Arnold at Ticonderoga, and volunteered
for the Quebec expedition.   At the assault on Quebec,
he led the forlorn hope under Arnold.   For a time he
served with distinction in the French army with Du-
mouriez.   In October, 1795, he died.   Oswald signed
his name at the end of the journal as "Sec'y pro tem."
For the journal, see No. 54, ser. 4, vol. iii., col. 1058.

5.   Henry Dearborn was born at North Hampton,
N. H., February 23, 1751, studied medicine, and was a
captain at the battle of Bunker Hill.   He served through
the war, and then settled at Augusta, Me.   His later
honors are mentioned in the text.   June 6, 1829, he died
at Roxbury (Boston).

6.   The MS. is preserved in the Public Library of
Boston.   A few differences may be found between it and
the reprint in No. 113, April, 1886, but none of any consequence.   For example, the distinction between a little

curl often occurring at the end of a word and a superfluous, but intentional, final *e* is not always observed.

7. Return J. Meigs was born in Middletown, Conn., December 28, 1740. He was engaged in mercantile pursuits in 1775, and also commanded a militia company of light infantry. When news of the battle of Lexington came, he and his men proceeded to the scene of action. His expedition from Guilford to Long Island in May, 1777, won him thanks and an "elegant" sword from Congress. Under Wayne, he took part in the storming of Stony Point. The end of the war found him a colonel. January 28, 1823, he died. His son became Postmaster-General. The following quotations suggest a close relation between his journal and Dearborn's: September 24th, Meigs (No. 6, Pt. II., p. 296) : " At Fort Western preparing for our march to Quebec ; this fort stands on the east side of the river Kennebec & consists of two blockhouses & a large house 100 feet long, which were enclosed with pickets ; this house is the property of Howard, Esq ; where we were exceedingly well entertained." Dearborn (No. 113, April, 1886, p. 277) : " We lay at Fort Western preparing for our March — Fort Western Stands on the East side of the River, and Consists of two Block-Houses, and a Large House 100 feet Long which are Inclos'd only with Picquets, this House is now the property of one Howard Esq: where we were well entertained." Such a similarity could not be accidental. There are, however, not many cases of the sort (see September 29th, October 23d and 26th, and November 13th). Of course the copyist would seem to be Dearborn, since Meigs's journal was published in 1776, but Meigs may have used Dearborn's notes. It does not matter very much, for each preserved his individuality ; but we have not quite two independent authorities here.

8. No. 112, second series, vol. 2. The society was given the MS. by Benj. Vaughan (No. 113, January, 1800).

9. I have tried to find the MS. but without success. As Colonel Meigs was living at the time of its publication by the Massachusetts Historical Society, it seems reasonable to suppose that he was consulted, but there is no evidence to that effect ; and, even if he was consulted, it does not follow that he carefully read the proof. As one specific instance of revision in the American edition, mention may be made of its combining the entries of September 25th and 26th, which are separate in Almon's edition. The main evidence is the style.

10. Isaac Senter, son of Samuel Senter, 2d, was born in Londonderry, N. H., in 1753. His medical studies were pursued at Newport, R. I., with Dr. Thomas Moffat ; but, while he was still a student, the tidings of Lexington impelled him to go to Cambridge as surgeon in the Rhode Island contingent. Retiring from the army in 1779, he practised medicine in Cranston and then in Newport, R. I. He was conspicuous as physician, writer, and public man.

11. No. 140, vol. i. I am greatly indebted to Mr. Charles Allen Munn, the owner of the MS., for an opportunity to compare the printed version with the original.

12. For further remarks, see the edition prepared by the author for the Rhode Island Historical Society, which will probably be published during 1904. The account comes to an end abruptly with October 27th. It is only an unfinished piece of work, full of repetitions and erasures ; and two pages are missing. Nothing of importance is added to what the journal gives. The differences between the penmanship of the two documents may be referred mostly to a tendency toward the easier forms of

letters, such as many people fall into in the course of
time.

13. Simeon Thayer (sometimes written Thayre,
though his signature was "Thayer"), son of David,
was born at Mendon, Mass., April 30, 1737, and as a boy
was apprenticed to a maker of perukes, probably in Providence.   During the French and Indian War he served
in a Rhode Island regiment, and when Fort William
Henry was taken by Montcalm, escaped death by the
narrowest of chances.   He then returned to Providence,
and followed his calling.   We soon find him an officer of
the "Grenadiers" of that city.   In May, 1775, he was
made a captain by the General Assembly, and in three
days had a full company enlisted.   When word came,
May 19th, that the British were marching on Dorchester
(near Boston), he called his company out, and in two hours
every man was on the way to Cambridge.   These troops
were the first to arrive from his State.   January 1, 1781,
he retired from the army, and three years later he opened
a hotel at Providence.   October 14, 1800, was the day of
his death.   Thayer's journal, advertisements of both his
earlier and his later businesses, with many further details,
may be found in No. 153, vol. vi.   Thayer seems to have
been in the habit of keeping journals, for, in an application to the government (No. 189), we find him using
these words: "An Extract from my Journal of some facts
relative to my Sufferings during the last French War &
the late War between Great Britain & America.   . . .
Many more Transactions of Importance I have omitted."
The handwriting of the journal is not Thayer's; but the
document evidently comes from him, for the heading
states that it is the record of one of Greene's captains.
This cannot mean Topham, as is shown by such entries
as that of September 15th, and by the fact that we have

a journal from Topham. Neither can it mean Hubbard, for this journal continues after the time of Hubbard's death. It must, therefore, mean Thayer. It is worth noting that in the heading of this journal this name is spelled " Thayre."

14. John Topham was a native of Newport, R. I., but no other facts of his early life are known. In 1775 he was appointed " captain-lieutenant " in the Rhode Island Army of Observation. (The captain-lieutenant was a lieutenant who acted as captain, because the captain served also as a field officer.) It is said that on hearing of the battle of Lexington he raised a company and marched for Cambridge at once. After his return from Quebec he continued to serve, became a colonel, and received the thanks of the Assembly. His later years were devoted to mercantile pursuits. September 26, 1793, was his last day.

Mr. Codman (p. 317) is in error in saying that Topham's journal has never been published. It may be found in several instalments in the Newport *Mercury*, beginning May 15, 1897. This version is substantially correct, but it does not begin until October 14th, whereas the MS. is in part readable as early as October 6th, and it contains many slight and some astonishing departures from the original. I am under obligation to the owner of the document, Mr. James G. Topham, a grandson of the author, for the privilege of revising the printed version by the MS. The latter is on small sheets of paper. Each line begins with a capital, and as there is practically no punctuation, and capitals are not employed at the beginning of sentences, there is some uncertainty at times as to the meaning. Owing to lack of time, I did not imitate the spelling, capitalisation, and punctuation of the MS.

15. Mr. George Humphrey, of Providence, the present owner of the MS., has kindly given me the following facts: William Humphrey was born in Rehoboth (afterward Swansea), Mass., in 1752, and died in Tiverton, R. I., July 1, 1832. He was lieutenant in Varnum's Rhode Island regiment, June, 1775. After returning from Quebec and being exchanged, he was appointed lieutenant in Colonel Angell's regiment. January 1, 1777, he was made first lieutenant in the Second Rhode Island regiment. October 22, 1778, he became a captain. January 1, 1781, he was transferred to the First Rhode Island regiment. He served till the close of the war, and probably was appointed a major, though the cessation of hostilities appears to have prevented the issuing of a commission. After the war he was captain of the Tiverton militia, 1794, 1798, 1799, 1800–1804, and member of the Rhode Island Assembly, 1802–1812. He was genial and kindly, a man of sincere piety, a deacon of the Baptist church for many years, and one greatly loved by the community. His journal, like Topham's, has a capital at the beginning of each line, and very little punctuation.

It is a pleasure to record my special indebtedness to Mr. Clarence S. Brigham, Librarian of the Rhode Island Historical Society, who guided me to both Humphrey's and Thayer's MSS.

16. The differences are curious. Under Sept. 30 we find in Humphrey: "This day proceeded toward the aforesaid falls through rapid water here is the second Carrying place we found that the course of the river differ'd From the draught that we had seen I carr'd my Battow across the island & encamped on the main On the west side of the river here is a new Mill erected & the worst Instructed I ever saw, the people Call this

place Canaan, a canaan indeed." Thayer's account is:
" Proceeded through the falls in rapid water, here is the
second carrying place. we found that the course of the
river Differ'd from the Draught we had seen. we encamped on the Main, on the west side of the river. the
carrying place is crosst an Island here is a new mill erect-
ing—the property of Mr. Coplin—the worst constructed
I ever saw. the People call this place Canaan, a Canaan
Indeed!"

It will be noted that Thayer's first sentence is an incorrect version of what Humphrey wrote, and also that he
added one fact to Humphrey's account.

September 21. Humphrey : "our Encampment grew
very uncomfortable especially For those who had no
tents and not being Us'd to soldiers fare." Thayer:
. . . "for those who had no tents, and not being
much used to the inconveniences that a soldier is obliged
to undergo, suffer'd exceedingly."

17. In both cases further evidence could be adduced.
E. g., compare Humphrey and Thayer for Sept. 18–22,
24, 25 and Oct. 25 ; and Humphrey and Topham for
Oct. 19, 21 and 28.

18. The name usually appeared as Heth. He came
from Frederick County, Virginia, and was blind in one
eye. Later he became a colonel.

19. Mr. William F. Havemeyer purchased those relating to the life of Washington, but he obligingly writes
me that he has no knowledge of Heath's journal. For
evidence that Marshall used it, see No. 109, vol. i., p. 53,
note.

20. See No. 138, second ser., vol. xv., p. 21.

21. Mr. Codman (No. 28) has spelled this name
Handchett; but I have found a number of the captain's
signatures in the Connecticut archives, and they are all

Hanchet, though his name was occasionally written Hanchett by others.   Mr. Codman (see p. 318) did not observe the difficulty connected with this journal.

22.   According to the genealogy of the Stocking family (No. 124, 1896) he was born June 2, 1753, and the British list of prisoners made him twenty-three years old in July, 1776.   Mr. Codman ranks him as a sergeant on pp. 85 and 100, but as a private on pp. 310 and 318. He was the latter.   See "Ware's" list (No. 206).

23.   Hanchet's company formed a part of the third division, as Arnold organised his army at Fort Western, and Arnold — fully corroborated by Oswald, Meigs, and Dearborn—states that the third division left Fort Western on September 27th ; but Stocking says that he left on the 25th, the day when the first division set out, and his stages all the way along correspond with those of the first division, as we have them from journalists of that party.   Had Stocking been specially detailed, he would have been pretty sure to indicate as much ; and indeed it is hardly possible to imagine that he was detailed with Morgan, especially as the first division consisted of riflemen, while he was a musketman.

24.   Until recently one gentleman named Stocking lived in Catskill ; but he knows nothing of Abner nor of his journal, not even whether Abner was an ancestor of his.   The oldest inhabitant of Catskill, almost one hundred years of age, is equally ignorant in this regard, and a search through the files of an old Catskill newspaper has thrown no light on the matter.

25.   Mr. Codman states (No. 28, p. 316) that nothing is known of Melvin except that he was a private in Dearborn's company, but the Massachusetts archives do not quite agree with that.

In No. 111, vol. x., p. 623, we find: " Melven, James,

Hubbardston. Capt. Adam Wheeler's Co., Col. Ephraim Doolittle's regt.; receipt for advance pay, signed by said Melven & others, dated Charlestown Camp, July 13, 1775; *also*, Private, same Co. & regt.; Company return dated Winter Hill, Oct. 6, 1775 ; reported as having gone to Quebec ; *also* list of men raised to serve in the Continental Army from 7th Worcester Co. regt. as returned by Capt. William Marean, dated Hubbardston, Dec. 29, 1777 ; residence Hubbardston."

" Melvin, James, Hubbardston, Private, Capt. William Marean's Co. of Minute-men, Capt. Doolittle's regt., which marched on the alarm of April 19, 1775 ; service, 8 days."

Evidently these two men were the same, and the one who wrote the journal. I looked up the original roll of October 6th, and found the date. Mr. Melvin (No. 116) seems to make the date October 15th by mistake.

James Melvin of Massachusetts Bay appears in Dearborn's company on the British list of men captured December 31st. After he was exchanged he seems to have re-entered the army, and, under three captains, to have served through the war. He was alive in 1801.

26. His brother-in-law was a sea-captain. Caleb was able in some instances to combine his two instincts, for I have seen a chair—one of four—that he is said to have brought from Spain. He was also a fifer, and served as such in Ezra Hunt's company of Moses Little's regiment of Newburyport men, but he seems to have gone to Quebec as a simple private.

27. By the kindness of the owner, the Rev. Edwin Charles Haskell. As the MS. is in Iowa, I have not seen it myself ; but Mr. Haskell spent two days on the work of making the comparison for me.

28. Mr. Codman concurs in this without question (p. 317).

29. He would have appeared there unless he had died between June 6th (the last date in his journal) and July 27th (the date of the list) ; and at that time deaths were not likely to occur.

30. This man is listed in the Massachusetts archives as Wilds, but his grandson states that the last letter was intended as a flourish. See No. 113, 1890–91, pp. 39 and 40.

31. It seems pertinent to add that Ebenezer Wild's grandson is satisfied that he did not go to Canada. Harvard University has a MS. copy of the journal, but the original has disappeared, though I have seen and examined the journals of Wild's own campaigns.

32. Mr. Codman follows without question the lead of Justin Winsor in regard to it (p. 316). Winsor edited the journal for No. 124.

33. I have searched for the Ware MS. in libraries and among members of the Ware family, but without result.

34. In the British list of prisoners (No. 20) the name is written Wire, very plainly. But I have no doubt this was a mistake. The list called Ware's was copied like the rest of the journal from Tolman, as is proved by the fact that a copy of Tolman's MS., now in the possession of his grandson, includes the list. It is not in the least probable that Tolman and Ware would conspire to omit Wire's name and insert Ware's, when the fraud could be so easily detected at the time. The British officer doubtless took Ware's name orally, and, if it was spoken a trifle indistinctly, he might easily call it Wire, as any one may find by trying.

35. No. 99, p. 323.

18

36. This is undoubtedly true, for Mr. Locke acknowledged the receipt of the MS. in a letter dated April 8th, 1852,—a letter that is still in existence. The MS. was sent him by William Tolman, and was never returned.

37. This is confirmed by the grandson of Ebenezer Tolman in a letter to me.

38. According to the son of William Tolman, who owned it in 1850, Mr. Locke was (he feels very sure) to have placed it for safekeeping in some historical library in Boston ; but I have not been able to find it. In 1850 Tolman's MS. had become a good deal worn, so that Ware's and Wild's copies were practically better. Mr. Locke's statement that the Tolman MS. differed but slightly from Ware's is supported by the fact that a document believed to have been copied from the Tolman MS. and now in the possession of the Tolman family, is substantially identical with Ware's journal, as I am informed by the owner.

Ebenezer Tolman was the son of Henry Tolman of Attleboro, Mass., and when fourteen years old was apprenticed to learn the carpenter's trade. About 1770 he removed to Fitzwilliam, N. H., where he was living on the outbreak of the war. He enlisted early enough to take part in the battle of Bunker Hill. His experience in the Quebec campaign did not discourage him, for he re-enlisted as sergeant. He died December 27, 1838. For these details and other assistance I am indebted to his grandson, Mr. W. O. Tolman.

39. Very little is known of Morison. In No. 141, vol. xiv., it is stated that he was a resident of Shearman's Valley in Cumberland County, Pa., when he enlisted in Captain William Hendricks's company. He was captured in the assault on Quebec, and, after his exchange, re-entered the army. One day, while acting as quarter-

master, he had a dispute with a colonel of the Maryland
Line.   The colonel drew his sword upon him, and he
promptly broke the colonel's sword-arm with a spade.
A court-martial sentenced him to receive one thousand
lashes ; and, although the magnanimity of the colonel prevented the execution of the sentence, Morison quit the
service in disgust.

40. "Provincial's" Journal : "Oct. 4.   Pushed and
dragged to Tentucket Falls (Hellgate).   Carried 40
perches and encamped, 8 [miles].   12, 13. Carried three-
quarters of a mile to a second pond, a mile over; then
two miles land to the third pond, two miles over, and
encamped, 5 [miles].   Nov. 1. . . . I myself saw
one of them offer a dollar, to one of our company, for a
bit of cake not above two ounces.   2. This morning,
when we arose, many of us were so weak that we could
scarce stand; I myself staggered about like a drunken
man. . . . 3. This day marched 20 miles, wading
several small rivers, some of them up to our waists. . . .
In the evening came in sight of a house, the first we had
seen for four weeks. . . . 5. Continued our march
down the river, the people kind and hospitable,—provisions plenty, at a high price. . . . 6. Came up
with Col. Arnold and the advanced party. . . . 7.
Marched this morning 3 miles, halted till evening, when
a Lieut. with 20 men, was ordered forward to see if the
way was clear."

Stocking: "Oct. 4. . . . We got forward 8 miles
to Tentucket or Hell-gate falls . . . The land carriage here was but about 40 rods.   12 and 13. We carried our bateaus and baggage three quarters of a mile
to another pond, one mile over,—then to a third, two
miles over. . . . Nov. 1. . . . Our hunger was
so great that many offered dollars for a single mouthful

of bread . . . 2. When we arose this morning, many of the Company were so weak that they could hardly stand on their legs. When we attempted to march, they reeled about like drunken men. . . . 3. This day we proceeded on down the river about 20 miles, wading several small rivers, some of which were up to our middles. . . . At evening we came in sight of a house, which was the first we had seen in the space of 31 days. . . . 5. We continued our march down the river. The people continued to be hospitable with some few exceptions. Knowing our need of their articles, some of them would extort from us an extravagant price. . . . 6. This day we came up with Col. Arnold and the advanced party. . . . 7. We this day marched down the river about three miles and halted until night. A lieutenant with 20 men was sent forward to see if our way was clear." It will be seen that Provincial says "I," but that Stocking does not. Up to Sept. 25 (not inclusive) Stocking does not resemble "Provincial." This is what suggested the remark in the text (p. 41) that perhaps he began a journal but gave it up.

Oct. 16, Stocking and Tolman agree in calling the advance six miles, while "Provincial" and Morison call it ten. This would suggest that one of them depended on the other; but the next day we find them disagreeing. It is clearly impossible to carry our inferences to a very fine point. No doubt the men talked things over, and as a rule used more or less independent judgment.

41. For a full account of Fobes and his recollections, see No. 77, vol. i. Mr. Codman does not mention Fobes (No. 28).

42. Ephraim Squier, son of Philip, was born in Ashford, Windham Co., Conn., on February 9, 1747—1748. Soon after the skirmish at Lexington, he marched to

Cambridge in Thomas Knowlton's company, re-enlisted before long in the artillery company of Captain Collander, and served at Bunker Hill. In July he entered a company at Roxbury under Captain Pomeroy, and signed for the Quebec expedition September 7, 1775. After coming back from Canada, he returned to the army. His death occurred August 19, 1841. His MS. was printed in No. 104, ii., 685.

43. Rev. Jacob Bailey was a missionary of the Church of England, and resided in Pownalborough (now Dresden), Me., from 1760 until, in June, 1779, his British sympathies—or rather his sense of obligation to keep his oath of allegiance—made it unsafe to remain there. His life has been written by W. S. Bartlett. He "was a close observer, an accurate writer." For Bailey's account of the expedition as well as other material my cordial thanks are due to Mr. Charles E. Allen, author of the *History of Dresden.*

44. Arnold's letters may be found in Nos. 54 and 106, i. The latter would seem to be the more reliable, for the paternity of the MS. is given (p. 341); but we find there some errors which do not appear in No. 54. I have not been able to discover the originals. According to No. 218, vi., p. 218, they have been preserved in the library of Bowdoin College; but nothing is known oɩ them there at present. For a letter from Captain Ward, see No. 185, p. 85. For one from Dearborn, see No. 106, i., p. 400, note. Others may be found in No. 72, appendix.

45. A journal was kept by Charles Porterfield, sergeant of Morgan's company. The MS. is in the hands of the Southern Historical Society, and a considerable part of it has been printed in No. 202, October, 1901. But the portion relating to the march is missing.

John Peirce, probably the surveyor attached to
Church's party, kept a journal, and the MS. was at one
time in the possession of Mr. Charles Congdon, treasurer of the Bradford Club, of New York. But I have
been unable to find any trace of its present whereabouts.
Other journals may come to light, but those we have
probably contain all the important points.

In quotations from the journals, errors in spelling,
punctuation, etc., though somewhat annoying and not
essential to our inquiry, have in most cases been retained, as illustrating the characteristics of the writer.

III: PAGES 56–73.

1. No. 113, October, 1876. (According to Mr. Codman, No. 28, p. 28, orders "to draft the men for Quebec"
were given on September 6th. He was probably misled
by the loose statement in Meigs's journal, September 20th.)
See the same for the order of September 8th, given below.

2. This was commanded by Captain, afterwards General, Daniel Morgan. Graham (No. 64) states that the
company marched six hundred miles in three weeks, on
their way to Cambridge, without losing a man. This
sounds incredible, but apparently is explained in No. 25,
p. 687, by the statement that the men were mounted.

3. The Lancaster County company was commanded
by Captain Matthew Smith, and the Cumberland County
(Carlisle) company by Captain William Hendricks.
The latter name has been given as Hendrick and Hendrickson, but his signature was "Wm. Hendricks." Mr.
Codman (p. 30) states that the Pennsylvania companies
marched more than twenty miles a day for twenty-two
days, but their average was less, as may be seen from
" Provincial's " journal.

4. Humphrey and Thayer state that there were two

adjutants (Christian Febiger was the principal one) and two quartermasters. There has been considerable question as to the spelling of Febiger's name. I have seen two signatures of his, and in both it was spelled as here.

5. Matthias Ogden (who afterward acted as brigade-major), Eleazer Oswald (secretary, and, in effect, aide), and Aaron Burr were volunteers, as were Charles Porterfield, John McGuire, and Matthew Duncan.

6. According to Mr. Codman each company of musketmen was "filled up" at Cambridge to the number of "eighty-four effective men, rank and file" (p. 29); but the order of September 5th disproves this. Possibly the subject may be worth some further remarks. As nothing like complete rolls exist, we cannot be sure about the names or even the numbers of the soldiers in the companies of the detachment. No. 86 gives Captain Hanchet's complement as one hundred.

McCobb's company, on the other hand, seems to have left Cambridge considerably short of its quota. On the official roll of his regiment, Winter Hill, October 7, 1775, it is noted: "The captain, 2 lieutenants, 4 sergeants, 3 corporals, and 44 privates gone to Quebec" (No. 149, p. 56).

The following statements from Mr. P. McC. Reed, the historian of Bath, Me., bear on the case: "My father said to me and others that 'McCobb took a company of soldiers on board of the Arnold fleet when it was anchored at Parker's Flats.' This took place when my father was in his prime, and he had a remarkably retentive memory. . . . Evidently, not having enough at Winter Hill to form a full company, he hastened down to the Kennebec to raise the necessary quota."

No. 173 states that men enlisted while Arnold was waiting at Newburyport, which seems to indicate that the proposed numbers had not been recruited previously. In No. 127, vol. i., there is a pay-roll of Dearborn's company (p. 214) containing seventy-seven names, with this commment signed by the captain: " This is a true roll of the Company under my command which marched from Cambridge for Canada, September, 1775."

Mr. Codman (p. 32) apportions the men to States as follows: Rhode Island, 250 ; Connecticut, 100 ; Massachusetts (including Maine), 400; New Hampshire, 100; Pennsylvania, 200; Virginia, 100; New Jersey, a few volunteers. But (1) these figures would make the total more than one hundred too great; (2) as the list of Arnold's men cannot be made up, the residences of some are not known; (3) there were men from New York, Maryland, and North Carolina, though not many; (4) there were very few, if any, over 88 from New Hampshire (No. 127, pp. 212, 213, 214). This statement, however, requires comment. No. 222 gives the names of 103 New Hampshire men as going with Arnold; and, while a few errors appear to have crept into the list, the author does make out that about one hundred went to " Canada." But does that prove that they went with Arnold ? It hardly seems so. Washington requested the New Hampshire authorities to pay up the New Hampshire men who were to march by the Kennebec; Deacon Brooks was appointed to do this; and he reported later to the Committee of Safety that the amount paid and expense of paying it were £348 7s. (No. 54, 4, iv., 1 and 2.) Now the amount paid the eighty-eight New Hampshire men in Dearborn's and Ward's companies was £345 16s. The difference, £2 11s., must have been required for expenses. It may be suggested that perhaps nothing was due the rest of the one hundred. But it is extremely improbable that these few were fully paid, when comrades enlisted at the same time were not; and Washington's message intimates that the pay of all was in arrears. How, then, did they go to " Canada " ? That question we are not bound to answer, but it occurs to me that possibly they went with Bedel to Montgomery's army. (5) The rifle companies did not contain one hundred men each. The rolls in No. 97 show that Hendricks had 85 and Smith had 80. By the act of Congress of June 14, 1775 (No. 195), each rifle company was to consist of 68 privates, 12 officers, and a musician. (6) There can have been but very few Virginians outside of Morgan's company.

I regret having to refer so many times to No. 28 in terms of disagreement ; but it has seemed necessary to discuss points of difference, else a reader might feel left in suspense between two opinions, and candor requires me to give a reference to the place where the other view may be found stated.

7. Meigs, also, had been at Roxbury (then a suburb of Boston).

8. Mr. Codman (p. 29) represents the whole detachment as remaining at Cambridge until the 13th; but (1) " Provincial" records a march of thirteen miles toward Newburyport on the 11th; (2) Morison recorded: " We began our march for Quebec " on the 11th; (3) Haskell and a small party reached Lynn on the 11th; and (4) Senter wrote under date of the 13th: " The detachment . . . had now been under marching orders since the 11th."

9. This was set off from Newbury in 1764. The distance from Boston to Newburyport was called about forty-five miles.

10. It is not recorded that all set out on the 11th; but it seems probable that these companies marched together and stopped at the same places, since we know

that they camped together at Newbury.   Their two
stopping-places I have not been able to identify.

11. Some of the journalists say "Mystick," taking the
name, apparently, from the river.

12. Melvin stopped for the night in Lynn.

13. Thayer and Humphrey put Beverly first, but this
is obviously a slip.

14. This arrangement of the battalions is given by
Dearborn's journal.   Mr. Codman (p. 31) puts McCobb
into the first, and adds to the second a Captain Oliver
Colburn.   This last gentleman is a surprise.   None of
the journalists includes in the army an officer of that
name, though more than one gives a list of the captains.
The order of September 5th called for only thirteen captains.   A list made out at a later time by Ward does not
mention Colburn.   Had there been fourteen companies
averaging eighty-four men (Mr. Codman's figure), the
total would have been about twelve hundred, instead of
ten hundred and fifty men.   In fact, only " Provincial "
gives more than thirteen companies.   And yet Arnold
wrote Enos in a letter to bring on " the carpenters of
Capt. Colburn's Company; " and later, speaking of provisions, he said: " The carpenters of Colburn's company
have more than they can bring up."   The fact appears
to be that a company of mechanics from the boat-yard
on the Kennebec, where the bateaux were built, followed Arnold part way to Quebec, and the man at their
head was named Colburn.   We shall hear more of this
later.

It should be added that possibly the army did not
march by battalions, as stated in the text.   There is no
evidence from Arnold or Oswald.   We only know that
the detachment (excepting the riflemen) was divided into
these two battalions, and that the reports of the journal-

ists fit into this scheme. From some of the companies we have no reports. Possibly these marched by themselves on a different schedule, but it does not seem probable.

Several of the officers were mentioned in the preceding chapter; a word or two may be added about a few others.

Christopher Greene was a descendant of one of the charter proprietors of Rhode Island under Charles II., and the son of Philip Greene, a judge of the Superior Court of the State. He was born in 1737; lived at what is now called Centreville; joined the " Kentish Guards " of East Greenwich, as lieutenant, in 1774, and in 1775 was appointed major in the Rhode Island army under his near relative and intimate friend, General Nathaniel Greene, but preferred to serve as captain in the Continental army. He rose to be a colonel, distinguished himself in the defence of Red Bank (Fort Mercer) in 1777, and was barbarously murdered by a gang of refugees near Croton Bridge, Croton River, N. Y., in the night of May 13, 1781. He was most highly esteemed.

Roger Enos was born in Simsbury, Conn., in 1729, but hailed now from Windsor, Conn. (Mr. Codman, p. 31, calls him " Roger Enos of Vermont," but he did not settle in Vermont until 1781). He served in the French and Indian War. In 1762 he was in the expedition against Havana. Died October 6, 1808.

Timothy Bigelow, son of Daniel, came from Worcester, Mass. On receiving news of the battle of Lexington, he marched at the head of some Minute Men to the scene of activity. After returning from Quebec, he became colonel of the Fifteenth Massachusetts regiment. He was born in 1740, and died in 1790.

Jonas Hubbard also was of Worcester, Mass. Though

an active business man, he interested himself in military
matters, was elected a lieutenant in a company of Minute
Men, and soon after going to Cambridge was made a
captain.   He was a typical patriot.   At the assault on
Quebec he was wounded and soon died.

Daniel Morgan was born in New Jersey in 1736, removed to Virginia in 1755, struggled for a rough liveli-
hood as farmer and teamster, served under Braddock,
raised a company of riflemen in 1775, and marched to
Cambridge.   His exploits during the war are familiar
to all.   Later in life he was sent to Congress.   He died
in 1799.

Samuel Ward, born at Westerly, R. I., November 17,
1756, was the son of Samuel Ward, Governor of the
State.   He studied at Brown University, joined the
Rhode Island Army of Observation, was made a captain
in May, 1775, and soon found himself at Cambridge,
burning with patriotic ardour.   After returning from
Quebec he rose to be a lieutenant-colonel.   When the
war ended he became a merchant, and settled after a
time in New York.   There he died in 1832.   He was
the grandfather of Mrs. Julia Ward Howe.

15.   His formal instructions were dated September
14th; but naturally there were final preparations to make
and last conversations to have with the Commander-in-
chief.   Mr. Codman thinks (p. 35) that he waited in order
to receive the latest possible news from Schuyler, but it
was not necessary to delay for that, since the manifestoes were to be sent on to him, and information could go
by the same express.

16.   At Salem he procured 200 pounds of ginger, received from the Committee of Safety 270 blankets, and
engaged a teamster to transport these articles to the
ships.   Perhaps he obtained also some hard money;

special efforts were made to secure it for him in that city.

Dr. Senter, the surgeon, went only seven miles on Wednesday, travelled via Salem to Ipswich on Thursday, and lodged Friday night at Newbury. He was attended by his mate (Mr. Greene) and by his assistants (Barr and Jackson).

The march of the soldiers through these towns doubtless interested the people deeply, but no incidents of their passage seem to have been recorded.

17. Oswald says that the whole detachment arrived Saturday evening. This means, I suppose, that *by evening* the last of the army had put in an appearance.

18. The riflemen camped "at the corner" of Rolfe's Lane, since known as Green Street, and a stone about seven feet high has been set up opposite the spot on the edge of the Common, with a bronze tablet recording the fact. (For the inscription, see No. 175, January, 1903, p. 352.) I should call it about a mile from this point to the Old South Church.

19. Mr. Codman (p. 34) puts all the musketmen in the Presbyterian Church, Davenport's Inn, and the ropewalks; but (1) it seems to me doubtful whether many soldiers lodged in the meeting-house. They would hardly turn the church of a highly respected and friendly minister into barracks. Besides, what did they do with the seats? It was in this church that many attended divine service the following Sunday: did they stand? Mr. Codman's authority was doubtless Thayer. Thayer says: "[Sept. 15. Arri]ved at Newbury Port about sun set and Quarter'd our men [in] the Presbiterian Meeting House," but under date of the 16th he records: "Capt. Tophams Company together with mine arrived." Humphrey agrees with Thayer for the 15th.

We may conclude that probably some of that company, but not the greater part, lodged in the church, unless we prefer to reject entirely this portion of the two journals on account of its evident and gross inaccuracy (Note 13). (2) Haskell states that his company were quartered in the Town-house. (3) So far as we are aware, no soldiers, but only the surgeon and his "company" went to the inn, and (4) Squier, not a rifleman, says: "We pitched our tents."

20.   Arnold wrote Tracy from Fort Western, thanking him warmly for "the many favors received" at Newburyport.   Mr. Codman (p. 34) speaks of the "lavish hospitality" of "old Newbury"; but I find no evidence of any entertainment there.   The hospitality appears to have been shown at Newburyport.

21.   Washington to Tracy, September 2, 1775; but later five suitable vessels were found at Beverly and two at Newbury, so that Tracy had to provide only four (Joseph Reed to Tracy, September 7th).

22.   Mr. Codman (p. 38) calls the 16th Sunday, and places the review on Monday: two slips.

23.   The church where they went, called the Old South, is in good condition still.   It was built in 1756, and the spire added in 1759.   Jonathan Parsons was the minister.

24.   According to Thayer the men embarked on Sunday and sailed on Monday, but this is plainly an error. Humphrey is correct, and apparently Thayer was careless in following him.   Meigs, on the other hand, places the embarkation on Tuesday.   This also is unacceptable, for there are ten witnesses against him.   Very possibly, however, the embarkation was not completed until Tuesday.

Mr. Codman (p. 38) gives the number of transports as

ten, and this requires a comment. Oswald's official journal says of them, "eleven in number," and four others corroborate him, while about as many say ten. My own conclusion is that originally there were eleven; but, as the *Swallow* got on the rocks, was relieved of substantially all her passengers, and was left astern, some of the journalists very naturally reckoned only ten. The *Swallow* rejoined the fleet in the Kennebec (probably carrying freight as well as twelve men), and so there were actually eleven transports. We have the names of nearly all the vessels: *Broad Bay* (which led the way under the command of James Clarkson), *Houghton*, *Eagle*, *Hannah*, *Britannia*, *Conway*, *Abigail*, and *Admiral*.

Mr. Codman (p. 38) speaks of "the *Commodore*, the flagship, carrying Arnold"; but (1) the sailing-master of the fleet, as Mr. Codman himself says, was the captain of the *Broad Bay*, and confusion might have resulted had Arnold been on another vessel; (2) Senter sailed on the *Broad Bay* and states that Arnold was on the same vessel; (3) Humphrey and Thayer say the same; and (4) Oswald states that the signals (*e. g.*, for boarding a hostile ship) were to be given from the *Broad Bay;* therefore Arnold must have been on that vessel. Dearborn observes that Arnold's vessel was "called the Commodore"; but either he made a mistake, or the term "Commodore" was applied to this ship to indicate that it was the commanding one. As Dearborn states that the signals were to be given from the "Commodore," he must, in view of what Oswald says, have meant that Arnold was on the *Broad Bay*.

25. Arnold's letter to Washington of September 19th might add interesting details, but I have not been able to find it. It can hardly have been important.

26. Half-tide Rock and Gangway Rock are near the

wharves of Newburyport, while Lunt's Rock, Black Rocks, and Badger's Rock await ships near the sea. Shoals and bars are not wanting. Mr. Codman remarks (p. 38) that the other vessels lay to while the *Swallow* was "gotten safely off," and the testimony of Senter points that way; but (1) Oswald states that she could not be got off at that tide; (2) he says: "whom I [*i. e.*, Arnold, in whose name he wrote] ordered to follow us," which implies clearly that the *Swallow* was left behind; (3) Melvin noted that Arnold did wait awhile for the grounded schooner, but finally transferred her passengers and went ahead; and (4) Arnold wrote Washington, September 25th: "a small vessel which run on the rocks but is since off, without damage, and arrived safe," which indicates that the *Swallow* did not go on with the rest of the fleet.

Still further: Stocking speaks of the "evening tide" (referring to a high tide) on the next day, and it must have come pretty late in the evening, for his vessel made thirty miles up the river, and then was helped farther by the tide. Haskell says it was high tide early in the morning, September 21st, and this confirms Stocking. So, as a high tide was necessary to get the *Swallow* off, she cannot have set sail until about evening.

27. Some time was spent after the bar was crossed in practising the signals.

28. Thayer says that they sailed along the shore; but it cannot be supposed that the fleet ran into and out of every bay. A straight line from the mouth of the Merrimac to that of the Kennebec runs "along shore." Oswald indicates that a direct course N. N. E. was followed. The wind was W. S. W.

29. The United States maps show two islands of this name near the mouth of the Kennebec; one is close to

Popham Beach, inside Seguin Island; the other lies on the west side of Phippsburg Point.

30. Mr. Codman speaks (p. 38) of the mouth of the Kennebec as "150 miles from Newburyport," but that is a mistake; the air-line distance is about 84 miles. Just how many miles the fleet actually sailed we cannot say, for we do not know how straight its course was. But the shortness of the time and the direction of the wind, as well as Oswald's testimony, intimate that the course was, in the main, direct. The statement in the text was intended to make a fair allowance for departures from a straight line. The vessels, we must understand, did not all stop at exactly the same time. Dearborn says 10 o'clock.

31. Mr. Codman (p. 39) states that this point was reached at 1 o'clock P.M.; but I find no support for this view, except that Haskell mentions 12 o'clock: he may have been on a belated vessel. Dearborn entered the mouth at 10 A.M.; Squier entered it early in the morning; Oswald says they were "in the mouth of Arrowsick" at 9 A.M.; "Provincial" says, "in the morning"; Thayer and Humphrey discovered the mouth about dawn; Meigs entered it soon after morning. In fact, Mr. Codman's statement is hardly consistent with itself: "They made sail early in the morning and arrived at one P.M. at the mouth of the Kennebec," since Wood Island, from which they "made sail," is close to the Kennebec.

32. Oswald notes that they anchored in Eel's Eddy (spelled *Ell* by Mr. Codman), but no such piece of water has been known at the mouth of the Kennebec for the past seventy years. Doubtless the name is a slip for Heal's Eddy. This lies at the very entrance of the river, east of Fort Popham. But it has never been

19

recognised as a proper anchorage, whereas Parker's Flats, a famous place for ships to lie, are within sight and only two miles distant. Some of the vessels are reported as anchoring there, and a direct tradition has it that Arnold himself did so. Putting these things together, and adding the fact that a local pilot was guiding the fleet, I have ventured to believe that Oswald is in error here,—as indeed would be very natural, since he was hearing many new names and had no reason to note them particularly. This view is confirmed by the fact that Oswald says they sent ashore for refreshments, while at anchor; refreshments were within easy reach from Parker's Flats, but not from Heal's Eddy. The Flats are merely extensive shallows.

33. Oswald says: "One of our fleet, viz, Capt. ——, overtook us," and, in his record of the next morning, adds: "After sailing a few miles discovered the other two of our fleet coming through Sheepscut Creek." Senter intimates that the fleet was pretty well scattered by the storm; but Oswald is explicit: "At 9 o'clock, A.M. arrived safe in the mouth of Arowsick [*i. e.*, the Kennebec below Arrowsic Island] with all our fleet except three."

34. At all events he began the practice of law there. Mr. Codman (p. 40) calls the place a hamlet, but it was considerably more than that. Meigs says there were "elegant buildings." The halt was made here.

35. See note 6. The journals, however, do not mention this. None of our authorities belonged to McCobb's company.

36. Formerly known as Chesepeake Bay and as Swan Pond.

37. Once called Garden Island.

38. The natural inference is that Arnold made the

last part of his day's journey in a rowboat or by land,—
most likely by boat.

39. The water just below Swan Island is quite shallow. The term " Flats " is locally applied to the spot.

40. This has been known as Calf Island.

41. Apparently what Senter calls Hellgate.

42. No. 107, 2d ser., v., p. 128.

43. In 1754. See No. 215.

44. Named after Thomas Pownall, a former Governor of Massachusetts Bay.

45. It is occupied by a great-grandson of the Major
Goodwin mentioned in the next sentence (1902).

46. No. 106, i., states that there was a blockhouse
called Fort Pownall at Pownalborough; but this is doubtless a mistake. There was a Fort Pownall on the Penobscot. Fort Shirley was at first called Fort Frankfort.
For a plan of it see No. 134, p. 47.

47. Mr. Codman has said (No. 28, p. 40) that the fleet
waited at Pownalborough " during the 22^d and 23^d " for
the vessels that ran aground. Such a delay would have
been serious, and we must examine the matter. (1)
None of the journalists mentions any such stop at Pownalborough; (2) it seems very improbable that the fleet
would stop there when time was so extremely precious,
and there was a deal of work to do a few miles above;
(3) we know that five at least of the vessels reached
Gardinerston on the 22d or earlier, and (4) the positive
statements of the journalists are inconsistent with Mr.
Codman's theory: Stocking and Tolman arrived at Fort
Western on the 21st, and Melvin came only six miles
short of it; Meigs was above Pownalborough on September 20th; Dearborn, Haskell, Senter, Squier, Humphrey, and Thayer were above Pownalborough on
September 22d; Morison and " Provincial " reached Fort

Western on September 23d; and a party *left* Fort Western September 24th. Some of the journalists speak of *passing* Pownalborough on the 22d.

Mr. Codman says also that the missing vessels which went up Sheepscot River rejoined the fleet at Pownalborough (No. 28, p. 40); but Oswald saw them approaching as he sailed on "a few miles" above Georgetown. Melvin, Humphrey and Thayer corroborate this.

48. Arnold states that "many" of the transports ran aground, and in a letter to Nathaniel Tracy, September 28th, he speaks of the voyage to Fort Western as "very troublesome indeed."

49. This appears to have been a night affair, for the *Swallow* did not reach Arnold until 4 o'clock P.M., and is significant as illustrating Arnold's anxiety to lose no time.

IV: PAGES 74–83.

1. Dr. Gardiner was a tory, and for that reason the name Pittston was commonly used for this region during the Revolutionary period. For a long time the two names were interchangeable. Gardinerston Plantation was incorporated as Pittston, February 4, 1779, and until 1803 comprised what is now Pittston, Gardiner, West Gardiner, Farmingdale, Chelsea, and Randolph.

2. In the journals we find Colborn, Coburn, Copelin, Coplin, and Coben (or Caben), evidently variants. Colburn himself and Arnold spelled the name in the present way, while General Gates wrote "Colbourn."

3. Preserved in the files of the House of Representatives, Washington, and previously unpublished.

4. The word "bateau" was hardly ever spelled correctly by the journalists. Their usual form was "battoe." We have no positive evidence as to the form

of the boats used by Arnold, but there are strong suggestions. The present Kennebec bateau, used by the
lumbermen, is very high and sharp at both ends, though
the stem projects rather more than the stern; and the
sides are high and flaring. There is a flat bottom; but,
on account of the flaring sides and long, overhanging
ends, it seems small. This boat is easily managed and
hard to overturn. So far as the memory of old boatmen
goes, it has always been the Kennebec type. My own
opinion is that a less developed form of it was probably
used by Arnold's men. It was easy to build, and comparatively light and cheap. The lake style of bateau
would not have answered here at all.

5. The "setting pole" was doubtless a pole such as
the boatmen use now to keep a boat off rocks or the
shore, or to propel it by pushing against the bottom.
At present the pole has a spike in the end. From
Colburn's charge—"Setten poles and pikes"—we may
infer that it was similar in 1775.

6. This indicates that Colburn was at Cambridge,
for, as the end of the letter shows, he was not expected
to come to Cambridge with an answer, and therefore he
must have made this inquiry on his way home. Colburn's bills presented to Congress (heretofore unpublished) bear on this matter, as one of them mentions
several trips to Cambridge. They throw light on a
number of other matters, and are well worth printing
in full:

The United States of America to ⎱
             Reuben Colburn ⎰   .   .   Dr.

1775
Septem. 3. To 14 Days going on an Express
              @ 6/ by myself   .   .   .   4: 4: 0

8	To Horse hire & my Expences going to Kennebeck with Joseph Farnsworth Comm[issary]	6:11: 2
15	To Dennis Gitchel going with an advance Party to [*i.e.* toward] Quebeck, by order of Col. Arnold, 17 Days @ 4/ . .	3: 8 —
	To Sam¹ Berry 20 Days for Ditto @ 4/	4 — —
	To Nehemiah Gitchel 16 Days for Ditto @ 4/ . . .	3: 4 —
	To Abraham Page 17 Days for Ditto @ 4/	3: 8 —
	To Isaac Hull 16 Days for Ditto @ 4/	3: 4 —
	To·an Indian Guide 18 Days @ 4/	3:12 —
	To paid 2 men for assisting in hawling Baggage across Norrigewalk Carrying-Place .	— 3: 4
	To 28 Lbs. Sugar for the men @	— 14 —
	To ½ Bushel of Meal . . .	— 2: 5
	To 8 Meals of Victuals for the men @ 8d	— 5: 4
	To Benjamin Fitch 2 Days going after the above Indian Guide @ 4/	— 8 —
20	To Victuals and Drink for 11 Indians one Day and a Night, they being a part of Col. Arnold's Army	1: 1: 4
	To victualling my Company 18 men, 2 Days	3:12 —

23 To a birch Cannoe delivered Col
      Arnold .   .   .   .   .   2 — —
    To James Stackpole's Bill for a
      birch Cannoe delivered Isaac
      Hull per order of Col Arnold .   2: 8 —
    To 200 Battoes @ 40/ .   . 400 — —
    To 100 lbs. Oakam .   .   .   1: 4 —
    To 4000 Nails .   .   .   .   1:12 —

                          £445: 1: 7

1786—July. 3^d—Errors, excep^d
                REUBEN COLBURN

Suffolk S—   Boston July 3^d 1786.

The above named Reuben Colburn personally appearing, made oath to the truth of the Forewritten Account,
by him Subscribed,
              Before me,
                  EDM. QUINCY J P

Another bill is as follows:

Gardnarston September yr [?] 1775 Dr
The younited staits of Amarika to Reuben Colburn

To 200 Battoes at 40/	400: 0: 0
To 480 Padels a /9	18: 0: 0
To 400 Setten poles and pikes a /9 . .	15: 0: 0
To 230 pair of oars a 2/ per pair . .	26: 0: 0
To 1 Barril of turpentine a 18 l . . .	0:18: 0
The a Bove Delivered to General arnold	
To vittelin 21 carpenters and guids [or guide] three Days a 1/ per meal . .	3: 3: 0
To Soplien the Ingon Guids [or Guide] .	2: 0: 0
To Cash paid the Ingon intarpentur . .	1:15: 0

To Cash paid Cap Dennes Getchel and five
    other parsons for going up Cannibeck
    River as an exspres to queback . .   28: 7: 9
To Sundri Soplies to Cap Getchel and [?] .   3:16: 4
To My Self Going on Expres from Cannibeck
    to Cambridge 3 times and expences and
    hors hires and procurin Beef flouer and
    other [?] for the arme with arnold .   23:15: 9

                                  522:15:10
    To the Contra
    By Cash at Sundri times   .   .   .   155:10:6

December 9, 1818, General Henry Dearborn took oath
to Colburn's claim (MS., Archives of Congress). Most
of the charges were the same as in the bill last quoted,
but the following items differed:
Myself going as an express from the Ken-
    nebec river to Cambridge 3 times, trav-
    eling expenses, horse hire, time, and
    procuring beef, flour, and other sup-
    plies for the army with Gen. Arnold .   27:15: 3

    Credit to the United States by cash re-
    ceived at sundry times 152:10: 6
    (The spelling of the original not followed.)

Why the three bills differ as they do I am unable to
explain, and the mystery seems deeper yet when we find
by a report to the House of Representatives, January 15,
1819, that Colburn's charge was £523 15s. 10d., while the
credit to the government was £159 10s. 6d.

Arnold wrote Washington on September 25, 1775:
" The Commissary has been obliged to pay for them [the

bateaux] with £100 I have lent him out of the pay."
In Washington's accounts appear these entries : " Aug.
20, Reuben Colburn, £10 ; Sept. 7, Reuben Colburn,
£16, *sh.* 6." Mr. Trofton, a member of the House of
Representatives, who urged Colburn's claim, stated that
these sums were on account of the boats ; but as Arnold's
letter of inquiry was not written until August 21st, this
could hardly be true of the first one, at least. Trofton
stated that Colburn received nothing except from
Washington, but how can that statement be reconciled
with Arnold's letter quoted above ?

General Henry Dearborn stated that he saw a letter
from Washington summoning Colburn to Cambridge.

It is said that Colburn went to Mount Vernon to consult Washington about the balance that he claimed, but
arrived the day after Washington's death. For a final
report on the claim see the Senate proceedings for March
12, 1824.

7. This sentence and the previous one help explain
the care taken, by Washington's orders, to send scouting
vessels out from Newburyport.

8. From the Archives of Congress ; hitherto unpublished. Meigs wrote in his journal under date of September 20th : " This day makes 14 only since the orders were
first given for building 200 battoes, etc.," and hence it
has always been supposed that these orders were issued
on September 6th.

9. Mr. Codman (No. 28, p. 29) states that " a company of carpenters was sent forward [from Cambridge]
to Colburn's shipyard " ; but Washington's order gives
no hint of this. On the other hand, the order would
allow Colburn no time to assemble a force of carpenters
ready for a march to Gardinerston. Further, the fact
that Colburn had a shipyard implies that he had work-

men, and as, of course, he would drop all other commissions for this one, they were perhaps able to do all the work that he had the facilities for handling. Again, Oliver Colburn, the major's brother, had a company of Minute Men in July and August, 1775, and thirty-six of them lived in Gardinerston, so that extra help could have been obtained there, no doubt. I do not know of any support for Mr. Codman's statement, and presume that it is incorrect for the same reason as the portion of the same sentence that precedes it (Chapter III., note 1). See also p. 301.

10. Here we have a definite and official reference to the mysterious "Colburn's Company," (Chapter III., note 14). The natural inference from the position of this paragraph is that what it orders was to be done after Colburn got home. This is confirmed (1) by the evident fact that guides could only be engaged near the region they were to traverse, and (2) by the fact that Colburn did go on from Gardinerston with a company, as General Henry Dearborn and Joseph North certified in support of his claim (MSS., files of Congress). Further, in Colburn's bill of 1786, appears a charge for "victualling my Company, 18 men, 2 Days." This indicates that Colburn charged for the board of his company of "artificers" when they were not engaged upon the bateaux. Just how to explain such a bill under date of September 20th we do not know, unless we assume that these men completed their work on the bateaux September 18th ; but evidently had Colburn brought a squad of workmen all the way from Cambridge his charge for subsistence would have been much more than this.

According to General Dearborn's certificate (sworn to on December 9, 1818), Colburn and his party went "to near the head waters of Kennebec River," *i. e.*, of the

West Branch, or Dead River.   A family tradition has it that Oliver Colburn, who bore the title of captain, was in command of this company ; and it is easy to believe that Major Colburn, while retaining the general direction of it, would prefer not to limit his movements by attending to the details of actual command.   But apparently Reuben himself was only "captain" in 1775 (note 16).

11.   This word is not clear, as the paper is worn.

12.   From the bill of 1786 we may infer that Joseph Farnsworth was appointed, and went to Gardinerston with Colburn.   Farnsworth appears later in Arnold's correspondence as his commissary.

13.   It will be seen that in drawing one of his bills Colburn made a charge for the oars, paddles, and poles, and that Dearborn did the same.

14.   "Nails etc." was interlined.

15.   Mr. Codman speaks (p. 29) of this as near Pittston, but it is *in* Pittston ; and of Colburn's shipyard as at Agry's Point (p. 40), whereas it was a little way *below* the Point.

There can be no doubt about the place where the bateaux were built.   Rev. Jacob Bailey recorded : " 200 bateaux were built at Colburn's."   The price paid for the bateaux (40*s.*) would seem to have been ample, for we find Dr. Senter buying (September 30th) for $4 a much better one than he set out with.

16.   These were evidently smaller or flimsier than the rest, for they cost much less.   Agry's receipt for payment (MS., Archives of Congress) is as follows :

GARDNERSTON Sept.[r] the 30th 1775

Then rec.[d] of Capt. Reuben Colburn Twelve Pounds Lawful Money it being in full for the building the Last Twenty Battoes   I Say rec.[d] by me

THOMAS AGRY.

This appears to prove, by the way, that in 1775 Reuben Colburn was called only captain ; and that he did not set out personally before September 30th.

Arnold's receipt (MS., Archives of Congress) runs thus:

Received Kenebeck Sepr 1775 of Mr. Reuben Colburn, Two hundred & Twenty Batteau's for the Publick Service   B.^t Arnold Col.^o

Mr. Codman says (p. 40) that the bateaux were " now nearly completed " (September 22d and 23d); but Arnold arrived there (Oswald's journal) September 21st, and wrote Washington (September 25th): " I found the batteaus completed " (No. 54, 4, iii., 960).

The use of " Mr." here and elsewhere with Reuben Colburn's name is evidence (1) that Washington's order to raise a company and attend the detachment did not make him and his men a part of the army, and (2) that Colburn held no regular captain's commission. Very likely his title came from service in the militia.

Certain other unpublished receipts are worth quoting (Archives of Congress):

Gardinerston Septr 15th 1775 Rec^d of Captⁿ Ruben Colburn the full Sum of Teen pound 14 and Eight pence Lawf^{ll} Money for fifty four days work at ye Battoes £10. 14. 8.   Nath.^{l.l.} Stevens.

Gardinerstown Septr 15th 1775

Rec^d. of Captⁿ. Ruben Colburn the full Sum of Nine pound Six & Eight pence Lawf^{ll} Money for 57 days Work done at Building Battoes

Edward Savage
Joseph Savag
Daniel Hilton
Michall Rierdan

Apparently, then, work on the bateaux began in July. But this cannot have been; and the explanation may be that each of these five men was the employer of several workmen, and the number of days charged for in the receipt represents the total number of day's works contributed by his gang. For convenience, the four whose gangs happened to have contributed the same number (57) signed the same receipt. Possibly we may see here a hint of the method used by Colburn to execute so large a contract. Each of his regular workmen may have been made the foreman of a gang of specially employed helpers. Of course in such a community every man knew something about the use of ordinary tools.

The quotation from Morison appears under the date of September 28; of course it may represent later feelings.

17. From Joseph Reed's memorandum (No. 54, 4, iii., 962). Colburn's bill states that they were sent by Arnold's order, but there is no inconsistency, for the orders of the Commander-in-chief would very naturally be conveyed through Arnold.

18. Vassalborough, the town above Augusta, was incorporated in 1771. At that time it was astride the river, half on each side. Sidney, on the west bank, was set off in 1796. John, Dennis, and Nehemiah Getchell were the first settlers there (1760), and a fourth brother, Jeremiah, lived in Augusta. All these men served Arnold, particularly as "pilots." One of my guides gave me some interesting bits of information that came down in the Getchell family,—valuable, of course, only as tradition.

19. This report was put in writing for them by Remington Hobby (the first moderator of the town of Vassalborough), and sent by him to Colburn. (See No. 54, 4,

iii., 962, for Hobby's letter.)   As the report was dated September 13th, it had, no doubt, been awaiting Arnold for some days.   According to Mr. Codman (p. 43) Getchell and Berry "made their appearance and submitted their report to Arnold" at Fort Western; but (1) their report was evidently sent to Colburn before Arnold's arrival; and (2) as to their personal appearing, we only know that Arnold saw the men before he wrote his letter of September 25th to Washington (*i. e.*, there is nothing to indicate that they did not meet him at Colburn's).   It is of considerable importance to note that Arnold received their report *before* reaching Fort Western, for this gave him time to mature the plan of sending off Steele's scouting party.   He reached Fort Western at 6 P.M., September 23d, and must have issued orders for this expedition very promptly, for it set out early enough the next day to make eighteen miles of hard paddling before night.   For a facsimile of the conclusion of the report (from the original in the Archives of Congress) see No. 175, January, 1903, p. 359.

20. Copied for me (very carefully, I have reason to believe) from the original in the Archives of Congress. An edited version is in No. 54, 4, iii., 961.   In writing Getchell's name, I spell it in the present way.

21. As shown by Colburn's bill, there were three others in the party, besides an Indian guide.   This is confirmed by the following bill (MS., Archives of Congress):

Cap.ᵗ Ruben Colburn to Dennis Getchell and Comp.ʸ Dr
1775
Sep.ᵗ 15 to 5 Men Fixing & going on their intended
    Journey to Quebeck 87 days   @ 5/ £21 : 15 : 0
    paid an Indian Pilot   3 : 4 : 0

6 Gallons Rum	4/	1 :	4 : 0
¼ cwt. [?] Sugar		0 :	12 : 6
½ bushel Meal		0 :	2 : 5
8 Meals Victuals	·		5 : 4

It will be seen that Getchell proposed to demand 5s. a day for services, while Colburn's bill shows that the charge was reduced to 4s. It will be noted that the day's works of the men were lumped, as was suggested may have been the case with the receipts given Colburn (note 16).

22. Partly confirmed by a receipt in the Archives of Congress:

GARNERS TOWN August the 31 Day 1775
Then I Received of Rueburn Colburn one Hundred and fifteen pound of salt Pork and one Hundred and Six pound of Shipp Brad one Half a Bushshall of Corn
SAMUEL BERRY

This shows that final preparations were made on the last day of August.

23. This appears from other evidence to have been at the site of Flagstaff village.

24. *I. e.,* " from."

25. According to Arnold's letter of September 25th to Washington (No. 54, 4, iii., 960) he was a Norridgewock Indian named " Nattarius." In reality his name appears to have been Natanis. More than once he appears as " Sataness " in the journals. The name Charlton in the next line means Carleton.

26. Natanis was not too hostile, however, to serve the party as guide, as is shown by a bill in the Archives of Congress:

Mr. Ruben Colburn to Dinis Gachel in behalf of the
United Colinies

To myself 17 Day going towards Quebeck at
    5/p Day   4 : 5 : 0

½ Day work of Morris Fling assisting with
    his oxen   2 : 0

Mr. Howard halling the baggage over the
    Carring [carrying-place]   1 : 4

Cash p'd Nattanes the Indin for Giding us
    on our Jurney towards Quebeck   0 : 6 : 0

The Archives of Congress contain another bill of
Dennis Getchell's, which is substantially like Colburn's
of 1786. This bill of Getchell's makes it clear that the
Indian guide "Went with us from Gaardnerstoun,"
and was paid for sixteen days. As Getchell and Berry
were back at Vassalborough on September 13th, it seems
plain that they went down to Gardinerston, and there
settled with Colburn on the 15th, charging for their
time from the day they first left home to the day they
finally returned there, as guides do now.

27. This must mean thirty miles *more* (nearly sixty in
all on Dead River), for it has just been stated that during the first thirty miles there was "good water"; but
the statement about the water shows that they did not
really go even forty miles up the stream.

28. Evidently Natanis served as guide on the 8th and
9th. This enabled him to earn some money and also
keep watch of the party.

29. *I. e.*, Sertigan (Sartigan, Sattigan).

30. Colonel Guy Johnson, British Indian Agent, who
led a body of warriors from New York to the vicinity of
Montreal to aid Carleton.

31. Blazed or "spotted" to indicate the way.

32. Mr. Codman's account (pp. 43, 44) errs at several points: (1) he says the scouts reported "the water, though shoal, no more so than was inevitable at that season of the year," while in reality the scouts mentioned only "the *dry* season." In fact, there had been a drought. (2) He says that the Indian reported "more spies, both whites and Indians, stationed near the headwaters of the Chaudière," whereas Natanis said nothing of white scouts there. The presence of white scouts would have been particularly serious. (3) He says the scouts had gone fifty or sixty miles up Dead River. Even fifty miles would have carried them quite through the shoal water that turned them back.

33. This will appear in Chapter XV.

34. No. 3 states that Lieutenant-Governor Cramahé sent a guard to " Sartigan," and No. 148 (September 14th) mentions that some Royal Fusileers arrived the day before from " St. Igan " (a corruption of " Sertigan " formerly common in the region).

35. September 25th, from Fort Western.

36. As Goodwin was the surveyor for the Plymouth Company, one might suppose that copies of all his maps would be preserved among the company's papers; but, after inquiry in all the likely places, I have had to give up the hope of finding them.

37. Mr. Codman (p. 41) calls the distance six miles,— a slip.

38. So Humphrey noted. Dearborn speaks of leaving " a sergeant, corporal & 13 men " " to take a Long the Batteau's."

39. Senter states that most of the transports were left at Colburn's; but (1) Oswald (September 23d) recorded that "all the vessels weighed anchor, and stood up the river, and anchored above five miles short

of Fort Western," and (2) we know that Dearborn, Stocking, Morison, Haskell, and ·Melvin sailed beyond Colburn's.

40. Every one of the 13 journalists who allude to their arrival at Fort Western (except Haskell) records arriving on the 23d or earlier, and he was only three miles below that point on Saturday night. It is important to note that time was not wasted. Mr. Codman (p. 41) represents the army as not going to Fort Western until the 24th. To be sure, Humphrey (and, after him, Thayer) speaks of " getting our men up and provisions from gardners town " on the 24th ; but we must conclude that these were a small minority.

V: Pages 84–92

1. Some consider Cushenoc a more correct form.

2. By the river. Mr. Codman (No. 28, table opposite p. 58) calls the distance 58 miles. Provincial " made it 45 miles; Senter, 46; Dearborn and Meigs, 50. The air-line distance is a little less than 40 miles.

3. He was Governor 1741–45, and began a second term in 1753. It was after him that the fort in Pownalborough was named. Fort Western was completed in the early autumn of 1754, equipped with light cannon, and occupied with a small garrison. Governor Shirley then withdrew with his troops.

4. The present arrangement of chimneys, also, is probably not the original one. It seems reasonable to suppose that they were built of stones, for bricks were probably not available here in 1754. I am indebted to Captain Charles E. Nash, of Augusta, for valuable information about Fort Western and the vicinity.

5. These are still used by woodsmen, and are called "splits."

6. The blockhouses were no doubt like the one still standing on the site of Fort Halifax. One of them is said to have existed as late as 1834. Humphrey and Thayer mention the "two large and two small blockhouses."

7. No. 215 states that remains of circumvallation could be traced in 1830.

8. Mr. Codman writes (p. 41): "the army built itself a board camp, as tents were few and wood plenty." This appears to be based upon certain words of Squier's journal: "There made us a Board Camp, wood cut very handy." No doubt boards could be had at Fort Western in 1775. In 1769 Captain Howard himself had built a sawmill about one and a half miles above on the same side of the river, and another mill had been erected by John Jones nearly opposite the fort. But still we can-

not believe that " the *army* " was housed in this way, for
(1) the fact is not mentioned by Oswald, Meigs, Dearborn, Thayer, Melvin, Morison, " Provincial," Stocking,
Senter, Tolman, Henry, or Haskell, and Squier only
says that " we " (*i. e.*, his party or company, as in previous sentences) built a board camp. (2) Haskell remarks that " several [not *all* or *many*] of the companies
have no tents here," but the barrack would lodge two
hundred men, I should say, and we read of men who
slept in private houses, so that the number to be housed
in a board camp would not have been large. (3) We
know that a considerable part of the army were employed in getting stores, etc., up from below, and so the
soldiers probably did not all lodge at Fort Western. (4)
While wood was plenty at Fort Western, boards, we
must suppose, were not, for the two sawmills probably
had but small stocks on hand. And (5) Haskell's
words appear to contradict Mr. Codman's theory,
for he says: " We are very uncomfortable, it being
rainy and cold and nothing to cover us," from which
it is to be inferred that out of " several " companies
which had no tents, a considerable number were left
without shelter. For all these reasons it cannot have
been true that " the army " built itself a " board camp."
Haskell's words indicate also that boards were not
" plenty "; for had they been, no soldiers would have
remained unprotected. The point is worthy of attention, for a great waste of time and muscle would have
been involved in building board cabins for the whole
army for so short a stay. It seems important to
note that, according to the record, Arnold pressed on
energetically.

9. Burned on June 12, 1866.

10. Senter indicates that headquarters were where

Howard's family resided. Dearborn and Meigs also mention Howard's hospitality.

11. The banquet is not mentioned by any of the journalists. Mr. Codman, however, accepts the tradition as history, and enlarges upon it (p. 41). But Arnold did not arrive at Fort Western until Saturday evening, and one whole division left on Monday, not late in the day. As the time when the army would arrive could not be foretold with certainty, the elaborate preparations and invitations to guests at a distance, described by Mr. Codman, were hardly feasible. On Sunday, Arnold was getting two scouting parties off, and Morgan's division was preparing to move,—a great labour; while some of the officers (Thayer and Humphrey, for example) and of course some of the men appear to have been employed in bringing things up from below. Humphrey wrote: "This Day we were busy'd in getting our men up and provisions from gardners town." On Monday, this last labour continued, Morgan's division was getting off, and Greene's division engaged in its final preparations. The amount of labour to be done was very great, and little time for elaborate festivities remained.

Further, had all the soldiers been "marched up" to the tables "to the sound of drum and fife" at "a monstrous barbecue of which three bears were" only "the most conspicuous victims," would not a hint of this event—truly grand for men just leaving the transports and just entering a wilderness—have crept into some one of the many narratives? Finally, Haskell tells us that Sunday, the 24th (the only day when the army was somewhat united), was cold and rainy (Mr. Codman is therefore in error in saying—p. 48—that fine "Indian summer" weather continued till September 29th). We all

know that when a storm comes at the autumnal equinox
it is rather likely to be somewhat long and serious.
"Tables" sufficiently ample to accommodate the army
would have had to be set up out of doors. Would it
have been agreeable to sit out a long feast under such
circumstances? And, even if the three bears could
have been properly barbecued, what would have been
the condition of Mr. Codman's "pumpkin pies"? As
before, it should be made clear that Arnold seems to
have understood the preciousness of time, and to have
kept himself and his army at work.

12. Apparently provisions were accumulated at Colburn's; and probably a part of the stores brought from
Newburyport were loaded into the bateaux at Gardinerston, in the hope that the transports, lightened in this
way, could carry the rest to Fort Western. But the
vessels were all, or nearly all, stopped by the shallow
water, and so had to be completely unloaded at a considerable distance below the Fort.

13. See note 19 on Chapter IV.

14. Arnold and Oswald agree that this party consisted of Steele and six men; but Henry, who belonged
to the number, gives the names of seven besides himself,
Steele and two guides. Henry may be in error, but perhaps Steele chose more men than he was directed to
take.

15. Lake Megantic.

16. Henry gives an account (the only one) of this
expedition. His narrative is full of interesting incidents, but it is so wanting in precision, and so inaccurate
as to dates, that we should gain nothing by attempting
to follow him. A number of his points will be mentioned
later.

17. Nothing seems to be known of Church, not even

his Christian name or his place of residence. He does not appear in Ward's list of the officers who made the march through the wilderness, the list of prisoners appended to Tolman's journal, nor the British list. I have advertised for information in a Vassalborough paper, as well as made many inquiries, but have received no information except that formerly there had been a noted Indian fighter in those parts named Captain Church. It seems natural to conclude that he was a man of the locality, and that his title was similar to Colburn's.

18.   Mr. Codman states (p. 44) that Church was to take the course and distances *of* Dead River; but (1) Oswald's journal says "to," (2) Arnold's letter of September 25th does the same, and (3) that is what Church did.   He was *later* despatched up Dead River.

Mr. Codman represents the two advance parties as going in two canoes (p. 45). But Steele's party had two; and apparently some importance was attached to that fact, for it is mentioned both by Oswald and by Arnold. Possibly the intention was to show that provision was made for the possible loss of a canoe. Such an accident was conceivable; in fact, in this case, both of Steele's canoes were broken.

19.   Strangely enough, Senter thought there were still only three divisions.

20.   In reply, Washington wrote (see also his letter of October 5th to Hancock) to both Arnold and Morgan that he had been misunderstood, if supposed to mean this; but Arnold permitted the arrangement to continue. For Washington's wise letter to Morgan (October 4th), see No. 54, 4, iii., 946.

21.   According to Mr. Codman the army did not reach Fort Western until the 24th, and then "lay" there "for

three days " (p. 41); it would then have been the 27th
or 28th before it began to move.   This would have been
dilatory.   But we have seen that by the evening of the
23d substantially the whole army had arrived.   The first
departures took place early on the 24th, and the four
divisions were scheduled to set out a day apart, beginning with the 25th.   Once again we note that Arnold
was urging things forward with great energy.

We must here note, however, that our authorities disagree in a surprising manner.   Oswald says that Arnold
reached Fort Western at 6 P.M., September 23d; sent
Steele and Church forward on the 24th; and despatched
the riflemen on the 25th, the second division on the 26th,
the third division on the 27th, and a part of the fourth
division on the 28th.   The account is circumstantial,
and seems perfectly consistent with the report of previous days.   Seven of the other journals bearing on the
matter confirm Oswald's reckoning; and Arnold's journal, which begins in the course of September 26th, confirms Oswald's statement that on the 27th the third
division set out.   Evidently Oswald's account must be
accepted.   To be sure, Stocking and Tolman, as already
pointed out in Chapter II., seem from this time on to
place themselves out of the division to which they are
supposed to belong; but this has perhaps been explained,
and, even if the explanation be wrong, their testimony is
not enough to shake Oswald and his support.   Henry
seems clearly to mean that Steele's party left Fort Western on the 23d; but he is so often mistaken about dates
and other details, that we need not regard his statement.

Now, however, comes testimony that we cannot ignore.
Arnold himself wrote Washington a letter that bears the
date of September 25th (No. 54, 4, iii., 960), and in
this he stated that he despatched Steele and Church on

the 23d, that the riflemen went "yesterday," that the
second division would go "today," the third division
"tomorrow," and the rest "the next day," *i. e.*, the 27th.
In short, he put everything one day earlier than Oswald
did.   How shall we explain this?

Did Arnold think that the 26th was the 25th, and
simply misdate his letter?   At first sight this looks probable, and such an error would explain the discrepancies.
Oswald states that Arnold wrote Washington on the 26th;
and the scrap of Arnold's journal for the 26th that has
been preserved has the words "With [possibly a copyist's
error for "write"] his Excellency, etc."

But an entry like that might refer to the completion
and despatch of a letter, and this letter of Arnold's certainly was not completed the day it was begun.   In fact,
on a closer look we find that this proposed explanation
does not answer.   The letter contains a postscript stating that since the preceding part was written, Lieutenant Gray had arrived with the manifestoes; and we know
from Oswald's journal (corroborated by Squier) that
Gray arrived at about 3 o'clock P.M., on the 25th.   Arnold's letter of that date, giving an account of the
despatch of the troops, was therefore written before that
day and hour, and not on the 26th.

So far as one can see, either Arnold blundered amaz-
ingly, or he intended to make Washington feel that he
was getting on more rapidly than he really was.   Washington had been very anxious that no time should be
lost (see article one of Arnold's instructions, No. 54, 4,
iii., 765), and Arnold evidently realised that his progress
had been slower than might be expected.   We shall find
him still later writing to Quebec a misstatement that
was sure to be discovered.   Indeed, this same letter of
September 25th gives an account of the arrival of the

fleet in the Kennebec which conceals the fact that two of the transports went up the wrong river.

In favour of the theory that Arnold simply blundered about things going on under his eyes and under his orders, it may be urged that later he forwarded to Washington a journal which did not agree with his letter. But Arnold was hasty and rash; and in the midst of the confusion he could easily forget just what he had written Washington, or trust that should Washington discover the disagreement, it could be explained as an accident.

Does this discredit his journal? I think not. His journal is particularly valuable for details that he would have no desire to misrepresent; we can check its dates by the others, and we do not find any other case like this.

22. A "carrying-place," "carry" or "portage" is a place where boats are carried from one piece of water to another.

23. This was also called the Twelve-mile Carrying-place. The portage over the height of land was in some respects greater than this.

24. Oswald is supported by Dearborn and Meigs. Arnold, in his letter to Washington, stated the point with somewhat less precision : "to clear the roads over the carrying-places." Mr. Codman (p. 45) adds considerably to their duties: "to follow the footsteps of the exploring parties, examining the country along the route, freeing the streams of all impediments to their navigation and removing all obstacles from the road." To free the Kennebec and Dead River of "all impediments to their navigation" would have been a commission worthy of demiurges.

25. Oswald states that the first division took provisions for forty-five days. Arnold in his letter to Washing-

ton, dated September 25th, says the same. Meigs and Dearborn record that the third division took forty-five days' provisions when they left Fort Western. As to the second division we have no direct information except in Arnold's rather loose letter of November 27th ; but, as Arnold states about twenty days later (October 15th) that the three divisions had twenty-five days' supplies, we may conclude (as would be the only rational supposition) that they left Fort Western with an equal stock, as his letter of November 27th says. Dr. Senter tells us, however, under date of October 25th, that "the first companies took only two and three barrels of flour with several of bread, most in a small proportion," and Mr. Codman (p. 46) accepts this account. But (1) Senter was neither an officer nor connected with the commissary department, and often betrays great ignorance as to inside facts (*e. g.*, note 19); (2) it is not easy to believe his story in the face of what we are told by Arnold ; (3) the facts of the march disprove it completely. There were certainly more than two hundred men (probably two hundred and fifty) in Morgan's division, since guides and other helpers went naturally in the front. As the scale of rations, after supplies began to run low, allowed twelve ounces of flour for each man per day, we may infer that at first Morgan's division probably used up a barrel of flour every twenty-four hours. If they took three barrels for each company, their flour would have given out, even if none was damaged, about October 3d. "Several" barrels or casks of dry biscuit or bread would not have lasted long. But there is not the slightest hint of such a state of things. Morison does not mention scantiness of provisions until October 23d, and "Provincial" does not until October 24th ; and they still had enough to last quite a while. The first division doubtless had less than its share of heavy baggage to carry, since it was to hurry forward.

26.   According to Mr. Codman (p. 46) each company had sixteen bateaux, and each bateau was managed by four men ; but (1) since, as he himself states, the forward companies carried much less weight than those in the rear, being regarded as " light infantry," they are not at all likely to have had an equal number of bateaux ; (2) according to Mr. Codman's view (he reckons fourteen companies), 896 men were required to manage the bateaux, while Senter estimated at 600 the number that went by land ; (3) the number of men in a boat cannot have been as precisely fixed as Mr. Codman represents, for the intention was to have each accommodate six or seven with their baggage, Senter says " about five," and Squier speaks of being alone in a bateau; and (4) Mr. Codman seems to disprove himself, for (p. 50) he says : " The bateaux crews were divided into two squads of four men each, the relief marching along the shore," so that 1792 men would be required by his theory.

Stocking, to be sure, makes a remark a month later about the bateaux having been reduced (by accidents) from sixteen to six for each company ; but this cannot be taken literally, for (1) Haskell says his company had only three left on October 24th, (2) the companies would not all lose the same number, and no general equalisation at frequent intervals or at any time was practicable, and (3) Stocking, a private soldier near the front, was in no position to know how companies miles in the rear had been, and were, provided with boats.   Stocking says that only six were carried over the height of land, but we are told that Morgan alone took more than that number. As for the crews, we can only say that in most cases there were probably from three to five men in each bateau.

27.   The journey of the troops will be studied in detail
presently ;   the object here is to give a general idea of
their progress.   Aaron Burr and "several other gentlemen " (Senter) went with Greene.

28.   Mr. Codman appears to take leave of Colburn at
this point, after representing him as one of Enos's
captains (p. 45).   The family tradition is that Colburn
returned with Enos.   This seems every way probable,
and agrees with Dearborn's statement (Chapter III.,
note 10).   In that case he was as truly with Enos, and,one
of his captains at the time of the council as at any previous time.   But on page 80 Mr. Codman writes : "the
three captains of his [*i. e.*, Enos's] Division, McCobb,
Williams, and Scott, held an informal council."   Colburn's company does not, in fact, appear anywhere as an
integral part of the army.   Arnold never refers to it in
that way, and Meigs spoke, October 12th, of "the 4th
Division of the army [with which Colburn marched],
consisting of three companies of musketmen."   Reuben
Colburn did not leave Gardinerston before September
30th (Chapter III., note 16).

29.   Very likely some of those ordered by Arnold
himself after he reached Colburn's, for they were not
paid for until September 30th.

30.   Apparently Colburn's company also.   Some
difficulties meet us here.   1. Oswald's journal does not
agree with Arnold's.   Oswald says, September 28th:
"Part of the fourth and last Division, McCobb's and
Scott's companies, embarked," but Arnold records,
September 29th, " Capt. McCobb's and Scott's companies
march at 10 A.M."   Squier, of Scott's, states that they
paraded on the 28th, intending to march, but proved
not ready.   The two accounts may be partially reconciled by supposing that some of McCobb's men left on

the 28th, but not all; and this seems in line with
Arnold's letter of September 29th: "forward on   .   .   .
the remainder of Capt. McCobb's."   2.   Oswald's journal and Arnold's journal do not agree with Arnold's
letters.   September 28th the journals noted : "Sent for
Col. Enos and the Commissary to come up from Colburn's with all the men and batteaus (boats)."   Now we
have letters to a similar effect from Arnold to these
gentlemen, and they are dated September 29th (No. 106,
i., pp. 358, 359).   But we may suppose that Arnold sent
written or verbal orders on the 28th, and the next day, as
he was leaving Fort Western, repeated the orders in writing.   Again, September 28th Oswald noted : "ordered
the sick and criminal on board the Broad Bay," but we
find Arnold directing Enos and Farnsworth on the 29th
to put the sick on the *Broad Bay.*   This discrepancy
may be explained in the same way as the previous
one.   A repetition of orders is not unusual.   In fact
Arnold's journal records the same orders as given on
the 27th and on the 28th.—viz., that the boats should be
sent up.

Mr. Codman says (p. 47): "That same morning [*i. e.*,
September 29th] the fourth Division, delayed in collecting provisions and finishing bateaux, left Colburn's shipyard"; but (1) as we have seen, Arnold and Oswald
agree in representing most of the fourth division as
having left Fort Western by about 10 A.M. of the 29th,
and there is no probability that they had already made
the nine hard miles from Colburn's that morning; (2)
Squier, the only journalist in that division, proves that
his company were at Fort Western on the 28th; (3) we
have no evidence that the men were "collecting" provisions except in the sense of moving them to Fort Western; and (4) there is nothing to show that soldiers were

employed on the construction of the bateaux; Arnold says some "were detained for Battoes to be mended, oars, paddles etc., etc."

31. James McCormick of Goodrich's company, who had killed Sergeant Reuben Bishop of Williams's company (the only man lost so far) and had been condemned to death by a court-martial, was sent to Washington for final judgment; the commissary was ordered to forward what provisions were left to Fort Halifax, to store there "such as the batteaux carry on," and to see that Howard should take good care of any articles remaining at Fort Western; Enos was directed to follow the route, ordering on the able-bodied stragglers, bringing with him the carpenters of Captain Colburn's company, and taking along all the provisions the bateaux would carry. Squier mentions that five men were punished for various offences on the 27th.

32. Mr. Codman speaks (p. 35) of Arnold's taking these with him from Cambridge; but (1) a letter from Joseph Reed to Arnold shows that they were despatched September 20th by the hand of Lieutenant Gray, (2) the postscript of Arnold's letter of September 25th mentions that Gray brought them, and (3) Oswald records that Lieutenant Gray arrived about 3 P.M., September 25th, "with a number of manifestoes."

33. Mr. Codman states (p. 47) that Arnold left Fort Western on the 28th, and was rowed by two Indians; but (1) both Arnold and Oswald record that he left on the 29th, (2) neither of them says that he was conducted by Indians, though he may have been, and (3) the Indians whom Arnold expected had not arrived (letter to Enos, September 29th).   As to (1) Arnold, and Oswald are corroborated by a comparison of their accounts of September 30th with Meigs's.

The word "pettiauger" of Arnold's journal is meant, I suppose, for periauger (pirogue, dugout).

34. One mystery remains. "Higgins" (or "Higgens") set out (apparently from Newburyport) by land with some Indians, but had not arrived when Arnold left Fort Western, and Enos was directed to hurry the Indians forward when they should appear. What Indians were these? I take it they were envoys from St. François (St. Francis) on the St. Lawrence, who had recently made a visit to Washington's camp. The bearing of this will be seen later (Chapter VIII., note 35).

35. Mr. Codman (p. 41) speaks of the army as lying at Fort Western to make "final preparations for their march,—at this, the last place where supplies might be obtained in the least adequate to their needs." He cannot mean that supplies could be transported to Fort Western and there delivered to the troops, for this would be true of Fort Halifax, or Vassalborough; but that stores of supplies adequate for the army existed, and were kept on hand, at Fort Western. This, however, was by no means the case. There was not the least occasion for maintaining there stocks "adequate" for a force of 1050 men.

In another place (p 51) Mr. Codman speaks of Fort Western as Arnold's "weak base of supplies." But Arnold wrote the commissary on September 29th from Fort Western: "You will forward on all the provisions [that are] here as fast as possible to Ft. Halifax, and such as the batteaux carry on, order stored there," so that Fort Halifax, rather than Fort Western, was the "weak base of supplies," though as the events showed, it was not in reality any base at all.

The surgeon's mate, sick with the dysentery, was left at Fort Western.

1. That was understood to be the distance, but perhaps this estimate was half a mile too large.

2. Sleds were used at Norridgewock Falls.

3. As already shown, the number of men in a bateau varied,—at least in the statements of the journalists. The bateaux were not all of the same size, and some doubtless carried more freight than others. .

4. 220 bateaux were constructed, and, although some had to be left behind for the transportation of stores to Fort Halifax, the army may be assumed to have taken more than 200 with it. If we allow four men to each, less than 250 are left to go by land, so that there could not be an equal division of the army into crews and relief-crews. To be sure, some country-people were helping the army, but on the other hand the officers probably did no regular work as bateaumen.

5. Vassalborough began to be settled in 1760. Eight years later it could boast of ten families, and the town records show that in 1775, twenty-five voters attended the town meeting. The chief settlement in the town was called Gatchell's (Getchell's) Corner, after the first family that came there (this is now Vassalborough proper). The Fort Halifax road went through it. Of the Getchells who served Arnold we have already heard. Dennis was captain of the town in 1774, and John, an active and soon-to-be-wealthy business man. The name is said to have been usually pronounced Gatchell or Gitchell in former times. See note 18 on Chapter IV.

6. Arnold's name was Three Mile Falls; Oswald's, Six Mile Falls.

As Washington's order of September 5th (Chapter III.), shows, the importance of enlisting experienced bateaumen was understood. Apparently they could not be obtained, for Arnold wrote Washington, October 13th : "The men in general, not understanding batteaux, have been obliged to wade & haul, etc."

7.   A Latin inscription indicated that the name was a compliment to the Earl of Halifax.

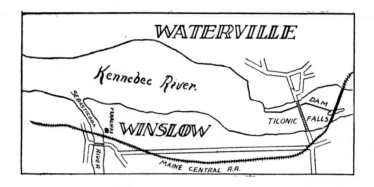

8.   As early as September, 1763, a trading post was established here.

9.   This redoubt was a blockhouse, surrounded with a palisade and perhaps a ditch, 61½ rods distant from the main fort.   The upper story of the blockhouse was twenty feet square.

10.   Lithgow was appointed by Governor Shirley before leaving the ground.   See No. 106, viii., p. 221.

11.   This was 960 feet from the main fort, 34 feet square, 2 stories high, with a sentry box on the top, and a twelve-pound howitzer that was fired every morning and night.   Mr. T. O. Paine has maintained that the two redoubts were 635 feet apart ; but we cannot be perfectly sure as to their positions.

12.   See No. 106, viii., p. 241.   A conjectural and doubtless incorrect picture of Fort Halifax may be found

on p. 198.   On p. 272 the two plans of the fort are given, and on p. 281 is a picture of the corner-stone with the inscription (now preserved in the State House at Augusta).

13.   Within the past few years a new roof has been put on it, and it has been otherwise repaired.   Originally the centre post, about six inches square, projected some four feet above the roof.   Like Fort Western, Fort Halifax was built of heavy pine timber.

14.   Lithgow remained for some time as a trader. Then he removed to Georgetown (p. 70).

15.   Some other names appear in the journals, and evidently a number of people resided in this locality ; but more than this cannot be said.   What are now known as Winslow, Waterville, and Oakland were then covered by the name Winslow (incorporated in 1771) ; but the town records make no mention of Arnold's expedition, and give no indication of the population at this time.

The gap in the quotation from Montresor is due to a break in the MS.

16.   This name appears in the journals in various forms : Taconic, Tacunnick, Ticonnick, Ticonic, Ticonick, Toconock.   Perhaps the correct spelling is none of these, for Tuconet, Ticonnet, or Taconnet is said to be the true word.   But it seems hardly worth while to spend time on the niceties of Indian orthography in this case or in other cases.   The territory around Fort Halifax is said to have been the seat of a tribe of Abenakis (or Abnakis) from whom the falls took their name.   Another version is that there were four chiefs who bore this name, the last of whom died in 1765.   See the Vassalborough (Me.) *Times*, June 17, 1902.

As Ticonic Falls were half a mile long, the statement of the text that they ran over ledges half a mile above Fort Halifax must, of course, be taken broadly.

17. Mr. Codman says (No. 28, p. 46) : " As they approached the Three Mile Falls, below Fort Halifax, the
crews of the bateaux were obliged continually to spring
out into the river and wade—often up to their chins in
water, most of the time to their waists. At the foot of
the falls a landing was made and the provisions and
bateaux carried around the rapids " ; but no carrying
was done at Three Mile Falls ; this is perfectly clear,
particularly because a number of the journalists state
that at Ticonic Falls was the first, or at Skowhegan Falls
was the second portage. Arnold seems possibly to give
Mr. Codman some support, for he says : " Arrived at
Ft. Halifax, where I found Capt. Dearborn's and Goodrich's companies just over the falls which are at 60 rods
over. Good carrying-place." But (1) a carry of sixty
rods would not have taken them around the Three Mile
Falls, and (2) Dearborn recorded : " Proceeded up the
river four miles to Ft. Halifax *against a very rapid stream*,
where we arrived at 11 o'clock A.M.," *i. e.*, he did not
carry around the Three Mile Falls. Arnold must therefore have said " Ft. Halifax " in a loose way, and have
referred to Ticonic Falls.

18. Mr. Codman says that the men " inserted two
handspikes under the flat bottom " (p. 50), but we have
no reason to think there was anything on the bottom
into which the handspikes could be inserted. Morison's
words are : " The method of carrying our bateaus was
by placing handspikes under them, carried by four men
alternately [in turn ?]."

19. Senter so states. Of course the present dam has
changed the aspect of the river.

20. The figures for the length of the carrying-place
differ widely. They are : Morison and Tolman, 40 rods;
Stocking and " Provincial," about 40 ; Squier, about 50 ;

Arnold, 60 ; Humphrey and Thayer, about 80 ; Dearborn and Meigs, 97 ; Haskell, 120.

21.   The first and third .divisions, as we have seen, left Fort Western with provisions for forty-five days ; the second had the same, no doubt ; the rear was supposed to have still more.   See note 25 on Chapter V.

22.   Or else of bread or biscuit.   Very likely this. is an underestimate, for at this time the men probably ate more than is suggested.

23.   Mr. Codman speaks of " extra muskets and rifles " (p. 47) ; but we have no evidence that such were carried. On the other hand we find Henry lamenting desperately lest the accidental loss of his weapon should compel him to go back with the invalids, and correspondingly elated when he found himself able to buy a damaged rifle at a high price from a man who was returning.   As is well-known, the Continental authorities had the utmost difficulty at this time to provide their soldiers with guns. Would they be likely to send an extra supply where it was practically certain that more or less of the men would soon be falling out, and might be induced to leave their arms behind, or, if necessary, compelled to do so, as was done in less urgent cases ?

The estimate of ammunition may seem, and very possibly is, too small.   The intention has been to avoid exaggerating the weight ; and besides, since Arnold planned to surprise Quebec and then coöperate with Schuyler, he may have taken a light burden of ammunition, expecting to replenish his stock after reaching Canada.   A great weight of it was highly undesirable.

24.   Arnold, in his letter of August 21st to Colburn, estimated the baggage at one hundred pounds per man. This would be a total of about fifty-three tons.   If we add forty tons for the boats, and allow for oars, paddles, and

poles, we get about one hundred tons in this way also.
The estimate of forty tons for the bateaux allows for
those lighter than the standard and those left behind to
carry provisions to Ft. Halifax, etc.

Mr. Codman says with reference to "carrying" the
bateaux (p. 46) : "Here, and *at all the other carrying-
places*, the bateaux had first to be unloaded"; but it is
evident that the bateaux were sometimes carried with
their lading (see Morison, October 12th). This was
very sensible, if the carry was short and the load light.
With reference to the transportation of the other things,
he says (p. 47) that they all "had to be packed across
on the men's backs, for they had no pack animals"; but
there were draught cattle, and these could move such
articles on carts, "drags," or sleds. Arnold states that
"baggage" was transported at Norridgewock Falls on
sleds drawn by oxen. Humphrey also mentions these
sleds. Senter mentions "teams," etc.

25. According to "Provincial" and Morison, the first
division went around Ticonic Falls on the 27th; Thayer
advanced three miles beyond them on the 28th; and
most, but not all, of the third division passed on the 29th.
Melvin speaks of going over on the 30th.

26. This form of expression is not intended to imply
that Arnold's journal was written by his own hand. That
question was touched upon in Chapter II.

27. Ticonic Falls are at Waterville. Fairfield comes
next on the north, and it is stated that in passing this
town the river falls thirty-four feet (No. 199). Here
are the chief manufacturing establishments of the Kennebec (No. 199). The total descent of the river in one
hundred miles above Fort Western is given as 1070 feet.

28. Fairfield began to be occupied in 1774 (No. 199).
The settlement was at East Fairfield. Here was Pishon's

ferry, with houses east of it, also.   Thayer records that straggling, *i. e.* deserting, began here.

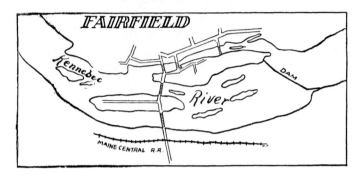

At this point we find the accounts of Arnold and Meigs disagreeing.   They camped together September 30th ; according to Arnold the camp was six and one-half miles from Fort Halifax, while according to Meigs it was twelve.   Meigs is wrong, for his reckoning would make the distance from Fort Halifax to Skowhegan Falls too large.

Mr. Codman's narrative would suggest an inadequate idea of the difficulty of the Five Mile Ripples, for (p. 48) he represents Arnold as camping above the Ripples with men whom he had met below the Ripples in the forenoon, *i. e.*, they went as fast by water as he with Crosier's team did by land.   They were in fact different men, though they belonged to the same division.   Meigs, with whom Arnold camped, had passed the Ripples the day before.

29.   This word is said to mean Place of Watch, and has been thought to have reference to the fishing.   A part of the Canaan of 1775 still bears that name, but it does not touch the Kennebec.

In Thayer's journal we find these rather odd words:

"The People call this place Canaan; a Canaan Indeed!" They would naturally be taken as ridiculing
the idea that Skowhegan resembled the "promised land."
Humphrey, however, while using similar language,
seems to convey the opposite impression: "the people
call this place Canaan, a canaan indeed for here is as
good land as I ever saw" etc. Perhaps Thayer misunderstood Humphrey's meaning, or had a different
opinion; or, possibly, Thayer did not intend his language
to be taken as ironical.

30. This I have from the grandson of one of the two
men. They were brothers named Weston. There is no
reason to disbelieve the tradition. (Arnold mentions
dining at "Western's," three miles below Skowhegan
Falls.) Both patriotism and self-interest would induce
able-bodied settlers to aid the troops. No doubt a
considerable, though constantly diminishing, number of
settlers attached themselves to the army while it was
within the borders of civilisation, and it can even be believed, as tradition affirms, that some of them marched
all the way to Quebec.

31. Mr. Codman says (p. 49) that after Greene's
division had passed the Five Mile Ripples, the river
"led them for 18 miles through a fertile country" and
they "encamped . . . three or four miles from the
next carry." This would make the distance from Ticonic
Falls to Skowhegan Falls twenty-six or twenty-seven
miles. (It is about twelve miles farther to Old Norridgewock. In his table, opposite p. 58, the *whole distance* is
given as nine miles.) It was in fact reckoned as twenty-
one miles between the two falls, but may be a mile less
than that.

Mr. Codman (p. 51) says: "Sept. 30 and Oct. 1, the
second division consumed in the herculean task of pass-

ing between the Falls of Skowhegan, and in ascending
'Bumbazee's Rips,' 7 miles to Norridgewock, which they
reached at noon"; which would seem to imply that
these rips were seven miles in length, and extended from
Skowhegan Falls to Norridgewock; but (1) Bombazee
Rips (Rapids) are only a few rods long; (2) they are
about seven and three-fourths miles above Skowhegan
Falls; (3) they are about three and three-fourths miles
below Old Norridgewock, while about two and three-
fourths miles above the Norridgewock of to-day; (4)
the total distance from Skowhegan Falls to Old Norridgewock was therefore about eleven and one-half miles;
but (5) the place at which Thayer says that he arrived
"about 12 o'clock," October 1st, was Norridgewock
Falls, nearly or quite a mile beyond Old Norridgewock,
and (6) the division as a whole did not reach that
point at all on October 1st, for according to Oswald,
Arnold "overtook Col. Greene, Major Bigelow, Capt.
Topham, and company" on October *second*, about six
miles below Norridgewock Falls. This, however, brings
us to a perplexing point. While Thayer says that
he reached Norridgewock Falls at noon on October
1st, Oswald states that he overtook Thayer at Skowhegan Falls at four o'clock P.M. that day. Which is
right? On examining Thayer's journal closely, we discover that it represents him as doing in three and one-
half or four days what Dearborn did in five. Next,
turning to Humphrey, we find two entries for October
2d, and none for October 1st. The two accounts might
be true of the same day,—one for the forenoon, the
other for the afternoon, but the first of them appears
under the date of October 1st in Thayer's journal. Accepting Humphrey's account as it stands, we find that
Thayer required four and one-half or five days to do

what Dearborn did in five (certainly much more probable), and that he was at Skowhegan Falls on October 1st,
as Oswald states.   It was, then, about noon on October
2d when he reached Norridgewock Falls.   This looks
the more reasonable because Oswald shows that Greene
did not reach that point until about midday, October
2d, and it is not likely that Thayer was twenty-four
hours in advance of his immediate superior.   It seems
plain that Thayer, finding in Humphrey's journal two
entries for Oct. 2nd and none for Oct. 1st, thought he
could improve the record.

Arnold called it twelve miles from Skowhegan Falls
to Norridgewock Falls, but the loggers' estimate (the
best we have) adds about half a mile.

Doctor Senter's journal is rather puzzling just here.
He mentions the Wassarunskeig Falls.   There are no such
falls in the Kennebec, but the Wesserunsett (formerly
the Wesserunsic) River goes over some high falls about
two miles before emptying into the Kennebec.   Senter
appears to mean that, as the Kennebec made a large
bend, across which ran a carrying-place, he decided to
go over by land in order to avoid the swift water ; that
the carrying-place took him to the foot of the falls in the
Wesserunsett ; that he crossed this river, carried past
the falls on the other side, and then carried on to the
Kennebec above the bend.

Senter's obscurity may fairly suggest, perhaps, that his
account was written some time after the events.   The
same inference may be drawn from the fact that he makes
the distance from Skowhegan Falls to Old Norridgewock
only five miles, and does not mention Bombazee Rips.

32.   Indeed, the opposite is suggested by Humphrey :
"proceeded towards the aforesaid falls Through rapid
water " ; and also, less clearly, by Dearborn.

33. Mr. Codman states (p. 49) that the fall *was* twenty-three feet high, but it cannot have been. The present dam has greatly emphasised the fall at this point,

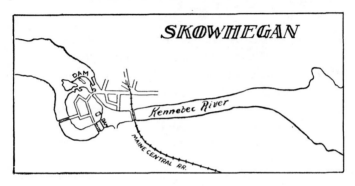

of course, since it concentrates a descent formerly distributed over several miles.   The river above is now like a mill-pond for a long distance, whereas Arnold recorded, "small falls and quick water." The total descent at Skowhegan — the falls and the half-mile below — is said to be twenty-eight feet. Besides Squhegan we find in the journals Scohegin, Scowhegan, Cohigin, Cohiggin, Cohegan, and Schouhegan.

34. Mr. Codman adds to the difficulties (p. 49) : "the heavy bateaux had to be hoisted and dragged up the steep rocky banks while the men struggled in the fierce rush of the swirling current " ; but (1) the current, being parted by the island, leaves a comparatively quiet place, of course, at its lower end, where the bateaux were taken from the water, and (2) it is difficult to see how the men could have been struggling in the river while they were going up steep, high banks.

35. But Meigs called it 250 paces ; Melvin, 40 rods.

36. This, reported by Thayer, was on the night of the 29th ; but by October 2d rain was again falling.

Humphrey tells it differently : "last night it froze so
Hard as to freeze our wet cloaths that we did not Lie
upon." The men are said by Thayer and Humphrey to
have " encamped on the main [mainland ?] on the west
side." This would not be the right, but the left, bank,
since the course of the river is here from the south-west.

37. "Bombazee" (formerly Bombazeene or Boma-
zeene, and spelled in still other ways) is said to come from
the name of Bomazeen, a great orator of the Kennebec
tribe, who was shot here. His residence was at Gardiner.
" Rips " means ripples (rapids).

38. This name also is spelled in various ways. The
form Norridgewog is preferred by some as the name of
the Indians of this region (simply those Kennebecs who
dwelt here, just as the Kennebecs were simply those
Abenakis who resided about the Kennebec River). The
Indian name of the village was Nanrantsouak. In the
journals we find such corruptions of the name as Nor-
ridgewalt or -walk, Norridge Walk, and Norrywok. Old
Norridgewock is now in the town of Starks,— not in the
town of Norridgewock at all.

39. See note 7 on Chapter I.

40. From Dearborn's account it would appear that
two or three families lived between Skowhegan Falls and
Norridgewock Falls, but that only one was living at Old
Norridgewock when the troops passed that point.

41. The loggers call it a mile ; Meigs said "about a
mile " ; Dearborn thought the distance only half a mile.
I should reckon it a short mile.

42. Oswald called it eleven and one-half miles from
Skowhegan Falls to Norridgewock Falls, while Arnold
thought it twelve miles to " Norrigewalk " (evidently referring to the falls). Dearborn called it twelve and one-
half to the falls, and this estimate seems about correct.

1. Of course the army would follow the military road here, especially as their starting point was on that side of the river.

2. Haskell expressly mentions going to Fort Halifax by land and crossing at that point. Crossing was necessary, for those who went by land were expected to help at the carrying-places, and this carrying-place was on the west side.

3. At present the highway on the eastern bank does not follow the river, presumably because there are obstructions, but the road on the other side does follow it. The inference is that better marching was to be found on the latter side. By going this way, the troops saved themselves the trouble of crossing the Wesserunsett River.

4. It seems clear that they did not march to Norridgewock Falls on the right bank, for (1) the left bank was shorter, (2) Dearborn mentions particularly the character of the land on the north (*i. e.*, left) side of the river, (3) Haskell speaks of encamping at Norridgewock, and this must mean the site of the Indian village (on the left bank), for he did not come to the falls until the next day, (4) Meigs passed the night at old Norridgewock village, which confirms our belief that a camp was there, and therefore that the army passed that way, and (5) we hear nothing about crossing Sandy River, which came in from the west. Thayer's and Humphrey's accounts seem inconsistent with this, for they did not see the village until after they arrived at the falls. But it is only necessary to suppose that they went by water, and this is probable.

The word "army" referring to the footmen at this

stage of the march will, of course, be understood as a convenient equivalent for "that portion of the army which went by land."

5.   The carrying-place at Norridgewock Falls was on the west side, for (1) Henry expressly says so ; (2) Arnold camped on the west side, and of course he needed to be on the same bank as the portage in order to supervise the operations ; (3) the same is true of Humphrey and Thayer ; (4) Meigs, after describing Norridgewock village, speaks of crossing to the carrying-place, and the village was certainly on the east side ; (5) from the nature of the ground one would think the west side must have offered the better way ; (6) toward the upper end of Norridgewock Falls the river turns sharply to the west, so that the distance by the west side was the shorter one.

6.   See No. 199.

7.   Arnold wrote " 1500 yards " ; Melvin, " about a mile " ; Morison, " a mile and 60 perches " ; Meigs, Dearborn, Stocking, " Provincial," Haskell, and Tolman, a mile and a quarter ; Humphrey and Thayer, "about" a mile and a quarter ; Squier, a mile and a half.

8.   Some of the oxen belonged to the army, perhaps, for later we find army oxen slaughtered for food ; but a good many must have been required to draw loaded sleds over bare ground and rocks.   Morris Fling helped here, no doubt.

9.   Senter says it all had to be discarded, but this is evidently an exaggeration.

10.   Each division in turn moved as soon as it was ready.   Mr. Codman states (p. 52) that " on Oct. 4 the leading companies began to push forward," but Arnold, Oswald, " Provincial," and Morison agree that the rifle-

men advanced on the 3d. He remarks also (p. 53) that
the fourth division arrived at Carritunk Falls on the
eighth ; but Squier did not reach that point until the
tenth. Further, on the night of the ninth, McCobb
camped about two miles below these falls, and Scott
was behind McCobb (Arnold and Oswald).   Arnold's
letter to Enos of September 29th indicates that
Williams also was behind McCobb. Further we know
that a part of the *third* division did not pass these falls
until the ninth.

On p. 62 Mr. Codman refers to a " base of supplies "
at Norridgewock ; but we find Arnold ordering the
commissary to forward the surplus provisions to Fort
Halifax, and then ordering them forwarded to the Great
Carrying-place (Arnold to Farnsworth, September 29th
and October 14th).   At these points there was a chance
to shelter and protect them, but there was none, so far as
we are informed, at Norridgewock, and we find no mention by Arnold of the latter place.   See also note 18 on
Chapter X.

Under date of the seventh, Senter makes the following record :   " By a council of the officers it was
thought advisable to send letters into Quebec informing
some gentlemen of that city of our movements, etc.
After the despatches were wrote it was concluded to
send one Mr. Jackquith, inhabitant of this river and
native of Germany, who spoke the French language, in
company with two Penobscot Indians, by name Sabattis
and Enneos."

Mr. Codman (p. 122) appears to accept this as
correct, for he says of the Indians who met Arnold
November 4th : "Among them also was Eneas, who with
Sabattis had been despatched express from Norridgewock with letters to Quebec."   But (1) this incident is

not mentioned by Arnold, Oswald, Meigs, Dearborn, or any other journalist; (2) "Jackquith" was no doubt Jaquin, of a French Huguenot family that settled in Pownalborough (C. E. Allen, historian of Dresden); (3) Sabatis is said by Henry (No. 72, p. 74) to have been a brother of Natanis, and the latter was a Norridgewock, not a Penobscot Indian (Henry was probably mistaken, however); (4) no real council of officers could have been held at Norridgewock on the seventh, for all the principal officers except Enos had gone on; (5) no such letter of Arnold's, dated October seventh, is in existence; (6) Arnold's journal contradicts Senter, for it states (and so does Oswald's) that Eneas was sent to Quebec on October 13th; and we have the letter bearing that date; (7) Arnold refers more than once in later letters to this one of the thirteenth but never to one of the seventh; (8) Mr. Codman, without observing the inconsistency, sends Eneas off on the thirteenth (p. 62) as well as on the seventh.

It is evident that Senter records under date of the seventh an incorrect version of what occurred on the thirteenth, and this is a very serious reflection upon his journal. Later we shall try to find out what was done on the thirteenth. Senter's Account seems to have repeated the error of the journal about this matter, but there is a gap in the MS. at this point. No other journalist blundered in this way.

11. Thayer speaks expressly of crossing the river, October 3d, but too much weight must not be given to this fact. The tradition is that the army marched past Carritunk Falls on the eastern bank, but Humphrey camped there on the other side. If it had remained on the west side, we should pretty surely find something in the journals about getting over the Carrabasset River

(Seven Mile Stream), which is quite wide for several miles from the Kennebec. On the other side there was no river to cross. Above Carritunk Falls the topography is such that it would have been scarcely possible to march to the Great Carrying-place on the west side.

12. The distance from Norridgewock Falls to Carritunk Falls is given as follows : Arnold, eighteen miles; Dearborn, eighteen miles ; " Provincial," nineteen miles; Haskell, nineteen miles ; Morison, nineteen miles. These estimates are substantially identical. Senter, .owever, makes it thirteen miles, and—curiously enough—this is the distance reckoned now by the loggers. It seems pretty certain that the neck of land which Arnold crossed has been cut through since 1775 by current and logs, and that the extra distance around what is now an island would have been a good mile ; so that Senter was not quite right. Mr. Codman (p. 52) gives the distance as eighteen miles.

13. The journalists have several names: Carratuncas, Carratunker, Caratuncah, Carritunkus, Carrytuck or Devil's, Divell's (Squier), Tentucket, Tintucket, Hellgate. Morison called them, by a slip, " Ticonic or Hellgate." The length of the carry is variously given : Arnold, " near 50 rods " ; Meigs, 433 paces ; Dearborn, ninety-five rods ; Morison, sixty perches ; several journalists, about forty rods ; Haskell, half a mile ; Humphrey and Thayer, about 8 rods. Dearborn's company passed these falls October 8th, at 3 o'clock, P. M.; Ward's passed them October 9th, at noon. The present spelling is either Carritunk or Carratunk.

14. Arnold observed here " a great number of small islands which appear very fertile " ; and he was not the only one to do so. Humphrey and Thayer speak of the

22

Seven Islands, on the east side of the river about seven miles above Carritunk Falls.

15. This is according to tradition, particularly a tradition in the Getchell family ; but the tradition is fully confirmed by topography. *Logan* is, I presume, a corruption of *lagoon.*

16. Melvin states that he arrived on the ninth, and Humphrey says that " two Companyes of the other Batallion " (*i.e.*, the third division) came that day. " Provincial " and Morison agree that they arrived on the seventh. Morgan very likely came the day before. Mr. Codman is thus in error (p. 54) in placing the arrival of the second division on the ninth, for Humphrey and Topham arrived on the seventh, and in placing the " appearance " of Meigs's division on the 10th.

The distance from Carritunk Falls to the Great Carrying-place is not given by Arnold, Oswald, Meigs, Dearborn, Senter, Melvin, Humphrey, Thayer, or Stocking. Haskell made it four miles by water plus fourteen miles by land. Morison estimated that it was eighteen miles. " Provincial " and Tolman called it twenty miles ; Squier, twenty or twenty-one by land. Getchell and Berry reckoned it as eighteen. The best estimate that I have been able to obtain makes it seventeen and one-half. The whole distance from Norridgewock Falls to the Great Carrying-place was therefore, in 1775, fourteen plus seventeen and one-half ; total, thirty-one and one-half. Mr. Codman makes it thirty-seven in his table of distances (opposite p. 58).

17. It is not in reality a conical peak, but the end of a long mountain, in line with which Arnold stood. Likewise the turn in the river is in fact slight, though seen from below it appears as Arnold states. A farmer half a mile above has ploughed up articles which have

suggested to him that some of the soldiers camped there, but this does not seem at all probable. To arrive at his place, they would have had to ascend rapids which have a vertical fall of about seven feet, and they would not have undertaken such a labour needlessly.

18. Others affirm that the initials on the rock were B. A., and some declare that Arnold's own hand cut them !

19. There were, however, some cases of diarrhœa and dysentery.

VIII : Pages 117–134.

1. Henry wrote in connection with crossing the Great Carrying-place: "Here are neither oaks, hickories, poplars, maples nor locusts; but there is a great variety of other kinds of excellent timber, such as the white and yellow pines, hemlock, cedar, cypress, and all the species of the firs " (No. 72, p. 25). His testimony is valuable on a general matter like this, and the other journalists confirm it. Melvin remarks of the third portage of the Great Carrying-place: "The woods are cedar and hemlock." Meigs says the third pond was surrounded with cedars. The last part of the fourth portage was called a spruce swamp by Dearborn, and a spruce and cedar swamp by Senter. October 3d, Stocking recorded that they were entering woods mostly of pines and hemlocks, with patches of spruce and fir. Other testimony might be added. The untouched forests of the region are still of this kind. There were, however, a good many birches in spots, no doubt. There is a note on p. 49 of No. 72 which is contrary to all this, but the writer must have been mistaken or have made a slip of the pen.

2. Lieutenant Church surveyed the route from the

Kennebec to Dead River, and Arnold gives his figures, so that it seems unnecessary to discuss others for this carrying-place, though when it is a matter of guessing, all opinions may be worth consideration. Church was sent forward from Fort Western, as already noted. Arnold met him and received his report at the Great Carrying-place on October 11th, but Church had been waiting three days. Church's figures for the first portage were three and one-quarter miles. The measured distance from the Kennebec to Arnold Camp (Lane's) is three and one-half miles and thirty-eight rods (*i. e.*, about three and three-eighths to the pond).

The map of the Great Carrying-place presented here is by no means scientifically accurate, but gives, I think, a fairly correct idea. It is based upon my own investigations and the reports of trustworthy and competent guides.

3. Mr. Codman (No. 28, p. 56) represents Arnold's men as bearing " further to the north " than the present route to Arnold Camp ; but this is because he held that the lake was a mile wide where they crossed it,—a view which, as we shall see presently, has no foundation. Is it conceivable that the soldiers would carry the bateaux and baggage, when these could be put into a lake and rowed? They would certainly seek the nearest point of the pond, and, as the course was 27° north of west, while the shore of the pond runs north at that part, this point was the south-eastern extremity. Again, had the trail borne more to the north, it would probably have been longer than Church made it.

4. Mr. Codman states (p. 56) that the trail was "well worn," but in that case there would have been no need of snagging and blazing. In another place, however, he says that the army found here " scarcely so much as an

imperfectly blazed trail" (p. 57). Morison, one of the advance party, called the way "trackless," but he was always looking out for effect.

5. October 3d, according to both Arnold and Oswald. "Provincial" gives that date for Hendricks's company.

6. Humphrey and Topham arrived that day. Mr. Codman says that if the riflemen had been "transported by magic" from Fort Western to the Great Carrying-place they would hardly have had time to cut their way through to the first pond (p. 57). This is worth looking into, for in that case Arnold was reprehensible for ordering anything so absurdly impossible as what the riflemen were told to do.

A road for the army needed to be eight feet wide, so that men carrying bateaux (the carriers stood at the ends of the bateaux, of course) could move in one direction, while empty-handed men filed past in the other; but, to make perfectly sure, let us assume that the road had to be of twice that width. The length of it was three and one-quarter miles, or ten hundred and forty rods. The number of working men in the three companies we will call two hundred and forty. Each man would have had, then, four and one-third rods of road to clear.

According to as good an authority as I could find, the trees may have stood as near together as four feet here in 1775, and have averaged a foot in diameter. This would have made it necessary to cut and clear away about fourteen trees in each rod of the road. An experienced "logger" tells me that this work would take seven hours. To clear four and one-third rods, then, would have required less than four days. But, had the riflemen been "transported by magic" to the point where their labours began, their axes would have been swinging on September 25th, and they would have had twelve days for the work. It should be added that the trail now passes, and probably passed then, for a long distance over smooth ledges where trees could not grow, so that much less work than here estimated needed to be done.

Mr. Codman represents the soldiers (p. 58) as "hacking with tomahawk and hunting-knife" at the "giants of the forest"; but, in the absence of evidence to the contrary, we may assume that they were adequately supplied with axes, especially as it was fully understood beforehand that they were to make their way through forests. Besides, what woodsmen like Morgan's soldiers would have undertaken to cut down a four-foot hemlock with a hunting-knife ?

7.   So Morison's journal and Senter's Account represent, but it was not so in every case. Thayer speaks of unbarrelling his pork here and stringing it on poles, in order to have it carried more easily.

8.   Mr. Codman says (p. 59): "All are equals till the line of march is re-formed at the other end of the carry." But there is a plenty of evidence, in addition to the strong probability, that the officers never ceased to be officers, though certainly they did not put on airs of superiority on account of their rank.

9.   It has been stated (No. 28, p. 56) that the pond "is one mile wide as the army crossed it"; but not a single journalist gives this as the length of the voyage over. Arnold's words are: "over the first pond half a mile, which pond is $1\frac{1}{4}$ mile long"; Squier gives the distance across as half a mile; Haskell as about half a mile; Meigs and Dearborn do not state the distance; Melvin says about three-quarters of a mile; "Provincial," a mile and a half (?); Tolman, two miles.   These last

figures really refer, probably, to the length of the pond.

10. See his journal for October 14th. Church's estimate of its width was three-quarters of a mile. In suggesting (p. 123) that Church's estimates were doubtless the best, I am comparing him with the journalists in general; Arnold's figures may be regarded here as Church's revised. The pond was probably more extensive in 1775 than at present.

11. Mr. Codman states (p. 56) that this inlet ran from "the extremity" of the pond. But Arnold indicates that his course was across the main axis of the pond (*i. e.*, he says the pond lay north and south and he went east and west), so that the inlet was doubtless the one to be found now on the side of the pond. The inlet was not, as Mr. Codman represents (p. 56), " overhung" with grey moss,—nothing in the journals or in its present appearance indicates this; but dead trees beside it are and were moss-grown.

According to Arnold the length of the pond lay from north to south, but that is hardly correct; it is nearer N. N. W. Apparently his statement that he crossed it from east to west must be taken with equal allowance. In general, Arnold's bearings are often incorrect, if taken literally.

12. The direction of this portage was 10° north of west in 1775.

13. Besides the facts that this would give a shorter path than the present trail (which makes a wide detour to avoid the swamp), and that the ground seems to correspond better to Arnold's description, there is another argument. Arnold says: "a small elbow running into it from the S. E., on the west side of which it empties itself." This shows that he was not at the termination of

the present trail, for the outlet is in fact at the opposite
end of the lake.   Again, Arnold saw Mt. Bigelow plainly
from the third pond, and therefore he must have been in
this quarter, though his bearing does not seem right.
The course over the third pond was " west by north."

It is rather curious that the three ponds empty in
three directions: the first one to the east, into the Kennebec; the second to the south, into the Carrabasset;
the third to the north, into Dead River.

14.   The direction is given as 20° north of west.

15.   Across this, as across the first of the four carries,
there is now a buck-board road.   The last mile does not
cross a swamp, as the trail did in 1775, but it seems natural to believe that the Indian trail followed a brook,
called the East Branch, which the present road crosses
and abandons.   In that case it soon entered a swamp.
The East Branch was not deep enough to carry the
bateaux.

16.   This is from Henry.   His usual inaccuracy is
shown all along here, but he could easily remember such
a broad fact as this, forcibly impressed upon his attention as it was, and Arnold fully confirms—as do others
—the general character of the morass.

It has been described as " the almost impenetrable
spruce and cedar swamp which covered the last mile
of the last portage " (No. 28, p. 61); but (1) Arnold
spoke of it as a " savanna, which is divided by a small
wood not exceeding a 100 rods,"—our only precise
description, and quite inconsistent with Mr. Codman's;
(2) Oswald's description is: " a savanna, wet and miry,
about six or eight inches deep "; (3) Montresor's description tallies with Arnold's ; (4) an important passage
of Henry's narrative (No. 72, p. 46) hangs largely on the
point that he could see across the morass, and as his life

was in danger there, the fact may well have become fixed in his memory; (5) Dearborn wrote of "a spruce swamp knee deep in mire all the way," and such deep and continuous mire is impossible where the interlaced roots of an "almost impenetrable" thicket exist; (6) Stocking called it a "sunken marsh"; and (7) what the men complained of was not "impenetrable" thickets but mire : "a sunken mire hole," wrote Squier. Doubtless there was more or less "low shrubbery" (Stocking).

Mr. Codman states that some of the men were "forced to spend a night there, camped in mud and stagnant water" (p. 61). But there is no need of exaggerating the sufferings of the army. Is it conceivable that officers so very solicitous for the welfare of their men as Arnold's officers were, would force them to camp in "mud and stagnant water" when good ground was not more than half a mile distant?

What makes all the struggles of the army on the last portage seem the more pitiful is the fact that they were probably needless. For about half a mile from the third pond its outlet is rapid and rocky, but my guide, who knows the stream very well, assured me that the rest of it is good water. Probably Arnold went the other way because there lay the trail, as Montresor's journal agrees. But why had not the Indians found the better route? Is it possible that the lake emptied at a different place in 1775? No, for Pownall (p. 16) spoke of its outlet as running northward. The route by the outlet was no doubt longer, and perhaps the Indians, using birch-bark canoes and having little baggage, did not mind carrying across. Possibly, too, Arnold, relying on Montresor's journal, gave Steele a wrong direction here. Montresor had special difficulty in finding this portage, and this suggests that it may not have been often used.   The Indians may have gone usually the other way.

17.   Mr. Codman says (p. 57) that at the end of the swamp "Dead River was reached," but the passage down the creek to the river is mentioned by Arnold, Dearborn, Senter, Thayer, and others, and the creek is there to speak for itself.

18.   Arnold says "about one mile." Dearborn speaks of coming to the stream within half a mile of the river. The former was the distance which Arnold rowed, while the latter was perhaps meant for the straight distance.

19.   The length of the Great Carrying-place was about 12½ miles, besides the journey on Bog Brook. This total was made up of four portages and three ponds: 3¼, ½, $\frac{9}{16}$, 1¼, 1⅜, 2½ (plus something on account of the obliquity of the course), and 2$\frac{5}{16}$. Mr. Codman is therefore in error in speaking (p. 57) of "16 miles of lake and forest" at this carrying-place. Church made the second pond ¾ of a mile wide, but Arnold reduced the estimate to ½ of a mile (exclusive of the inlet), and I have accepted his opinion (note 10).   Slips are found in both Arnold's and Oswald's journals at this point, but one can easily detect and rectify most of them (see, however, note 11).   To help the reader judge of later estimates of distance (since we have measurements here for comparison), some of the figures may be quoted:

First portage (3¼ miles): Dearborn, 4 miles; Haskell, 4 miles; Melvin, 4 miles; "Provincial," 3¼ miles; Squier, 3½ miles; Stocking 3¼ miles; Thayer, "about 4 miles"; Tolman, 3½ miles; Humphrey, 4¼ miles.

Second portage (180 rods): Dearborn, ½ mile; Haskell, 1 mile; Melvin, about a mile; "Provincial," ¾ mile; Squier, ¾ mile; Stocking, ¾ mile; Humphrey and Thayer, ½ mile; Tolman, ¾ mile.

Third portage (1¾ miles): Dearborn, 1¼ miles; Haskell, 2 miles; Melvin, 1½ miles; "Provincial," 2 miles; Squier, 3 miles; Stocking, 2 miles; Humphrey and Thayer omit this portage; Tolman, 2 miles.

Fourth portage (2¾ miles plus 60 rods): Dearborn, 4 miles; Haskell, 2½ miles; Melvin, 4½ miles; "Provincial," 3¼ miles; Squier, 5 miles; Stocking, 4 miles; Humphrey and Thayer, 4¼ miles; Tolman, 3 miles; Morison, 3 miles; Senter, 4 miles. Meigs only says that the whole distance was 12½ miles.

20. As Morgan left Norridgewock Falls on the 3d and led his division, he very possibly reached the Great Carrying-place on the 6th.

21. Mr. Codman states (p. 61) that "by Oct. 16 the little army was at last across the carry"; but Haskell of Ward's company reports passing the night of the 16th near the third pond, and Squier's comrades of the fourth division did not reach Dead River until the 20th. Arnold's journal (October 13th) states that two divisions reached Dead River that day.

22. Mr. Codman has expressed the opinion (p. 60) that sickness "threatened already [*i. e.*, October 12th, when the hospital was erected—see note 26] to destroy the effectiveness of the force." This is clearly very important, if true, and requires investigation. (1) Arnold was unaware that his army was in such danger. Under date of October 12th, he reviewed in his journal the physical and moral condition of the men, and mentioned one death, as well as a very few accidents by water; but he had not a word to say of sickness, except that he mentioned having to leave sick men, "eight or ten in number," behind. Eight or ten in an army of one thousand were practically none at all. Arnold noted the spirit, industry, and great cheerfulness of the men,—

all of them inconsistent with general sickliness. (2) In fact there were not as many sick as Arnold counted on, for he wrote Enos, October 15th: "I expected to have found some subaltern unwell, who might have been detained," etc. (3) Senter, it must be noted, speaks of the sick on the 16th as having "increased to a very formidable number"; but this was four days later than the time referred to by Mr. Codman, and in the meanwhile the army had been getting the consequences of drinking the unwholesome water of the second pond. It was to the bad pond water, which the use of salt meat compelled the men to drink in large quantities, that Senter attributed what sickness there was; and, as the cause would soon cease to act, since the army was moving on, it was not a serious matter. (Senter was, however, mistaken in speaking of the water of the first pond as bad, for that is fed entirely by springs. His remarks apply to the second pond.) (4) Senter mentions by name only two persons as ill here (both of them, he adds, had been ill at the beginning of the march); and though he says the hospital was filled with the sick, we cannot infer that patients were very numerous, for the building was a log house, quickly put up, and no doubt small. Neither was the condition of the sick bad enough to detain the surgeon. (5) Morison recorded, October 25th: "Until this period we had in general enjoyed good health and spirits." (6) Up to the time the hospital was erected, Dearborn had sent back two sick men—a very small part of a company—and that was nine days before. (7) The very day after the hospital was erected Arnold wrote Washington, "The men are in high spirits," and this does not sound as if disease were threatening to paralyse the expedition. (8) Arnold wrote at the same time that he had "about 950 effective men," and after allowance is made for the feeble (not sick, but not rugged), for men working in the rear with the commissary and on other details, for the "straggling," *i. e.*, deserting, that began as soon as Fort Western was left, for the persons getting lame, and for those injured more or less by accidents of various kinds, the number to be set down as sick does not seem excessive. (9) According to Stocking the hospital was "designed for our sick in case they should return this way"; evidently he did not think a great part of the army were on the verge of invalidism. (10) None of the journalists, except the surgeon, shows any feeling that there was much sickness, or mentions being ill up to this time. (11) The condition of the army was not such as to require any change of plans. (12) The men did, as a matter of fact, go right on through greater and greater hardships. Our conclusion must be, I think, that while a good many persons were somewhat afflicted with such ailments as rheumatism, vomiting, and diarrhœa, and some with dysentery, so that the aggregate looked formidable to a young surgeon just out of the apothecary's shop, the efficiency of the army as a whole was not by any means endangered by sickness at this time.

23. So Senter states. This perhaps explains how Dearborn came to think that the log-hospital was erected by the first division.

24. Mr. Codman (p. 59) applies one of these names to the log-hospital, and the other to the log-house mentioned in the next paragraph. But Senter says that the house for the sick was "christened by the name of Arnold's Hospital," and Stocking's words are: "Between these ponds we built a blockhouse and gave it the name of Fort Meggs, designed for our sick," etc. The only building erected beyond the first pond was the hospital.

As no other journalist mentions either name, we must
conclude that some soldiers gave one name to the hospital and some gave the other, which is not at all surprising.

25. Serving as ensign in Morgan's company. Senter
(MS.) also spells the name "Irvine," while Morison
wrote "Irwin."

26. Dearborn records the building of the house by
the Kennebec under date of the 11th, and Mr. Codman says (p. 59) that when the hospital was erected a
house "had been already erected on the Kennebec side
of the first portage." But (1) the house on the Kennebec was not erected until the 12th, for Arnold, Oswald,
and Meigs (who says he received the orders from Arnold
and had them executed) agree that the orders for it were
issued on that day, and nobody but Dearborn says anything else; and (2) the hospital was put up the same
day, for Arnold, Oswald, Melvin, and Haskell testify to
this and nobody differs, except that Stocking throws
together the events of the 12th and 13th, and so cannot
be counted either way. It is, therefore, clear that the
house on the Kennebec had not been "already" built
when the hospital was put up.

27. Mr. Codman (p. 62) states that Farnsworth was
to establish a dépôt of "supplies brought up from the
Kennebec country below," which might seem to imply
that further supplies were to be gathered from the inhabitants. This would be an interesting fact, but I do
not find any reference to such a procedure at this time.
October 13th Arnold wrote Washington: "I have ordered the commissary to. . . forward on *the provisions
left behind* (about 100 barrels) to the Great Carrying-
place." Apparently Farnsworth did not carry out this
order, for Squier drew provisions at Fort Halifax on his

way home, and evidently did not do so at the Great Carrying-place.

28. Church had been waiting for him since the 8th (Humphrey).

29. What river was this? William Allen evidently thought it was Spider River (No. 106, i., p. 395). But I can see no good reason to doubt that it was Arnold River, since in all probability Steele followed the trail which the army took afterward. In fact his mission was to find and reconnoitre this trail. As we shall see, it led to Arnold River. But Henry's account is vague, and probably some or many of his statements are more or less erroneous. For this reason we cannot be sure.

30. Arnold's words are: "the Dead River from the last carrying-place he judges to be 80 miles." This figure included the Chain of Ponds, for Arnold adds: "the carrying-place from the Dead River to the Shordair pond about 4 miles," *i. e.*, Dead River was regarded as running through the ponds, as it still is, and as we find the journalists expressly saying later. Mr. Codman makes a threefold error, then, in his table of distances (on the map opposite p. 58): (1) he accepts this hasty and excessive estimate of Steele's; (2) he adds six miles to it; and (3) he understands Steele as excluding the ponds (see his p. 60).

Though Steele's canoes broke (p. 114 of text), they were repaired enough to be serviceable.

31. Mr. Codman (p. 60) represents Steele and his two companions as staggering into camp, "emaciated and exhausted," and adds (p. 61) that "as soon as Lieut. Steele was able to undertake the duty," he was sent on again. But (1) Arnold records unconcernedly that he ordered Steele off again the very day of his return. This does not look as if he was not able to walk. And

(2) Henry's account, vague as it is, shows plainly that all of Steele's party suffered hunger for a while, that a plenty of moose-meat then came their way, and that at first this meat was very good food. After a time, when all the fat of it had been used up, *those who were left behind* suffered from innutrition and diarrhœa. Steele, however, had gone on. So we may believe that he reached the camp in fair condition.

32. "Chaudiere Pond." According to Mr. Codman (p. 61) Church was to go down the Chaudière River, but Arnold implies clearly that this was not intended: "Lieut. Steel[e] to go down the Chaudair," etc. (October 12th).

33. St. François (St. Francis) on the St. Lawrence River (Lake St. Peter).

34. The letter was directed to "John Mercier, Esq. [the American copy as printed in No. 54 and No. 106 says Manir, but the English copy, sent to London on November 9th by Cramahé, gives the name as Mercier] or, in his absence, to Capt. Wm. Gregory or Mr. John Maynard." The letter was headed, "Dead River, about 160 miles from Quebec." Arnold stated that he had "about 2000 men," though he wrote Washington that day that he had about 950 effectives. Mr. Codman (p. 63) attempts to explain this by stating that Arnold "thought he might muster" 2000, including Indians and Canadians, before reaching Quebec. But (1) his own numbers were sure to dwindle from sickness and desertion; (2) Steele had reported that there were no savages on the route; and (3) in the small settlements on the Chaudière he could not have expected to raise 1100 or 1200 volunteers. Indeed (4) he had no thought of stopping to gather a large body of recruits, as is evident, for example, from his letters to the Commander-in-chief.

(5) Washington's instructions contain no hint of raising
French troops, and gave him no authority to do so.
The statement was, of course, knowingly false, and was
doubtlessly intended—a trick of war—to give confidence
to his Quebec friends.

Mr. Codman speaks of Arnold's sending an express to
Washington (p. 62); but, in fact, his letter was taken by
" a person going down the river."

35. Who was this Eneas ? The question is important,
because the answer may enable us to say whether Arnold
was prudent or foolhardy in trusting him. Mr. Codman
holds (p. 64) that Eneas was a brother of Natanis, and
that he met Arnold later at Sertigan. But I have not
been able to find the least evidence for either of these
statements, and infer that Mr. Codman must have been
thinking of Sabatis, to whom — according to Henry —
they would both apply. Arnold would be very likely to
make inquiries about the Indian whom he thought of
sending (his letter of November 8th to Montgomery suggests that he did so), and he would hardly have entrusted
such letters to the brother of a person (Natanis) whom
he had ordered Steele to kill or capture as a British spy
and a villain. Senter declares that Eneas was a Penobscot Indian, but Senter's account of the matter has been
proved suspicious and inaccurate (Chapter VII., note
10). The name Eneas has been called a mistake for
Natanis; but this is an error, for Natanis did not appear
until considerably later.

It seems fairly clear that Eneas belonged to the St.
François tribe. Some reasons for thinking so are : 1.
Washington expressed the opinion that Arnold could
communicate with Schuyler by the aid of the St. François Indians (see his instructions to Arnold, 8). 2. This
could only be through Indians of this tribe *in Arnold's*

23

army, for their home was far away, and they were not at all likely to be met with by accident.   3. We infer from Arnold's letter to Washington of September 25th (No. 54, 4, iii., 960) that a party of Indians set out from Newburyport by land to join him, and he says he shall send one of these Indians to Schuyler "as soon as they arrive."   4. St. François Indians visited the camp at Cambridge not long before Arnold set out, and several of them were detained there for some reason after the chief left (No. 54, 4, iii., 339).   William Allen, in No. 106, states without qualification that Eneas was a St. François Indian.   He does not give his authority, but the early time at which he wrote, as well as his carefulness and his personal acquaintance with Dearborn, gives weight to his opinion in spite of his numerous errors. As there is nothing, so far as I am aware, against this theory, I am inclined to believe that since Eneas was the sort of Indian recommended by Washington, Arnold cannot be blamed for trusting him.

Who was his Indian comrade?   Senter states that he was Sabatis, a Penobscot Indian.   Henry mentions that on November 4th "*we for the first time* had the pleasure of seeing   .   .   .   Natanis and his brother Sabatis." Mr. Codman accepts this as proving their relationship. But it does not seem correct.   Perhaps Henry misunderstood a general use of the term "brother" in Indian phraseology for the limited use of the word to denote close blood relationship.   According to Arnold, William Allen, and others, Natanis was a Norridgewock Indian. Allen says he was the last of his tribe; if so, he did not have a living brother.   There certainly was a Sabatis connected with the army, and Allen, who personally knew his daughter, brings proof that he was a Penobscot, and therefore not of the family of Natanis (No.

106, i., 394, note). A further argument against this relationship is the fact that—as pointed out above—Arnold
would not have trusted the brother of Natanis with such
a mission. Allen believed that Sabatis went with Eneas,
and there is no evidence against that opinion, I think,
after his relationship to Natanis is disproved, except the
italicised words in the remark quoted above from Henry.
But it is not surprising that Henry had not seen or did
not remember having seen Sabatis prior to November
4th, even if Sabatis had been with the army.

Besides the Indians there was one, and, so far as we
know, only one white man in this party. Arnold, Oswald, and Senter agree about that. Who was he ? Senter
says it was " Jackquith," and Mr. Codman follows him
(p. 64). Allen says the name was Jakins. There is no
doubt that this man—his name was really Jaquin, in all
probability—was at some time sent to the French settlements (Arnold's journal, October 27th); but that does
not prove at all that he went at this date, for Arnold
wrote, November 1st, to his friend in Quebec: "I have
several times on my march wrote you by the Indians," and
if he thought it wise to send a white man with his Indians
once, he may have thought so again. This receives
some confirmation from two facts: Senter (October 28th)
calls " Jackquith " " one of his [*i. e.*, Arnold's] expresses,"
and Arnold's way of alluding to him in his journal (October 27th: "one Jakins, whom I had some time since
sent down to the French inhabitants ") implies that nothing had previously been said of despatching him.

On the other hand there is clear evidence that Jaquin
was not the man sent by Arnold at this time. We have
a letter of this date from Arnold to Lieutenant Steele:
" I have sent the bearer and another Indian to Quebec
with letters, and must have John Hall, as he speaks

French, to go to Sartigan with them." (Hall was a deserter from the British forces at Boston.) This was a positive order from the supreme authority of the army, and we cannot doubt that it was obeyed. Hall was there, for we find him later at Quebec. We have other evidence. Arnold expected to reach Lake Megantic about October 20th or 21st, and the white man sent off on October 13th was to meet him there (see Oswald, October 13th), but Jaquin did not reach the lake on his return until October 26th or 27th. The inference is that he was sent later than October 13th. There is, indeed, another possibility. Steele was given permission to send a second white man with Hall in case Hall should not be willing to go alone; Jaquin may have been selected and may have been delayed on his return. This, however, is guesswork, and is opposed by the statement that one white went with the Indians, as we learn not only from Arnold and Oswald, but from Humphrey and Thayer, who appear to have seen the messengers on their way. It may be objected that we have no mention in Arnold's journal of Hall's return ; but neither have we a record there of his despatching more than one letter by Indian hands, and yet we know that he did so.

Hall was to go to Sertigan and there hire a Frenchman to accompany the Indians to Quebec, picking up information from the people. Although, as suggested in the next paragraph of the text, Hall may be supposed to have done good service, Arnold seems to have thought it expedient to obtain further information through Jaquin.

36. See his letter of November 7th.

37. This is surprising. As the three first divisions left Fort Western with forty-five days' provisions and about eighteen days had passed, Arnold's statement

would indicate that but little had been lost, for we have no evidence of any transfer of supplies from the fourth division. Yet he himself (October 3d) speaks in his journal of a "great part" of the bread of Thayer's and Hubbard's companies as damaged, and the same causes were likely to have the same effects in other cases, as we know from the journals. This and later developments appear to show that Arnold did not keep himself as well posted about the state of the provisions as he should have done.

38. Enos was also to send on a yoke of oxen belonging to the army, to be slaughtered. (Meigs noted on the 13th that up to that time four moose had been killed by "our men.") Arnold wrote Enos about his "proposal in regard to Mr. North": "When we arrive at the Dead River, will determine that matter, where you will hurry as fast as possible. There I design holding a council of war and expect particular advice from Canada." What was to be the source of this "particular advice"? Not Hall or Eneas, for Hall was to meet the army at Lake Megantic, and the Indians, who were to go farther than he, would be still longer away. In fact Arnold had written Washington two days before this: "I have had no intelligence from Gen. Schuyler or Canada, and expect none until I reach Chaudiere pond." It would appear, then, as if he wrote thus to Enos merely to stimulate him. The next inference would be that he suspected Enos of lukewarmness. If this was the case, we can understand why he expressed so little surprise on hearing than his division had returned.

39. He also ordered forty men of Meigs's division "to work on the roads that the rear might pass with less difficulty." Arnold seems to have camped, October 11th, on the west side of the first pond, for Senter found

him in camp there on the 12th, and to have remained there until 4 P.M. on the 14th.

40. Our only authority for this is Henry (No. 72), one of the scouting party. He says it took place on October 17th. Of course the date is wrong, but that does not authorise us to reject an incident which could not fail to fix itself in his mind. See note 31.

With reference to this incident, Mr. Codman (p. 60) says of Steele and his two companions that "having wrecked both canoes . . . they had left *two* of their party several miles up the Dead River too weak from lack of food to retreat further towards succor." But (1) Henry, our only informant, indicates that at least four were left behind (p. 46); (2) they were left, not several miles up Dead River, but about opposite the mouth of Bog Brook (pp. 24, 43, 45); (3) they remained, from choice, to complete the process of "jerking" the moose meat, which would require six days (p. 45), and, after losing strength for some days, were still able to cross Dead River and walk to the third pond (pp. 46, 47); (4) the canoes, though damaged, were repaired and continued to be used (pp. 40, 41). (The references are to No. 72.)

IX: 135–146.

1. Tradition has it that Major Bigelow climbed this peak to see the spires of Quebec, and from him the range is supposed to have taken its name. Sparks has scouted the idea that an officer in the army "had the courage as well as the leisure" for such an excursion; but Meigs has recorded that he and Hanchet made the attempt, though they set out too late in the day to succeed. We have no evidence that Bigelow did so; neither can one believe that a major in the army could

have expected to see anything of Quebec from this point. Lieutenant Steele had reported that Dead River was eighty miles long; beyond that were Lake Megantic and the Chaudière River; Bigelow must have had some knowledge of Steele's report; or, at the very least, he knew that when baggage was a deadly burden, it was Arnold's will that his men should be loaded down with provisions for about three weeks. He must have known also that the "height of land" lay between Dead River and Quebec. Mr. Codman (No. 28, p. 66) gives the height of Mount Bigelow as thirty-eight hundred feet, but the United States Geological Survey makes it thirty-six hundred feet.

2. I went the entire distance up Dead River and the ponds by canoe, so as to study carefully all the landmarks. A part of the river I have travelled over several times, and most of the way I have gone by land, also. Besides my personal observations, I have employed several of the most competent guides to make investigations, and have obtained data from a considerable number of the best-informed residents. To make the journey by water is particularly necessary, since the journals describe the march in terms of the river, which was, of course, essentially the highway of the expedition.

Possibly it needs to be added that all figures for distances on Dead River are estimates. Careful and experienced boatmen can reckon distances pretty closely by repeatedly timing themselves. When a number of such estimates are compared and corrected by one another, and further rectified (as they are) by comparison with known surveys of the land, a fairly close approximation can be made. It is not a measurement, but is certainly worth far more than the hasty guess of Steele, who went over the route only once and back, and, so far

as we know, was not specially trained in such work.   As
a map of Dead River could not be drawn accurately, a
diagram, showing the relations of things, seemed the best
expedient.

3. This is not positively certain, but seems extremely
probable.   Now it was (October 18th) that Major Meigs
ordered the last yoke of oxen killed for food, so that
Mr. Codman is in error in saying that the last of the
oxen were slaughtered "before the Dead River was
reached " (p. 47).

Mr. Codman observes that (the mouth of) Bog Brook
"formed a convenient harbor and landing place near
the first camp of the army on the Dead River" (p. 66).
But the camp one mile up Dead River (*i. e.*, a mile from
the mouth of Bog Brook) was the "first camp" on the
river for Meigs, Dearborn, "Provincial," Morison, Haskell, Stocking, and Tolman.   All the rest whose first
stopping-place is indicated went farther.

4. The name Dead River is due to the fact that at
low water there is no perceptible current here, or for
a good many miles above, probably because the shallows
below act as a dam, and convert the stream into a mill-
pond.   At high water the current runs four or five miles
an hour, but on account of the stillness of the stream, due
to its depth, might easily be thought much less.   To
this fact we may partly attribute the large overes-
timates of distance on Dead River, I dare say.   The
water was now of medium height probably, for there
had been heavy rains, and Humphrey says that in this
part of the river the current was so strong that it was
necessary to pull the bateaux along by the bushes on
the banks.   To be sure, Arnold wrote, October 21st,
that the stream was low before; but he then had for
standard the freshet that had come upon him.   Besides,

the river seems low even when it is pretty full, because the banks are high. One may assume, therefore, that even in this part of its course the river probably flowed at least one and one-half or two miles an hour.

It is interesting to find evidence here how closely Arnold kept his eye on Montresor's journal. He wrote under date of October 16th: "We were now near the large mountain mentioned the preceding day. Here the river by its extraordinary windings seemed unwilling to leave it—two hours had passed away and we had gained nothing in our course, but at last by slow degrees it became more regular and returned to its proper course." In Montresor's narrative for July 16th we find: "We had now passed the mountain, but the river, by its extraordinary windings, seemed unwilling to leave it. Two hours passed away and we had gained nothing in our course, but at last by slow degrees it became more regular and returned to its proper course" (No. 106, i., p. 355).

5. Humphrey and Thayer mention this, giving as the reason the strength of the current. But had there been a plenty of oars and paddles, the boats could probably have been propelled.

6. Unlike the courses on the river, the portages had been surveyed, and Arnold was probably in possession of the results. To be sure, he had not yet overtaken Church and the surveyor; but, as the surveys were made for the sake of having the information to use, we must assume that in one way or another the figures were communicated to the commander. At all events he would receive them later if not sooner, and whenever they came to hand, they would be used in his journal. This view seems confirmed by the fact that his figures for the portages are evidently not estimates. We seldom meet

with the word "about" in connection with the carries, while it is commonly applied to river distances and sometimes to bearings. For these reasons we may accept Arnold's statements about the portages, and usually neglect the others.

Mr. Codman expresses the opinion that "probably the whole third division" camped at Hurricane Falls "on the 16th" (p. 68); but Meigs and Hanchet camped, as Meigs says, "one mile up the river"; Ward's company (as Haskell shows) had not reached Dead River; and we know by comparing Meigs and Dearborn that Goodrich's company was a long way behind Dearborn's on the morning of the 16th.

7. Mr. Codman (p. 67) seems to call the distance from Bog Brook to Flagstaff Point "about 21 miles." It is really about ten or ten and one-half by the road, and between twelve and one-half and fourteen by the river. Arnold reckoned it fifteen.

8. This is not absolutely certain, but the distance and the description of the spot seem to point unmistakably to this conclusion. At Flagstaff one meets with a number of stories about this expedition. It is believed that Arnold camped for at least two weeks on the point (some assert all winter) and that the name of the village is derived from a flag-pole that he set up there. Indeed, it is said that Arnold himself climbed the pole, and fastened the flag at the top. As to the pole, I found in Flagstaff and neighbouring places three circumstantial descriptions and histories of it derived from old inhabitants,—stories not capable of being harmonised, so far as one could see. One hears also of muskets, and even cannon, buried there by the army, whereas there is not the least probability and is still less evidence that Arnold took any cannon (Senter's Account states expressly that

he did not), and the soldiers were not ready yet (however they may have felt later) to bury their guns.

I have spoken of these tales as " stories," not " traditions," because, when Arnold went up Dead River, there were no inhabitants to pass traditions down, and he left nobody behind him there. The belief that he camped at Flagstaff can readily be explained, it seems to me. When the first settlers arrived, it was easy to see (if we are correct in believing that the house of Natanis was there) that a clearing had been made by some one. Every sign of human work dating apparently from somewhere near the period of Arnold's expedition was naturally attributed to his army, as is often done still; and so it was inferred that the Indian clearing had been his camp.

9. Mr. Codman (p. 67) represents most of the men who went by water as crossing " on foot the points of land between the serpentine windings of the river "; but (1) the journals do not mention this; (2) nothing would have been gained, for, after crossing the point, they would have had to wait for the bateaux; (3) much would have been lost, for the steep, high, and crumbling banks would have been hard to ascend and descend, if the river was at all what it now is (Thayer says the shores were " bold "); good landings are not easily found on this part of Dead River; and (4) most of the bateaux must still have been laden, as Henry states, for boats seem to have been smashed about as fast as their contents were used up, and some went adrift down the Kennebec; and a laden bateau, we are particularly told, carried only men enough to navigate it. If, then, the crew had got out to walk, what would have become of the boat ? Boats not otherwise loaded probably carried the infirm or ill.

10. For the exact wording of the journals see below.

Thayer says at the end of his account of the 16th: "in the morning our company had," etc. This could not refer to the 16th, for on that day they had enough for half-rations, *i. e.*, six ounces per man, which would mean, as there were now, according to Thayer, sixty men in the company, twenty-two and one-half pounds (Humphrey says fifty men); also because Humphrey remarks, "in the morning *here*," etc., and he was not in Camp Greene on the morning of the 16th. Arnold, in his letter of the 17th to Enos, stated that Greene's division had four barrels of flour and ten barrels of pork. This would have given the men full rations of bread for nearly six days, and of pork for nearly fifteen days. We might infer from this that Hubbard's company must have been better supplied than Thayer's and Topham's; but we find Arnold providing for an equal distribution among the three of whatever Enos should send.

What shall we do, now, about these very different reports on the provisions of the second division? According to Humphrey and Thayer there was not enough flour for breakfast on the 17th; according to Arnold's letter, probably written just after breakfast, there were four barrels.

The impulse would be to say that two witnesses are stronger than one. But (1) if the statements of Thayer and Humphrey were strictly correct, what did the men live on until Bigelow brought some flour four days later? Salt pork would hardly have answered as an exclusive diet. Had the men been reduced to that, the journals would probably say so; and there is no mention of fish or game. (2) Thayer and Humphrey are in general less authoritative than Arnold. (3) Arnold's letter to Enos is an official and strictly contemporary document, qualified only by the chance of a misprint; but we do not know just when the two journals were written as we have them, nor just how independent of each other they were on this point.   Had Arnold intended to misrepresent, he would have made the supplies appear smaller, not larger, than they were.   (4) Topham's account, while it does not agree exactly with Arnold's, differs very significantly from Humphrey's and Thayer's.   Humphrey says: "in the morning here our company Had not five or 6 lbs of flower to 50 men."   Thayer, by changing "not" to "but" and "50" to "60," appears to make the rest his own.   But Topham, though following Humphrey in general, says, "not more than 5 or 6 lbs per man." Arnold's figure would allow a trifle more than four and one-third pounds per man, but Topham's statement was evidently not intended to be exact.   On the whole, then, it seems fairly clear that Arnold's account is the one to be accepted, though it is very possible that he ignored a partly used barrel, which did actually bring the amount of flour up to five pounds per man.

Arnold's journal might seem to imply that Greene's division, though short of flour, had bread; for he says, "great part of their bread being damaged."   But the fact that the men were on short rations before it was found that fresh supplies could not be obtained, indicates that there was not enough bread to signify; nobody else gives a hint of bread; and it is very possible that "bread" was used as a synonym for "flour."   This seems, in fact, probable, in view of Humphrey's words: "Arnold . . . hearing of our wants of *bread*," etc., for Arnold speaks of their wanting *flour*.

It should be added that Senter corroborates the journalists of Greene's division.   He reached their camp on the evening of October 21st, and under date of October

22d, says: "This day for the first [time] I was oblig'd to come on half allowance, as the advanced party [by which he doubtless means Greene's men, thinking—as he did—that most of the army were behind him] had been for several days."

Mr. Codman, doubtless reflecting Senter's erroneous statements (note 25, Chapter V.) remarks (p. 68): "The inequality in the distribution of the provisions among the different companies . . . had now conspicuously appeared." But Arnold has recently said that the first three divisions (*i. e.*, each of them) had enough for twenty-five days, and we have just seen that the companies of the second division appear to have been equally in want. So far as one can discover, the only inequality of distribution was the intentional assignment of an extra supply to the last division as a reserve fund.

11. Mr. Codman says (p. 68) that he arrived at 3 o'clock in the morning; but (1) Thayer says "in the evening," (2) Topham adds " 8 o'clock in the evening," (3) Humphrey says, " about 8 O Clock," and (4) Arnold writes in his letter of the 17th, " last night late," which would seem quite true of boating on the river until eight o'clock, when it was almost dark at half-past four.

12. In his journal, Arnold says that Bigelow was sent back to "assist the rear in bringing up their provisions," but this meant, as the letter to Enos said, that he was to "bring up as much provisions as you can spare." Just here we find a suspicious spot in Humphrey's journal. October 16th he says he was " sent back " with Bigelow, yet October 17th to 20th he records what went on at the camp. Did he then copy from Topham or Thayer? That does not follow, for (1) orders were issued to Bigelow on the 16th, but he did not set out until the next day; and, as Humphrey states that he was ex-

tremely reluctant to go, we may infer that he obtained an excuse from the trip; (2) his journal for October 17th to 20th could not be made from Topham's and Thayer's; and (3) October 21st he alludes to Bigelow's return in terms which seem to indicate that he did not go: " Major Bigelow who had been down With our boats return'd," etc.

13. Topham says *one* barrel, Thayer and Humphrey say *two*.

14. Dearborn mentions arriving on the 17th. According to Arnold, however, Dearborn's and Goodrich's companies arrived at 10 A.M. on the 18th. This perhaps means that the greater part or the last of them came at that time. They were set at making cartridges. Melvin records at this point: " Had orders to put ourselves in a defensive condition," and Dearborn mentions that the powder-horns were filled. This implies that until now the usual military observances and precautions had been neglected. Indeed, why should they not have been ? This was a rough-and-ready army, out for work, not for pomp, and until now there had been no danger to fear. If Carleton were going to attack the army, he would certainly not weaken and endanger his forces by coming down to the Great Carrying-place. He would wait until fatigue and hardship had reduced the strength of the Americans, and they had become involved in the more difficult region above. Then, nearer his base, he could attack with far greater certainty of success. For these reasons it does not seem at all probable that sentries were kept on guard at the Great Carrying-place, as Mr. Codman supposes (p. 58).

15. They worked at this under a Mr. Ayres. By Chaudière River is here meant Arnold River, no doubt. This is from Meigs.

16. In Topham's journal, October 21st, occur these words: "600 men came up to us at 11 o'clock, & thought to find Col. Arnold, but not finding him returned back and drove up his rear." It is impossible that six hundred men, two-thirds of the whole detachment, can have appeared in this Melchizedek style. Doubtless the statement is to be disregarded as somehow a total mistake. This is the more evident because Thayer reports what appears to be the same incident in a way that looks perfectly sensible: "Col. Enoe came up with us about 11 o'clock in expectations of finding Col. Arnold. but on his disappointment return'd and drove up [*i. e* urged on (?)] his rear." Humphrey says the same. Williams's company arrived in the afternoon under command of a sergeant.

The fact that Williams seems to have marched in the rear of the fourth division, and that he arrived at Camp Greene just after Enos went back to "drive up" his rear, suggests that Scott and McCobb had gone ahead. But Williams appears to have been in the van of his division now. Scott was behind him, and apparently the same can be said of McCobb.

17. Mr. Codman (p. 69) says "ceased," but Arnold's word is "abated," and also, "small rains the whole of this day." The 18th was very rainy, according to Dearborn, and Morison's journal might be construed to agree with that; but no other journalist gives the same report, and Humphrey, Thayer, and Haskell refer to the weather as pleasant.

18. The wind has been described (No. 28, p. 71) as "swinging to the S. S. W." during the morning of the 21st. This is based evidently on Senter's record: "Wind S. S. W."; but Senter says nothing about "swinging," and Arnold mentions that the wind was from the same

quarter the day before: "wind to the So. wd." It was a steady, heavy storm.

19. Mr. Codman states (p. 71) that all the divisions except the first were in motion October 21st; but Humphrey, Topham, and Thayer agree that the second division did not budge till the 22d, and Senter corroborates this. It was not until the 21st that Bigelow returned with the boats, and after that the sick had to be sent back, and the preparations made for breaking camp.

20. Arnold's estimate. The forward portions of the army received the brunt of the flood, because they found themselves in the foot-hills, where the stream was more rapid and the valley narrower than below.

21 Mr. Codman states that Arnold "saved himself only by sacrificing his baggage" (p. 73), but Arnold says the baggage was conveyed to a small hill, and the next day was dried.

22. Henry says this took place during the night of the 22d, but as in so many other cases his date is wrong.

23. Squier estimates the rise of the river at twelve feet, Senter at ten (October 22d), Arnold at eight, Dearborn at eight or nine. Mr. Codman assumes (p. 71) that fires could not be kept going on the night of the 21st; but Arnold, Senter, and Squier indicate the opposite.

24. What had become of their tents does not appear. Washington stated at Cambridge that tents were provided for all. Some may have been lost, but it would not be easy to lose tents. The men may have wearied of carrying them. Perhaps so many bateaux had smashed that there was no way to transport all the tents. Possibly the supply was not what Washington supposed it to be. Or perhaps, on account of the gale, it had not been feasible to set up the tents.

24

25. Mr. Codman says (p. 72): "The few guides became confused, and the copies of Montressor's map which
some of the officers had were *therefore* worse than useless." But (1) there is no evidence that the guides
were confused, for the guides were apparently at the
head of the army, and that portion did not go astray;
(2) why should Montresor's map become worse than
useless *because* the guides were confused? Guides do
not go by a map; if they did they would not be guides.
When guides fail, maps become peculiarly valuable.
And (3) as no detailed information about this locality
could possibly be derived from Montresor's very meagre
map, how could it become *worse* than useless? The
situation was bad, but it is possible to exaggerate the
freshet and its evil consequences.

26. During the time of the great storm and flood (October 19th to 22d) the riflemen advanced only some five
miles. One reason for the delay, according to Mr. Codman (p. 70), was that they "were counting upon the rear
divisions to bring them supplies"; but, if that was the
case, why did they move on before the rear divisions,
i. e., Greene's and Enos's, came up?

X : PAGES 147-163.

1. The South Branch rises not far from Rangeley
Lake.

2. Arnold's words are: "Oct. 21. . . . At 7 A.M.
embarked and proceeded up the river 3 leagues, when
we came to a small fall of water, the portage over W. N.
W. ab^t 10 rods—ab^t $\frac{1}{2}$ mile higher up came to another
fall more considerable. Portage over ab^t 26 rods c° W.
N. W. Continued our route up the river for ab^t $\frac{1}{2}$ mile
and came to another fall. The portage 75 rods, c° over

W. N. W.—about 90 rods higher up met with a fourth fall very considerable and long—Portage over W. N. W. Distance 73 rods—here we overtook Capt Morgan and his division, but as his encampment was bad proceeded about one mile higher up. . . . It was now quite dark so that we had little time to encamp." Where the Eustis dam now stands there was formerly a wall of rock which compelled the river to make a sharp turn, and run where the mill has been built. There is one difficulty here. Arnold says the portage was W. N. W., and I do not see how the carry at Eustis dam can have run in that direction; but (1) it is impossible to tell just how the river went, or just where the portage was in 1775, (2) we do not know how to interpret such bearings,—a portage is not often straight, and (3) apparently Arnold was not very careful here, for he gives W. N. W. as the direction of four successive portages,—exceedingly improbable on a stream like Dead River. Perhaps, on account of the rain, he was not using a compass, as he may have done elsewhere. In that case, as the sun was hidden, he would be likely to err.

3. By the road eighty-two rods, but " across lots," in a pretty direct line, only four hundred and forty-three short paces,—say about seventy rods. The reader may wonder why I did not have the distances on Dead River measured. On account of the windings and swellings of the stream, it would have been necessary to measure the middle of the channel, and this would have been quite difficult. The results, even if correct, would probably have been of little help, since Arnold's figures for distances by water were only estimates, no doubt. Careful, averaged estimates appear to be as good as anything for our purpose.

4. A little way above Upper Ledge Falls a back

channel (now closed by a dam) runs down to the piece
of smooth water between the Upper and the Lower Falls.
From all that I have been able to learn, however, it
seems clear that this channel was never full except in
flood times, and that the river now runs where it did in
1775. The Indian carry is said to have been across the
island formed by the two channels. The Upper Ledge
Falls dam has gates to regulate the flow of water and a
sluice for the logs to pass through. The same is true of
the dam at the foot of the first pond.

5. Arnold's words. He describes no other falls on
the river in such emphatic terms; they fit Upper Ledge
Falls exactly, and there are no other falls on the river so
"very considerable and long."

6. The river makes a turn of sixty degrees just below
Lower Ledge Falls.

7. If the portage of twenty-six rods was on the upper
side of Black Cat Rapids (on account of swift water or
some other difficulty), and the portage of seventy-five
rods began fifty rods below Lower Ledge Falls, we get,
with Arnold's half-mile, near three-fourths of a mile.
Possibly the river has lengthened its course since 1775.

8. An error. Hendricks is meant.

9. We may assume that Meigs, after reaching Camp
Flood on the 22d with "part of his division," went back
and brought up the rest the next morning.

10. *I. e.*, "distance."

11. Allowing for the difference in the declination of
the compass.

12. The reader will recall several cases in which
Arnold's bearings do not seem right. Still others might
be mentioned. It seems as if, in some cases, at least, he
must have guessed.

Mr. Codman does not undertake to identify the branch

which the men went up by mistake; but, as he places
Camp Disaster at Ledgè Falls, his theory requires us to
believe that it was (1) some temporary stream produced
by the rains, (2) the South Branch of Dead River, or (3)
Tim Brook.   I have searched in vain for some stream
besides these and Alder Stream that could have made
the "crotch."

(1) Nobody can go up and down that region as I
have done, besides employing guides to do the same,
without feeling satisfied that a temporary stream, navigable for four miles the second day after the freshet, is
inconceivable.

(2) As already suggested, it seems tolerably clear that,
according to Henry, some of the riflemen took the South
Branch for Dead River.   Henry (No. 72, p. 33) says
that, on the afternoon of the day he passed the cabin of
Natanis on the scouting expedition, he came to a stream
entering Dead River " from the west or rather the north-
west," which the party were inclined to take; and that
later he was told by a boat crew of Morgan's men that
they did follow this westerly stream and went seven
miles up it.   The only navigable affluent from the west
that Henry can have seen on the day he passed Flagstaff
Point is the South Branch, which empties eight or nine
miles above, and this is the only affluent of Dead River
that is navigable for seven miles.   But Mr. Codman is
wrong in representing " the riflemen " (p. 73) in a body
as making this mistake, and also in representing any
riflemen at all as going up this branch on the 22d, for
Arnold's journal renders it practically certain that they
passed its mouth late on the 17th, or early on the 18th,
and quite certain that they had got a long way above it
by the evening of the 21st.   Mr. Codman says that when
the riflemen discovered their mistake they " made a bee

line across the land" to Dead River. But our only
authority for the blunder of the riflemen, Henry, says
they were a boat crew. Is it supposable that a boat
crew would thus abandon their bateau and stores, especially as it would have been vastly easier to go by water?

Now Mr. Codman (p. 74) sends the erring party of
the third division up the same stream, and apparently on
the same day, October 22d. But Arnold, Meigs, Dearborn, and in fact all who allude to this accident, place it
on the 23d, and the musketmen who blundered were at
that time far beyond the mouth of the South Branch, for
Arnold's journal shows that Meigs's division was within
a quarter of a mile of this point at noon on the 20th,
and still advancing; Meigs and Dearborn prove that the
division advanced six or seven miles on the next two
days; and Arnold proves that at 7 A.M. on the 23d, it
was nearly four leagues above. Further, to think of
their "cutting across" from four miles up South Branch
to Dead River and reaching Upper Ledge Falls (where
Mr. Codman represents them as arriving) the same day,
is practically impossible. We conclude, then, that the
"crotch" was not at the mouth of the South Branch.

(3) As what has been said implies, if Camp Disaster
is placed where Mr. Codman places it, at Ledge Falls,
the only plausible theory about the "crotch" is that it
was the junction of Tim Brook with Dead River, forty-
eight rods above Black Cat Rapids. This is the view of
people in the locality. But the difficulties involved in
this theory are insuperable. (a) Dearborn says that his
bateau went four miles up the affluent, but there are falls
about two miles up Tim Brook that no boat could ascend,—in fact a sort of gorge, and to cut a road and
carry around and back would have caused a far greater
delay than we have any trace of; (b) Tim Brook is less

than ten miles above Arnold Falls, but Arnold called the distance between Arnold Falls and the " crotch " fifteen miles; (*c*) Tim Brook is about fourteen miles below the first pond, but Arnold called it less than fourteen and a half miles from the " crotch " to the first pond, and this was where he was quite sure to exaggerate distances; (*d*) Tim Brook, much smaller than Dead River, does not make with it what any one would call a " crotch "; (*e*) for three miles below the " crotch " Arnold did not have to carry, but within less than a mile below Tim Brook two carries would have been necessary; (*f*) the portages of seventy-five and seventy-three rods were about four miles below the " crotch," but, on the Tim Brook theory, falls requiring such carries cannot be found; (*g*) the country is so desperately bad that had the men found themselves up Tim Brook they would soon have given over trying to " cut across," and would have followed that stream down to Dead River. Other arguments could be presented, but these appear quite sufficient.

The fact that the men went up a stream coming from the westward shows on which side of Dead River they marched; and Henry (p. 52) states that they went on the south (*i. e.*, the south-west) side.

13. " Lower Shadagee Falls " is a somewhat indefinite name. It may be said to cover about half a mile of shallow swift water and " ripples " below Upper Shadagee.

14. This has been considerably reduced in height by blasting.

15. Mr. Codman (p. 74) places Camp Disaster at Ledge Falls, and, though he does not expressly say so, it seems evident from his description (p. 75) that he means Upper Ledge Falls. There is, no doubt, a local

belief that the mishap occurred here, and Mr. Codman appears to have accepted it without question. But this local belief is entitled to no weight. Like the Flagstaff stories, it is not even a tradition. Apparently it is based upon the fact that several quarts of bullets were found near the site of the upper dam. But bullets have been found elsewhere. Boats were capsized in more places than one; and it was very easy, in loading or unloading at a carry, to let a bag of them slip into the river. The objections to the Upper Ledge Falls theory seem decisive: (1) the "crotch," we have satisfied ourselves, was at Alder Stream, and Camp Disaster was above that point; (2) if we place Camp Disaster at Ledge Falls, the distances come right neither above nor below; (3) Camp Disaster was at a portage of seven rods, but one would have to carry many times that distance to get around Upper Ledge Falls; (4) the theory would compel us to suppose that Arnold failed to mention Lower Ledge Falls, for below the portage of seven rods there was no other for about seven miles; (5) on this theory we cannot place the portages of seventy-five and seventy-three rods, and the "very considerable and long" falls. Were Lower Ledge Falls suggested as the point where Camp Disaster was pitched, the difficulties would prove substantially the same.

16. It will be remembered that most or all of the riflemen were marching at this time with Meigs's division (the 3d).

17. October 22d, Morgan passed Arnold. Beyond Camp Disaster Arnold pressed forward in advance of the army, but does not mention overtaking Morgan. The natural inference is that Morgan camped with the rest of his division at Camp Disaster, and so left that point at about the same time as Arnold.

18. This is Arnold's and Dearborn's figure. Others add slightly to it. Of course the lack of food increased the number of invalids, but the cases of disease do not seem to have been many. October 23d, Senter writes: "Several of our men were excessively exhausted with the diarrhea, with [a] few rheumatic cases" (MS.). The sick were furnished with three days' provisions, and Enos was ordered by letter to give them supplies enough to carry them on to the commissary (at the log house on the Kennebec?) or to Norridgewock. The mention of Norridgewock in Arnold's order does not prove that any dépôt of supplies existed there, especially as it is shown that the commissary was elsewhere. (Arnold's letter is incorrectly printed—p. 84—by Mr. Codman; "in" Norridgewock should be "or" Norridgewock.) The people at Norridgewock were few, but they had now laid in their winter's supplies, and could give a simple meal or two to a good many men. Squier's account of his return trip makes no mention of a dépôt at Norridgewock. At Ft. Halifax, not at Norridgewock, he "drawed provision." And our inference is confirmed by Arnold's letter of October 24th to the commissary: "I wrote you the 14th instant to send forward to the Great Carrying-place all the provisions you had. This I make no doubt you have done"; *i. e.*, there was no thought of establishing a dépôt at Norridgewock.

19. That it was a picked company is clear, for we know that one of his men, Stocking, did not go with him, while men not of his company did go. Haskell informs us that a sergeant and seven men were taken from Ward's company. See also Chapter XIII., note 19. Each man was allowed ten pounds of flour and five pounds of pork, equivalent to the full rations for ten days. According to Mr. Codman (p. 76), this company consisted

of fifty-five men; but seven journalists give the number as fifty and nobody gives it as fifty-five (Melvin and Thayer say sixty).

20.   It surprises one to find Arnold writing Enos, October 24th, that " we" had on that date twelve or fifteen days' provisions.   Eight days before this, Greene's division was put on reduced rations, and had been able to get only a barrel or two of flour.   Apparently Arnold did not keep well posted as to the state of things behind him.   In accordance with his order, forty-eight men were sent back from the second division.

21.   A difficulty confronts us here, however.   In dating his letters written at Camp Disaster Arnold spoke of being thirty miles from Chaudière Pond; here he says he is " about 20."   This would seem to make the interval at least nine miles, whereas the distance from Shadagee Falls to Sarampus Falls is probably not over four and a half or five miles.   But the figures for the interval in his journal amount to only seven miles plus eighteen rods plus one hundred yards, which can be discounted to the actual distance with a fairly good conscience.   Or he may have received information in the meantime that changed his opinion.

22.   Senter, who camped a few miles below with Greene's division, speaks of " nigh six inches."

23.   There is a buckboard road from Eustis village to an abandoned (1902) farmhouse on the first pond, about opposite which the outlet must have been in 1775.   The treasurer of a lumber company writes me that some years since he had the road chained from the Shaw House at Eustis to the farmhouse, and found the distance to be eleven miles and one hundred and ninety rods.   Owing to changes in the road, the present distance may be a quarter of a mile less or more than this.

The length of the road has no close bearing, however, on our opinion of the distance by water.

24. After Arnold, Dearborn gives the best account, though his estimates of distance are much too large. Up to Arnold Falls we can follow him perfectly; but after that, in consequence of the incompleteness of his record, we cannot be sure. His account falls into the scheme of the text except that Arnold's carries at Eustis Falls and Black Cat Rapids appear two miles apart in Dearborn, and are longer than Arnold's (perhaps because the river had risen). Dearborn gives a group of three portages of 74 rods (evidently a slip for two), and he gives only three more carries, without specifying their order: 4, 4, and 90 rods, against Arnold's 12, 6, 40, and 100. (Possibly, if Arnold's boats were light, he made a carry that the others did not make.) Meigs agrees with Dearborn, except that he mentions only two portages of 74 rods. He calls the portage at Camp Disaster 15 rods long. These two journals show distinct signs here of mutual dependence yet of independence. It is particularly to be noted that both journals place Camp Disaster at the first portage above the 74-rod carries, which were almost certainly Ledge Falls. In the list of Dearborn's portages (p. 148 of the text) the one following the 74-rod carries is omitted because he gives no figures for it.

No help can be obtained from Melvin, Tolman, Henry, Fobes, or Stocking. Morison and " Provincial " throw scarcely any light. Haskell travelled by land, and his estimates of his marches do not aid us, for the flood compelled him to follow a circuitous route. His portages above Arnold Falls are 20, 30, 50, 70, 15, 4, 5, 160 rods. He mentions going four miles up the wrong stream on October 23d, but he " had to go back again " instead

of cutting across.   Humphrey, Thayer, and Topham
are extremely vague about the features of the river.
Senter, travelling with the second division, speaks of
having to make roads at two carrying-places (apparently
Eustis Falls and Black Cat Rapids), which shows that
the portages used by the first and third divisions had
been submerged, and so may help us understand disagreements about the portages.   His recollection of
Ledge Falls represents falls half a mile long, separated
by " not more " than that distance from falls of the
same length,—certainly far from a correct picture.   He
suggests the falls at Camp Disaster (Shadagee) only by
mentioning the wrecks of bateaux.   Beyond this he
speaks of passing one waterfall and three carrying-places.
Squier (his journal is not accurately printed here) evidently boated over the carrying-place at Arnold Falls;
how far beyond that he went on the 22d, cannot be told.
The next day, after advancing eight miles, he carried 60
rods (Eustis Falls ?) and camped half a mile above.
On the 24th, after going a mile, he carried 50 rods
(Black Cat Rapids ?), boated two miles, carried half a
mile (Lower Ledge Falls ?), boated 40 rods, carried
half a mile (Upper Ledge Falls ?), and camped two miles
above.   The next day he marched until two o'clock
(though not all the time), and seems to have nearly but
not quite reached Shadagee Falls.   Then the fourth
division retreated.

Dearborn and Meigs called it ten miles, plus something
more, from Camp Disaster to the first pond.   As the
"something more," made on the morning of the 26th,
cannot have been a great deal, they are supporters of
the Shadagee Falls *versus* the Ledge Falls hypothesis;
for their figures require liberal discounting, and Ledge
Falls are probably thirteen or possibly fourteen miles from

the pond.   The figures of "Provincial" and Morison are extravagant.   According to Dearborn it was about forty-one miles from Flagstaff to Camp Disaster.   Even liberal discounting cannot bring this down to the distance between Flagstaff and Ledge Falls, about twenty miles.

25.   Mr. Codman states (p. 74) that among the losses at Camp Disaster was a considerable " sum of money destined to pay off the men "; but Morison, whose words these are, puts the event on the next day.   This is confirmed by his remark that it was after the Colonel took his departure.   Arnold did not push on ahead of the main body on the 23d, for he speaks of despatching the troops on the 24th; but on the 24th he did so.   We have other testimony to the upsetting of boats on the 24th (Tolman, Haskell, "Provincial," and Stocking).

26.   Melvin's journal intimates that he did no more on the 26th than reach the first pond.

27.   According to Montresor there was a large beaver dam at the foot of the first pond.

28.   Mr. Codman (p. 75) remarks: "The valley narrows as it reaches these lakes, and the intervale is cut up by steep hills and deep ravines.   The circuits the army was obliged to make in order to avoid the overflowing of the river became wider," etc.   But of course the circuits did not become "wider" where the valley narrowed.

29.   For Humphrey, Thayer, and Topham say that Greene, Thayer, and Topham *stayed* by desire of Col. Enos to hold a council on the 25th.   Williams's company reached Camp Greene, where the second division still lay, on the 21st, and Scott's cannot have been far behind, for they called themselves twenty-one miles from Bog Brook that night.   McCobb's had at other times led the division.   Senter speaks as if the fourth division

might easily have come up with the second at the time of the council.

30. For the distance from where they encamped at the close of that day to the first pond seems to have been about what this theory would require. Besides, they heard on the 24th that the carrying-place over the height of land was twenty-five miles distant. According to Arnold the foot of the first pond was about eighteen miles from that carrying-place. On this basis Greene's division had then arrived within seven miles of the first pond, almost exactly where we have placed Camp Disaster.

Humphrey, Thayer, Topham, and Squier seem to agree in representing the camp as farther along than Ledge Falls. It cannot have been at Sarampus Falls, for Arnold was near there on the night of the 24th.

The journals coming from men of the second division do not represent it as moving on the 24th. Senter, who overtook it at evening on that day, states that he found these troops "waiting for the remainder of the army to come up, that they might get some provisions ere they advanced any further. Upon enquiry I found them almost destitute of any eatable whatever." But this does not assert that they had been waiting all day. Apparently they had not been, though the journals are silent. Senter advanced, yet did not pass them.

31. Topham said on October 25th: "We are in absolute danger of starving," and Humphrey said about the same. Thayer wrote on the 24th that only half a pint of flour per man was left, and Senter, the same day, that there was almost nothing eatable in the division except a few candles! But see note 33.

32. Greene, of course, did not know when he set out that Arnold had left the army and pressed on in advance. He must have returned before or about noon, for by two

o'clock the council had been held and orders given for the retreat of the fourth division.

33. It should be added that all this is not positively certain. The principal data are: 1. Thayer: "Oct. 25. We stay'd for Colonel Green to consult [with Arnold] about our situation . . . in the afternoon [the men] went about three miles and encamp'd waiting for our boats [that went down the river to get provisions]. Here [*i. e.*, at the camp] col. green capt. Topham and myself stay'd by desire of col Enoe to hold a counsel of war. . . . Mr. Ogden . . . and myself took the Boat in which we ran rapidly down with the current where we expected to receive from the returning party 4 Barrels of flour and 2 of Pork . . . working . . . up against a most rapid stream for a mile and half . . . I reach'd and met some of our boats coming to me [sent from the camp three miles above] . . . Mr. Ogden and myself . . . lied that [night] disagreeably in the snow . . . about 9 o'clock [the next morning] we overtook our troops who were just ready to march." The fact that Thayer met boats of his division so long after setting out in a boat (provided, it will be noted, by Colburn) is explained by the hypothesis adoped in the text, viz., that during the council the men advanced three miles, so that time was necessary to send them orders, unload the boats, and bring them down. As it was already afternoon, the men camped, awaiting the return of these boats. 2. Topham: "Oct. 25. We stayed for Col. Green who is gone forward to hear what we must do for provisions . . . [The men] Proceeded on our way about 3 miles and encamped for our boats to come up, which could not be done very quick on account of the rapidity of the river. Col. Green, Capt. Topham and Thayer stay [behind] by desire of Col. Enos in order to hold a

council of war." 3. Humphrey: "Oct. 25. This day
we stay'd for Col. Green who is gone Forward to here
what we must do for provision . . . in the afternoon
went about 3 Miles and encamp'd and to wait for our
boats; here Col. Green Capt. Topham & Thayre stay'd
by desire of Col. Enoe," etc. One's natural inference
again would be that the officers stayed at the camp
pitched in the afternoon; but the whole division remained there, while the tarrying of the officers is represented as done specially at the request of Enos. Possibly
the meaning might be drawn that the whole division
advanced three miles ; then Greene and the officers
stopped the march and stayed for a council, and the
division encamped to wait for them. But the encamping seems to be represented as done "to wait for our
boats," and the boats did not go down the river until after
the conference, hence the army did not go into camp for
the sake of the conference. 4. Senter: "Wednesday,
25. . . . We now waited in anxious expectation
for Col. Enos' division to come up, in order that we
might have a recruit of provisions ere we could start off
the ground. An express was ordered both up and down
the river, the one up the river in quest of Col. Arnold
[but Humphrey, Thayer, and Topham show that Greene
himself went.] . . . The other express went down
the river to desire Col. Enos and officers to attend in
consultation [but it was for the interest of *Enos and his
officers* to hold a council, and Humphrey, Thayer, and
Topham state that he asked it]. They accordingly came
up before noon. . . . After debating upon the state
of the army with respect to provisions, there was found
very little in the division then encamped at the falls
. . . the other companies not being come up, either
through fear they should be obliged to come to a divider,

or to show their disapprobation of proceeding any further. . . . Received it [*i. e.*, the provisions from the
fourth division], put it on board our boats, . . .
bid them adieu, and away — passed the river, passed
one W. falls and encamped [but it was Thayer who went
for the supplies, and his account is different]." Senter
also says: " To compel them to a just division, we were
not in a situation, as being the weakest party "; but if the
conference took place at the camp of the second division,
Greene had the officers of the fourth division entirely in
his power. 5. Squier: " Oct. 25. This morning by a little
after Break of day went up to the rest of our company
[1½ miles ahead] there stopt till Capt. Scott and Lieut.
Sprague went up to the Lieut.-Colonel Eanos a mile
forward and we marched on I went by land We marched
till 2 o'clock in the afternoon then was ordered to march
back to our camp."

Mr. Codman (p. 83) calls this council or conference
" a general council of war," which, of course, it was not,
for it was not summoned by the commander.

What, now, was the duty of Greene and Enos? On
the day before, Arnold had written them both. Enos
was directed to " proceed with as many of the best men
of your division as you can furnish with 15 days' provision." Greene was directed to " proceed on with the
best men and 15 days' provisions for each [man]."
The two orders were evidently intended to mean the
same, and that meaning is most clearly stated in the
first. Obviously, Arnold supposed both divisions better
provided with supplies than they seem to have been, and
supposed that the log house on the Great Carrying-place
contained a plenty of provisions. His plan was that
Enos and Greene should press on with as many men as
could be furnished with provisions for fifteen days, after

provisions for, say, four days had been set apart to get all the rest of the two divisions back at least to the log house. The question of duty becomes then a question of fact. How much provisions had the two divisions?

If Greene had 180 men (as Thayer intimates in two ways), and had four barrels of flour (Arnold's figure, Chapter IX., note 10) after breakfast (the time when Arnold's letter was probably written) on October 17th, and he continued to give half-rations of flour until after breakfast on the 22d (very possibly full rations were resumed when Bigelow brought more flour on the 21st); then, after providing dinner and supper (half-rations) for his division on October 24th, and three meals on the same short allowance, October 25th, he had left 456 pounds.

This does not seem at first to agree with statements of the journalists. Humphrey, under date of the 24th, writes: "We are almost destitute Of provision, being brought to half pint of flower Pr man and having no more to deliver out, it Being the last we had." But (1) this is only a repetition of the difficulty encountered on October 17th (see Chapter IX., note 10); (2) it seems hardly possible to take Humphrey literally, for it would compel us to suppose that for about twenty-four hours the division had no bread at all, while he only says on the 25th: "We are absolutely in a dangerous situation." He even expects to be able to live until "Supplies from the french side" can be obtained. If none come from that source, "we shall be poorly Off," he thinks. (3) The "had" (cf. "are" above) suggests that the last six words may have been added when Humphrey's journal was copied; *i. e.*, perhaps the original record meant only that the company was reduced to half a pint per day (half-rations), while the entry as it stands appears to mean that one half-pint apiece, given out on the 24th, exhausted the stock.

In short, while the matter is far from clear, it looks as if the supply of flour—very small indeed it must have seemed under the circumstances—was actually inadequate, and it is possible that exaggerated reports of the situation found their way into the journals. Senter's statement that Greene's division had nothing eatable but some candles on the 24th appears clearly extravagant, for the division, if it had no other flour, would not have used up in three days the two barrels brought by Bigelow ; and the other three witnesses are not independent.

But Greene's supply of pork needs to be considered. Accepting Arnold's account of the situation on October 17th, calling a barrel of pork 200 pounds, and assuming that one pound a day was given out (to make up for the shortage of bread), we find that, after furnishing his division with supper on October 25th, Greene had 440 pounds of pork. His supplies were equivalent then to 608 rations of bread and 586⅔ rations of meat, *i. e.*, food enough for one man for 597⅓ days. Four days' rations for the division would more than have exhausted the supply. In short, Greene could not have equipped any men for the advance according to Arnold's orders,—that is to say, after providing for those returning.

The state of Enos's supplies came out at his trial by court-martial (see note 39). The upshot of the testimony (No. 54, 4, iii., 1710) was that after supplying Greene with certain provisions on October 25th, the fourth division had left only enough for three days. Enos himself in his report to Washington (November 9th) stated that, after sharing with Greene, the fourth division found itself with only food enough for three days (No. 54, 4, iii., 1610).

But it has to be borne in mind that the testimony at the trial of Enos was given exclusively by his officers, and that they had the strongest possible inducement to colour or misrepresent facts. Squier informs us that on the 28th all " took 2 days' provisions for each man." This proves that on the 25th, Scott's company, at least, had enough for five days (and Squier reports the loss of a part of a barrel on the 26th). It took Squier until afternoon on the 30th to reach the " inhabitants " at Norridgewock. He went by water, and therefore rapidly, but he says that some " could not go by water"; these must have had still ampler supplies. Twenty of Scott's company, and (we may assume) an equal detail from each of the other companies, went back to Bog Brook on the 29th to get flour from Dead River across the Great Carrying-place. The transportation of this flour would have been a slow affair, so that these men must have needed provisions for, say, eight days; and there must have been at that time a large undivided quantity of flour, else such a detail would not have been necessary. It looks, therefore, as if the fourth division began their retreat with provisions for, at the very least, six days, so far as flour was concerned.

As to their pork, we have no such data; but we may assume that the stock was at least as good, for (1) when the ration was fixed, equal quantities of flour and of pork were allowed, which implies that equal quantities were in stock, (2) pork was less likely to be injured, and (3) Enos had given some flour, but no pork, to Greene's division previously.

Greene had probably 125 men after supper on October 25th, and we know that he then (counting the two barrels just received from Enos) had full rations for about seven days (flour equivalent to pork).

It may be asked, if Enos had an ample supply of pork, why did he not give Greene some on the 25th ? The reply is easy: it was hard for Greene to get the flour which he urgently needed, and of pork he still had a considerable supply.   Another question is this: if the second division now had supplies for seven days, why did they complain so bitterly of Enos? Again the reply is obvious: they did not know how soon they would reach the "inhabitants," and, allowing for accidents, their stock seemed dangerously small.   Arnold's orders implied that provisions for fifteen days were needful.

Enos had, after the conference, perhaps 250 men of his own (including Colburn's), and was said at the trial to have had 150 from the other divisions.   A simple computation will show that provisions for one man for 3275 days were on hand in the two divisions.   These would supply 107 men for fifteen days, and 418 men for four days.

In all this figuring, we have adopted underestimates, but—to be perfectly safe—let us now throw off the seven men at a venture, and say that at least one hundred men could have gone forward as Arnold ordered.   If there was a broken barrel on the 17th besides those mentioned by Arnold (Chap. IX., note 10), if Greene's division did not resume full rations on the 21st or 22d, if he did not have 180 men, and if the fourth division had more than the above minimum estimate of their supplies, then this number would have been more than 107.   Mr. Codman would therefore seem to be in error in saying (p. 87) that the precise execution of Arnold's order was " an impossibility," and that if Enos had undertaken to obey it some of the men who advanced would " undoubtedly have perished " by starvation.

Some may feel that the testimony at Enos's trial has

been rather too summarily dismissed. A comparison of the journals (*e. g.*, see p. 395), probably unbiased testimony, with the interested statements of the officers seems to justify scepticism. But let us now look at the matter from another point. Let us assume that when Bigelow returned on October 21st he found Greene's division absolutely destitute of food. Captain Williams testified that he gave Bigelow eight barrels of provisions. These were enough to make full rations for about six days. Yet Enos wrote Washington that he " overtook Colonel Greene with his division, entirely out of provisions," and this occurred in the forenoon of the 25th. Bigelow's party, to be sure, lived a day or two, perhaps, out of what he received; but this does not invalidate the argument, —especially as we may be sure that under such circumstances Greene would not have dealt out full rations. Further, Greene must have had some supplies Oct. 21st.

34. Mr. Codman (p. 75) represents the men of the second division as discouraged by the boat-loads of invalids sent back from the first and third divisions, who " assured them of the hopelessness of any further progress . . . and exhorted them to turn back." But no journalist except Senter mentions such exhorters, and he names but one. It should be remembered that these returning soldiers were not stragglers. Their being sick did not make them poltroons. They were going back by order. Morison tells us how the riflemen tried to conceal their condition as they grew feeble, and, if spoken to about returning, declared " that they would soon be well enough." When ordered to the rear " they lamented that their indisposition prevented them from sharing in this grand adventure throughout." We have no reason to doubt the substantial accuracy of this picture.

35. Mr. Codman (p. 81) quotes Senter, without question, to the effect that the men on this side were Enos, Greene, Bigelow, Topham, Thayer, and *Ward*. But I cannot believe that Ward attended the council, and think his name was an error for *Hubbard;* for (1) Hubbard, one of Greene's captains, would hardly have been absent; (2) Ward belonged to another division, now more than a day in advance, and so would not be likely to be there ; (3) Haskell, of Ward's company, says that they went forward (from Camp Disaster) on the 24th, and continued their advance on the 25th. Senter, the doctor, might easily be misinformed about this matter, as about so many others. The probability that Senter was ill-informed on this point is shown by Thayer's statement that six voted in the negative and seven in the affirmative on the question of advancing, whereas according to Senter the numbers were five and six. Further, Lieutenant Hyde testified at the trial of Enos that he was present at the council, and " we found " certain things, and Lieutenant Buckmaster in his testimony "confirms what Lieut. Hyde deposes." How could Buckmaster do so if he was not at the council ? Yet Senter does not mention him. Still, in default of better evidence, the text follows Senter as to the persons present at the conference (except in the case of Ward) and other points. Certainty is unattainable here.

36. What made this defection seem peculiarly exasperating to the rest was the fact that the fourth division had a comparatively easy time of it. Being in the rear they found roads, and often huts, all ready for them. As Colburn does not appear again it is probable that he and his company of " artificers " retreated with Enos.

37. So Thayer, our best authority at this point, says. Senter calls it two and a half barrels. Four barrels of

flour and two of pork had been promised.   Thayer, under date of October 28th, says that before reaching Arnold River, men cut up and boiled rawhide, and lived on
the " liquid " " for a considerable time." Thayer does not
say who did this, and it is of course possible that some
party of troops were actually reduced to such straits at
this time.   It seems equally possible, however, that
Thayer, relying on his memory, carried back to this
date something which occurred later.   The passage does
not appear in Humphrey's account.

Mr. Codman intimates (p. 79) that Arnold had given
"peremptory orders" to the fourth division *after* the
flood to divide their provisions with Greene, but I do not
find any evidence of this.   Arnold must have supposed
Greene had received supplies, since on the 24th he
ordered him to go on with as many of his best men as he
could furnish with rations for fifteen days.

One is a little surprised to hear nothing of the
"game" reported plentiful by Steele's scouting party.
Very likely the leading companies were able to bag
some (though we do not hear of it), but the passage of
such a body of men must have frightened the deer and
moose away.   The fish, however, were not too much
scared to bite.   Senter and Arnold had no difficulty in
catching a plenty of large trout in Dead River after
many of the army had passed.   This may help to explain how the men were able to live when supplies were
so scant; but they seem, as a rule, to have had no time
for fishing.

38.   This is from Senter.   As there is no mention in
the journals of Humphrey, Thayer, or Topham that the
division broke camp that afternoon (it must have been
late when the boats got back), we may suppose that it
refers to a party that went on with Senter.

39. Mr. Codman (p. 83) represents the failure of the expedition as due to Enos's defection, and the defection as due to the failure of "an express, despatched by Greene," to reach Arnold and apprise him of the situation. His words are:

"From the failure of this courier to reach Arnold may be traced Enos's defection and return, the failure of the Expedition . . . and the loss of British America to the American Union."

But Senter is the only one who states that an express was sent in search of Arnold, and he adds that the express was sent that Arnold "might be inform'd of the state of the army, many of whom were now entirely destitute of any sustenance." This means that he (if there was an express) went to see about supplies, not to say anything about Enos. In fact Senter indicates that he went before the council was held. But Humphrey, Topham, and, by implication, Thayer, say that Greene himself went forward to see Arnold. Evidently then, he did not send an express, and Senter misunderstood the matter. But Greene certainly went *before* the council, and for the purpose of securing provisions; and his failure to reach Arnold can have had no bearing in any way on Enos's defection, because when he went he did not know that Enos was intending to abandon the enterprise.

But let us concede to Mr. Codman (what is impossible, for Greene then knew that Arnold was out of reach) that an express was despatched *after* the council to notify Arnold of the threatened defection; would his overtaking Arnold have changed the result, as Mr. Codman holds? Arnold had a start of more than a day, and was pushing on with all possible speed. Consequently it would have taken a person under the most favourable circumstances two and a half days to overtake him, and at least a day and a half would have been necessary for Arnold or an order from him to come back to Camp Disaster. Enos's division would, then, have had a start of fully four days. Six days at least would have been required to overtake it. By that time Squier reports being below Fort Halifax (November 4th). Arnold certainly would not have quitted the rest of the army to go on such a quest, and, if he had, could not have induced the men to return then. An order from him, arriving at that point, would have had no effect; they would have reasoned that he did not understand the situation, and it was now quite impossible to march for Quebec. Neither would Arnold have sent them a peremptory order to advance, unless he had made sure there was food enough to keep them alive,—this we know from the orders that he did give. In short, this lack of communication with Arnold, to which Mr. Codman attributes the defection of Enos, had really no bearing upon it. Whether the defection of Enos caused the failure of the expedition, it does not lie within the scope of the present study to inquire.

The fortunes of the returning party have no direct interest for us. It is enough to say that they reached Cambridge. Enos was placed under arrest, tried by a court-martial, and honourably acquitted; but none of those whom he abandoned was present to testify, for his commission was about to expire when he reached Cambridge, and it appeared necessary to try him at once. He was acquitted, therefore, on the testimony of men in the same awkward position as himself. This has deprived the verdict of its efficacy, and the fact that the men who decided to go on succeeded in reaching Quebec has tended, of course, to increase the feeling that he should not have retired. That feeling was very strong at the time. It is not within the province of this book to inquire how just it was.

Some of the testimony given at the trial must, however, be considered a little more in detail than in a previous note. Captain Williams testified that he let Bigelow have eight barrels of provisions (whereas Topham stated that Bigelow obtained one barrel, and Humphrey and Thayer that he obtained two), that he was *informed by Bigelow* (which implies that Williams was not present at the conference) that the " council of war " decided that Enos's whole force should return (whereas Humphrey, Thayer, Topham, and Senter state the contrary), and that the fourth division had but three days' provisions when they turned back (disproved by Squier's journal). Captain McCobb testified that it was " agreed " at the council " that the whole division under Col. Enos should return," and that " we left " Greene's division " with about five days' provision." Captain Scott confirmed McCobb. Lieutenant Hyde (" Hide ") testified that " it was adjudged that there was about four days' provision for those who went forward, and we returned with 3." Lieutenant Buckmaster supported Hyde, and said that there were 150 men (Mr. Codman, p. 84, erroneously quotes him as saying " invalids ") from other divisions with the fourth.

A few things may be said: 1. While these witnesses had a strong motive for colouring, if not misrepresenting, the facts, the journalists had little or none. 2. We cannot accept Williams's testimony as to the amount that he delivered to Bigelow; it is contradicted both by Humphrey, Topham, and Thayer, and by the fact that Greene was again in need on the 24th. 3. If, as the witnesses represent, it was agreed that the fourth division should go back, why did the journalists represent it otherwise, and why were the army in general so bitter against Enos and his men ?   4. Hyde disputes McCobb.

How did it happen that Enos, who possessed a disproportionate share of the provisions to start with, could not afford to be more liberal with Greene, even after keeping back an ample reserve for himself ? Of course he had the sick and the stragglers to feed, and Lieutenant Hyde said there were 150 of them; but it was only on the 24th that invalids began to be sent back in large numbers. It would seem, then, as if he must have lost a good deal of provisions. But the rear division ought to have profited by the experience of those before it; and, according to Senter, it had a disproportionately large share of flour, which suffered less than bread (biscuit) because in better barrels. (Thayer tells us that on the 25th the fourth division was " overflowing in abundance of all sorts "; this must be taken with some allowance, but Squier noted on October 23d, " fare plenty here.")

Mr. Codman (p. 79) attributes a part of his loss to the freshet; but while the water rose considerably in the lower part of Dead River, where the fourth division was, the force of the flood must have been far smaller there, and the current far less dangerous, so that, as the provisions were in boats, no special losses need have occurred. The matter must therefore be left somewhat in the dark, especially as we do not know precisely what the fourth division had at first. Enos, in writing Washington on November 9th (No. 54, 4, iii.), said: " When we arrived at the Great Carrying Place, [thinking], by what I could learn from the division forward, that provisions was like to be short, I wrote to Colonel Arnold, & desired him to take an account of the provisions forward.

He wrote me word that there were 25 days' provisions
for all the divisions ahead." This seems trustworthy
for we have Arnold's reply (October 15th) to a letter of
Enos's written the day before. It is therefore clear that
Arnold received a warning or at least a hint of danger at
this time. There was little that he could do. He had
(October 14th) ordered the surplus provisions sent up
from below, but to wait for them might ruin the enterprise. So he evidently concluded to push on and take
the chances, hoping that after all there would prove to
be food enough on hand.

But what of the one hundred barrels or so of provisions that Arnold ordered sent on from Fort Halifax
to the Great Carrying-place ? They do not seem to have
been sent. Squier records drawing four days' provisions
at Fort Halifax, but gives no hint of getting supplies
at the log house. So, if Arnold had retreated from Lake
Megantic or the ponds, counting on obedience to his
order, the results would have been disastrous.

Arnold himself did not hear of the defection of Enos
for some time. Mr. Codman, to be sure, says (p. 85)
that Stocking was with Arnold and Hanchet, and Stocking's journal indicates that he heard of the retreat on
October 25th. But Mr. Codman is mistaken. October
28th Arnold supposed that Enos was advancing, for he
recorded in his journal that he " Dispatched one Hull to
Col Enos & the rear Division to Pilot them up." Mr.
Codman was no doubt misled by assuming that Stocking was with Hanchet's advance party. He was not ; as
is clearly shown, for instance, by the fact that on October 28th Hanchet's party was on Lake Megantic at 6
A.M. (as we know from Arnold, who saw them there),
while Stocking records that he was crossing the height
of land that day.

XI: Pages 164–181.

1.   Senter says that he went on in a birch canoe ; but
(1) Senter was not near him and did not overtake him for a
long time; (2) Arnold abandoned his original birch canoe
at Vassalborough for a pirogue, and we have no hint of
his obtaining another ; (3) under date of October 25th
he wrote : " we were obliged to go on shore several times
to Bail our Battoes," which certainly implies that he was
not in a canoe, since a canoe would have required bailing
quite as much ; and (4) he wrote also that it was very difficult to keep the bateaux above water in the storm.   How
then could a canoe have lived?   I feel sure from my
own experience there that in such a storm as met him he
could not have gone up the ponds in a birch canoe.

2.   The purpose of building this dam was to facilitate
logging operations.   When a "drive" of logs is to be
sent down Dead River, the gates of the dam are opened,
and a flood of water carries them along.

3.   Montresor calls what was unmistakably this first
pond (including both of the present names) only half a
mile long, but this must be a mistake.   Arnold had Montresor's journal in his hands, for as we saw, under date of
October 16th, he used the language of that journal verba-
tim.   Therefore, when we find him giving figures so different from Montresor's, we may feel sure that he did it
knowingly.   Arnold overestimated distances by water as a
rule, but we cannot suppose that he multiplied the length
of this pond by seven.   The map of the Chain of Ponds
(p. 165) is based upon an excellent map by Mr. Austin
Cady, slightly modified by observations of my own.   The
figures on the map indicate the height of the mountains.

The name "Chain of Ponds" covers the series from
Lower to Round, inclusively.

4. At this point is now situated a camp of the Megantic Fish and Game Corporation, which very courteously admitted me to its privileges.

5. This name does not come from our friend of Arnold's time, but from an Indian woman who lived and died (or was killed) on the tongue of land that separates Natanis and Round Ponds.

6. Arnold states that Long Pond lay north and south, but its direction is nearer to north-west and south-east — another instance of his fallibility in the matter of bearings. A strong wind down this lake produces a considerable " sea."

7. This is worthy, perhaps, of explanation. None of the maps that I was able to obtain showed such a pond as this, though Arnold's journal seemed to require it. The first time I visited the ground I had my guide follow the Stream, while I went by land at a varying distance. We both arrived at Horse Shoe Pond (out of which the Stream issues) without finding any pond, and my guide was sure there was none, else he would have known of it. I concluded that Arnold had underestimated the distance he went on the Stream, that the portage of twelve rods was required to get around some obstruction, that his next pond was Horse Shoe Pond, and that as I went on I should discover some explanation of his enumerating one more pond than Nature seemed able to afford. This explanation, however, I did not find; when I had examined the whole ground I had to admit that either the journal was incorrect, or I had failed to discover a sheet of water that Arnold crossed. In favour of the first alternative was the fact that Meigs mentioned one pond less than Arnold ; but it is far easier to omit an item than to insert one that does not exist, and Arnold's journal bore many marks of carefulness.

It was not convenient for me to retrace my steps at that time, but I sent my guide back to reinspect the locality. He found nothing, and the guides and sportsmen with whom I talked and corresponded knew nothing of the missing pond, though some among them had been tramping over the region for many years. Finally I determined to make a fuller investigation myself, and at length I found the object of my search. Then I understood why it was unknown. It lies parallel and very close to the Stream, separated from it only by a steep ridge from fifteen to forty feet high, which sinks into a piece of wet ground perhaps ten rods wide near the lower end. Here is the outlet of the pond into the Stream; but, as the pond drains only a basin a little larger than itself, there is no overflow except in the spring or after rains. No outlet-channel exists, and, as the low ground is covered thickly with alders, there is no reason why a passer-by on the Stream should suspect the existence of a pond at that point.

Beyond the low ground just mentioned rises a very steep hill, which suddenly drops down again into a sort of cleft, where water, no doubt, escapes during flood times; so that the pond has in reality two outlets separated by the high hill. Beyond the cliff this hill resumes, and continues until it unites at the head of the pond with the ridge on the other side. In this way the pond is concealed very effectually.

Without knowing of Lost Pond one cannot explain Arnold's journal. As Mr. Codman's guide, with whom I happened to become acquainted, was not aware of its existence, I infer that Mr. Codman himself was not. This may explain why his account of the march is practically a blank so far as the most difficult portion of the narrative is concerned.

8. My description is of course based entirely on present conditions. The pond is probably about thirty rods wide in the middle, as Arnold said.

9. Montresor evidently considered this outlet the main stream, for he wrote: " Here [at the short portage] the river turns off to the [gap in MS.] although a rivulet [*i.e.*, Horse Shoe Stream] which falls into it here springs from lakes I have yet to mention [*i. e.*, Horse Shoe, Mud, and Arnold Ponds]." This passage was inexplicable to me for a long time, but the explanation is simple. Hathan Stream expands itself into a sort of lagoon just before it empties into Horse Shoe Stream, and so appears to be the main channel.

10. Arnold called the direction of this portage W. 35° N. The ridge, if one may judge from present indications, was almost a natural highway. It is quite sharp and dry, and the trees probably did not stand near together. It is evidently a thoroughfare for the deer at present, and one finds there a well-marked path made by them.

11. Montresor called Horse Shoe Pond " about 700 yards long and 270 in breadth." He mentions " leaving the brook, which has a cascade, on our right hand," as he set out for the next pond; and this fits Horse Shoe Pond exactly.

12. The present trail from Horse Shoe Pond to Mud Pond runs in about the same direction as the trail of 1775. The distance was called five hundred yards by Montresor, seventy-four rods (that is, 407 yards) by Arnold, and about five hundred yards by myself and guide.

13. Of Mud Pond Montresor says: " This is much smaller [than Horse Shoe Pond], its form very regular, the shore rocky." This is unmistakable. Big boulders

26

are thickly set along parts of the shore. In a single group one may count thirty. This is true of no other pond in the region.

14. According to Arnold this portage was only forty-four rods (that is, 242 yards) in length. The present path is about 550 yards long. Evidently Arnold went by another trail. As nearly as one can judge, he probably followed the brook which connects the two ponds. The ponds appear to be nearest each other there, and the distance that Arnold gives (forty-four rods) may well have been correct for that route, it seems to me. Montresor seems to confirm this surmise, for he says that he entered Arnold Pond "nigh the source of the brook [connecting it with Mud Pond]." He also calls it "a short portage" which implies that it was short in comparison with the previous one of five hundred yards.

An expert in such matters called my attention to what seemed a line of lighter foliage running from Arnold Pond toward Mud Pond, which, in his opinion, showed that a road had been cut there long ago. This line was where I have just suggested the trail may have run in Arnold's time.

15. Arnold calls this pond one and one-half miles long, but that is certainly excessive, as I know by talking with sportsmen who had shot at a mark that stood about half-way across the pond, and of course knew how far their rifles could carry. Montresor says "about three fourths of a mile," and that is close to the truth. Though not so long as Long Pond, Arnold Pond is wider and therefore larger. Montresor called it "almost 500 yards wide," and Arnold "½ a mile." Its irregular shape causes the width to vary greatly.

16. It is necessary, of course, to allow for the change in the declination of the needle since 1775. On apply-

ing to the Coast and Geodetic Survey, I was favoured with the following letter:

"We have no data for the precise locality 'Dead River'; however, according to the information we have on file for various places in the vicinity of Portland, we find that the needle pointed on the average in October, 1775, $8\frac{1}{10}°$ West of North, and that at the present time it would point on an average $14\frac{6}{10}°$ West of North." (August, 1901.)

It will be noted that I have here accepted Arnold's bearings, which have proved erroneous in certain other places; but I accepted them only as hypothetical, until they seemed to be proved correct. Further, since this was a well-known portage, it is easy to believe that the bearings had been carefully determined, and that Arnold was not dependent for them on his own compass or his own guess.

17. Morison: "Attempts were made to trail them over" (Oct. 27th). What he meant by "trail" may be seen from another passage (October 25th): "It was a magnificent spectacle to behold a long line of boats trailed up an almost impassible river by their mooring ropes, by men," etc. A sufficient reason why we find no other mention of such an attempt may be that the attempt failed; or, even if the boats went by water a little way, this was as nothing compared with the terrible portage that remained, and so did not seem worthy of mention.

18. There are some additional arguments of uncertain value. The fact that the pond, the river, and a mountain overlooking the pond all bear the name Arnold might appear significant; but we do not know when or by whom the names were given, and there can have been no real tradition about it, since there were no inhabitants hereabouts. Still, President Allen (No. 106, i., p. 395, note)

knew in 1831 of the name Arnold River (in 1775 it was called the Seven Mile Stream.)   Stories are told of the finding of boats and the discovery of a great quantity of rotting oars leaning against a tree; but the finders of such things are mostly not within the reach of questions now. Somewhat more valuable is the statement of a man over eighty-five years old, reported to me by one of my guides, that he came upon the irons of a lot of bateau poles on the shore of Mud Pond near the outlet, and that when he was first there, as a boy, it could be seen that men had camped on the spot many years before.

A Boston gentleman has told me of finding a bayonet in a spring north-west of Arnold Pond.

19.   See No. 106, i., p. 395, note.   President Allen was of the opinion, as already mentioned, that what Steele's party took for the Chaudière (*i. e.*, Arnold River) was Spider River.

20.   Mr. Codman does not undertake to throw any light on our problem.

21.   The word *bog* is here used in the sense understood in this region,—*i.e.*, a rather narrow expanse of open water surrounded by a swamp.

22.   At the same time, I recognise the fact that my investigations about the height of land were not entirely satisfactory, for they were not scientifically conducted.   In reality, the first step should have been to survey and map the region.   I thought of having this done, but found the objections too serious.   The cost of even an approximately correct survey and map would have been $1500 or more, probably.   It would have been necessary for me to superintend the work, and this would have involved camping for weeks in the midst of the flies, mosquitoes, and midges.   Neither would the results of such an approximate survey have been scien-

tific after all. There was another objection: the data
given us by Arnold are not scientific. The directions of
his portages can only have been approximations, for a
trail is never straight for long. The distances by pond
and stream were only estimates. Besides, assuming that
his estimates were exactly correct, we should not be
greatly helped, for we have often no means of knowing
precisely where he went between two points. It seemed
to me, as already suggested, that perhaps after all the
best results might come from pursuing his method,—*i.e.*,
making as careful estimates as possible. Of course
when the region is cleared, if that day ever comes, it
may be possible to do better than can be done at
present.

23. One of Getchell and Berry's reconnoitring
party.

24. We do not know at precisely what time these
events occurred, but apparently it was at the close of the
day. It may be supposed that Steele's and Church's
men were helping clear the path over the Boundary
Portage.

25. Arnold wrote: "The Carrying-places from lake
to lake are so many and difficult, that I think the whole
will get forward much sooner by leaving all the batteaux.
If there are any people sick you will perhaps be under
a necessity of bring on some batteaux." This was addressed to " Col's. Green, Enos and the Captains in the
rear [portion] of the detachment."

Arnold's ground for issuing the order was a report
from Hanchet (see Arnold's letter of October 27th just
mentioned) that the "roads" through the woods (around
the lakes) were well spotted and preferable to the water.
This shows that Steele and Church's party had done a
great deal of work. Evidently Hanchet had either

gone by land all the way, or had obtained his information from this party. (By "spotted" Arnold meant "blazed.")

XII: Pages 182–195.

1. Mr. Codman states (No. 28, p. 88) that at this time Arnold had crossed the height of land, and "was paddling rapidly down the Chaudière Lake"; but Arnold says, under the date of October 27th: "At 4 P.M. we entered the Chaudeire Pond."

2. Arnold met the two lieutenants on Arnold River about noon on the 27th, after overtaking their men the previous day, apparently at evening. In his letter written on the morning of the 27th Arnold said: "Lieut. Steele has gone over the pond. His party are here." This evidently means that Steele's men so reported.

3. Mr. Codman states (p. 88) that at this time Captain Hanchet was "marching around the lake [Lake Megantic] on its eastern shore"; but Arnold says: (1) that Hanchet left the Boundary Carrying-place with him on the 27th, and (2) that at sunset on the 27th Hanchet was on a point of land not very far from where Arnold River empties into Lake Megantic (Chaudière Lake).

4. Mr. Codman (p. 88) separates the first and third divisions here by a good many miles. But neither Morison nor "Provincial" supports this position, for neither states that the riflemen entered the first pond on the 25th. On the other hand, Morison represents himself as arriving on the evening of that day at a notable point of transition, and this can have been only the beginning of the ponds. (Henry's journal is quite unreliable here.) As the first and third divisions had been travelling in company for some time, it is difficult to see why they

should now be separated by about the whole length of the Chain of Ponds.

5. Mr. Codman states (p. 88) that at this time Enos "was beginning his retreat"; but according to Squier, the only journalist in that division, the retrograde movement began the previous day (October 25th) at 2 P.M.

6. The number of men lost between this point and Quebec seems to have been quite small.

7. On reaching Quebec Arnold had about six hundred and seventy-five men (Arnold's letter to Washington, December 5th); deducting the advance parties and allowing for a few deaths, we have about six hundred.

8. The reader is referred to the map on page 171. This is based largely on my own observations, but, though not scientifically accurate, is probably correct enough for the present purpose. The bearings were taken with a good pocket compass. Distances I measured only by traversing them and counting paces, or noting the time, or both. Experience gives one a fair judgment as to the rate of a walk. My guides rendered material assistance in this work, for they are accustomed to such reckoning. I also got the best information I could from other reliable guides. But in this direction one has to be extremely cautious. An intelligent and experienced guide, while often surprisingly accurate about the things he is familiar with, may not draw the line between them and what he does not know. Guides are liable to accept and represent as knowledge what they have only heard from others of their guild, and it is not at all easy for them to confess, particularly to an employer, that they are in ignorance about any such matter. I tried in every suggested quarter to find exact data, but obtained little. A prime difficulty lies in the fact that the country is all wooded. One cannot see far

along a trail for instance; and in the course of a mile one has to take the bearings forty times, perhaps, and strike an average. The various parts of my map, based on many independent data, came together with a consistency that rather surprised me.

9. Arnold's journal is always excepted in this chapter, of course.

10. It may appear singular, but it is a fact that no guide with whom I talked knew where the outlet of Lower Hathan Bog ran. I had to follow the outlet all the way down through about a mile and a half or a mile and three-quarters of alder swamp to find its connection.

11. The question of the outlet of Crosby Pond is an interesting one; but, as it did not directly concern me, I did not follow it to a conclusion. I found no evidence of outlet except what is suggested in the text. Of course the overflow is little or nothing, except in spring or after a heavy rain, for the pond has but a very small drainage area.

12. Haskell speaks of it as seven miles to "Shedoer Streams," but it is not perfectly clear where he began to reckon, or where he stopped. See Chapter XIII., note 14.

13. Steele and Church were together on Arnold River; their men were together on the Boundary Carry; Arnold met the men there; Arnold looked for, and doubtless followed, the marks of the scouting party; Hanchet was with Arnold on the farther side of the Boundary Carry.

14. Mr. Codman's account (p. 77) of this part of the march cannot be endorsed unreservedly. It is little more than a rewording of this portion of Dearborn's journal, which is relied upon rather than the somewhat more accurate account given by Meigs, but it is represented as telling the story of "Meigs's men." All Dear-

born's errors are reproduced and several errors are added.
The first are the mistakes as to the sizes of the ponds,
statements that there was a strait half a mile long between Long Pond and Round Pond (not supported by
Arnold, Meigs, or the fact), that the pond next after
Round Pond was half a mile over (not supported by
Arnold, Meigs, or the fact), and that there were only
three ponds beyond Round Pond, whereas Arnold and
the facts prove that there were four.   The errors that he
adds are the statement that the passage between Lower
Pond and Bag Pond was two rods long (both Dearborn
and Meigs, our only authorities, say four rods), the omission of one pond of the " chain," so that two straits join
(his words are: " They passed   .   .   .   to a narrow gut
two rods over, then poled up a narrow strait," etc.; both
Meigs and Dearborn, as well as Arnold, mention the
pond omitted by Mr. Codman), the statement that the
" narrow tortuous gut " (Horse Shoe Stream) was " 3 or 4
miles in length," whereas it is no doubt nearly or quite six,
and the statement that " Meigs's men " encamped at the
fifteen-rod portage, whereas Meigs, describing " our "
movements, indicates that his men crossed Lost Pond and
encamped " on the northwest side, upon a high hill, which
is a carrying place."   Mr. Codman does not attempt to
make his account fit the topography of the region, which
would evidently have been impossible; neither does he
deal with statements differing from Dearborn's.   He
calls the Boundary Portage four and one-half miles long
without comment, whereas, according to the measure,
it was not quite four and a quarter.

Both Dearborn and Meigs make the strait between
Bag Pond and Long Pond one and one-half miles long.
Arnold says " half a mile," which is far more reasonable.

15.   It is not certain that the men marched on this

side; but they had been on this side below, and the nature of the ground made it easier to continue there.

16. This carry is to my mind somewhat doubtful. Meigs and Dearborn, the only two (besides Arnold) who give a fairly good account here, do not mention it. Thayer and Humphrey refer to it distinctly; and "Provincial," Haskell, and Tolman seem to allude confusedly to it. Topham's record is somewhat mixed. It may be that some of the boatmen poled up the swift, narrow, crooked stream between Bag Pond and Long Pond, while others preferred to carry. According to Arnold, the stream was half a mile in length, and we can believe him; but the carry may not have been more than half as long, or the stream may have been good a part of the way.

17. See Chapter XI., note 25. But the letter was addressed to the second and fourth divisions.

18. Mr. Codman (p. 77) says he was "unwilling to leave the spare ammunition [i. e., the reserve stock] of the detachment which had been entrusted to his company of Virginians"; but it would be remarkable if Morgan's company, considered light infantry and charged with the work of clearing roads, had also been loaded down with the general stock of ammunition. There is no evidence that the riflemen carried more than their share of powder and ball. Indeed, we should suppose that the reserve stock would have been entrusted to Enos, and Dearborn states (October 27th) that the retreating division took with it more than their "part or quota" of the ammunition. Tolman (October 24th) says they carried back "large stores" of ammunition. Morison concurs.

19. According to Morison, Hendricks's men carried their boats a part of the way, left them in the woods,

and obtained their officers' consent to let them remain there, preferring to march by land and get on without tents. They then returned to them the next morning, took their guns out of the bateaux, and marched. This appears to be the only way to harmonise his statements (October 27th and 28th); but his account does not seem quite correct here (note his distances for October 28–30).

20. Meigs does not mention giving such orders, and the reference may be to Arnold's letter. The men seem to have regarded the orders as the result of a conference of the officers. Stocking says, " It was resolved "; Tolman, " It was agreed." Such a conference may have been held, and Dearborn, being in the rear of the division, may have received its conclusions as "orders."

Mr. Codman says (p. 79): " The bateaux of Meigs's Division were hauled up . . . and all but six for each company abandoned "; but this is evidently based on a misreading of a passage in Stocking's journal: " It was resolved to leave here most of our batteaus, which had already been reduced from 16 to 6 for each company—but 6, I think, were carried from this place." This means that most of the six which each company still had were left behind. But, as pointed out (Chapter V., note 26), this passage is not trustworthy.

The story of the damaged powder also is from Stocking. In itself it is perfectly credible, but we cannot positively say to how large a part or to what part of the detachment it applies.

21. Ward seems to have camped at the beginning of the portage. Dearborn mentions at this point " one Mr. Ayres, the Capt. of our Pioneers," who agreed to become his travelling companion. It may safely be assumed, I think, that Mr. Ayres was a captain only in the sense of being at the head of this gang. The pioneers

belonged to Meigs's division (see his journal, October 19th), but a civilian, if a good woodsman, was the proper kind of a person to direct them.

22. The position of this division seems to be fixed by the mention in Topham's, Humphrey's, and Thayer's journals of a pond beyond a carry three-quarters of a mile long. This would seem clearly to be Horse Shoe Pond, especially as Topham adds that the river ran through it,—a fact that distinguished it sharply from Lost Pond, which they had just left. Something is wrong, however, with these journals here. They mention on the 28th three portages and three ponds before the Boundary Carrying-place was reached, which is inconsistent with the record of the previous day.

Here must be considered the surprising fact that "Provincial" and Tolman give the length of the carry just before the last pond as fifteen rods, and Morison as sixteen. It appears beyond doubt that this is erroneous. Possibly it is a confused recollection of the distance from Horse Shoe Stream to Lost Pond. The error is significant as evidence that the journals were written some time later than the events, as well as another hint that the writers were not independent. Stocking, the fourth of their group, does not mention the length of the portage.

XIII: Pages 196–216.

1. It certainly is surprising that the four men should have met in this way, but nothing else would agree with Arnold's statements. In a letter dated "Chaudiere River, 27th Oct." he says: "I have this minute arrived here [a statement without significance unless it meant that he had just arrived *at the river*] and met my express from the French inhabitants. . . . I have just

met Lt's. Steel and Church." And in his journal he wrote: "On this stream we met Lieut^s Steel and Church with one Jakins, whom I had sometime since sent down to the French inhabitants." It would appear that the meeting took place just after Arnold "entered" the river. How did Steele and Church happen to be there? Steele had been ordered to go down the Chaudière River "near the Inhabitants, & examine the falls, portages, &c., & return to the [Chaudière] Pond as soon as Possible." He would not be at all likely to go alone on such a mission, for the danger of accidents was great; and we may infer that he took Church with him. Jakins, called also Jackquith, was probably a member of the Huguenot family Jaquin (Anglicised as Jaqueen and Jakin) that settled in Pownalborough (see Chap. VIII., note 35).

2. This letter, dated "Chaudiere River, 27th Oct. 1775," must have been carried along by Arnold and sent back the next morning, for (1) a postscript adds information about the land where the river empties into the lake; (2) the letter was sent by Hull, who, according to Arnold's journal, was sent on the 28th; and (3) Hull carried also a letter for Washington written after Arnold's arrival at the lake.

3. This letter illustrates Arnold's indifference about rigid accuracy. It was dated "Chaudiere Pond, 27th Oct. 1775," but according to the journal was written (was it ante-dated to give Washington a false impression?) on the 28th. It said: "I have this minute arrived here with 70 men [counting Hanchet's evidently], and met a person on his return, whom I sent down . . . to the French inhabitants." But this "person" appears to have been met near the meadows on Arnold River.

4. Arnold wrote that he hoped soon to see Enos in Quebec.

5. Apparently he added ten of Steele's men to his original fifty. Arnold wrote (October 27th) that most of Steele's party were " going forward."

6. Mr. Codman's account of Hanchet's march on the 27th (p. 92) was sure to be erroneous, because he assumed that Stocking was with him (p. 85) and therefore followed Stocking's journal. Hanchet evidently had a picked company (Chap. X., note 19). Stocking's journal represents him as not crossing the height of land until the 28th.

7. Arnold's estimate. These facts prove (1) that there must have been deep water to the east of Hanchet's men, else they could have followed the shore of the lake around; (2) that men could go to the actual edge of the lake, for Arnold, two miles distant, would not have seen Hanchet's party had it been at a distance from the shore, and Arnold says the men were discovered " on a *Point* of low Land "; (3) that Arnold entered the lake a considerable distance west of the place where Hanchet was, for it was two miles from the wigwam to this place (which was on the *eastern* side of the lake), while it was three miles to the point where Arnold entered the lake; and (4) that if Hanchet carried a boat over the height of land it was not now in his possession. With reference to (3) it must be concluded that Arnold miscalculated a little, as was very natural. His three miles may have been two and one-half.

How could Arnold "discover" Hanchet's men even two miles away? Perhaps they made signals. It is safe to assume that Arnold's party built a fire as soon as possible after landing. Hanchet's men could see the smoke. Perhaps they halloed; so large a company at the water's edge would have been visible, if something drew attention to the spot where they were.

8. Isaac Hull, one of Getchell and Berry's scouting party.

9. Arnold seems to have laid emphasis on the size of his party, for he mentions the number of his men and boats in his journal, in the letter to his officers, and in his letter to Washington. Where did he get his men and boats? According to Mr. Codman (p. 88) Arnold had them on the eastern side of the mountains; but (1) why, then, does he suddenly begin on the 27th and 28th to talk about his determination to proceed " with 4 batteaux and 15 men " ? This emphasis suggests change; there is no reason to suppose that he *reduced* the size of his company; hence the suggestion is that he added to it. (2) We know that he here took on two or three men, viz., Steele and Church, and probably Jaquin. And (3) apparently he took others from Hanchet on the morning of the 28th, for Hanchet (see Arnold's journal) had sixty men on the 27th (Mr. Codman, on p. 92, says fifty-five, but Arnold's figures are sixty), and on the 28th proceeded with only fifty-five. One was left behind because out of provisions, and Hull was sent back as messenger and guide, so that Arnold seems to have taken three. In all, then, he added five or probably six to his party here. And as he then had only fifteen, his original company was probably nine, besides himself and Oswald. If this conclusion is correct, he had with him at the bark house Hanchet's sixty men, his own original nine, Steele, Church, and Jaquin—total, seventy-two, in round numbers seventy, as he wrote Washington. This tallies with another way of figuring: Hanchet left the bark house with fifty-five and he with fifteen; Hull went back, and one man remained at the wigwam—total, seventy-two.

(Arnold excluded Oswald from his count, and I have assumed that Captain Hanchet also was not included among the "men.")

The theory that Arnold took men from Hanchet is somewhat confirmed by the fact that he waited for him. He did not wait in the fear that Hanchet was going to get into trouble, for in that case he would have lingered near the mouth of the river. What other reason had he for delaying, when time was so precious?

Next, where did Arnold get his four bateaux? Mr. Codman thinks they, too, came from the other side of the mountains (p. 88). But how could Arnold's nine men have transported four bateaux so quickly and easily across the many portages? Steele's party did not do the work, for Arnold seems to have found them two and one-half miles along on the Boundary Portage. Possibly Hanchet helped, but Arnold does not mention Hanchet before this same point; and, as Hanchet had a good start of Arnold, it is natural to suppose that he kept ahead, at least until a number of portages were crossed. Arnold and his party could have gone in two bateaux. Steele and Church were met on the river,—so they probably had a bateau. The fourth was possibly taken from Hanchet after he had carried it across the height of land; for, even if his party went partly or mainly by land, we can hardly doubt that he took at least one boat. Neither would he have left it on the eastern side of the Boundary Portage; and yet, when he reached Lake Megantic, he evidently had no boat. This matter is perhaps of considerable significance. Somewhere on the wilderness journey Hanchet seems to have become thoroughly hostile to Arnold, and this hostility came near upsetting Montgomery's plans for the assault on Quebec. Arnold's sending Hanchet in advance seemed to give him a place of honour as well as the best chance of safety. But if the Colonel, after doing so, took away his boat and some of his best men in order to deprive him of the glory of being first at the settlements and of sending back provisions to save the army,—that would have been a natural cause of complaint.

This would explain why Arnold wrote that he was "determined" to proceed with four bateaux and fifteen men; an expression that suggests opposition.

Where now did Arnold obtain his canoe? See Chapter XIV., note 1.

10. Senter says that he arrived at the meadows by Arnold River at 4 P.M. on the 27th, and *found* there not only Morgan but "all the advanced party, saving Col. Arnold, &c." But "advanced party" must mean simply "leading troops," for (1) by sunset on that day Hanchet and his men had made the extremely tedious and slow march of six miles to Lake Megantic; (2) two companies of musketmen went on from the meadows before four o'clock, as Humphrey, Thayer, and Topham show ("at 4 o'clock an express came from Col. Arnold . . . two companies of musquetry are gone forward."—Thayer); and, in fact (3), as we shall find, not only two but four companies had gone on.

11. Arnold himself did not receive news that Enos had returned until after the evening of the 27th, for at that time, as we have found, he wrote Enos that he hoped to see him soon in Quebec. Mr. Codman is therefore in error when he implies that Arnold knew of it on the 25th by quoting (p. 85) Stocking's record of the news under that date, and stating that he was with Arnold at the time.

12. We are told that the officers resigned to the men their share of the pork, but this was not true in every

27

case. Dearborn's and Haskell's accounts place the division of provisions on October 27th on the eastern side of the height of land, but the testimony of Meigs and others is decisive against them. Eight journalists place the fact on the 28th, and Melvin does not mention it. Thayer says the provisions were divided among ten companies. It is rather surprising to find journalists recording that all fared alike, and yet on comparing their accounts discover that all did not fare alike. The statements are: Henry, 5 pints; "Provincial" and Morison, 4 pints; Humphrey, 5 pints flour and 2 ounces meat; Thayer, 7 pints; Topham, 1 pint flour and 2 ounces pork (doubtless a slip); Stocking, 4 pounds flour and 40 ounces pork (evidently a slip); Senter, 5 pints (pork not properly divisible as it would not have averaged one ounce per man); Goodrich's men (according to Melvin) about $4\frac{1}{2}$ pints flour and 12 ounces pork; Tolman, 4 pints flour and 4 ounces pork. These inequalities may have arisen from mistakes in distributing the supplies. We are informed that they were divided into ten parts for the ten companies. Scientific accuracy was not practicable. If a company had fewer men than it was supposed to have, of course each man received more than the average. The intention evidently was that all should fare alike. According to Meigs, ammunition also was divided, and this appears very probable. Mr. Codman (p. 94), following Senter, states that each man received 5 pints of flour and no pork. The flour was cooked (there was now no salt, for it had been washed out of the boats) in different ways: a sort of gruel was made, or the flour was stirred up thick with water, and baked more or less thoroughly on coals or in the ashes.

13. I infer so, because Dearborn, Melvin, Henry, Tolman, and Haskell do not mention the letter, and pursued

a route that Arnold strongly condemned; but they would not have moved without drawing rations.

14. Did Smith's company go down the river? According to Henry's account, it seems quite clearly to have done so; and here the evidence is not a detail, about which he would very likely err, but certain large features of his experience, which he could not have invented unconsciously. Besides, it is impossible to see how Smith came to occupy the advanced position that we find him in later, if he did not follow this route. In the negative appears this remark from Humphrey, repeated by Thayer: "two companies of The muskettry are gone forward but the 3 rifle Companies staid with us." These words come after the mention of Arnold's letter. But (1), as Morgan and Hendricks are admitted to have passed the night on or near the meadows, Humphrey may simply have taken it for granted that Smith did the same, and (2) Smith's company was an unruly one, and may have been determined to go down the apparently easy route by the river in spite of Arnold's warning. It is noticeable that Topham omitted the words quoted above from Humphrey.

What shall we say of Ward? At first sight his company would not seem to have set out at this time. Tolman appears to indicate that the march began the next day, and Haskell speaks of going six miles that next day; but (1) Tolman's account is completely muddled here, and (2) Haskell's account of the 28th indicates that he went beyond the meadows, and, while the direct distance from the meadows to the pond was only six miles, no one following the river could reach the lake without travelling much farther. The evidence that Ward's company marched this way is: (1) the omission of all reference to Arnold's letter and the news from

Schuyler in Tolman's and Haskell's journals; (2) Haskell's statement that he marched by land seven miles on
October 28th and "encamped in Shedoer streams,"
which suggests that he marched about two and three-
quarters miles down Arnold River from the meadows
that day; (3) Haskell's statement that he reached Lake
Megantic and went the whole length of it in a bateau;
and (4) Tolman's statements that in the course of their
wading the men were annoyed by waves from the passing bateaux, and that they were taken across a river in
a boat.   See also note 22.

15. One infers that the messenger *told* of these things,
because they were not in Arnold's letter.   Hull, the
messenger, would naturally know of the news brought
by Jaquin.   Some, at least, of the troops supposed that
this information was sent by Arnold.   According to
Stocking's account the messenger seems to have been
Jaquin; but (1) why should Arnold send him back now,
if he took him along on the preceding day? (2) Arnold
would need Jaquin as guide and interpreter; (3) evidently Jaquin was not going home, for in that case the
letter to Washington could have gone by him; (4) Jaquin did not need to go back to the army to carry any
of the letters, for Hull was the bearer of them, and
(5) had Jaquin gone back there would have been two
guides for the army; but only one is mentioned.   Evidently Stocking heard of news as coming from below by
Jaquin, and made his own inference.

16. Senter states that several companies marched
down by the river, and then passed around the lake by
the western side of it; but (1) the other journalists give
no evidence of such a course, and unless some captains
parted from their companies (extremely improbable) we
know the route of every company except Hubbard's;

(2) such an attempt would have plunged the men into a dreadful swamp at the lower end of Annance River; and (3) the men would have seen that such a course would place a long lake between them and their comrades, besides unknown difficulties that might make reunion impossible. As for (1), Senter says that Greene and "most of his officers" went by the easterly route, and this might seem to exclude the men; but it is very common to mean troops, as well as their commander, when the commander and officers are mentioned. As the companies marched singly in most cases, Hubbard may have been with this part of the army without Senter's knowing it, for Senter was in the fore with Greene. Probably Senter wrote merely from hearsay. There is no likelihood that Hubbard flew off at a tangent alone (see note 25). With reference to Hanchet's company (not his advance party) it should be added that we have no information unless we accept Stocking ; but, as Stocking's account seems quite independent here, we may probably infer that it represents his own experiences.

We know that Greene and Bigelow went back to the high ground, for Meigs tells us of paying them money there. For the same reason we know that Getchell and Berry had accompanied the army to this point.

17. The proofs that they came to or near the shore are: (1) Hanchett's men did this (see note 7), Goodrich's men could go as far as Hanchet's, and they were just as anxious to do so; and (2) Dearborn says, "When we *Came to the Pond*, I found Cap.t Goodrich's Company, who Could not proceed by reason of finding a River which leads into the Pond"; and also, "going into the Pond and round an Island, where Cap.t Goodrich was with Some of his Men who had Waded on, He informed

me . . . that there was no way to pass the River without Boats." The only testimony pointing the other way is from Henry. He remarks that after getting across the second river they skirted it " to its mouth " ; but (1) Henry's narrative is as usual unreliable here as to details,—*e.g.*, he places this event on November 1st, whereas we know from Dearborn and Melvin that it occurred on October 28th, and (2) his words need be taken to imply only that the river was crossed a *short* distance from the lake; the men may have withdrawn a little to make the passage more conveniently. As for the existence of the two rivers, no further proof need be cited. Dearborn, Melvin, and Henry are clear and emphatic upon that point. Dearborn, for example, says, "after we had got them over this river, we had not marched above 50 Rod before we Came to Another River." Mr. Codman is therefore mistaken in saying (p. 97) that the men were stopped in the angle (B on the map) where Arnold River meets the outlet of Rush Lake, for (1) Arnold could not have seen Hanchet's men there, (2) men in that place could not be said to have come " to the Pond," for the lake is at least three-quarters of a mile below, and (3) it would have been necessary to cross only one stream, viz., Rush River.

18. Melvin's language seems at first very puzzling. His words are: "Being Sunday: crossed a river after much fatigue and loss of time, in a birch canoe, and then waded to another river, about 40 rods from the first, which we crossed last night." (As it has just been stated that Melvin went in a canoe, it needs to be added that his narrative does two things: it tells his own experiences and also those of the company.)

As a matter of fact, Melvin's inference was not literally correct, for it was the live Arnold, not the

Dead, that the men crossed Saturday evening; but it could be considered the same waterway, and by him it naturally would have been.

19. This is another proof that the men with Hanchet were not his own company, as Mr. Codman supposes, but a picked body. Other proofs are: (1) Stocking, a member of Hanchet's company, was not with his advanced party, as already pointed out, and (2) we read that when the general distribution of provisions took place they were divided among ten companies; therefore the organization of Hanchet's company must have been preserved (see note 6 and Chap. X., note 19). The quoted words are from Dearborn.

20. Apparently Morgan's men did not appropriate all of Melvin's supplies, for he speaks of using up the last on November 1st. Mr. Codman (p. 94) represents Morgan as setting out before Smith, but certainly he reached the lake later than Smith's bateau. If he set out first why did he not arrive first? Mr. Codman speaks (p. 94) of Smith's men as tramping "along the east bank of the river" and having to go in single file because "the country was mountainous"; but the land beside the river, like all flood-plains, is very low and very flat. He also (p. 94) says that Smith began his march October 30th; but this is an error due to relying on Henry.

21. According to Henry (p. 65) Smith's men fell into a difficulty not mentioned by the others, a tract of water, covered with ice, three-fourths of a mile across. Here two women who had followed their husbands, Mrs. Sergeant Grier and Mrs. Warner, became conspicuous,—the former for lifting her skirts and wading through the water, the latter for going back to her sick husband and lingering with him to give assistance. I have tried in vain to

identify this marsh.   There is no considerable body of water along this route that could possibly fit the story except Island Bog; and that, while about a mile long, is only a few rods wide.   My conclusion about the tract of water is that it was a temporary one.   The ground is higher along the river bank than away from it; the river had overflowed the swamps, no doubt, during the recent flood; and the overflow could not escape from the low ground rapidly.

22.   That Ward's company was the hindmost of those which marched down the river appears from the facts that (1) this company is not mentioned by Dearborn or Melvin as arriving, though both Haskell and Tolman indicate that it went this way; (2) Haskell's account shows that by the time he came to the lake, arrangements had been made to transport men across the rivers; and (3) Tolman indicates the same thing, though his narrative is confused.

Mr. Codman (p. 96) states that " Ware's Company " (*i.e.*, Ward's) went with Meigs.   This is probably because it is evident that some troops went with Meigs, and Mr. Codman held erroneously that Hanchet had his company with him.   These points have been sufficiently discussed (notes 6, 14, and 19)

23.   Mr. Codman evidently believed that Greene's division did not join the rest at the river.   He speaks of it (p. 101) as going into camp " on the high ground," and waiting "all day " for the rear to come up; but (1) they cannot have waited " all day," for they had come from Horse Shoe Pond since morning ; (2) Humphrey says ; "came to a small rivulet," evidently Arnold River; (3) Topham writes, " proceeded close to the rivulet in a large meadow " ; (4) Thayer says, " here we divided our remaining flour equally in 10 companies," implying that

he was with the rest of the army, so that, as we know that most of the army went to the meadows, we may be sure that he did; and (5) Greene's men, it would seem, must have shared provisions with the rest; for otherwise, having had a good supply of pork on October 25th, they would have had far more than they did on the afternoon of October 28th (see Chap. X., note 33).

As a result of this mistake, Mr. Codman finds it necessary (p. 93) to suppose that Arnold may have written two "similar" letters, one of which went to the meadows and the other to Greene on the high ground; but (1) there is no authority for this; and (2) is it conceivable that Arnold, in his haste, would write a second letter when the first one was directed "To the Field officers & captains in the detachment," and contained these words: "N.B. To be sent on, that the whole may see it"?

24.   Mr. Codman (p. 101) confines the distribution to Greene's division and some of Meigs's men: but Thayer's statement quoted above and the statements of nearly all the journalists are against this view, and there is nothing to support it.

25. Topham went back a mile, "turned into the woods and encamped"; Thayer went three miles; Meigs "marched back upon the height & encamped." According to Mr. Codman (p. 94), Hendricks's men went down the river like Smith's; but that seems hardly possible. To be sure "Provincial" and Morison say nothing about retiring to the high ground Saturday evening; but, as one of them speaks of setting out the next morning through woods, and the other tells of going over mountains, it is evident they did not go down beside the river. Neither journal supports the theory that the company marched by the stream; and as both mention Arnold's

letter, it is the more improbable that Hendricks did so. Hendricks's one bateau went down the river carrying Lieutenant McClellan, who was ill. Stocking testifies that he withdrew to the rising ground and encamped.

Mr. Codman expresses the opinion (p. 103) that a portion of the army went around by the western side of the lake. In this he follows Senter, who represents three or four companies as doing so. Objections to this view have already been presented (note 16). We are now in a position to offer more. What companies took that route? Not Goodrich's, Dearborn's, Smith's, Ward's, or Morgan's, for we have followed them elsewhere. Were they some of the companies that camped Saturday night on the high ground? Then they went back Sunday morning to the low ground which they had just left in obedience to Arnold's orders, and followed the river route that he had warned them against, got over the marsh on the lower Annance nobody knows how, and struck off alone into wilds they were totally unacquainted with for a destination they had no certainty of being able to reach by that route, and along the opposite side of the lake to that which they had been commanded to take; and all this in preference to obeying orders and following a guide that Arnold had sent them! But this is not all. The journals of Stocking, Morison, and " Provincial " show that their companies did not go by the western route. Topham's and Thayer's journals indicate that they themselves did not, while references to their men imply that their companies were with them; besides which it is inconceivable that captain and company would put a lake and unknown wilds between them purposely. The possibility is narrowed down to Hubbard (see note 16); so that Senter's testimony (since he said that three or four companies went this way) is over-

thrown.   Senter was perhaps thinking of the companies
that went down the river, whose further course he very
likely did not know.

26.   Hull, the bearer of Arnold's letter.   He was sent
to pilot up the rear, and this group of companies con-
stituted the rear.

27.   Mr. Codman says (p. 103) of Greene's movement:
"The division passed quickly down the Seven Mile
stream [*i. e.*, Arnold River]"; but (1) that was just
what Arnold had told them not to do; (2) it was just
what they had moved back from the river to avoid doing,
and (3) it was just what the accounts indicate with perfect clearness that they did not do.

28.   They cannot have gone "north and by east," as
Arnold suggested.   It seems plain that the five companies followed about the same route, for (1) they were
all acting in obedience to the same directions of their
commander; (2) they all set out to follow the guide sent
by him, and had no other; (3) they all had nearly or
exactly the same point of departure; (4) they all had
the same destination in view; (5) as comrades in a wilderness, they would naturally wish to keep in touch; (6)
it was easy to follow the same route, even though not in
one body, for the snow indicated where the forward
party had gone; (7) a comparison of the accounts shows
striking similarities and nothing inconsistent with this
view; (8) the nature of the ground, added to the facts
that we are sure of, makes it almost certain that they
pursued substantially the same route: (*a*) they were sure
to strike either Rush Lake swamp or a brook running
north-west into it; if they struck the brook they would
infer (especially if they had Montresor's map) that it
led into Lake Megantic, and would be likely to follow it;
in both cases the result would be the same.   (*b*) They

crossed neither Arnold River, Rush River, nor the outlet of Spider Lake, for in either of these cases they were almost sure to reach the southern end of Lake Megantic. (c) The only thing left was to go around the eastern end of Spider Lake, and the length of their journey is evidence that they did this. (9) Each account contains features that fit this route peculiarly well, e. g., Senter: a small pond, and then a stream leading to a lake; Thayer: going *south* in order to find a place to ford the stream (Spider River); Topham: going N. ½ W. after the river had been forded; Meigs: marching from 1 o'clock till night along Nepiss Lake.

Mr. Codman says (p. 101) that Greene's division (1) marched on October 28th over the "chain of lakes" (which in fact they left on the 27th), crossed the height of land and camped; (2) that they waited all one day for stragglers, etc.; (3) that "the next morning the advance was promptly begun" (p. 103); and (4) that "at daylight of the 29th we [*i. e.*, they] started *again*, and at 11 o'clock sank into the fatal spruce and alder swamp between the Seven Mile Stream [Arnold River] and Nepess Lake" (p. 103). In other words, he makes four days' work out of the events of two. I have not undertaken to point out all the errors in this part of his account.

29. The brook is not mentioned in the journals, and they may have headed so as not to cross it until after they came to Rush Lake; but this does not seem probable.

30. Mr. Codman says (p. 103) that the outlet of Spider Lake was not crossed because there was too much water. This means that the water ran more than about four feet deep, for a stream of that depth was soon to be forded; but (1) this is not indicated by the journals, and (2) the water cannot have been so deep, for (a) Spider

Lake drains but a small area; (b) the effects of the
storm of October 19–21 had no doubt passed; (c) since
that storm, snow only had fallen and had not melted,
and (a) the ground was frozen. The water in the outlet
must have been less than normal. Under normal conditions the stream is rather wide for a brook, but very
shallow,—a small boy can wade it.

31. Meigs found a place where Indians had camped;
no one else alludes to such a spot. Thayer mentions
getting a partridge for supper.

32. Mr. Codman says (p. 104) there was "no cooking to do," and represents the men as making all their
flour into cakes before starting (p. 102). He may have
relied on Henry (p. 62), but on p. 65 Henry mentions
cooking later. Thayer says that "daily" the flour was
mixed with water and laid "on the coals to heat a little"
as follows: a gill for breakfast, two gills for dinner, and
a gill for supper; and Morison speaks of making such
cakes this particular day. Senter says under date of
November 1st that they had water stiffened with flour,
which shows that flour was still carried. It must surely
have been easier to transport three to five pints of flour
than the same stuff in the form of half-baked cakes.

33. The name is not given in the journals, but this
must have been the river. It is formed of streams that
rise on the slopes of the height of land, flows north-
westwardly, and enters the eastern end of Spider Lake.

34. One feels amused at first to find the men thinking of going around Spider River, but probably the slug-
gish water that they found in it near the lake suggested
that it was only a lagoon or "bog." Indeed, Senter intimates as much.

35. We cannot identify this. What is called Moose
Hill is probably too far away.

36.   All the rest of the army except those who went by water had now passed along the eastern side of Lake Megantic.   Doubtless the lake could be seen, but there was at first no way to be sure what body of water it was.

37.   It is not certain that all camped just here.

XIV : PAGES 217–234.

1.   We have inquired where Arnold obtained his men and bateaux.   Whence came the canoe?   In Mr. Codman's narrative (No. 28, p. 92) it suddenly appears on the Boundary Portage.   But Arnold does not mention it until after he reached the bark house.   Indeed, he says that he "rowed," not *paddled*, to that spot, whereas beyond it he "paddlcd."   So it seems a reasonable inference that the canoe was found there.   See Chapter XI., note 1.   Dearborn's journal shows that Indians did lay up canoes in that region.   He found two.

2.   According to No. 37, 1092 feet above sea level.   I have been unable to find any reliable figure for the length of the river.   The lake is commonly called thirteen miles long, but ten would be nearer the fact.   Arnold thought he paddled thirteen miles on it, October 28th, but probably his voyage was less than nine.   He gives the direction as north by east, but it was almost due north.

3.   I was obliged to make the trip with a boatman from Maine who had never seen the river.   We secured the best canoe to be obtained within fifty miles, and took all possible care, yet we had several narrow escapes.

4.   Mr. Codman (p. 108) represents the Chaudière for seven miles below Lake Megantic as having been "a broad sheet of black water, perhaps 100 yards in width, owing to the recent freshet, moving swiftly through a

vast tract of overflowed forest "; but (1), as suggested in note 30, on Chapter XIII., the effect of the rains of October 19–21 had no doubt passed; (2) the banks of the river are too steep, much of the way, to allow such a width of water, except during an extraordinary flood; (3) such a flood would have been more white than black; and (4) Arnold's statement that the river was twenty rods wide the next day intimates that it seemed even less on the first day, for it broadens rapidly.   Moreover, we find proof in the journals that the Chaudière was not in a state of flood at this time, for we read in Henry's account how men dug roots out of a sand beach exposed by the lowness of the stream, and his description is so detailed that we can hardly think of rejecting it.   Mr. Codman himself accepts it, though it contradicts his theory of a flood.   Meigs says the river was " very shallow " in places.   Dearborn found it " Shole."

The question of the state of the river is decidedly important, for the water, if as high as Mr. Codman represents, would have added immensely to the difficulties of the army by covering lowlands, changing brooks to deep inlets, and sometimes burying the trail.   See note 7.

5. It seems quite possible to identify this place by the severity of the rapids, the correspondence of the river above and below with Arnold's description, and its estimated distance from the lake.   The point is certainly a dangerous one.   My guide was able to avoid the rocks only by sending the canoe into the wildest of the water. Sitting in the stern, he was unable to see the bow for a few seconds,—it was so buried in the waves.   I sat as close as possible to the prow, and great quantities of the water were thrown to right and left by my body; but, in spite of this, the canoe was barely able to float by the time we got through.   This place is called by some

the Devil's Rapids. It is safe to say that had Arnold's party undertook to pass it in their bateaux the consequences would have been serious. According to reports, more men than one have been drowned there. Mr. Codman (p. 109) says that Arnold went twenty miles before an accident occurred, but Arnold's journal states that his mishap was "ab^t 15 miles" from the lake. Mr. Codman also remarks (p. 109) that the men "used their poles and paddles where they could, but it was seldom"; but I feel very sure that they were using pole or paddle or oar all the time. It was certainly possible to do so, for my canoeman did.

Mr. Codman (opposite p. 110) gives a picture of what are named the Great Falls, to show the place where Arnold met with this mishap, and his text (p. 110) concurs; but Arnold's journal indicates unmistakably that the disaster occurred nearly sixty miles, by the river, above these falls. Besides, it is easy to recognise the Great Falls later, in their proper place, in his journal. Further, Arnold's letter of October 31st is inconsistent with Mr. Codman's opinion. Again, the falls are only about three and a half miles above the mouth of the Du Loup. Arnold reached the Du Loup on the 30th, but this mishap occurred on the 28th. Mr. Codman was probably misled by an error of Henry's, or a local tradition, or both.

Mr. Codman (p. 110) says that "only two of the bateaux and Arnold's periagua were saved from the general wreck, and the periagua was so badly damaged that it had to be abandoned"; but (1) Arnold speaks twice of his boat as a "Birch [bark] Canoe," not a periagua (pirogue, dugout); and (2) Arnold states that the canoe was abandoned in consequence of damage received the following day.

It would appear that while three of Arnold's boats were " staved," one of these continued to be usable.   To be sure, in his letter of November 27th, he speaks of setting out with five bateaux, but apparently he forgot at the moment that one of his five boats was a canoe.

6.   Arnold adds: " for 5 days,"—a slip somewhere, for he had expected to reach the settlements on the 30th and actually did so.   Arnold, in a letter dated November 27th, speaks of going on from this point with five men. This would imply that the rest walked.   His journal says, in a blind way, " 3 men."   As he did not count himself nor Oswald usually, this might perhaps be interpreted as equivalent to the statement in his letter.   In a letter to Washington, November 8th, he speaks of going on with only six men after his first shipwreck, but this may have been a slip of the memory.   When these letters were written, Arnold's mind was full of other concerns, and errors are not surprising.

7.   There is a break in the journal just here, but this appears to be the meaning.   According to our estimates, the Chaudière is 60 feet wide below the dam, 125 feet wide below the Devil's Rapids, 200 feet wide thirty miles below the dam, and then as much as 400 feet wide in many places long before the Du Loup comes in.   The water is swift almost all the way, and the rapids could not be numbered.   Once we estimated there were about four miles of nearly continuous white water.

I have tried in every way I could think of to obtain reliable information about distances on the upper Chaudière.   There is a government map (1898), but it cannot be called wholly correct.   This is due very largely, perhaps, to the fact that it follows the older maps of the geological survey.   Roads do not appear where they now run, and of course the windings of the river have not

28

been accurately drawn. The French people along the
banks are not intelligent and precise. Figures from the
most reliable persons to be found do not always agree.
Fortunately, nothing hinges upon an exact knowledge of
the distances here, though it would be satisfactory to
have it.

8. Arnold's account makes it plain that, as stated in
the text, he refers here to the Great and Lesser Falls.
The portage of a half-mile was necessary in order to
leave the river before entering some rapids which are
above the falls, and far enough above them to avoid
having to climb the bluff, which here becomes very high
and steep. According to a local story, Arnold was capsized between the rapids and the Great Falls, and lost
his money-box as well as other things; but the story is
valueless and every way improbable. Henry, recalling
events over thirty years after they occurred and vaguely
remembering these falls, erroneously associated them
with Arnold's mishap on the 28th.

Mr. Codman (p. 110) says that Arnold crossed "several
long portages" on the 30th; but Arnold mentions only
one of half a mile and one of fifteen rods. Mr. Codman
(p. 111) states that Arnold travelled the last forty miles
(up to evening on October 30th) "half by water, half by
land,"—*i. e.*, that he went twenty miles by land; but the
total length of *all* Arnold's portages on the Chaudière up
to the evening on October 30th, as given by his journal,
is a mile and a rod. Had it been necessary to "carry"
twenty miles, he would not have been able to arrive
at the settlements before the next day.

9. The half-sentence which here ends Arnold's journal seems to state clearly that the first house was four
miles below the Du Loup.

10. The next day Arnold wrote this letter:

"SARTIGAN, Oct. 31, 1775.

"GENTLEMEN—

"I have now sent forward for the use of the detachment 5 bbls. and 2 tierces and 500 lbs. of flour by Lt. Church, Mr. Barrin and 8 Frenchmen, and shall immediately forward on more as far as the falls. Those who have provisions to reach the falls will let this pass on for the rear; and those who want, will take sparingly as possible, that the whole may meet with relief. The inhabitants received us kindly, and appear friendly in offering us provisions, &c. Pray make all possible despatch.

"I am Gent. your's &c.

"B. ARNOLD."

"Officers of the Detachment."

Mr. Codman (p. 111) speaks of Arnold as " purchasing supplies " " two days after leaving Lake Chaudière " ; but he was more than two and a half days on the river.

11. At this point, for obvious reasons, the journals become peculiarly unsatisfactory. For example, Tolman writes, November 1st, "we having been four days without any provisions"; but as the division took place late on October 28th, this appears incredible. Stocking says that " many " of his company had been without food for five days on the morning of November 2d; but that is impossible, for he records that all shared in the division of October 28th. Senter states (November 1st) that "several had been entirely destitute of either meat or bread for *many days*." Dearborn mentions two dogs eaten on November 1st. One of them belonged to him. But Melvin, of his company, puts these incidents on October 31st, and adds another dog, while Humphrey, far behind Dearborn, saw men kill and eat a dog on November 1st.

Were there four dogs? Dearborn wrote Wm. Allen that there were but two in the whole detachment. Mr. Codman (p. 116) says that Burr's half-breed girl, Jacataqua, "and her dog were now constantly hunting for any sort of meat for the starving soldiery; and, skilful with herbs and roots, she became indispensable to the sick." This is, however, supported by nothing better than tradition, so far as I know. He adds: "When, therefore, Dearborn's dog and those of other soldiers were sacrificed, hers escaped." The statements about dogs made above appear to clash with this pleasant theory. Stocking speaks of a calf as taken from the body of a cow on November 2d, and Thayer of the same thing on November 3d; but it is highly improbable that two such incidents occurred. Mr. Codman (pp. 114–116) quotes Morison's account at length as a true picture; but Morison writes on November 2d of having been four days without eating anything, while his journal implies clearly that he had supper on October 30th; he tells us that he roasted and ate his shot-pouch, while roasting would have made it drier and harder than ever, and only boiling could have got anything out of it; he tells of a "huge mountain" and "lofty hills" through which the Chaudière ran, whereas these terms cannot be applied with propriety to the region. With such data it is impossible to make out exactly the march of the army.

In the hope of clarifying the reader's thought a little, a diagram, connecting events of the march with features of the river, has been presented (p. 223).

12. Apparently Morgan must have begun the descent of the Chaudière pretty early in the forenoon of October 30th, and two hours would have brought him to the place where Arnold's disaster occurred (see note 13). Senter and Stocking, however, speak of overtaking Morgan's

company at the scene of their mishap at evening on the 31st. Would Morgan have waited there a day and a half? We may be sure he would not; and "Provincial" says that after their shipwreck the company "then all took to the land, and made the best of their way towards the inhabitants." In view of what we have learned of Senter's and Stocking's journals, these slips do not surprise us. According to Senter, Morgan's men lost everything except their lives, while Stocking intimates that a very small part of their provisions was saved.

13. Apparently Arnold, Morgan, McClellan, and Smith met with disaster at the same place. That is what we should expect. As to the last three the journals leave no room for doubt. Dearborn speaks of encamping near a fall where ten boats were wrecked,—all except Arnold's and his, he says. This was eight miles by land from the lake, which may answer fairly well to Arnold's "ab^t 15" by water. (Arnold's bateaux suffered, but his canoe, like Dearborn's, escaped injury here.) As there was a camp where Morgan met shipwreck, Dearborn was likely to spend the night there. The connection appears complete when we note further that just below the place of wreckage mentioned by him, Dearborn passed a carry of "a Bout Half a mile," and that Arnold carried one hundred and forty-six rods just below the scene of his mishap; therefore Arnold's and Morgan's wrecks occurred at the same place, for the "ten" boats cannot be made up without Morgan's. Haskell puts the place of disaster just where Arnold does, fifteen miles, by the river, from Lake Megantic. Where misfortune overtook Ward's and Goodrich's bateaux we do not know. Morgan's, Smith's, Goodrich's, and Ward's may have made the ten mentioned by Dearborn.

Mr. Codman (p. 112) places McClellan's mishap where
he does Arnold's, viz., at the Great Falls. Aside from other
objections to this, (1) we find "Provincial" and Morison
meeting with McClellan on October 31st, while they
cannot have passed the Great Falls until November 3d,
and (2) Henry states that three days were required for
two active Indians to go from the first settlement with a
canoe to the place where McClellan was left, and bring
him down. Had he been lying at the Great Falls this
would have required only three or four hours. Mr. Codman (p. 113) accepts Henry's account. No. 28 (p. 112)
speaks of the bateau in which McClellan lay as having
been "carried further than the others"; but evidently
it was carried no farther than the others which were
transported across the Boundary Portage.

Mr. Codman states (p. 113) that Dr. Senter "with
the few instruments which he carried in his knapsack
tried the Sagradoine method to relieve the sufferer."
Senter's word, however, is Sangradoine. He evidently
means the method of Dr. Sangrado of "Gil Blas," *i. e.*,
blood-letting. What he needed for this was the lancet,
which he says that he had in his *pocket*.

14. If a road followed the general course of the river
from Lake Megantic to the Du Loup without meandering
at all, it would be, I judge, about forty miles long. To
that we may add at a venture, since the Chaudière is
extremely crooked, fifty per cent. for the footmen and
seventy-five per cent. for those who went by water. Arnold called it "upwards of eighty miles" from the lake
to the first inhabitants (No. 106, I., 384). Mr. Codman
(*e. g.*, p. 113) accepts estimates of distance that we find
in the journals, but this is unsafe.

15. Henry says there was no path at all, but this appears hardly credible. Even if some of the Indians who

went up the river travelled in canoes, others must have been sensible enough to walk.   Arnold's letter of October 27th states that he was told there was " a good road . . . all the way down "; but this is equally hard to believe.

16. The only large tributuary of the Chaudière is the Du Loup, but there are several other streams which would be very uncomfortable to wade in November.

17. Dearborn was ill, and for this reason, perhaps, he hurried on in advance of his men, though apparently not more than an hour's march.   One may infer that the two companies were together here from the fact that they were together later.

18. Morgan's men disappear after they are wrecked, but we have glimpses of Goodrich's.   Melvin (October 31st) speaks of Captain Smith's overtaking Goodrich's company; but we can infer little from this, for (1) Melvin states that Goodrich's company broke up the day before, (2) we do not know whether Smith was in advance of his men or behind them, and (3) Melvin says Goodrich's men stopped, but does not indicate where or how long.

19. For they were told that the first inhabitants were fourteen miles away.

20. Mr. Codman (p. 119) pictures the Canadians as coming back to the camp " with the bodies of half-frozen and insensible provincials, slung in place of their flour-sacks across their horses."   But this is certainly fanciful.   Mr. Codman's authority just here is plainly Morison, and Morison's words are: " They [the Canadians] gave them bread and saved them from death, placed them upon horses," etc.   Here is nothing about carrying the soldiers like meal-bags.   On the other hand, if the men were able to eat bread, they were then

able (if not before) to sit on the horses, aided, perhaps, by Canadians walking beside them.

21. We may perhaps infer that Thayer and Topham were alone, whereas Meigs speaks of the men with him.

22. Haskell was of this party; Tolman came later.

23. Both Thayer and Topham had been in the rear of the division, but Topham seems to have gone ahead.

24. Of course Arnold or Hanchet may have had something to do with these people.

25. See note 10. In Arnold's letter of November 8th to Washington he speaks of sending "fresh provisions, flour, &c." The first item refers, perhaps, to the cattle.

26. See Chapter XIII., note 12.

27. But possibly his illness may have been the reason.

28. Melvin spoke of Morgan's men as stealing his provisions at the bark house on Lake Megantic, but records eating the last of his supply on November 1st. Evidently a part of his food was not taken, for he mentions (November 2d) that his comrades would not give him anything although they gave "to strangers." (Perhaps they suspected that he had not lost his rations, but was hoarding them). November 2d, Melvin says, "I shot a small bird, called a sedee, and a squirrel, which I lived upon this day"; but, as he met the relief "about noon," he did not have to subsist in this way very long. Mr. Codman is, therefore, not quite correct (p. 114) in representing one man as saving his life by means of a sedee and a squirrel. Game seems to have been frightened away; or the men were too exhausted and too anxious to reach the settlements to go in pursuit of it.

29. Topham's record of the day is evidently based on Humphrey's, but these words are added.

30. There appears to have been at least one case of concealing supplies. Henry states that on the appearance

of relief, Captain Smith gave him a thick piece of bacon-fat as large as a man's hand, done up in a paper. For certain exaggerated reports, see note 11.

31. Mr. Codman (p. 133) accepts this as "probably not far from the truth," only he represents Morison as saying that "the effectives at Point Levi" numbered 510. Arnold wrote Washington, November 8th, that all were "happily arrived (except one man drowned and one or two sick—and Colonel Enos's division)"; but manifestly this was not correct. It should be noted that Morison ignored desertions. Henry thought seven starved.

32. No. 106, i., p. 386. With reference to the Indians (next sentence of the text) it may be added that Arnold's bargain with them seems to have made no mention of clothing (see p. 244).

33. At the trial of Lieutenant-Colonel Enos (No. 54, 4, iii., 1710) Lieutenant Buckmaster testified that when the fourth division returned there were 150 men with it but not of it. If we deduct 30 for Colburn's men and others who were not soldiers and allow 250 for the three companies, we get a total of 370, which, added to Arnold's 675, make 1045. But this figuring is really of very little value, since we are ignorant how many had deserted or been sent down the river sick, or how many of the sick had died, etc.

XV : Pages 235-246.

1. Spelled also Sattagan, Sattigan, etc. Sattigan has been said to have been the Indian form. Between Sertigan and Sartigan one is inclined to look upon the former as the correct French spelling, because we find— even in the Quebec *Gazette*—the form St. Igan, and this would come more naturally from Sertigan than from Sartigan.

2.   For example, a map of the British Dominions in America, by Thomas Kitchin, places Sertigan pretty near Quebec; Sayer and Bennett's map of August 14, 1776, puts it about one-third of the way from the St. Lawrence to Lake Megantic; and a map of "Canada, Louisiane et Terres Angloises par le Sr. d'Anville" (1775), places it just below the mouth of the Du Loup.

3.   For this and other valuable points relating to this region I am happy to acknowledge my indebtedness to Mons. J. Edmond Roy, author of No. 159 and other valuable works on the local history.

4.   Senter, however, as well as Dearborn, appears to have acquired some idea of the truth, for after he had gone five miles from the village that he called "Sartigan," he began his next entry: "Sartigan, Saturday, [Nov.] 4."
By " Sertigan " or " Sartigan " (in quotation marks) is meant the first settlement entered by the Americans.

5.   No. 106, i., p. 401.   It needs to be added that Allen had little besides the journals of Meigs and Henry.

6.   Arnold's journal ends with these words: " 3 miles further [beyond the Lower Falls] bro't us to the crotch of the River where the Des Loups enters, which is ab^t 7 rods over—4 miles further brought us to the first house on"

7.   To be sure, Senter represents the second stream as the larger; but (1) Senter, as we have found, was often inaccurate, and (2) the depth of the stream was perhaps the significant dimension in Senter's mind, and the Du Loup, on account of its width, is very shallow except at flood times.   It is very possible that like other streams the R. la Famine has shrunk since the land was cleared.

8.   Senter says this came from the S. W.; but, as no

considerable affluent flows from that quarter, he must
have meant the S. E.

9. There is a Rivière St. André between these two,
but (1) it does not seem large enough to fit the case, and
(2) had the settlement stood there, it would have been
less than three miles from the Du Loup, while the R. la
Famine is four miles distant.

10. The mere fact that, according·to Allen, Hanna's
house was that of a "lord," would make one doubt ,very
much whether it had been standing in 1775, for we
are told by Haskell that the dwellings in the first settlement were "small." Besides, Allen says there was but
one other house near Hanna's, while Haskell mentions
"three or four" in the first settlement.

11. Mr. Codman (No. 28) makes several mistakes
here: (1) he accepts "Sartigan" as the actual name of
a village ("there were but 3 or 4 small houses . . .
in Sartigan"—p. 120). (2) He represents that there
was a "house on the Du Loup" (p. 120). The only evidence in favour of this is that of Allen, which has been
analysed, and that of Henry, which is inconclusive as
well as untrustworthy. Henry states only that the first
house was within "a few hundred yards" of a river that
had to be waded. (Since Mr. Codman uses these quoted
words, we may infer that he relied upon Henry.) According to our hypothesis, this stream was not the Du
Loup but the La Famine. Against the theory that a
house stood on the Du Loup we have a plenty of evidence: (a) No village exists there now. (b) In 1824
fewer houses were there than existed in 1775 in the first
settlement, whereas settlements had been growing. (c)
Arnold says that four miles beyond the Du Loup brought
him "to the first house." (d) Dearborn places the first
house about four miles below the Du Loup. (e) It took

Senter until half past ten o'clock to go from the Great Falls to the first inhabitants that he mentions. (f) Thayer places the first house five miles beyond a river, which cannot well have been any stream above the Du Loup. (g) Humphrey and Topham represent the first house as five and six miles below the Falls, which does not permit us to fix it on the Du Loup. In short, there is very strong evidence against such a theory and practically none for it.

(3) Mr. Codman (p. 120) represents Dearborn as stopping at a "house on the Du Loup," which his journal proves he did not do, even if a house stood there.

(4) He represents Dearborn as going six miles to "Sartigan" the next day. But (a), as shown above, no journalist represents the distance from the Du Loup to "Sartigan" as six miles; (b) since Dearborn's journal shows that he went over four miles below the Du Loup on November 2d, to say that he had to travel six miles farther to arrive at "Sartigan" is to place the settlement ten miles below the Du Loup, which is clearly inadmissible. (c) Meigs states explicitly that the first house was in "Sertigan," not six miles from it. (d) Mr. Codman himself (p. 120) describes "Sartigan" in Haskell's terms, and Haskell says: "We espied a house—then we gave three huzzas, for we have not seen a house before for thirty days. We came to the inhabitants; the village is called Satagan," etc. How, then, can Mr. Codman place six miles between Haskell's first house and Haskell's "Satagan"?

(5) Mr. Codman (p. 120) says that Dearborn found Arnold at "Sartigan" ($i.\ e.$, at the first settlement) on November 3d. But Arnold wrote from "Sartigan" on November 1st: "I am just preparing to go down the river," and we have no "Sartigan" letter from him of

later date. Besides, Dearborn's account makes it clear that he found Arnold on that day at least ten miles below the Du Loup, while Mr. Codman places "Sartigan" about six miles below that river.

Further evidence that Arnold was not in "Sertigan" on November 3d is suggested by Senter. At 10:30 on November 3d Senter arrived at "the first town, principally inhabited by aborigines," which corresponds with Mr. Codman's description of the first settlement: "Sartigan, a settlement largely Indian." Then, Senter says, he went on five miles farther to find Arnold.

12. No. 54, 4, iii., 1328. Force again gives the name of the Quebec gentleman as Manir, but it was really (J. D.) Mercier, as already mentioned. Mr. Codman writes "Manier."

13. I infer that this money was some of the specie referred to by Washington, because paper would have been useless here.

14. It is very discouraging to try to identify places in this region, for the French *habitants* are not only ignorant, but sublimely indifferent about history. All along the way I did what I could to gain local information, but obtained the smallest possible results. At St. Francis (St. François) Mons. Taschereau Fortier, Registrar of Deeds, and a member of the most distinguished family of the district, drove about with me most courteously to interview the oldest people, and continued his researches after I left, but without securing much valuable information. Even a priest and local historian, Father Demers, whose kindness I desire to acknowledge, was unable to tell me anything about the state of things in 1775. No light could be obtained from parish records, for the oldest do not quite reach that year. I had hoped to be able to identify the sites of certain taverns referred to by

journalists and possibly find the buildings, but I failed to satisfy myself. One thing told me was that about half-way between St. George and St. Francis there always had existed an inn; but this does not fit any of the journals well. Another was that about a mile below St. Francis there stood formerly a small wooden fort on the west side of the river, and the "Bostonnais" (as the Americans were called) left a garrison there; but (1) the journals give no hint of such a thing; (2) Arnold could spare no men for garrison duty; and (3) why should he have cared to hold a fort there?

15. Evidently vigorous work was done to prepare for the hungry army. Henry mentions Steele and John M. Taylor of Smith's company as co-operating actively with Arnold.

16. Mr. Codman says (p. 125): "they were not averse to receiving fair pay for their provisions"; but the journalists agree that the prices were exorbitant. Dearborn writes: "ask a very great price"; Topham: "ask a prodigious price"; Thayer: "mighty extravagant with what they have to sell"; Tolman: "provisions plenty but very dear"; Morison: "Milk one shilling per quart," etc. But it should be remembered that the people on the Kennebec also had charged round prices.

17. Natanis, Sabatis, and Eneas appear to have been present.

18. The speech is given by Senter. He was there.

19. Arnold, in his letter of November 27th, states that about forty Indians joined him before he sent provisions to the army, and that some of these went with the relief party; but this was probably a slip of the memory. Senter's figure is "about fifty"; Dearborn's, 22.

A "Portuguees" appears to have been equivalent to forty shillings, for that is the sum, according to Dear-

born, that Arnold was to pay.   Probably, then, the word
means the Portuguese gold coin called commonly the
Johannes or Joe.

20.   Mr. Codman (p. 120) places at about this time
the return of "Burdeen," a private in Topham's company, who, with a number of other invalided men, was
saved by finding and killing a horse that strayed from
the relief party.   But the fact is really much more interesting and significant, for, according to Topham's and
Thayer's journals, the man did not rejoin the army until
November 22d.   This shows that the Canadians continued friendly.   Topham spelled the name Brudeen.

21.   Mr. Codman says (p. 126): "The river ceased to
curl madly over rock and shingle, and, though still white
with foam, became quieter and broader," etc.   But this
is not true of the river above the St. Francis Rapids,
since these are the worst of all, nor below them, since
there is no foam, but only dead stillness for many miles.

22.   The French name of St. Mary (sometimes written
St. Mary's) is Sainte Marie, of course.

XVI : Pages 247–257

1.   Mr. Codman states (No. 28, p. 126) that Arnold
was "entertained handsomely" by Taschereau.   This
would be an important statement, if true.   But (1) had
Taschereau been at his home, he would have left it on
Arnold's approach, for he could not have forgiven himself or been forgiven by his friends for striking hands
with the enemy.   He was, in fact, conspicuous for loyal-
ist zeal, served as officer and paymaster, and fought the
Americans at the assault on Quebec.   See No. 225, September 23, 1809, and No. 148, December 21, 1809.   He
particularly proved his enmity toward the invaders by

undertaking to punish one of his tenants who refused to take up arms against them (No. 159, iii., 49). So marked was his hostility, that the Americans sold his effects at public auction in February, 1776. (2) According to Sir James LeMoine (No. 91, p. 62) the tradition is that Taschereau was in Quebec. (3) This tradition has been confirmed to me by a descendant of Taschereau. (4) Senter's allusions to roast turkey and Spanish wine (which probably suggested that Taschereau entertained the American officers) may be sufficiently explained by the fact that the manor house and its contents were doubtless freely used by the Americans, since the political sentiments of the proprietor were of course reported to them. And (5) Roy states that Taschereau left his manor house before the Americans arrived there (No. 159, iii., 49).

Taschereau's place belongs now (1902) to Mr. Charles P. Lindsay; but the old mansion was destroyed by fire, and the present house stands on the other side of the road.

2. Just what was done we cannot perfectly make out. Thayer is the one who says most about it, and his style is here at its worst: "[Nov.] 7 Col. Green being one of 10 order'd Capt. Topham & myself to remain there 3 Days in order to bring up the men in the rear, and push off from thence to S Mary's. again from thence I was sent back to Santigan by Col. Arnold in order to hire Boats to bring up the invalids. . . . [Nov.] 8 Major meigs met me at S Mary's with the 96 invalids in order to purchase canoes to help them of which we perform'd & bought 20 then major meigs left me whom I never saw *since* (means during ye march), and had to carry them 30 miles on our Backs 4 men under each canoe to Point Levi going 12 miles without meeting an house then 15

more & staid at S. Arey's parish at a house near the chappel of the same name.   there we dined and set out again for Point Levi where we arrived about 8 o'clock."

The only way I can get a meaning from this is to paraphrase it thus: "Nov. 7, I, though no more bound to do this extra work than any other of the ten captains, had been ordered by Lieut. Col. Greene to remain with Capt. Topham up the river three days to urge on the rear, and then to go to St. Mary.   When I reached St. Mary, Col. Arnold sent me back to "Sertigan" to hire boats for the invalids and bring them to the rest of the army. Nov. 8, when I reached St. Mary with 96 invalids, Major Meigs met me, and proposed that we buy canoes in order to take the invalids around to Point Levi by water.   So we bought 20.   But then Major Meigs left me; and I, not knowing how to go by water and understanding that the canoes were to be used for crossing the St. Lawrence, decided to carry them overland.   This we did, four of the invalids carrying by turns under each canoe.   [" 16 remaining men were not able to do duty."— · *Marginal Note.*]   From St. Mary I went 12 miles without seeing a house, dined at St. Henry at a house near a church of that name, then went 15 miles more, and reached Point Levi at 8 o'clock P.M."   But according to Humphrey and Topham twenty canoes were carried by Meigs; and it does not seem possible that this was another lot.

3.   In French, the *Route Justinienne.*   Justinien was a Récollet priest.   He spent seven years in this field and died in 1760.

4.   In French, St. Henri.

5.   In French, the *Route du Pavé ;* called also *Le Vieux Chemin,* and *Le Chemin du Petit St. Henri* (a

29

place near the northern end of it). This road was begun in the summer of 1746, and completed a year later.

6. No. 91, p. 162.

7. At this point we are very much in the dark. Arnold's journal is missing. Dearborn and Henry were sick and behind. Meigs, Thayer, and Topham marched in the rear. Senter hired a horse and went with the chaplain. Stocking and Tolman seem again to be reflections of "Provincial." "Provincial" and Morison, though members of the same company, here disagree. Melvin is clearly inaccurate. Haskell, though good, does not give us all we wish to know. "Provincial" mentions one march of three miles on November 7th, while Haskell mentions very distinctly two such marches.

8. This letter is headed "St. Mary's 4 leagues from Point Levi." Both the distance from Point Levi and the fact that the letter was written on the 7th show that it probably should have been headed "St. Henry." The letter stated that near a third of the detachment had returned, "short of provisions."

9. Here is curious evidence of the way Tolman wrote his journal: "*They* [the lieutenant and *30* men] marched till near two o'clock in the morning, when *we* halted. *We* were in sight of Quebec," etc.

10. Where was the "Point Levi (or Levy)" of 1775? A map drawn by "A Captain in his Majesties Navy" in 1759 (page 451) applies the name to a strongly marked point of land projecting into the St. Lawrence somewhat more than half-way from Quebec to the Island of Orleans. E. Antill's map (No. 218, vi., 226), puts it at the same place, and indicates St. Joseph's church near at hand. Still other maps agree substantially with these. Caldwell (No. 24) wrote: "The 8th, they got to Pointe Levy,

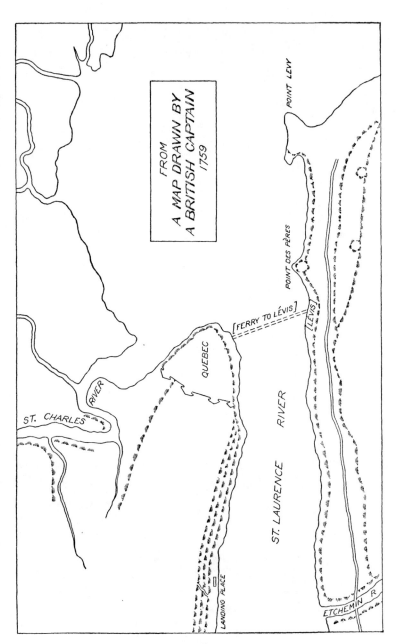

FROM
A MAP DRAWN BY
A BRITISH CAPTAIN
1759

POINT LEVY

POINT DES PÈRES

[FERRY TO LÉVIS]

[LÉVIS]

QUEBEC

ST. CHARLES

RIVER

ST. LAURENCE   RIVER

LANDING PLACE

ETCHEMIN R

where they took post, as also at my mill," which implies that the mill was not at the Point.

Sometimes the name appears to have belonged where Lévis is now. Ainslie's journal (No. 3) speaks of Caldwell's mill as "three or four miles above Point Levy," which would place the Point about opposite Quebec. Melvin has it : " Nov. 8. Came to Point Levi, . . . opposite Quebec." And the battery opened by the Americans on April 3, 1776, which was opposite Quebec, is spoken of as being at Point Levi in Nos. 3, 70, 98 (Finlay's journal), 224, etc.

Finally, we have good evidence that the name was applied still higher. The *Journal of Remarkable Occurrences* (No. 131, 1880) speaks of " Col. Caldwell's mill at Point Levy." November 8th or 9th, a midshipman named McKenzie was captured by the Americans while trying to obtain something from the mill ; No. 3 says of this event, " A boat from the *Hunter* sloop was fired at from Major Caldwell's mill " ; Henry (No. 72, p. 79) states that the mill was " on our left " and about a mile from his quarters, which fixes his quarters as about three miles above a point opposite Quebec ; Henry says that at the time the *Hunter's* boat approached the mill, all the soldiers ran that way, and that " Morgan and the Indians, who lay nearest to the commander's quarters, were foremost," *i. e.*, Arnold's quarters were farther upstream than Henry's ; yet Arnold headed his letters, " Point Levi." (Henry is confirmed at one point by No. 3, which says that McKenzie was captured by Indians.)

Meigs wrote : " Our men, that were gone forward to *Point Levi*, made prisoner of Mr. M'Kenzie " ; but he was captured at Caldwell's mill, and must have been taken (aside from Henry's testimony) by men quartered somewhere near. Haskell wrote, November 13th : " At Point

Levi the carpenters were all drawn out to making ladders and paddles ; this evening [*printed* morning] all were ordered down to the river to a place of rendezvous, in order to cross over." Now the rendezvous was Caldwell's mill, so that Haskell appears here to apply the name Point Levi to some spot on the bluff above the mill. No. 3 says : " A party of the rebels was lodged in it [the mill]," yet all of the Americans are reported as being at " Point Levi." Humphrey speaks of arriving at "Point levy," and then says that "we spied them [McKenzie's party] and fir'd Upon them." This places the mill at Point Levi, and also places Arnold there, for Humphrey speaks of coming up with Arnold. Thayer's account is the same. Senter states that the Chaudière emptied "but four miles above Point Levi," and the mouth of that river is seven miles above the part of Lévis opposite Quebec.

The effect of all this, after every necessary allowance has been made, is to prove, it seems to me, that the name —whatever its original application — was used loosely in 1775, and often applied in a general way to the great promontory opposite the promontory of Quebec. This was natural. There was no other convenient designation for that locality. Careful persons spoke as Ainslie (No. 3) did, perhaps : " on the Point Levy side " ; but this was very sure to pass over into " at Point Levy," and the name is at present applied in this broad way. A confirmation of our conclusion is found in these words of Arnold's (letter of November 27th) : " those [*i. e.* the boats] on Point Levi being all destroyed to prevent our crossing." The reference is evidently to a large area.

11. The Americans crossed this highway probably about one-fourth of a mile from the present church of St.

David de Lauberivière. At that time the present road along the river had not been constructed.

12. *Chemin du Moulin.* There can be no doubt, I think, that these were the roads travelled by the Americans, for it is known exactly what roads were in existence at that time, and these are the lines that fit what information we have as to the movements of the army. The pivotal point of the route was St. Henry. Dearborn states expressly that the troops went by that village, while Humphrey, Thayer, and Topham speak of dining at "St. Arey's," evidently an attempt at the French pronunciation of St. Henri. Meigs lodged there, he says.

13. Senter arrived on the 8th, and says that few of the troops came that day. Dearborn states that the "main Body" arrived on the 9th. It seems clear that the Americans lodged at the top, not at the foot, of the high bank of the St. Lawrence; for (1) Henry indicates as much very plainly, (2) Haskell speaks of being "ordered down to the river" so as to cross it, and (3) there was no road at the foot of the bluff.

14. *Rivière de la Scie.*

15. A mill that is believed to be a close imitation, or perhaps a reproduction, of this is now standing on the spot. It was built in 1781. My information on these points comes from Mons. J. Edmond Roy, who not only is the accomplished historian of the region, but was formerly a part-owner of the mill. I have also made two personal visits to the place.

16. Haskell so states, and Melvin implies the same.

17. No. 3: On the third of November ". . . we learnt that a great body of men were not far from Quebec. . . . The Lieut.-Governor ordered that all the canoes, boats, shallops & craft shou'd be brought off from the opposite shore & from the Island of Orleans."

18. Cramahé to Howe (MS.), November 8th, No. 220, Eng. and Amer., August, 1775—December, 1776, p. 109.

19. According to No. 3 and the *Journal of Remarkable Occurrences* (No. 131, 1880), this took place on the 8th; but they state that, in consequence of the capture of McKenzie, the sloop battered the mill the next day. It hardly seems probable that the captain of the *Hunter* would have waited so long before opening fire on the rebels who had taken his brother prisoner. Indeed, Senter intimates that the capture was immediately followed by the cannonade. With the exception of Morison, all of the American journalists who date the affair place it on the 9th.

20. "Provincial" and Tolman (followed by Mr. Codman, No. 28, p. 137) state that the boat came for flour, while Morison says "flour & other provisions"; but the first two accounts are undated, the third is dated wrongly (November 10th), and all of them are inaccurate. Humphrey, Thayer, and Topham state that it came for oars, and Henry that "oars & spars" were the objects of their quest.

21. According to Mr. Codman (p. 137), he was a brother of the captain of the *Pearl* frigate. But Ainslie (No. 3), whose testimony is particularly valuable because he was on the British side, states that his brother commanded the *Hunter;* and as a matter of fact, Thomas McKenzie was captain of the *Hunter* sloop-of-war from April 9, 1773, until May 11, 1776, as is shown by the British official records (Ticket Office Pay Books, Series I., vols. 1432 and 1433). (See also note 25.)

22. Henry is here confirmed by No. 3.

23. Or Haulstead. See No. 24, supposed to have been written to General Murray. The date of it is June

15, 1776. Halstead was a partner in the business to the extent of having a share of the profits. Caldwell says he detained "some flour and 200 bushels of wheat." He was appointed commissary of the American forces. The information that he could give did not throw much light on the exact condition of things in Quebec, for he had been suspected of holding communications with the enemy, and, several days before, had been sent down to the Island of Orleans. He was originally from Jersey. At Quebec he had been a merchant. The text follows Senter as to the date of Halstead's appearance; but Arnold's letter (postscript) of November 8th mentions the arrival of a friend from Quebec, and perhaps this was Halstead.

24. As fast as beeves were killed the skins were made up into these moccasins (Senter).

25. It is very needful to determine as well as we can where these vessels were stationed. Our only official information is a letter from Captain Hamilton, of the *Lizard* frigate, to Admiral Graves, November 9th (No. 20, Admirals' Dispatches, No. Amer., vol. vi.), which says: "Yesterday the [Lieutenant] Governor sent me advice of the advanced Guard of the Rebels being within two leagues and a half of the Main River, and desiring the [*Hunter*] Sloop might move higher up the River to keep a good look-out on the Enemy. I therefore ordered Captain MacKenzie on that service; he is within our signals." This implies that the frigate remained at the usual anchorage near the city, but that the *Hunter* proceeded a considerable distance up the river. Fobes states that the British "stationed a sloop-of-war up the river." Senter mentions that young McKenzie was captured "in sight of two of their ships of war." One of these was apparently the *Hunter*, for she opened

"fire," and we naturally assume that the other was the *Lizard*. This seems to imply that the frigate was hardly four miles distant. Arnold wrote Washington, November 13th: "To prevent which [*i. e.*, our crossing] the *Hunter*, sloop, and *Lizard*, frigate, lie opposite—however expect to be able to evade them." This he wrote just before the crossing was made, and when, therefore, the point of departure had probably been fixed ; and for this reason, as well as the fact that we have placed Arnold's headquarters—not with absolute certainty, however—more than three miles above the Lévis ferry, we are inclined to infer that Arnold's point of view when he said "opposite" was not far from Caldwell's mill, whence he set out to cross.

Another point needs to be considered. It was known that the Americans came to attack Quebec, and of course their most obvious plan would be to cross at the city, where the river was narrowest; therefore Captain Hamilton would naturally be on his guard there. But probably he knew that easy access to the Plains of Abraham could be had from Wolfe's Cove, and perhaps that most of the Americans were near Caldwell's mill; and he would therefore keep a lookout in that quarter.

Senter, who informs us that he crossed in the boat with Arnold, gives very explicit information: "The enemy had advantageously posted to [*i. e.*, two] vessels of war in the river, in order to obstruct our passing the river to the Plains of Abraham. . . . Crossed between the two vessels." Humphrey seems to support this, for he says that the *Hunter's* boat rowed *down* to the Americans. Meigs writes that two men-of-war were "stationed to prevent us," and Dearborn states, like Senter, that the crossing was made "between" two war vessels. Dearborn, however, was not on the spot.

Perhaps, then, we may conclude that Captain Hamilton placed the frigate as far above Quebec as he could without losing command of the narrow passage there, and sent the *Hunter* a little above Caldwell's mill, where the river narrowed again at Point Pizeau. McKenzie would still be within his signals.

26. See Arnold's letter to Washington, November 13th. This is the only reason given by him for the delay in crossing, though he also mentions that he has waited three days for the rear to come up. His words are: "The wind has been so high these three nights I have not been able to cross the river." To Montgomery he wrote: "As the wind has moderated, I design crossing this evening"; *i. e.*, but for the wind he would have crossed sooner. Mr. Codman does not allude to this vital difficulty.

27. Topham, in particular, was ordered on this business (Humphrey), and he notes: "Borrowed of some Frenchmen some wooden canoes" (November 10th).

28. November 13th, Arnold wrote Montgomery, "near 40," and Washington, "about 40"; November 27th, he wrote "about 30." Dearborn and Meigs say thirty-five.

29. The mouth of the Chaudière is about three miles above the mill. Senter, as printed, reads "were to be drawn from the cave of the Chaudiere," and Mr. Codman (p. 143) follows this; but the MS. is quite rational: "were br^t down from the cove of the Chaudiere."

30. Arnold wrote Montgomery, November 14th, that the crossing was "effected between 9 and 4." Meigs recorded: "at nine o'clock we began to embark our men." Morison wrote, "At about 9 began to cross." Senter, to be sure, noted that the men assembled at two o'clock A.M.; but why should they wait so long, and how

could three trips have been made over and back in two hours? Henry's time for embarking is "between 10 and 11." The mill is mentioned by Senter and Henry, and that was in fact a good place to go from.

31.   Senter so states, and one of the boats is mentioned by several of the journalists.

32.   From about a mile to about a mile and a half according to the route followed.

33.   Marshall (No. 109), who used Lieutenant Heath's journal, states that the first landing was about a mile and a half above Wolfe's Cove, but that it was found impossible to scale the bluff. Senter also mentions that a landing was made above the Cove, though he says the intention was to go directly there.

34.   Arnold speaks of the weather as not "suitable" for another trip. Wind was of course the thing to make trouble.

35.   Here is a difficult point. Senter calls the night "exceeding dark," whereas Humphrey states that "it was a calm moonlight night," and Haskell that it was "pleasant." Henry's account is: "The moon, now about three o'clock, shone brightly, and the tide run out rapidly." The natural inference from all the data would be that the moon crossed the horizon at three or four o'clock. I have, however, thought it necessary to have the hour of moonrise at Quebec calculated, and Mr. John M. Poor, Instructor in Astronomy, Dartmouth College, who has kindly made this investigation for me, reports that it was about 10 o'clock P.M. on November 13th. The only possible conclusion seems to be that the sky was heavily clouded until about four o'clock the next morning; for, with a clear moon in her fourth quarter, six trips of about thirty-five boats across the St. Lawrence under such difficulties would have been impossible.

36.   Henry states that it was built by those who landed first; Senter, that it was made to warm the men who were wrecked, and these do not appear to have belonged to the first party that crossed.

37.   Senter affirms that the firing was contrary to orders; but Thayer says that he, Arnold, and four more hailed the boat, and that "we" fired on her.   Topham and Melvin affirm that the Colonel fired.   Arnold himself (letter of November 14th) wrote: "we fired."

38.   Marshall (No. 109) states that the leaders held a council on the north side.

39.   Henry says, "the following night."   Thayer writes: "Topham and I . . . could not then bring the whole party over. whoever [*i. e.*, however] We brought the remainder over the second attempt."   Dearborn says that "all our men that were fit for duty which was about 500" crossed in the night of November 13–14.   Arnold's letter of November 20th to Washington indicates that he had with him about 550 effectives : but does not indicate precisely at what time. On the 14th, Arnold wrote Montgomery of his "party of 500" as having "nearly all" got over, though he sent word to Hanchet: "many of the men I expected are left behind." Meigs says that "about 500" crossed in the night of November 13–14.

Stocking and Tolman mention some harmless fire from the frigate early on the 14th, and the former represents some of the men as crossing after daybreak.

40.   Arnold to Hanchet, undated (No. 106, i., p. 375).

41.   The principal points requiring notice in this portion of Mr. Codman's narrative (not to mention omissions) are the following : (1) The name "St. Marie" is used (*e. g.*, p. 130); but of course the correct form is Ste. Marie in French or St. Mary in English.   (2) He

states (p. 126) that Arnold received Montgomery's letter of October 29th at St. Mary and "at once" despatched a reply. The reply, then, went from St. Mary. But Montgomery's letter was not received until November 8th; Arnold left St. Mary November 6th, in all probability; and, as we have seen, he headed his reply, "2½ leagues from Point Levi," so that it was written more than twenty miles from St. Mary. (3) He writes Eleazar instead of Elzéar (Taschereau); Cramahè instead of Cramahé. (4) He speaks (p. 130) of "some of the officers" riding on horses from St. Mary on; but we hear of none who rode except the surgeon and chaplain. (5) He speaks (p. 130) of the soldiers leaving St. Mary as refreshed by "four days of rest"; but the facts are that few reached the first settlement before afternoon or evening on Nov. 3d; then they had over thirty miles to march before reaching St. Mary — a sufficient task for two days, considering their condition; on the sixth, as is clear from the accounts of six journalists, they left St. Mary and marched from two o'clock P.M. (6) Mr. Codman (p. 131) says that the troops "covered 18 miles on the 7th"; but he should have said "on the 6th." (7) He states (p. 131) that the men carrying the twenty canoes went "along the river bank" "twelve miles" from St. Mary, then left the river, and followed the main body eastward. But it is inconceivable that invalids should have *carried* canoes along the river, ignored the *Route Justinienne*, and turned west, when their course lay toward the east, merely in order to go then through a trackless forest.

(8) Mr. Codman (p. 131) represents these men as going beside the river twelve miles, then fifteen miles to St. Henri, and thence to Point Levi, "a total carry of thirty miles." This would make the distance from St. Henri to Point Levi (*i. e.*, the St. Lawrence) only

three miles. It is in fact over eight miles in an air-
line. (9) He says (p. 131) that at this time "the
severe Canadian winter had begun." This expression
would imply at least a freezing temperature; but, as he
recognises on page 130, the mud was deep in the road.
(10) He represents (p. 131) both the army as halting and
the lieutenant with his squad as going forward to Point
Levi, on November 8th; but "Provincial" says (November 7th), "halted till evening, when a Lieut., with 20 men
was ordered forward to see if the way was clear."
Morison's journal places this in the *morning* (evidently
a slip) of November 7th. Tolman has it: "7th . . .
halted till night, when [*i. e.*, at nightfall] a lieutenant was
sent," etc. Stocking's record is: "7 . . . halted until night. A lieutenant," etc. (11) He states (p. 131)
that Arnold went to Point Levi with the lieutenant; but
the only evidence bearing on this is Arnold's letter of
November 8th to Montgomery. This proves that at 1
o'clock A.M., November 8th, he was at least "2½ leagues
from Point Levi." It is hardly possible that, besides
reading a letter from Montgomery and writing a long
reply, he could have reached Point Levi, as the lieutenant did, by 2 o'clock, with danger, darkness, and a rough
road to hinder him. (12) He states (p. 132) that on the
9th "the whole army now advanced to Pt. Levi"; but
Arnold wrote Washington on the 8th that his army "are
here and [*i. e.*, or] within two or three days march";
some, then, reached Point Levi before the 9th. "Provincial" speaks of being quartered there on the 8th. Senter
indicates that a portion of the army arrived that day.
On the other hand, we have many intimations that some
did not appear until after the 9th. (13) He says (p. 132)
that the falls of the Chaudière tumble "into the great
river," *i. e.*, the St. Lawrence; but these falls are two and

a half miles from the St. Lawrence. (14) He says (p. 132) that "by the 13th all the survivors except a few, who, like Capt. Dearborn and Henry, were too ill to be moved from hospitable shelters found by the wayside, had come up"; but, as already pointed out, Brudeen and others did not turn up until the 22d, and they were not in such shelters. (15) He quotes (p. 133) Morison's estimate that seventy or eighty had died in the wilderness as "probably not far from the truth"; but Morison himself adds that he was "inclined to believe that some of these got to the inhabitants" (see note 31 on Chap. XIV. and text). (16) Mr. Codman says (p. 134) that Caldwell's mill stood "about a mile to the west of Point Levi," but if the name "Point Levi" is used in its broad sense (see note 10) the mill was *at* Point Levi; if in its narrow sense, it was several miles distant. (17) He gives (p. 134) the distance from Caldwell's mill to "King's wharf, Quebec," as "1100 or 1200 yards"; but the site of King's wharf is below the flagstaff of the Quebec citadel, so that this distance by an air line was close to three miles. (18) He states (p. 134) that "The mill was the property of Major Henry Caldwell"; but the mill, an appendage of the seigneurie of Lauzon, was *leased* by Caldwell in 1774, and not *purchased* by him until February 28, 1801 (No. 159, iii., 357). (19) He says (p. 134) that "The person whom they found in charge [at the mill] joined them and became a commissary." This has reference, of course, to Halstead. But we have no evidence that he was "found" at the mill, and Senter mentions his "arrival" on the 9th, adding that he had been banished from Quebec to the Island of Orleans "several days" before. (20) He speaks (p. 134) of the "impregnable battlements" of Quebec as within sight of the Americans; but such terms could only be applied to the citadel, and the citadel did not exist in 1775. (21) He says (p. 135) that " a detail of carpenters under Lieut. Savage was told off to make scaling ladders, spears, and hooks " ; but (*a*) could carpenters make the hooks of scaling ladders ? (*b*) Thayer and Humphrey represent the spears and hooks as made by the blacksmiths under Captain Hanchet, and Haskell confirms this. (22) He places (p. 136) the capture of the midshipman on November 11th as Henry does; but very many of Henry's dates are wrong. Topham, Thayer, Haskell, and Melvin agree that the incident occurred on the 9th (see note 19). Senter, to be sure, mentions it under date of the 11th ; but so does he mention Halstead's arrival, which, he adds, took place on the 9th.

Addendum to note 2 on Chapter II. : " Provincial's " journal, as printed in Glasgow, begins, " The Journal of Capt. William Hendricks, and Capt. John Chambers, of the Rifle-Men, from Carlisle," etc. Hence Egle, and also Codman (p. 318), speak of it as Hendricks's journal. This, however, it cannot have been, for it continues after Hendricks died. Chambers was a private. Hence the above remarks, due probably to somebody in Glasgow, have no authority, and the journal is anonymous. Possibly Chambers was the author, but the theory of the text seems more reasonable.

APPENDIX

ARNOLD'S JOURNAL OF HIS EXPEDITION
TO CANADA

From the Sparks Manuscripts in the Library of Harvard University, No. 52, vol. ii., p. 1. The MS. is endorsed as follows: "The original in possession of Judge Edwards of New York. This copy given me by Mr. R. R. Ward, Feb., 1831."

N. B.—In quotations from the journal it has not always seemed desirable to reproduce exactly all the rather annoying peculiarities of punctuation, capitalisation, spelling, and abbreviation, though enough have been given to show how the journal was written; but they are here printed as they appear in the MS. In several cases the MS. is not perfectly clear, however. A very conspicuous instance of obscurity is the spelling of "Chaudière." In a few cases abbreviation is indicated in the MS. by a mark not exactly imitated in type fonts.

A number of our Men employed in bringing Provisions, &c, with his Excellency Gen! Washington and Dispatch bark. Five of the Transports [1]—

WENSDAY 27.TH SEP.^{R} 1775.*

Major Meigs with Cap^{ts} Hanchets, Wards, Dearborns & Goodrichs Companies Marched at Noon—Send down a number of Boats to bring up all the flour from below—Wrote to my Sister Hannah—Sent to the Commissary to forward on all the Battoes &c.

* Of course the MS. does not use capitals in these headings except at the beginning of the day and the month.

THURSDAY 28[H] SEPT. 1775.

The whole Detachment marched, except Scott, McCobbs & Williams Companies, who are detained for Battoes to be mended, Oars, Paddles, &c &c.[2]

Sent for Col[s] Enos & the Commissary to come up from Colburns, with all the men & boats—ordered the sick & criminal on Board the Broad Bay Cap[t] Clarkson with stores &c—

FRIDAY. 29 [?] SEPT[R] 1775

Capt[n] M[c]Cobbs & Scotts Comp[is] march ab[t] 10 A.M. at noon—left Fort Weston in a Bark Canoe for Fort Halifax—left Col Enos with Capt Williams Comp[s] to bring up the rear with the Provisions behind. Our canoes proving very leaky stopped at Vassalborough 8 miles above Fort Western & changed her for a Pettiauger—Lodged ab[t] 4 miles short of Fort Halifax. C[e] of the River from F Weston to Halifax is No. N. E. 18[m].

SATURDAY SEPT 30[H] 1775.

At 6 A.M. crossed the 3 mile Falls & at 10 arrived at Fort Halifax where I found Cap[t] Dearborns & Goodrich's Comp[ns] just over the falls which are at[3] 60 rods over—Good carrying Place—

SATURDAY SEPT 30. 1775.[4]

At 10 A.M. dined at Crosiers & hired him with his team to carry over baggage over land about 5 miles to avoid the riples or quick water above the falls which are very dangerous & difficult to pass. At 5 P.M. left the landg & proceeded up the river one mile & half where we lodged in the Woods with Major Meigs & his Division—

SUNDAY OCT 1. 1775.

Mounted the River at ab[t] 12 miles, over several Rips & swift water—Dined at one Westerns [5] 3 miles before Sou heagan [6] falls at 4 P.M. Reached Sou heagen falls which we passed & went up the river 5 miles where we lodged

at one Widow Warrens—great part of the way small falls
& quick water.[7]

MONDAY OCT. 2^D 1775.

At 10 A.M. arrived at Norridgewalk Falls 6½ miles from
where we lodged—great part of the way swift water &
Rapids. The Land from Fort Western to this place
appears in general very good & fertile & is thickly inhabited. Here we leave the English settlements, no
Inhabitants being above the falls, which by the best
estimation are 50 miles from Fort Western—Here I overtook Capt Morgan with his division, who had just got
his baggage over the Carrying Places, which is about
1500 yards over, so high there.[8]

N.B.[9] Course from Fort Halifax over the Ripple

	N° Dist.	5^m
From Ripple to sou heavyon falls—very crooked, ab.^t N°		16
From sou heavyon falls to Norrigewalk S. W. 5 & N. W. 7—		12
		33

SUNDAY OCT^R 3^D 1775—

The Rifflars proceed for the G Carrying Place some [10]
Thayers & Hubbards Comp^s employed in getting over
their baggage, examining Bread great part of which is
damaged by the Boats leaking, & the difficulty of passing
the Rapids, where it is impossible for People unacquainted to get up the Boats without ship.^g water. here
is some small vestiges left of an Indian Town, (destroyed
by the English ab.^t 10 years [11] since) the foundation of
an Old Church and alter the monument over the fort [12]
St Francis. the founder of the Church & the whole
tribe we are told are extinct except two or three—

WENSDAY OCT 4.^H Carpenters employed in repairing

Battoes, & the several Companies in carrying over their Provision, some of which proves unfit for use. Col Grants[13] division proceeded forward. Major Meigs Division arrived with Colburn &c.

THURSDAY OCT 5^H 1775—Companies employed as on preceeding day—

FRIDAY OCT 6^H Major Meigs with his Division went forward—Col Enos with the last Division arrived—

SATURDAY OCT 7^H The last division employed in examining their Bread (part of which is wet and unfit for use) carrying their Baggage & Provision over the Portage

SUNDAY 8^H OCT^R We have not been able to get all our baggage over the Portage until this morning, tho' we have constantly had two sleds going with oxen, owing to the height of the Hill & the bad road—a storm of rain prevents our proceeding this day—

MONDAY OCT 9^H—Struck our Tents—carried our Baggage across the Portage—embarked & proceeded up the River about 3 miles 6° N. N E here the River takes a remarkable turn to the E N E. ab^t $\frac{3}{4}$ of a mile & then turns W B N ab^t $\frac{3}{4}$ of a mile more. we crossed the elbow over land being ab^t 30 rods, which saves more than a mile of rapid water—here the River takes its proper course ab^t N. at 12 o Clock passed the 7 mile Stream — at 3 dined at one of the Islands, & at 5 encamped with Capt McCobb on another Island, within 2 miles of Carratunk falls, the whole dist^{ce} this day 16 miles course N N E. Easterly the water very rapid, the land from the Mo. of the River, to Corratunk falls appears[14] & in general fertile & tolerably well wooded with some Oak, Elm, Ash, Beech Maple, Pine, Hemlock, &c

TUESDAY OCT^R 10—AT 9 A M—

Arrived at Curratunk falls—the fall of Water is ab^t 15

feet—the Portage near 50 Rods over—We proceeded up
the River ab^t 5 miles ag^t a very rapid stream C° ab^t N°
— here the mountains begin to appear on each side the
river, high, & snow on the tops and appear well wooded
—the River from Norridgewalk to the G Carrying Place
is very uneven in wedth, but in general about 400 yards
& full of a great number of small Islands which appear
very fertile land—We ascended the River this day ab^t 12
miles in general very rapid & shallow water—we encamped late at night much fatuiged—

WENSDAY OCT 11^H 1775—We embarked early this morning & proceeded up the river, the Stream very rapid
indeed—At 10, arrived at the Great Carrying Place which
is very remarkable, a large Brook emptying itself into
the River just above which comes out of the first Lake—
When abreast of the Carrying Place in the River, you
will observe at ab^t 400 yards above you a large mountain
in shape of a shugar Loaf—at the foot of which the
River turns off to the Eastward—This Mountain when
you are at the carrying Place seems to rise out of the
middle of the river—Here I overtook Capt Morgan &
his Division, Col° Grain [15] & Division—part of each had
proceeded as far as the Second Lake Major Meigs arrived
just before me—Met Lieut^r Church who had been at the
dead River on a survey & reports as follows—From Kene-
ler [16] over the Portage to the first Pond or Lake course w^t
27° N° Distance 3¼ miles rising ground, bad road but
capable of being made good.

Over the first Pond half a mile, which Pond is 1¼ mile
long [17]—here our People caught a prodigious number of
fine Salmon Trout, nothing being more common than a
man's taking 8 or 10 Doz in one hours time, which generally weigh half a pound a piece—The Second Portage
is W. 6° N° — half a mile & 20 rods—very hard, but ruff

roads—The second Pond is in length from N° to S° 2½ miles long, & ¾ mile wide.[18]

The Third Carrying Place is ¼ mile[19] & 40 rods The Road very bad—Course West 10° N—

The Third Pond is in length from N°. to S°. 3 miles Width 2 miles—Co over W. B N.

The fourth or last portage is West 20°. N°. Distance 2¾ miles & 60 rods—the first part of the road tolerable good —the last mile a Savanna, wet and mirey ab.ᵗ six or eight inches Deep—

THURSDAY OCT. 12.ᴴ—Lieut.ᵗ Steel returned from Chaudiar [?] Pond & says he discovered no Indians that the dead river from the last Carrying place he judges to be 80 Miles—most part of the way a fine deep river—the current hardly perceptible—some five falls & short carrying places, and rapid water—The carrying place from the dead river to Shordair [?] Pond ab.ᵗ 4 miles—very good &   ground most part of the way & Plenty of Moose and other game on the River—This Day employed Capt Goodrichs company in building a Logg House on the 2ᵈ Carrying Place to accommodate our sick, 8 or 10 in number who we are obliged to leave behind—Also a Party at the E.ᵗ side of the first portage to build a small Logg House for men & provisions

Ordered Lieu.ᵗˢ Steel & Church with 20 ax men & a surveyor to Chaudair [?] Ponds to Clear the Portages & take a survey of the Country—Lieut.ᵗ Steel to go down the Chaudair [?] near the Inhabitants & examine the falls, portages, &c—& return to the Pond as soon as Possible. Our men are much fatigued in Carrying over their Battoes, Provisions, &c, the roads being extremely bad—however their spirit and industry seems to overcome every obstacle—& they appear very cheerfull—We have had remarkable fine weather since we left Cambridge, and only one death has happened, & very few accidents by water, which is the more remarkable as there seldom passes a season without some People being drowned in the Kenebec, which is very difficult & dangerous to ascend—

Oc.ᵀ 13ᴴ This morning dispatched one Eneas & another Indian with Letters to some Gentlemen in Quebec & to Gen.ˡ Schuyler—sent a white man with[20] who is to proceed as far as Sartigan & after discovering the sentiments of the inhabitants, & procuring all the intelligence he can, is to return to us at Chaudair Pond where we expect to meet him in abᵗ 7 or 8 days. Two divisions have this day reached the Dead River.[21]

N. B. The foregoing transmitted to Genˡ Washington—

SATURDAY OCTᴿ 14ᴴ 1775—

Left our encampment at 4 P.M. carried over the Portage, which accordᵍ to Lieut. Church's survey, is W 6° N ½ mile & 20 Rods—ground hard—we soon arrived at the second Pond which makes as desolate an appearance as the first does bountifull, the Lake being very irregular, long & narrow—the trees all dead & full of moss—the water very thick & muddy. Our course over it for abᵗ ½ mile was West, then stand N. B W. abᵗ ¾ a mile up a narrow creek, or arm of the Lake. Our course over the Third Portage was Wᵗ 10.° N.° 1⅛ of a mile — Road extremely Bad, being choaked up with Roots, which we could not clear away, it being a work of time—reached the third Pond or Lake—there the prospect is very beautiful & noble, a high chain of mountains encircling the Pond, which is deep, clear & fine water, over which a forked mounttain[22] which exceeds the rest in height bearᵍ N. West, & covered with Snow, in contrast with the others adds greatly to the beauty of the scene.   it being late made no attempt to cross but encamped for the night.

SUNDAY OCT 15ᴴ 1775. AT 10 A.M.   We embarked and proceeded over the Lake.   our course was N. W.   This Lake appears to be 3½ miles long & 2½ broad—very uniform—a small elbow running into it from the S. E. on the west side of which it empties itself.   We entered on the Portage at 1 o clock P. M.   We ascended the hill about 1 mile the Portage conducting us thro' the Gap or breach in the mountain—After descending the hill a mile we came to a low Savanna, where we encamped for the night.

MONDAY OCTᴿ 16ᴴ   Early in the morning continued our Route over the Savanna which is divided by a Small wood not exceedᵍ a 100 rods.   The Road excessive wet and miry, being near up to our knees. (but thanks to our Boots) we got over without being much wet.   Our course was nearly W. 20° N. 2¾ miles & 60 rods—Here the men had a most fatiguing time in getting over their Battoes, baggage &c.   at half after one P.M. we arrived at a small brook, where we lanched our Battoes & after rowing abᵗ 1 mile arrived at the Dead River which is abᵗ 60 yards wide uniformly deep & gentle with current. Prior to which ordered 10 men of each Company of Major Meigs Division to work on the roads, that the rear might pass with less difficulty—Continued our voyage up the River—we were now near the large mountain mentioned the preceding day—Here the river by its extraordinary windings seemed unwilling to leave it—two hours had passed away & we had gained nothing in our course, but at last by slow degrees it became more regular & returned to its proper course [23]—when we had got 3 leagues we found a small fall,[24] the Portage over 40 yards—The course this 3 leagues was nearly S. Wᵗ here

we passed Capt. Morgans Comp[y] & continued our course
2 leagues where we found an Indian House.[25] One
league further up we overtook Cap[t] Green & Division,
with whom we encamped much fatigued—our course
was ab[t] W. N W[t]—

TUESDAY. OCT. 17[H] Finding Col Greens division
short of flour (great part of their Bread being damaged)
ordered a Sub[t] 2 Serg[ts] & 29 privates, out of each company under the command of Major Bigelow, to return &
assist the rear in bringing up their Provisions, the remainder of the division to be employed in making up
their Cartridges—Caught a number of fine Trout on the
River. At 12 o Clock Capt Morgans Division passed us
& went on for Chaudire Pond

WENSDAY OCT[R] 18[H] 1775—At 10 A.M. Capt. Goodrich's & Dearborns Companies arrived—gave orders for
their making Cartridges as well as those who are up—
at 5 P.M. Major Meigs arrived with the last of his division.

OCT 19[H] THURSDAY—Small rains the whole of this
day — at 3 P.M. the storm abating, Major Meigs went
forward with his division, & soon after followed & proceeded on our way abt 2½ leagues to the second carrying
Place.[26] our course was various —part of the way was
S. W. & gradually shifted to S. E[t] with many turnings
and windings. We passed 6 small rips, very swift water
& shallow, which brought us as near the mountain as
we had been at any time before. The course over this
carrying Place is S[o] 35[o] E[t] distance 15 Perches. Night
coming on & the rain increasing we encamped on the
Portage & caught a plenty of fine Trout near the Falls—

N. B. rained very hard all night. The whole Country
since we came into the Dead River appears a flatt for a
great dist[c] to the N[o] ward & Ew[d] tolerable land & some

part well wooded, but in general covered with Spruce, Cedar, Firr, Birch, &c. the soil cold and in general barren—

FRIDAY OCT 20—Rainy morning—at noon major Meigs's Division came up, & being very wet &. the storm continuing, they proceeded on, intending to encamp early, Continues rainy the whole of this day—wind to the So. w^d.—

SATURDAY OCT^R 21—Storm continues tho' something abated, a Prodigious fall of rain for 2 days past—has raised the River upwards of three feet, which except the loss of time we instance in our Travels as the river was low before. At 7 A.M embarked & proceeded up the River 3 leagues when we came to a small fall of water, the Portage over W N W ab^t 10 rods [27]—ab^t $\frac{1}{2}$ mile higher up came to another fall more considerable.[28] Portage over ab^t 26 rods C^o W. N. W. Continued our Route up the River for ab^t half a mile & came to another fall.[29] the portage 75 rods Co over W N W— about 90 Rods higher up met with a fourth fall very considerable & long[30]—Portage over W. N. W. Dist. 73 rods—here we overtook Capt Morgan and his Division, but as his encampment was bad proceeded about one mile higher up, very wet & much fatigued, having Paddled up near four leagues, thro' the rain which continued incessantly. It was now quite dark so that we had little time to encamp, & it was near 11 o clock before we could dry our Clothes & take a little refreshment, when we wrapped ourselves in our Blankets & slept very comfortably untill 4 o clock in the morning, when we were awaked by the freshet which came rushing on us like a torrent, having rose 8 feet perpendicular in 9 hours, and before we could remove wet all our Baggage & forced us from our comfortable habitation very luckily for us we had a small hill to retreat to, where we conveyed our baggage & passed the remainder of the night in no very agreeable situation—

SUNDAY OCT. 22ᴰ—This morning presented us a very disagreeable prospect, the Country round entirely overflowed, so that the course of the river being crooked, could not be discovered, which with the rapidity of the current renders it almost impossible for the Battoes to ascend the River, or the men to find their way by land or pass the small brooks, arms of the river, &c—Add to this our Provisions almost exhausted, & the incessant rains for three days has prevented our gaining anything considerable, so that we have but a melancholy prospect before us, but in general in high spirits. At 9 A.M. Capt Morgan with his Compʸ passed us up the River, & at 5 P.M. Major Meigs with part of his Division came up with us, were employed the whole of this day in Drying our Baggage, &c, the whole of which was sometime under water (last night) and very wet—

MONDAY OCTᴿ 23ᴰ 1775—

At 7 A.M. Capts Smith, Hendrickson,[31] & Major Meigs with his Division came up & passed on — At 10 A.M. embarked & proceeded up the River — the stream by reason of the freshet very quick: in abᵗ 3 miles we came to the crotch[32] of the River. Our Cº was abᵗ wᵗ — Here we found that the Land [party] had by mistake taken the S. W. or wrong course which we rowed up two miles, & sent men ahead to inform them of their mistake, & direct their march. This mistake occasioned a detention of the Battoes & whole division near 2 hours, when the whole were formed we proceeded up the River against a very Rapid Stream abᵗ 3 miles to the 7ʰ Carrying Place,[33] Cº over Nº 35-E distant 7 Perches: here we had the misfortune of oversetting 7 Battoes & loosing all the Provisions. Here the whole Division encamped — the River continues high & Rapid, & as our Provisions are but short & no intelligence from Canada, I ordered a counsell of warr summoned of such officers as were Present, who came to the following resolutions [34]

TUESDAY OCT.ᴿ 24. Sent back the sick 26 in number & ordered Col Green & Col Enos to send back as many of the Poorest men of their Detachment, as would leave 15 days provision for the remainder, who are to follow on as fast as possible. Capt Hanchet with 50 men set out early for Chaudier Pond, in order to forward on provisions from the French inhabitants of Sortigan [35] for the use of the army.— Dispatched the Division inward & at noon set forwᵈ. Went about 7 miles — very rapid water — when we came to two falls — the Portages over the first was N° 20° W. 12 Perches the second which was abᵗ 100 yards above the first was N° 12° Eᵗ 6 Perches.[36] N. B. this is the 10 carrying Place since we entered the Dead River. We are now about 20 miles from Chaudiere Pond — We proceeded abᵗ 1 ᵐ higher up, when night coming on, & the rain increasing, which had begun abᵗ an hour before, we encamped — It continued raining & snowing all night At 4 in the morning the wind shifted to N° & it cleared up—Abᵗ two inches now on the ground—

WENSDAY. 25ᴴ OCTᴿ. We embarked early this morning & proceeded up agᵗ a rapid stream, about 1½ mile came to a Portage of abᵗ 40 rods, C° abᵗ W. Nˡʸ — the fall very inconsiderable—abᵗ 1 mile higher up found another fall, the Portage over 100 Rods, N. Wᵗ Water continues rapid ½ a mile, when we entered the first Lake [37] which is abᵗ ½ a mile wide, but contracts itself in several Places— We rowed abᵗ 2 miles when the Lake is no more than 2 rods wide, when it again opens to its former length [38]: one mile & a half brought us to a marshy ground—

passed on in a small Rivulet for half a mile which brought
us to a Lake [39] ab^t 5 miles long & ¾ wide—Several Points
make out into it — All these Lakes are surrounded with
a chain of prodigious high mountains—At the cut of this
Lake which lies N. & S, we found it contracted to ab^t 3
rods wide for a short distance which brought us to a
small round Pond [40] or rather the N° end of the Lake —
Here we were a long time at a Loss for the Portage — at
length we found a small brook [41] which we entered &
rowed up ab^t 1½ miles with much difficulty being obliged
to Clear away the drift Loggs in many places — Snowed
and blowed very hard.—the wind at N° All this day in
the last Lake the Sea ran so high we were obliged to go
on shore several times to Bail our Battoes, which was
with much difficulty kept above the water — Night coming on & we being much fatigued and chilled with the
cold, we were obliged to encamp without being satisfied
whether we were right or not as our guides gone forward
had made no marks or we had missed them—We made it
11 o clock before we could get comfortable to lie down.
The whole distance this day appeared to us near 14
miles, but as we rowed ag^t sea & wind we might possibly
be deceived 3 or 4 miles in the distance —

THURSDAY 26^H OCT^R

Early in the morning despatched one of my men up the
small stream to see if he could discover any signs of
a Portage while we got Breakfast, & packed up our baggage He returned without making any discovery; we
continued our Route up a narrow & very crooked &
rapid brook ab^t 3½ miles which brought us to a Portage
of 12 Perches. C° W. 20° S. to a small Lake [42] ab^t 80
rods long & 30 broad. In a few minutes we arrived at
another portage C° W. 35° N. Dist^t ¾ of a mile & 53
rods—carried over & entered another Lake [43] ½ a mile in

length another Carrying Place of 74 rods C⁰ W. 5° N. brought us to another Lake [44] of abᵗ ½ a mile long.   Another Portage of 44 rods Course Wᵗ brought us to the last lake,[46] which is 1½ miles in length & ½ a mile broad. At 4 P.M Entered on the great carrying Place into Chaudiere Pond: the length of the portage 4 miles & 60 rods—the first 2 miles abᵗ N. 1¼ miles W. 10° S. then N to the brook—abᵗ 2 miles of the First Part of the Portage you ascend, which brought us to the heighth of Land at an elevation of abᵗ 35° from that we then descended the Hill to the Brook.   We advanced on the Portage about 3 miles this evening (at Dusk) much fatigued.   The whole of our baggage did not arrive until very late, & we made it near midnight before we could pitch our tents; the whole distance this day abᵗ 10 miles.   All these small Lakes [46] have a communication with each other by a small Brook or river, & between most of them are considerable Falls, which occasions so many Portages.   N. B.   Sent back Nehemiah Petchell [47] to Pilot up the rear—here we met 20 men of Lᵗ Steels & Churche's Party—

FRIDAY, 27. OCT.   We continued our course over the Portage.   1 Mile Broᵗ us to a beautiful Meadow, ¼ of a mile more to the stream [48] which we entered at 11 o clock Bidding adieu to the Southern Waters, we followed this River which is abᵗ 2 rods wide abᵗ 10 miles which is very crooked & runs all points of the Compass: we met many obstructions of Loggs, &c. which we were obliged to cut away.   On this stream we met Lieutˢ Steel and Church with one Jakins, whom I had sometime since sent down to the French inhabitants.   He left Sartijan [49] the 22ᵈ inst & says the French Inhabitants appear very friendly & were rejoiced to hear of our approach, that there is very few Troops at Quebec—Govʳ Carleton at

Montreal, & one small Frigate at Quebec—at 4 P.M. we
entered the Chaudeire Pond or rather Lake Magantuck
which is in length from N° to S° ab[t] 13 miles, & 3 or 4
wide—We rowed on ab[t] 3 miles to the E[y] side & encamped: here we found a very considerable wigwam: we
waited here for the arrival of Capt Hanchet & 60 men
who left the carrying Place with us to come on by land.
At ab[t] Sun set we discovered them on a Point of low
Land on the E[y] side ab[t] 2 miles from us.   I immediately sent all the Battoes for them who discovered them
on a low marshy ground, to gain which they had waded
two miles thro' water to their waists: This error was
occasioned by their endeavoring to keep the Stream,
whereas they should from the carrying Place kept on the
high land & steered in about N B E or N. N. E. which
would have brought them to the Lake clear of the
sunken ground—It was near Midnight before all the
men were brought over, as the Battoes were obliged to
go three & four times each—

SATURDAY 28[H] OCT[R]—Dispatched one Hull to Col Enos
& the rear Division to Pilot them up, wrote his [50]

Genl Washington & enclosed the letter to Col Enos with
orders to send it forward by Express.   Capt Hanchet
with 55 men marched on at 6 o clock—at 7 embarked
with Capt Oswald—Lieut! Steel and Church & 13 men in
4 Battoes, & a Birch Canoe, being Resolved to proceed
on to the french Inhabitants, & at all events send back
provisions to meet the rear, who are at a very short
allowance of Provisions, and the men much fatigued &
some sick—We paddled on briskly, & at 10 A.M. reached
the N° End of the Lake, where the Chaudiere takes its
rise—C° N° B E. Dist. 13 miles—Went a shore, made a
fire.   I waited for the rear Battoes who were near 4
miles astern of us.   At 11 entered the Chaudiere which

31

is very Rapid, full of Rocks & Dangerous, & the more
so to us as we had no Guides—We lashed our Baggage
to the Boats, & the current carried us down the stream
at the rate of eight or ten miles an hour: after having
gone ab^t 15 miles we came to a very long rapid in which
we had the misfortune to overset & stave 3 Boats—lost
all the Baggage, Arms, & Provision of 4 men, & stove
two of the Boats to pieces ag^t the rocks—But happily no
lives were lost altho' 6 men were a long time swimming
in the water & were with difficulty saved. This misfortune, tho' unfortunate at first view, we must think a very
happy circumstance to the whole, & kind interposition
of Providence for no sooner were the men dry & we embarked to proceed, but one of the men who was forward
cried out a fall ahead which we had never been apprised
of, & had we been carried over must inevitably have
been dashed to pieces & all lost—We soon found the
portage, which is 146 rods. C? E. 30° N? & after carrying our Baggage over it, entered again on the River, but
with more precaution than before, & after going ab^t ½ a
mile discovered more dangerous Rapids—Went on shore
& examined them, & finding they were long & night
coming on, made no attempt to pass them but encamped,
& divided our provision which amt^d to ½ ^lb Pork & 2^oz
Flour to each man for 5 days.

SUNDAY 29TH OCT^R At 7 A.M. embarked in two Battoes & a Birch Canoe 3 men—We had not proceeded far
when the Canoe by running ag^t the rocks sprung a leak
& could not proceed—the men took their hands leaped
on board—We proceeded this day ab^t 40 miles found it
less dangerous than before, as the river had widened
near   ab^t 20 rods over in general, but still very difficult to pass—the wind at E^t & some snow renders it very
cold—

MONDAY 30ᴴ OCT—
Early this morning embarked & proceeded down the
River abᵗ 10 miles when we came to rapid water—filled
one of our Battoes, but luckily lost nothing: here we
were obliged to lower down the stream by our Painters:
about 2 ᵐ lower we came to Falls [51] and a Portage half a
mile over Cº Nº here we met with two Penobscot Indians who appeared friendly & assisted us over the Portage—½ a mile lower down brought us to another Portage[52]
of abᵗ 15 rods—3 miles further bro't us to the crotch of
the River where the Des Loups [53] enters, which is abᵗ 7
rods over—4 miles further brought us to the first house
on

NOTES

1.   Oswald's journal for September 26th concludes
thus: "a number of our men employed in bringing up
provisions, etc; wrote his Excellency General Washington, and despatched back five of the transports."

2.   Oswald's journal for the 28th begins: "Part of the
fourth & last division, McCobb's & Scott's Companies,
embarked; Captain Williams's Company being left for
batteaus, oars, paddles, etc." Certainly this is not "a
copy" of Arnold's journal, neither do the differences
seem attributable to Force. Perhaps Oswald kept a
journal of his own, and incorporated some of his own
record with Arnold's, when the latter was written off for
Washington.

3   Perhaps a copyist's error for "abᵗ."

4.   It will be noted that there are two headings for
this date. In Oswald's journal there is but one, and Arnold is represented as dining at 2 P.M. There are other
differences.

5. *I. e.* Weston's.

6. In pencil: "Scowhegan." It is not perfectly clear how the copyist intended to spell the name.

7. It does not seem necessary to point out all the differences between Arnold's journal and that signed by Oswald, since the latter is easily accessible, but Oswald's record for this day may be quoted: "Left our encampment early in the morning; at ten, A.M. passed the seven & fifteen mile streams; dined at one Western's; at four, P.M., reached the Scohegan Falls, where we overtook Hubbard's and Thayer's Companies; after crossing the carrying place, which is about one hundred rods, launched our batteau again, and proceeded up the river about five miles, and at eight, P.M., encamped at the Widow Warren's, distance seventeen miles; course to Scohegan Falls, about N.; from the falls to where we lodged S. W., water quiet part of the way; quick and small falls." It does not look as if Oswald could have written this from Arnold's journal and his own memory.

8. Oswald's journal says here: "which is one mile; course N. W." One is tempted to suppose that the last words of Arnold's entry should be: "over a high hill."

9. The rest of the entry for October 2d does not appear in Oswald's journal. "Sou heavyon" means "Skowhegan." "Sunday," below, was a slip.

10. Oswald's journal has in the place of this word, "Topham's," which makes the meaning sound.

11. In Oswald's journal, "fifty."

12. Oswald omitted "the fort."

13. In pencil, "Greens" and also "Greenes." The latter is, of course, correct.

14. The word "level" of Oswald's journal seems to belong here.

15. In pencil, "Greene."

16. In pencil, "Kenebec." In the next line, Oswald's journal has, "three-quarters of a mile," a clear error.

17. Oswald: "a quarter of a mile," another error.

18. Oswald: "half a mile."

19. An evident error for "$1\frac{1}{4}$," which Oswald gives. See Arnold for October 14th.

20. The word "them" from Oswald's journal fits well here

21. Here Oswald's journal ends.

22. Evidently Mt. Bigelow, though Arnold's bearing is not right.

23. Compare Montresor's journal.

24. Hurricane Falls.

25. The cabin of Natanis.

26. At Arnold Falls.

27. Probably at Eustis dam.

28. Probably Black Cat Rapids.

29. Probably Lower Ledge Falls.

30. Probably Upper Ledge Falls.

31. Hendricks.

32. Probably at the mouth of Alder Stream.

33. Probably Upper Shadagee Falls.

34. At this point comes in the MS. a blank sheet; but the entry for the next day shows what the resolutions were.

35. "Sartigan."

36. Sarampus Falls, probably.

37. Lower Pond.

38. Bag Pond.

39. Long and Natanis Ponds.

40. Round Pond.

41. Horse Shoe Stream.

42. Lost Pond.

43. Horse Shoe Pond.

44. Mud Pond.

45. Arnold Pond, formerly called Moosehorn Pond.

46. Except Lost Pond.

47. Or Getchell.   Undoubtedly Getchell is intended.

48. Arnold River, called in 1775 the Seven Mile Stream.

49. Or Sartigan.   Just below, "Lake Magantuck" signifies "Lake Megantic."

50. The lacuna should doubtless be filled with the word "Excellency."

51. Great Falls.

52. At the Lesser Falls.

53. Known now as the Du Loup.

For further explanations, consult the text and notes which precede.

INDEX

A

Abenaki, spelling of, 259; 323
Adams, Seth, old settler on Kennebec, 117
Agry, Thomas, a shipwright, 77; receipt, 299
Agry's Point, 77, 299
Alder Stream, 155, 373
Allen, William, 178, 239, 354, 355, 403, 442
Almon's *Remembrancer*, 28
Amaguntick Lake, *see* Megantic (Lake)
Amherst, General, sent message to Wolfe by way of Kennebec, 16
Annah, Mr., called Seigneur in Sertigan, 239; 443
Anville, Sieur d', maps, 4; 442
Apportionment of troops, by companies, 279; by States, 280; by battalions, 58, 282; by divisions, 88
Arnold, Benedict, his route, 3; had Montresor's map and journal, 17; used Goodwin's sketches, 18; his own journal, 26; his letters, 55, 277; his forces, 56, 57; left Cambridge and reached Newburyport, 61; sent three scouting vessels, September 16th, 62; at Gardinerston, 73; letter to Colburn, 75; reasons for stopping at Gardinerston, 77; 80; trouble with boats, 78, 79; met Goodwin, 82; reached Fort Western, 83; talk with Getchell and Berry, 87; sent Steele and Church to reconnoitre, 88, 312; rearranged army, 88; plans on leaving Fort Western, 91; his progress to Great Carrying-place, 91; passed Five Mile Ripples, 101; arrival near Norridgewock, 1, 105; at Norridgewock Falls, 109; at Great Carrying-place, 113; estimate of Little Carry Pond, 125; of West Carry Pond, 126; arrival at and departure from Great Carrying-place, 128; ordered building of hospital, 129; ordered building of dépôt for supplies, 129; received lieutenants' reports, 130, 131; letter to friends in Quebec and to Schuyler, 131, 352; sent journal to Washington, 132; began to ascend Dead River, 133; at Camp Greene, 143; at Arnold Falls, 144; at time of flood, 145; account of Lower Dead River, 149; error in journal? 152; account of Ledge Falls, 153, 154; passed riflemen at Upper Ledge Falls, 154; at Camp Flood, 154; error about direction of river at Alder Stream, 156; description of Upper Shadagee Falls, 156; at Camp Disaster, 156; held council of war, 156; advanced from Camp Disaster, 157; estimates of advance and of Sarampus Falls, 158; estimates to

Index 489

Huddlestone, Captain, at Fort
Halifax, 99
Hull, Isaac, bearer of Arnold's
letter, etc., 198; 413, 415, 420,
427
Humphrey, William, his journal,
33 ; *cf.* with Thayer's, 34, 269 ;
cf. with Topham's, 36, 270; at
first house, 228 ; biographical
note, 269
Hunter, English sloop-of-war,
253, 255, 451, 456 ; position
of, 457
Hurricane Falls, 139, 362
Hyde, Adjutant, voted to retreat,
162 ; at Enos's trial, 395

I

Iberville, proposed attack on
Boston, 19
Indians, *see* Eneas ; *see* Natanis ;
see St. Francis Indians ; Indian guide, 216 ; two Penob-
scots aid Arnold, 220 ; council
with Arnold, 244, 446 ; some
enlist, 244, 446 ; two sent for
McClellan, 245 ; two sent to
Quebec with Jaquin, 250
Ipswich, musketmen quartered
there, 61
Irvin [e], Dr., at hospital, 129;
232, 350
Island of Orleans, 253, 457, 464

J

Jaillot, Hubert, his map, 4
Jaquin, report at Arnold River,
196 ; sent to Quebec ? 250 ;
Senter's statement concerning,
335 ; not sent to Quebec Oc-
tober 13th, 355; 413, 420
Jeffreys, Thomas, his map of
Kennebec region, 4; explan-
ation of his map, 10
Johnson, Guy, 304
Justinian Road, 249, 449
Justinien, Récollet priest, 249,
449

K

Kennebec River, in map in
French Navy Department, 3 ;
Mitchell's map, 4; Nolin's and
Seale's maps, 5 ; early missionaries in its vicinity, 9 ; Pownall's description, 10–16 ;
Goodwin's maps, 18 ; early
suggestions for use of route,
19–21; route as given by
Washington, 22 ; Arnold set
sail for, 65 ; fleet at mouth,
66, 289 ; fortifications at
mouth ? 69; navigation of lower part, 69 ; shallow above
Gardinerston, 83 ; falls above
Fort Western, 93 ; falls above
Fort Halifax, 99; falls at
Skowhegan, 102 ; about Norridgewock, 105–109 ; beyond
Carritunk Falls, 112 ; forma-
tion of, 113 ; descent of, 326 ;
islands near Carritunk Falls,
337
Kitchin, Thomas, his map, 442

L

La Famine, Rivière, 240, 442
Ledge Falls, Upper and Lower,
nature of, 152 ; Arnold's ac-
count of, 153; 371, 372, 375,
376
Lesser Falls (in Chaudière
River), 220, 434
Lithgow, William, 97, 322, 323
Little Carry Pond, size, etc., 125,
343 ; change of level, 189
Little Swan Island, 71, 291
Lizard, English frigate, 254, 255;
position of, 457
Lovejoy's Narrows, 71, 291
Lynn, musketmen passed
through, 58; 281, 282

M

Malden, musketmen passed
through, 58; 61